Daytrips and Getaway Weekends in the Mid-Atlantic States

NEW YORK, NEW JERSEY, PENNSYLVANIA, DELAWARE, MARYLAND, WASHINGTON, D.C., AND VIRGINIA

Sixth Edition

by
Patricia & Robert Foulke

The Globe Pequot Press

Guilford, Connecticut

The information in this guidebook was confirmed at press time. We recommend, however, that you call establishments before traveling to obtain current information. Travelers should exercise due care and caution in using information, following recommendations, and making plans.

Cover design by Saralyn Twomey
Cover photo © Laurence Parent Photography, Inc.

Interior photo credits: page 191, courtesy Chester County Tourist Bureau; page 285, courtesy Office of Tourist Development, Maryland Department of Economic and Community Development; all other photos courtesy of tourist bureaus and convention and visitors bureaus where the attraction is located.

Library of Congress Cataloging-in-Publication Data
Foulke, Patricia.
    Daytrips and getaway weekends in the Mid-Atlantic states: New York, New Jersey, Pennsylvania, Delaware, Maryland, Washington, D.C., and Virginia / by Patricia & Robert Foulke.—6th ed.
        p. cm.
    Includes index.
    ISBN 0–7627–0758–5
        1. Middle Atlantic States—Tours. 2. Family recreation—Middle Atlantic States—Guidebooks. I. Foulke, Robert, 1930-   II. Title.
F106.F68   2001
917.404'44—dc21   00-063614

Manufactured in the United States of America
Sixth Edition/First Printing

Contents

ITINERARIES

Introduction

We hope that this book will arouse your historical imagination, inspire you to explore a variety of interesting places, and provide you with details about what to see and do at the sites you choose to visit. Some people want to hit only the highlights; others prefer to poke around in places off the beaten track. In either case, once you are on your way, you will want to strike a nice balance between knowing what you are looking for and having the fun of discovering something unknown to most travelers. This book provides much of what you need to know, and the people you meet and circumstances of the day will often lead to the most surprising and memorable finds.

Travelers notoriously display the urge to collect things on trips. We would like to suggest a different kind of collection—not things, but the sights and sounds of places or man-made objects. How many rushing waterfalls can you find in the western part of New York state? How many lighthouses can you spot along the Hudson River? Look at the different kinds of construction of the bridges all around Manhattan, from the pioneering Brooklyn to the soaring Verrazano. Pennsylvania is famous for covered bridges; how do they vary from the Pennsylvania Dutch country to the Bucks County region? How many atria can you visit in New York City? How do the barns in Maryland differ from those in Pennsylvania? Make a study of the beaches along the Maryland, Delaware, and New Jersey coasts. Let your imagination refine your observation and put some focus into your travel.

This book suggests a variety of activities while you travel. If you have a strong interest in history, we have tried to provide just the right amount of information, letting you know what to look for when you are at an historic site. We have interviewed people with expertise in the museums and houses listed in each itinerary, and they have often given us more information than we can use in a book of this size. We try to include enough of it to whet your appetite and give you background for your visit.

For those of you who want to build a trip around doing more than seeing, we have suggested recreational areas that can provide both exercise and fun during your trip. This six-state region provides almost any setting that one could wish for active sports—mountain, lake, river, seashore—and each has its own character and ambience. In New York alone, for example, you can surf on the ocean beaches of Long Island; hike or ski in the Catskills or the high peaks of the Adirondacks; ramble through estate gardens in the mid-Hudson or run white water on the upper Hudson; cycle along the shores of the Finger Lakes or the towpaths of the old Erie Canal; or fish, swim, water-ski, and sail almost everywhere, from Peconic Bay at the tip of Long Island to the shores of Lake Erie.

Trip Planning

Within a city or region, we have tried to cluster or group sites of interest so that you will know what is available nearby. We don't like to drive or walk back and forth randomly looking for something and know you won't want to either. Whenever possible we have also suggested, for your convenience, a pleasant place for lunch or dinner in the area.

Our planned itineraries will save you the time and trouble of gathering information and deciding on a route. You can choose to travel all of any itinerary, or part of one, or combine parts of several. We have moved around the mid-Atlantic states in a way that makes geographic sense, so you can connect easily from one itinerary to another. Some of the longer itineraries are not meant to be traveled in one chunk of time—unless you have a lot of it or are visiting from another part of the country or world. For example, from New York City you might choose to travel to the end of Long Island at one time and explore the Hudson River Valley and Catskills on another trip. From Philadelphia you may want to head west toward the Pennsylvania Dutch region or north to the Delaware Water Gap and the Poconos, or, nearer home, into Bucks County or the Brandywine Valley for day or weekend trips. The map accompanying each itinerary shows the route from place to place so that you can quickly visualize the possibilities.

Each itinerary contains sightseeing tips and a good bit of detail about places of special interest. The description is not meant to be comprehensive but represents a selection of the highlights of each site, plus some little-noticed details that may give you the feel of the place. At times our enthusiasm runs away with us and we write a great deal; perhaps you will feel as inspired as we were.

Itineraries

A: New York City, Long Island, and the Hudson River Valley. The old cliché is right: Even if you might not want to live there, the Big Apple is fun to visit. Long Island is a microcosm containing great variety for you to enjoy, including those gorgeous beaches. The Hudson River Valley, caught between mountain ranges, has castles on the cliffs and legends galore.

B: Upstate New York. From Saratoga Springs, with its horse racing and summer ballet or symphony, to the Adirondacks—cool, green-blue water and the peace of stream, lake, and mountain—you can have it all on a single circuit. The Thousand Islands have the special charm of diamond-like fragments filling a massive river from shore to shore, and the Mohawk Valley has rolling hills and villages with "Leatherstocking" charm.

C: Western and Central New York. Cities such as Syracuse, Rochester, and Buffalo are being revitalized and have much of historic interest to recommend them. The Finger Lakes, lined with vineyards and stretching into rolling hills, also have strong connections with American cultural and political history. Chautauqua has a special ambience that gets into your blood, and it represents a unique development in nineteenth-century thought. Niagara Falls is not only for honeymooners—the escarpment has geologic and practical dimensions that must be seen to be appreciated.

D: Northern Pennsylvania. Erie and Presque Isle have both the lure of lake recreation and a history ranging from the War of 1812 through rum-running during Prohibition. This itinerary continues across the northern section of Pennsylvania from Erie to Kinzau Dam, Coudersport, the Grand Canyon, Williamsport, and Lewisburg.

E: Western Pennsylvania. Pittsburgh is no longer a smoky city but a beautiful one—go and see for yourself! After seeing Pittsburgh you can visit Fort Necessity, Ohiopyle, Fort Ligonier, Bushy Run Battlefield, Johnstown, and Huntingdon.

F: South-Central Pennsylvania. The Revolutionary and Civil wars ravaged much of this beautiful rolling area, but you can relive the events without the misery. Pennsylvania Dutch country lures visitors with its special foods and living history of one of the country's most interesting religious groups. The Brandywine Valley developed one of the first industries in the country and provided the setting for flourishing architecture, gardening, and art.

G: Eastern Pennsylvania. The streets and buildings of Philadelphia are a living museum of our independence, and they offer the visitor a full range of cultural opportunities. Bucks County, with its horses, inns, and canal, provides rural peace within easy reach of the city. The Delaware Water Gap and the Poconos go hand in hand, joining the natural beauty of mountain and river and furnishing the visitor with a full range of recreational opportunities.

H: Delaware. The shore has impeccable beaches and interesting remnants of nineteenth-century Americana, as well as all forms of water sports. The coast has tales of shipwrecks to tell, as well as nature preserves; and inland areas have fine colonial homes for you to visit.

I: New Jersey. This diverse state is not all megalopolis. The Pine Barrens, beaches, and harbors are treasures waiting to be discovered. Princeton is a college town, full of charm.

J: Maryland. Although small in size, this state is rich in contrasts between cities and almost untouched rural areas, and it surrounds a bay with two distinctive shores and a maritime life all its own.

K: Washington, D.C., and Virginia. Our nation's capital is one of the world's most carefully planned cities and contains a wealth of art and culture in addition to its public monuments and government buildings. We have added several historic sites in Virginia and West Virginia. All fit in with Washington and the development of our country, and all are within easy reach of the city.

Information

The Internet can provide you with travel information, and your local library is a good source of books as you begin to plan a trip. Later you may want to buy some of them to take along on your trip. State tourism offices offer maps, information about historic sites, lists of accommodations and restaurants, and sightseeing suggestions. It's a good idea to write before you go.

Delaware: Delaware State Travel Service, 99 Kings Highway, P.O. Box 1401, Dover 19901. Phone: 800–282–8667 in Delaware or 800–441–8846 outside of Delaware. Fax: 302–739–5729; www.state.de.ustourism

Maryland: Maryland Tourism, Redwood Tower, 217 East Redwood Street, Baltimore 21202. Phone: 800–394–5725 or 410–333–6611. Fax: 410–727–2308; www.mdisfun.org

New Jersey: Division of Travel and Tourism, One West State Street, CN 826, Trenton 08625. Phone: 800–537–7397. Fax: 609–633–7418; www.visitnj.org

New York: New York Department of Commerce, Division of Tourism, One Commerce Plaza, Albany 12245. Phone: 800–225–5697. Fax: 518–473–8347; www.Iloveny.com

Pennsylvania: Bureau of Travel Development, Department of Commerce, 416 Forum Building, Harrisburg 17120. Phone: 800–847–4872. Fax: 717–787–0687; www.experiencepa.com

Virginia: Virginia Department of Economic Development, Division of

Tourism, 1021 East Cary Street, Tower II, Richmond 23219. Phone: 800–847–4882 or 804–786–2051. Fax: 804–786–1919; www.virginia.org

Washington, D.C.: Washington, D.C., Convention and Visitors Association, 1212 New York Avenue, N.W., Washington, D.C. 20005. Phone: 800–422–8644. Fax: 202–724–2445; www.washington.org

West Virginia: West Virginia Division of Tourism, 2101 Washington Street East, Charleston, WV 25305. Phone: 800–225–5982 or 304–558–2200. Fax: 304–558–2873; www.callwva.com

If you would like information on a specific city or town, write: Name of city, Convention and Visitors Bureau or Chamber of Commerce, City, State, ZIP code.

Before You Go

When you've considered where you want to go, weather and road conditions, crowds in high season, ferry schedules (if applicable), and any other contingencies, you're ready to get organized. Make a list of the areas you want to cover, the activities you would like to enjoy, and possible side trips. A destination for each night with estimated mileage and driving time is the next step. Addresses and phone numbers you'll need along the route are added to the list. Then put your lists, brochures, travel articles, books, and other information you've collected into a large envelope for easy reference along the way.

Food

You will want to try the local cuisine as you travel. Be alert to special foods that are featured locally. Is there an unusual restaurant you've heard wonderful things about? It doesn't hurt to write or phone ahead for a reservation. (We have listed phone numbers for each of our suggestions.)

Activities

Enjoy! Remember that you are not working and not following a rigid schedule. Let the ages and interests of your family set your focus. Leave some time for relaxation (time to do nothing) and flexibility (the freedom to change your mind according to weather and mood).

ITINERARY A:

New York City, Long Island, and the Hudson River Valley

VANDERBILT MANSION

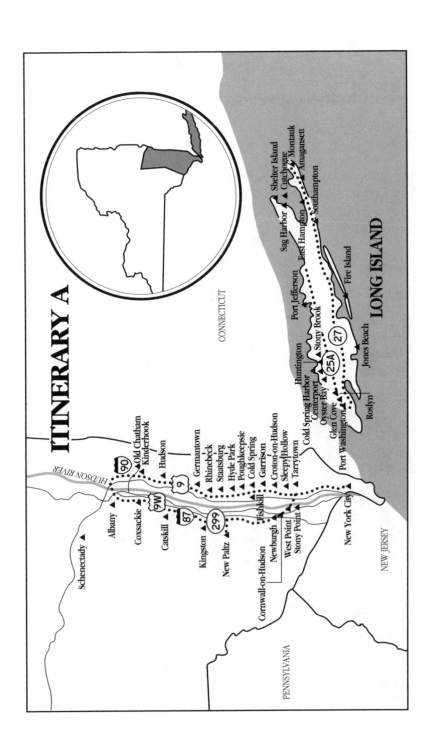

ITINERARY A

New York City, Long Island, and the Hudson River Valley

3

This itinerary can begin in the New York City area, or it can continue from Itineraries B, G, or H. Like all of the itineraries, it can also be traveled in reverse.

～ *New York City* ～

New York, a city of eight million people that overwhelms visitors who often don't know where to begin, contains 303 square miles, 578 miles of waterfront, 6,400 miles of streets, 3,500 churches and synagogues, 100 skyscrapers, 65 bridges, 230 miles of subway lines, 999 miles of bus routes, 25,000 restaurants, 150 museums, 400 art galleries, 90 institutions of higher learning, and much, much more. The sheer magnitude of the statistics is staggering in itself, and visitors often find that the noise of honking horns and squealing brakes, the motion of cars and taxis speeding along the streets, and the confusion of dodging so many people while walking further add to their uncertainty. The trick is to become oriented to the various sections of the city and then select a manageable area to enjoy, perhaps on a walking tour. If you want to preplan your visit, free information will be sent to you from the **New York Convention and Visitors Bureau** (810 Seventh Avenue, New York, New York 10019; 800–NYC–VISIT or 212–424–1200). You can also call the New York State tourist office in Albany for New York City information (800–CALL–NYS).

For an overview of the city, visitors can choose a bus tour, helicopter ride, cruise ship, or a skyscraper observation deck. We tend to climb the tallest tower for a bird's-eye view of a strange city when traveling in Europe, but in New York the sea of other buildings viewed from above may be fascinating to the eye but hardly helpful for orienting yourself. For arranging an initial tour, useful addresses include **Circle Line Statue of Liberty Ferry** (Battery Park, South Ferry, New York 10004; 212–269–5755); **Circle Line Sightseeing Yachts, Inc.** (Pier 83, foot of West 42nd Street, New York, 10036; 212–563–3200); and **Gray Line of New York** (254 West 54th Street, New York 10019; 800–669–0051 or 212–397–2600).

We managed an overview of the city by land, sea, and air. The helicopter trip swung around the Statue of Liberty, ran along the riverfront, and hovered above the peaks and pinnacles of skyscrapers. The experience is both breathtaking and suggestive of the power that many see in the irregular pattern of buildings thrusting upward. For those who want to stay closer to the ground, bus tours are available in several sections of the city;

the guide's narration will give you lots of anecdotes about the sites you are passing. Cruising by ferry or ship gives yet another dimension to your orientation.

Interested in collecting? As you tour New York, you will find a variety of sites pertaining to almost any special interest. If you like bridges, you can see one after another ringing the island and linking the boroughs, each with a tale or two to tell. In recent years hotels and corporate buildings have upgraded their interior spaces by the use of atria—peaceful havens of greenery, splashing water, and courtyards removed from outer confusion and noise; see how many you can "collect." Some atria are ringed with restaurants, galleries, and shops. Our favorites include **Trump Tower,** 56th Street at Fifth Avenue, with an 80-foot waterfall; **IBM Atrium,** 56th Street at Madison Avenue, with tall bamboo trees; **Crystal Pavilion,** 50th Street at Third Avenue, with two water walls; **Citicorp Center,** 53rd Street between Third and Lexington avenues, under a slant-roofed silver tower; **Park Avenue Plaza,** 52nd to 53rd Street off Park Avenue, with a waterfall; **Equitable Center,** 52nd to 51st Street at Seventh Avenue, with American art from the Whitney Museum; and **AT&T,** Madison Avenue between 55th and 56th streets, which includes the InfoQuest Center on technology information. Parks, churches, museums, galleries, and theaters are found all over New York. A historical theme can be traced through the many sites that have been restored. More than forty islands lie within the New York City boundaries, bearing names like City Island, Roosevelt Island, Broad Channel Island, Governors Island, Staten Island, Ellis Island, Rat Island, The Raunt, Shooter's Island, Cuban Ledge, and Liberty Island. They make a fine addition to anyone's collection of interesting islands in the world.

Manhattan

Manhattan, named by the Algonquin Indians, "island of the hills," is the smallest of the five boroughs of New York City. It is 13.4 miles long and 2.3 miles across at the widest point. Moving from north to south with map in hand, you can visit the Upper East Side and Upper West Side, which bracket Central Park from 110th Street to 59th Street; Midtown, the Theater District, and the Garment District from 59th Street to 34th Street; what we call the Neighborhoods, an area of five neighborhoods from 34th Street to Houston Street; and Lower Manhattan. We will group sights within each of these areas for your convenience. Our selections are not meant to be comprehensive; it would take a lifetime to see them all.

<table>
<tr><td>

Belvedere Castle
Central Park West
& 79th Street
New York 10024
212–772–0210

</td></tr>
</table>

Central Park

Central Park contains 840 acres from 110th Street to 59th Street devoted to landscaped recreational areas designed by Frederick Law Olmsted and Calvert Vaux. Ponds, lakes, woods, and flowers fill this area in the middle of the largest city in the United States. In the center of the park is **The Ramble,** with its twisted, hidden paths leading up to **Belvedere Castle,** designed in 1867 by Calvert Vaux. The name Belvedere was derived from *bellevedere,* or "beautiful view," which is available from the Gothic tower. The U.S. Weather Bureau moved into the building in 1919, and in 1930 an automatic weather recording system was installed. Restoration of the building took place in the 1970s, and now, as the Central Park Learning Center, the place provides educational programs for children and for the public.

The geologic history of **Vista Rock,** with Belvedere Castle perched on the summit, stretches back 450 million years. Black mud lay on the floor of an ancient ocean, built up layer upon layer of sediment, and then was squeezed, heated, and crystallized as Africa and North America moved closer together. Mountains formed, eroded, and crowded up again and again. The two continents split apart, and the Atlantic Ocean rose to submerge the entire eastern part of the United States. During the Ice Age, Vista Rock was covered with 1,000 feet of ice. As the glacier moved, boulders scraped and striated the rock; look at the twisted layers of this schist rock to see the record of its erosion.

The Lake contains an iron bridge with a graceful curve that makes a fine photographic frame; boats may be rented at the east end of it. To the north are the **New Lake, Shakespeare Garden,** and **Delacorte Theater,** which presents free "Shakespeare in the Park" performances during the summer. The Metropolitan Museum of Art is just beyond the New Lake. **The Mall** juts through the middle of the park and is lined with two rows of busts of famous persons, leading to a bandshell at one end. The southern part of the park contains playing fields and **The Central Park Zoo. Tavern on the Green** (212–873–3200), on Central Park West, has Baccarat chandeliers and provides a glassed-in view of the park during lunch or dinner.

Sadly, the pleasures of this beautiful park are no longer free of peril. The general caution given to visitors is simple: Never enter the park at night; some people feel that its more remote sections are not fully safe at any time. On the other hand, many New Yorkers continue to use and enjoy their magnificent park, and you will probably want to join them during daylight hours.

Upper East Side

Museum Mile is the name given to an extraordinary string of major museums along Fifth Avenue from 103rd Street down to 53rd Street. If you find museums compelling, this strip can be the centerpiece of your visit to the city. We will list some of them, from north to south.

The **Museum of the City of New York** traces the history of the city from its days as a Dutch trading post to the present. Exhibits include models of the *Half Moon* and *Dauphine,* a scale model of Nieuw Amsterdam in 1660, a collection of silver, a ship's figurehead of Andrew Jackson from the USS *Constitution,* life-size rooms of a Dutch nineteenth-century home, nineteenth- and twentieth-century dollhouses, and the bedroom and dressing room from the house of John D. Rockefeller. The **Conservatory Garden** is across the street, in Central Park.

The **Cooper-Hewitt Museum,** the Smithsonian Institution's National Museum of Design, is in the renovated Andrew Carnegie mansion. The museum functions as a design reference center—a working museum with changing exhibits. The collection includes original drawings dating back to the fifteenth century; embroidered, woven, and printed fabrics; silver, bronze, and metal pieces; and jewelry, wallpaper, porcelain, furniture, and clocks.

The **Solomon R. Guggenheim Museum** is housed in a building that Frank Lloyd Wright designed in 1943. This cream-colored concrete building looks like a corkscrew. Inside, the spiral ramp ascends for a quarter mile up to a 92-foot-high glass dome. We suggest you take the elevator to the top and then proceed down on foot. The collection includes paintings by Chagall, Picasso, Mondrian, Klee, Pissarro, Renoir, Monet, Cézanne, Van Gogh, Gauguin, Toulouse-Lautrec, and Degas. The museum was renovated in early 1992.

The **Metropolitan Museum of Art** contains collections dating from prehistory to the present. You will need a map in this immense structure that, including its wings, covers over thirty-two acres. Only one-fourth of the total collection is on display at any given time, and the volume is mind-boggling. Its departments include American, Ancient, Medieval,

Museum of the City of New York Fifth Avenue & 103rd Street New York 10029 212-534-1672
Cooper-Hewitt Museum 2 East 91st Street New York 10128 212-860-6868
Solomon R. Guggenheim Museum Fifth Avenue & 89th Street New York 10128 212-423-3500
Metropolitan Museum of Art Fifth Avenue & 82nd Street New York 10028 212-879-5500

Whitney Museum of
American Art
Madison Avenue &
75th Street
New York 10021
212-570-3676

Frick Collection
Fifth Avenue & 70th
Street
New York 10021
212-288-0700

American Museum
of Natural History
Central Park West &
79th Street
New York 10024
212-769-5100

Hayden Planetarium
Central Park West &
81st Street
New York 10024
212-769-5900

The New-York
Historical Society
Central Park West &
77th Street
New York 10024
212-873-3400

European Sculpture and Decorative Arts, European Paintings, Primitive Art, the Lehman Pavilion, Arms and Armor, Musical Instruments, Islamic, Far Eastern, Costume, Drawings, Prints and Photographs, and the Uris Center for Education.

The **Whitney Museum of American Art** owns the largest collection of American art in the country. Begun in the Greenwich Village studio of sculptress Gertrude Vanderbilt Whitney, the museum was founded in 1930. A sunken sculpture court in the center is the focal point for three cantilevered gallery floors. The collection includes works by Benton, Bellows, Prendergast, Hopper, Sloan, Calder, Nevelson, O'Keeffe, Rauschenberg, Reinhardt, and David Smith.

The **Frick Collection** comprises works by European artists from the fourteenth through nineteenth centuries. The house was designed in 1913 for Henry Clay Frick and contains his personal furnishings and art collection. After his death his wife lived there until she died in 1935, when the house became a museum. The collection includes works by Boucher, Hogarth, Romney, Reynolds, Gainsborough, Fragonard, Vermeer, Bellini, Titian, and El Greco.

Upper West Side

The **American Museum of Natural History** is one of the largest natural history museums in the world. Among the more than thirty-four million species and substances exhibited are dinosaurs, elephants, a blue whale, minerals and gems, reptiles, primates, and birds. Other displays portray Eskimos, Indians, Africans, Mexicans, and Central Americans. The museum has a rare books section, and free lectures, concerts, films, and plays are offered during the year.

The **Hayden Planetarium,** which is part of the Museum of Natural History, offers a sky show, the Guggenheim Space Theater, and the Hall of the Sun. Adjoining galleries contain exhibits on astronomy.

The New-York Historical Society is both a museum and a library. The collection contains decorative arts, watercolors by John James Audubon, folk art, toys from the eighteenth century, furniture, and paintings by Stuart, West, Peale, Durand, Cole, and Church.

Lincoln Center was constructed between 1962 and 1968 to promote music, theater, and dance. The complex can seat 13,747 persons at one time. It consists of the Avery Fisher Hall, the New York State Theater, the Metropolitan Opera House, the Library and Museum of the Performing Arts, the Vivian Beaumont Theater, The Walter Reade Theater, and the Juilliard School of Music. Tours of Lincoln Center are offered daily. Free concerts are given outside during the summer.

Midtown

Carnegie Hall seats 2,804 persons in a building with perfect acoustics. Dating from 1891, with Tchaikovsky conducting at the first performance, this building has witnessed concerts by the finest musicians in the world. Faced with possible destruction at one point, the building was saved by Isaac Stern and a group of New York patrons. The **Weill Recital Hall** (212–903–9600), seating 297 persons, features performances by contemporary music ensembles.

The **Museum of Modern Art,** although founded during an inauspicious time, just after the stock market crash in 1929, has amassed a major collection devoted to the twentieth century. Disciplines exhibited include painting, sculpture, architecture, film, prints and illustrated books, photography, and drawings. The museum has been in its present location since 1939, and considerable expansion took place during the early 1980s. The expansion has doubled the space of the collection and provided an intriguing new structure with glass domes on a series of levels. Visitors can stop for a meal at the Garden Cafe and look out at the Sculpture Garden. Among the famous paintings hanging in the Museum are *Water Lilies* by Claude Monet, *The Bather* by Paul Cézanne, *Monument to Balzac* by Auguste Rodin, *Dance* and *Memory of Oceania* by Henri Matisse, and *Starry Night* by Vincent Van Gogh.

Also on 53rd Street is the **American Craft Museum,** which exhibits contemporary craft making. Galleries are reached via a curving 40-foot-high "stairatrium" that flows up and down. The permanent collection includes work from World War II to the present in clay, glass, metal, wood, and fiber. Artists demonstrate their work in the "Meet the Artist" program.

For a meal in a brownstone with a waterfall in the garden room, try the **Courtyard Cafe,** nearby at 130 East 39th Street (212–685–1100).

Lincoln Center
Broadway & 65th
 Street
New York 10023
212–875–5350

Carnegie Hall
Seventh Avenue &
 57th Street
New York 10019
212–247–7800

Museum of Modern
 Art
11 West 53rd Street
New York 10019
212–708–9480

American Craft
 Museum
40 West 53rd Street
New York 10019
212–956–3535

9

Rockefeller Center
Fifth to Sixth
  Avenues and 47th
  to 52nd Streets
New York 10020
212–632–3975

Radio City Music
  Hall
Sixth Avenue & 50th
  Street
New York 10020
212–247–4777

St. Patrick's
  Cathedral
Fifth Avenue & 50th
  Street
New York 10022
212–753–2261

Grand Central
  Terminal
Lexington Avenue &
  42nd Street
New York 10017
212–935–3960

Rockefeller Center is one of those places some visitors want to see every time they return to New York. Romantic images of the "real New York" from earlier decades seem to flow around Rockefeller Center. One of our favorite diversions is having a drink in the **Rainbow Room** (30 Rockefeller Plaza; 212–632–5000), sixty-five floors up, watching the city turn on its lights at dusk; then we feel we have really arrived. Renovated in 1930s Art Deco style, the Rainbow complex offers a view, with artwork including a Norman Bel Geddes ocean liner over the bar. Rockefeller Center is a collection of nineteen office buildings covering twenty-two acres and employing 65,000 persons. The **Channel Gardens** were so named because they are situated between the French and British buildings. Their blooming plants are changed seasonally, and benches provide respite from walking. **Rockefeller Plaza,** on the lower level, is filled with ice skaters in the winter, and flags of the United Nations countries flutter in the breeze all around it. Shops and restaurants line the concourse area, and underground passages connect the buildings. The **GE Building,** at 30 Rockefeller Plaza, soars seventy stories into the air. José Maria Sert's painting entitled *American Progress* hangs in the lobby.

Radio City Music Hall is the place to go for a Christmas "spectacular" if you are in New York after mid-November. Other shows, movies, and pop concerts fill the hall throughout the year. The Rockettes have been dancing at Radio City since 1932. In 1979 the hall's elegant Art Deco architecture was completely restored. The chandeliers in the Grand Foyer can be lowered mechanically for cleaning—two tons of crystal and steel notwithstanding. Gold mirrors and gold-leaf ceilings make the mezzanine floors dazzle.

St. Patrick's Cathedral, dating from 1858 (although it did not open until 1879), was once thought to be too far out of town, if you can imagine that. Spires rise 330 feet, and the bronze doors open into the nave adorned with seventy stained-glass windows from Chartres and Nantes, France.

Grand Central Terminal, which was recently renovated, is a Beaux Arts building with a gigantic concourse area leading up to a 125-foot-high vaulted ceiling decorated with constellations of the zodiac. For years the **Grand Central Oyster Bar** (212–490–6650) has been touted as the best place around for seafood; its popularity is quite evident during the lunch hour.

The **United Nations** consists of a narrow glass building (the Secretariat) adjacent to the General Assembly, begun in 1947 by a committee of international architects. The dramatic complex is adorned by flags of the member nations arranged in alphabetical order. To your right as you enter is the Meditation Room with a Chagall window, dedicated to Dag Hammarskjold. The oval Assembly Room is fascinating to visit, and you may wish to take a tour or sit in on a session. The Delegates Dining Room is open to the public for lunch by reservation.

The **New York Public Library** was built in 1911 to house the Astor, Tilden, and Lenox libraries. The Beaux Arts building is guarded by two friendly marble lions named Patience and Fortitude. An architectural tour of the structure is free. It has been newly renovated. Beautiful Bryant Park is just behind.

South of the theater district is one building few tourists miss. The **Empire State Building,** once the tallest building in the world, has now been topped by many others. The observation level on the 102nd floor will provide an 80-mile view if the visibility is good. The top of the Empire State Building is brilliantly lit at night—a treat to spot when you are on an evening cruise. Runners might like to get in shape for the annual Empire State Building Run—that's right—up all 1,575 steps. In an internationally popular contest, runners tend to make it up to the top in twelve to fourteen minutes (the winners, that is!).

The **Guinness World of Records** is located on the concourse level of the Empire State Building, next to the Observatory Ticket Office. Look for Vincent Van Gogh's *Irises,* which sold for a record $53.9 million in 1987; statistics on volcanoes, the universe, and space; the longest soft toy (250 feet), which looks like a pink-plush centipede; a model of the world's tallest man at 8 feet 11.1 inches; a display on crazy eating; and much more.

United Nations First Avenue & 46th Street New York 10017 212-963-7713
New York Public Library Fifth Avenue & 42nd Street New York 10036 212-869-8089
Empire State Building Fifth Avenue & 34th Street New York 10018 212-736-3100
Guinness World of Records 350 Fifth Avenue New York 10018 212-947-2335

Theater District

Most of the theaters lie between 40th and 57th streets on a north-south axis, bounded by Eighth Avenue to the west and Avenue of the

TKTS
Broadway & 47th
  Street
New York

Poe Cottage
Grand Concourse &
  Kingsbridge Road
Bronx 10467
212–881–8900

Americas to the east, but 45th Street is noted for its cluster of legitimate theaters. **Shubert Alley,** between 44th and 45th streets, is the heart of the theater district and is used only by pedestrians.

Ever since 1753, when the Hallam Company arrived from London to produce drama in New York City, the public flocked to be entertained. In the 1830s Walt Whitman and Washington Irving encouraged serious theater as well as pure entertainment. Between 1850 and 1900 melodramas, plays with a message such as *Uncle Tom's Cabin,* and operettas were popular. Later the classics returned, as well as plays depicting themes of World War I. Eugene O'Neill was instrumental in presenting satire, expressionism, and realism. Plays presented real problems faced by people during that time. The theater of the absurd played with features of a world that didn't make sense. During the 1960s and 1970s, current social problems, political assassinations, and war played dominant roles in drama. If you're interested in half-price tickets for Broadway, Off-Broadway, Lincoln Center, and other performances, go to **TKTS** in Times Square or at the World Trade Center. Tickets for matinees are sold on Wednesdays and Saturdays from 10:00 A.M. until 2:00 P.M. Tickets for evening performances are sold Mondays through Saturdays from 3:00 to 8:00 P.M. On Sundays the hours for ticket sales are from noon to 8:00 P.M.

In addition to drama, New York City has fostered a rich literary heritage from its beginning. Washington Irving poked fun at the first Dutch settlers in his *History of New York.* Edgar Allan Poe, who lived in and out of New York during his lifetime, was a literary critic for the *New York Mirror.* He caused an uproar when he accused Longfellow of plagiarism. **Poe Cottage** in the Bronx is open to visitors; there Poe lived a life of poverty— his wife died of tuberculosis with Poe's cloak around her, hugging the family cat for warmth. Herman Melville was born at 6 Pearl Street, near State Street, in 1819. After his marriage in 1847, he lived at 103 Fourth Avenue in Greenwich Village. He worked for a time as a deputy inspector at the New York Custom House and reflected the life of the city in stories like "Bartleby the Scrivener, A Story of Wall Street." Walt Whitman lived in Brooklyn in 1839 and in Manhattan in 1841. His New York works include "Mannahaata" and "Crossing Brooklyn Ferry."

Many novelists have found their material in both the high and the low life of the city. Henry James, born in 1843, lived at 21 Washington Place in Greenwich Village and later at 58 West 14th Street. He was very fond of his childhood neighborhood and wrote about it in *Washington Square.* Even after he moved to England, New York society provided one of the touchstones of value in his later, more complex novels. Edith Wharton was born to wealth, and her novels about old New York society include *The Age of Innocence, False Dawn,* and *New Year's Day.* Stephen Crane was born into a family of writers; as a young man he lived on New York's Lower East Side, where he wrote his first book, *Maggie: A Girl of the Streets.* He wanted to experience life in the Bowery for his writing and once slept in a Bowery shelter to observe the men who lived there; *Midnight Sketches* was developed from these experiences.

> Algonquin Hotel
> 59 West 44th Street
> New York 10036
> 212–840–6800
>
> *Intrepid* Sea-Air-Space Museum
> Pier 86, foot of West 46th Street at Hudson River
> New York 10036
> 212–245–0072

Theodore Dreiser came to New York in 1894 as a newspaper reporter and wrote *Sister Carrie.* John Dos Passos lived in Greenwich Village in the 1920s, producing *Manhattan Transfer* during that time. Thus, many of the traditions of realism in nineteenth-century American fiction are inextricably linked to the life of New York, not to mention poetry—Hart Crane and the Brooklyn Bridge—or drama—Eugene O'Neill and the life of the waterfront. And because New York remains a mecca for writers, that close relationship between experience in the city and literature continues in the twentieth century.

The **Algonquin Hotel** has been a gathering place for literary wits and critics since the 1920s. For almost fifteen years one such group met every day and was known as the Algonquin Round Table, the Algonquin Wits, or—to those on the inside—as the Vicious Circle. Alexander Woollcott was the instigator of this group, which included writers, artists, musicians, and socialites. Their focus was to shape cultural and literary taste and to further their own careers; in some ways they were not unlike the Bloomsbury group in London, though more self-conscious and perhaps less talented.

Another restaurant to try after the theater is **Sardi's** (234 West 44th Street between Broadway and 8th Avenue; 212–221–8440). Caricatures of Broadway stars line the walls, and the flavor is definitely theatrical.

West of the theater district is the ***Intrepid* Sea-Air-Space Museum,** a technology museum housed in the famous aircraft carrier that saw action in World War II and the Vietnam War. Exhibits explain air, sea, and space technology within five theme halls: Navy, Intrepid, Pioneers, Space Technology, and the Hall of Honor. You can climb into the control bridge and command centers of the carrier and see a variety of aircraft close at hand. A wide-screen film simulates what it is like to be on the flight deck as jets scream off.

13

Madison Square
Garden
4 Pennsylvania Plaza
Seventh Avenue
between 31st
& 33rd Streets
New York 10001
212–465–6741

Visit **Madison Square Garden,** a sports, entertainment, convention, and office complex. Over six million spectators pass through its doors every year. The building is the third Madison Square Garden in the city; it opened in 1968. The New York Knicks—professional basketball team—and the New York Rangers—professional hockey team—call Madison Square Garden home. A wide variety of performances and exhibitions are given there, including rodeos, circuses, dance productions, tennis matches, gymnastics exhibitions, and horse shows.

Neighborhoods

This section of New York runs from 34th Street south to Houston Street. The neighborhoods include Chelsea, Gramercy Park, Stuyvesant, Greenwich Village, and the East Village. Each has its own character and history.

Chelsea (from 14th Street to 25th Street, from Eighth Avenue to the Hudson River) was the name of the estate of Captain Thomas Clarke, who bought the land in 1750. Clement Clark Moore inherited his grandfather's land and gave a sizable chunk to the General Theological Seminary. Moore is perhaps best known for his poem "A Visit from St. Nicholas." The motion picture industry got its start in Chelsea in 1905 but eventually moved to Hollywood. Chelsea is known for its many antiques shops on Ninth Avenue between 20th and 22nd streets.

Gramercy Park, a former marshland, was later converted into a London-style square surrounded by town houses. The park remains private; only residents have keys. In the center of the park stands a statue of Edwin Booth in his *Hamlet* costume. As you walk around the square, note the ornate street lamps and ironwork on some of the houses. A number of actors are memorialized in the windows of the **Little Church around the Corner,** which is also a popular place for weddings.

Stuyvesant (from Second Avenue to Third Avenue and 15th Street to 18th Street and Rutherford Place) was an elegant residential district during the nineteenth century. The square was a gift from Peter Stuyvesant, and his statue, complete with his peg leg, stands in the square in front of **St. George's Episcopal Church.** The **Friends' Meeting House and Seminary** was a stop on the Underground Railroad.

Greenwich Village has a flair all its own. The people who live there gravitate to **Washington Square** for soapbox orations and a parade of the most amazing outfits and hairdos anywhere. They really go all out for special events, such as the Halloween parade, which attracts a crowd standing six deep along the streets to ogle costumes that are more elaborate each year. Greenwich Village was settled by British colonists in 1690; they named the area for their village in England. During the early part of the eighteenth century, a number of large estates were built; the maze of winding roads evolved as the boundaries of those estates. Lavish town houses were built around Washington Square and along Fifth Avenue. You may want to walk along Washington Square North, where there are two rows of red-brick townhouses (numbers 1–13 and 21–26) dating from the 1830s. Look for both Doric and Ionic columns beside the entrances and note the cast-iron fences. Walk around behind Washington Square into Washington Mews and MacDougal Alley for a glimpse of renovated stables and servants' quarters of the old town houses. Gertrude Vanderbilt Whitney once had a sculpture gallery in one of the stables—leading eventually into the development of the Whitney Museum. One of the pleasures of Greenwich Village is spending time looking at the menus posted in front of the many restaurants before making a choice. These posted menus remind us of evenings spent strolling the streets in European cities and villages.

The **East Village** was once the residence of wealthy New York families, but when they moved out it became an industrial area. **St. Mark's-in-the-Bouwerie,** dating from 1799, was once a country church. It stands on the site of Peter Stuyvesant's chapel. "Little Ukraine" is a grouping of Byzantine churches with rounded onion domes, and Ukrainian restaurants and shops. The area's boundaries are Broadway and First Avenue and Houston and 14th streets.

Lower Manhattan

Lower Manhattan includes SoHo, the Bowery, Little Italy, TriBeCa, Chinatown, Wall Street, and the Battery. The original Dutch settlement of Nieuw Amsterdam flourished for forty years on what we now call Lower Manhattan. All traces of this village have disappeared, as well as buildings from Revolutionary War days.

SoHo, which means "south of Houston," was occupied by Indians during the seventeenth century. More recently the area's outdated industrial buildings have suddenly sprung to life with avant-garde galleries, boutiques, and restaurants. Sunday brunches are popular there. SoHo's boundaries are Houston and Canal streets, the Bowery, and Sixth Avenue.

The Bowery, located north of Canal Street to Houston, was once a farm, then an entertainment mecca, and eventually a skid row, inhabited by the poverty-stricken, drifters, and alcoholics. Recently revitalized, it is

New York Stock
Exchange
20 Broad Street
New York 10004
212–656–5165

now home to many wholesale and retail shops.

Little Italy is the place to go for Italian cuisine or to buy special Italian foods not readily available elsewhere. The **Feast of San Gennaro** is held during September. **SPQR Ristorante** (133 Mulberry Street between Hester and Grand; 212–925–3120) is recommended for Italian cuisine and atmosphere, complete with a strolling musician. Their pasta is homemade. Little Italy covers Mulberry Street from Houston to Canal streets, and Lafayette Street to the Bowery.

TriBeCa, which means "Triangle Below Canal," has a group of Federal homes on Harrison Street. The area is seeing new life, as SoHo did, with the renovation of outdated industrial buildings into studios. TriBeCa is a trapezoid in shape, south of Canal Street, bounded by Broadway on the east and Chambers on the south.

Chinatown celebrates the Chinese New Year over a fifteen-day period with a parade featuring lions, dragons, and firecrackers. The lions go from door to door receiving red envelopes containing money in return for banishing evil spirits from homes and shops. Chinese legend says that Buddha invited all of the animals of the world to visit, but only twelve came, so he rewarded them by giving each in turn the honor of being animal of the year. The motif appears in Chinese celebrations as well as on gift items sold that year. You can spend time wandering along Mott, Bayard, and Pell streets past grocery stores displaying ducks, bean curd, and dried fungi and mushrooms. Before you go make a list of special herbs and condiments you may need to create your own Chinese meals at home.

Shops offer a variety of goods, including china tea sets and bowls, brocade jackets and dresses, ivory carvings, jade jewelry, lanterns, fans, and wall hangings. Look for the unusual telephone booths, which resemble pagodas.

Wall Street needs no introduction as the financial center of the city and the nation, but visitors are often surprised to find it shrouded in shadows created by the many skyscrapers soaring up from extremely narrow streets. The origin of the name is even less well known: In 1653 Dutch Governor Peter Stuyvesant had a wall built to protect the village from the Indians who lived on the other side. For a nineteenth-century response to being enclosed in Wall Street, read Melville's "Bartleby the Scrivener."

The **New York Stock Exchange** was designed by George B. Post with Corinthian columns and sculpture reminiscent of a Greek temple. Fortunes are made and lost on the trading floor. You can view the chaos from a visitors' gallery above and hear narration on the procedures in process. Exhibits show the history of the stock exchange and the financial organization of member companies.

The **World Trade Center,** known as the "United Nations of Commerce," provides a center for international banks, custom house brokers, exporters, importers, trade associations, manufacturers, freight forwarders, trade development agencies, and transportation lines. The six-building complex was designed by Minoru Yamasaki and completed in 1970. The twin towers that soar 110 stories into the atmosphere are second in height only to the Sears Tower in Chicago. Construction of these massive towers without disturbing adjacent buildings was engineered by building a concrete wall entirely around the foundation area; then work could proceed inside the wall without worrying about water seeping in. The 1.2 million cubic yards of earth removed from the excavation area were deposited as fill in Battery Park.

> Observation Deck
> 2 World Trade Center
> New York 10048
> 212–435–7397
>
> National Museum of the American Indian
> 1 Bowling Green
> The Battery
> New York 10004
> 800–242–NMAI or
> 212–825–6700

The five-acre plaza within the World Trade Center is the site of concerts at noon, surrounded by people having lunch. The large bronze globe revolving in the pool was designed by Fritz Koenig, and the granite pyramid on the Plaza by Masayuki Nagare. The **Observation Deck** on the 107th floor and the open-air deck on the 110th floor provide a view you won't forget. You can also have lunch or dinner at **Windows on the World** (call 212–524–7000 for reservations), which is on the 107th floor of 1 World Trade Center.

The **Battery** (the southern tip of Manhattan between State and Battery streets) was the spot where Giovanni da Verrazano, Estaban Gomes, and Henry Hudson came ashore. Twenty-one acres reach from the junction of the Hudson and East rivers to Bowling Green. In 1693 the British built a fort on an offshore island, and in 1870 the island and mainland were joined by filling in the gap. Castle Clinton, built in 1807, was developed into Castle Garden in 1824 and used for entertainment. Lafayette attended Castle Garden in 1824, and in 1850 Jenny Lind was the star performer in a concert there. **Castle Clinton National Monument** (212–344–7220) is open and features exhibits on the original fort.

Battery Park City is a ninety-two–acre landfill with an esplanade. Don't miss the Winter Garden.

The Smithsonian Institution has opened the **National Museum of the American Indian** with the move of the Heye Collection into the old Custom House on Bowling Green in the Battery. Cass Gilbert designed the building, which was completed in 1907 for $5.1 million. Four Daniel Chester French sculptures depict Asia, Africa, Europe, and North America. Look up and you'll see his Beaux Arts flair with dolphins, shells, and sea creatures on the cornice.

Ellis Island National
Monument
New York
212–883–1986
212–269–5755;
(ferry info)

Inside, the grand stairway and the rotunda are lit from a skylight dome. Reginald Marsh painted the dome's frescoes. The new museum required a shell inside a shell in order to reconcile the need for windows and for protection from sunlight.

The George Gustav Heye Center is the first of three NMAI sites. The other two will be on the Mall in Washington, D.C., near the National Air and Space Museum, and in a Cultural Resources Center in Suitland, Maryland. Heye bought and collected vast amounts of artifacts from many Native American communities, as well as sponsoring archaeological digs and ethnographic studies.

Richard West, director of the museum, describes the collection as Indian culture seen through native eyes. He is Southern Cheyenne and the son of a Native American artist. Objects to be displayed are chosen by a selected panel of Native Americans, including religious elders, tribal leaders, and artists. They have been chosen with care. For example, Susan Billy found that baskets were part of her background, and she selected a coiled basket with shell beads and feathers, used for the ritual washing of a newborn baby. Linda Poolaw chose a pouch, made by the tribe of her Kiowa father, which depicted nomadic life in its geometrical patterns and she chose another from her Delaware mother that is reminiscent of sedentary woodlands life. Visitors are welcome to walk into each of the galleries circling the rotunda.

Near the main entrance there's a Resource Center with four touch-screen multimedia programs. Visitors can learn about native life and traditions through these programs and can also work with objects that may be handled. Discovery boxes are available for you to enjoy—ask for the "Powwow" Box, which offers experience in dance and pageantry. The "Tatanka" Box contains quilts, beadwork, and hide boxes made by Ina McNeil, who is a descendant of Sitting Bull.

The **Staten Island Ferry** is one of the few free rides of New York City. For no charge, you can board at the foot of Whitehall Street in Battery Park, chug out into the harbor, past the Statue of Liberty and Ellis Island to Staten Island, and return past that unmistakable skyline.

You can also take a ferry (Circle Line; 212–269–5755) from the Battery for a fifteen-minute crossing to **Ellis Island National Monument.** Take the same ferry to the Statue of Liberty.

Imagine what it must have been like to leave friends, family, and home and step onto a ship with a piece or two of luggage. Passages across the Atlantic were miserable in steerage, with abominable living conditions and the real chance of storms to face. The sight of the Statue of Liberty extending her welcome must have lifted spirits with visions of a better life in the New World. But as the ship neared Ellis Island, people were full of apprehension, wondering if they would be accepted—or

Statue of Liberty
New York 10004
212-363-3200

turned back. Everyone had to undergo a medical examination, some were detained, and 2 percent (12 million) were separated from their families and returned to their homeland. It must have been devastating. Ellis Island was called "the island of hopes and the island of tears."

Ellis Island has now been restored to the tune of $160 million. With about half of all American families remembering someone who came through, the urge to visit is real. The first wave of about 5,000 immigrants arrived just after the Revolution, then 150,000 during the 1820s, 1.7 million in the 1840s, and 2.5 million in the 1850s.

Begin your tour with a film, commencing with poignant photos of families leaving their homes in Europe, traveling steerage across the ocean, and arriving at Ellis Island. Scenes of the derelict Ellis buildings give way to the restoration that has now been completed. Museum displays trace the first moments of the peak immigration years, from 1880 to 1924, when people tried to adapt to their new lives in America. Often their children were "go-betweens," and they had to walk a fine line between two opposing cultures—that of their parents, ingrained with ethnic mores, and that of their new friends and teachers, who often frowned on foreign ways. The children learned English and served as translators and envoys to the New World. Photographs throughout the museum bring visual impression to a new life. And voices of those immigrants who are still living can be heard describing their feelings at various stages in their adjustment.

We were especially touched by the Treasures from Home room. You'll see a lamb-shaped sugar dish brought from Russia in 1911; a copper coffee pot from Finland in 1923; a samovar from Germany in 1910; a copper cauldron from Italy in 1919; a green wooden ale bowl from Norway in 1900; a spinning wheel from Norway in 1894; a mangle board with carved pattern and "horse" handle, also from Norway, in 1890; a wedding dress from Armenia in 1890; a Black Madonna painting from Poland in 1909; a black Aragonese dress and fan from Spain in 1890; a regional dress from Moravia in 1920; and more. We recommend taking the first boat in the morning, before crowds appear. You can spend a number of hours on Ellis Island and then take a boat to the **Statue of Liberty.**

She was refurbished in time for an extravagant 200th birthday in 1986, including complete reconstruction of her torch, by French craftsmen. Gold leaf was applied to the torch, and sunlight makes it glimmer. This favorite monument of every American was built by the sculptor Frédéric

Fraunces Tavern
Museum
Broad & Pearl
Streets
New York 10004
212–425–1778

Auguste Bartholdi in 1886. She stands 151 feet high as she welcomes people to our shores. Many of us find tears streaming down our faces as we glide by her when returning by ship. The same thing happened to us more than forty-eight years ago when we saw a smaller replica of her on the shore of the Seine in Paris.

As you enter the museum, you'll come face to face with a copy of a lady's face—the Statue of Liberty herself. Her giant toes are on display a little farther on. A nearby plaque certifies that France gave her to America as a gift in 1886 as a token of friendship and liberty to enlighten the world. The idea had been proposed in 1865 by Edouard Réne Lefebvre de Laboulaye in his Paris home. Displays chronicle the development of the idea with sculptor Auguste Bartholdi, who was influenced by the Colossus of Rhodes from 300 B.C. Gustave Eiffel used his engineering skills to devise the support system and exclaimed, "It will hold!" During the 1980s restoration stainless steel replaced the rusted iron inside the statue. Wafer-thin sheets of copper were used with the "repoussé" method, and you can see a movie showing workmen hammering the copper into shape.

The museum displays a collection of medals, programs, and books, as well as the sword of the captain of the Lafayette Guard, which led the land parade on October 28, 1886. Don't miss the display of "popular culture" items sold for the celebrations—plates, spoons, a Tiffany-style lamp, clock, quilt, whirligig (wind-up toy), and more.

You can walk partway up the pedestal for views all around or climb twenty-two stories up inside the lady into the crown.

Fraunces Tavern Museum is located upstairs in a historic building. This museum of early American history and culture was the site of George Washington's farewell to his officers on December 4, 1783, when forty-four officers attended a dinner in his honor. Washington toasted them, walked to Whitehall, where he took a boat to New Jersey, went to Annapolis, Maryland, and resigned his commission at a ceremony in the State House there. You can see the Long Room, now renovated and set for a dinner as it would have been that night. The Clinton Dining Room, across the hall, features wallpaper printed by Jean Zuber in 1834. This "historic" wallpaper depicts a number of important events against a background taken from various scenic spots in America. The furnishings are of the nineteenth century, mostly of Duncan Phyfe design. The room is named after Governor George Clinton, who used to entertain guests in Fraunces Tavern.

The museum houses a permanent collection that includes Chinese export porcelain, silver, documents, prints, paintings, maps, clocks, weapons, and sculpture. Special exhibitions are held, as well as a full roster of educational programs on topics such as science and witchcraft in colonial times, native American fare, reviving eighteenth-century etiquette, New York City folklore, and medicinal plants in colonial America.

> South Street Seaport
> Fulton & Water
> Streets at East
> River
> New York 10038
> 212-748-8257

South Street Seaport is a new restoration of a nineteenth-century port district. In 1625 the Dutch West India Company established a trading post called Nieuw Amsterdam, and the British took possession of it in 1664. After the Revolution, in 1784, the *Empress of China* sailed to Canton, providing a link between the Orient and New York. In 1793 Peter Schermerhorn consolidated his waterfront lots on Fulton Street, and the Schermerhorn Row landfill began to reclaim land from the sea. In 1811 he built a row of counting houses. Robert Fulton's ferry docked on Fulton Street in 1814, and soon a packet line began service between New York and Liverpool. In 1822 the first Fulton Market opened, and the Erie Canal was completed in 1825 to extend the linkage by water from the Hudson to the Great Lakes. The Brooklyn Bridge construction began in 1870. Thomas Edison lit up South Street, the first commercial district in the world to have electric light, in 1882. A tin structure was built for the Fulton Fish Market in 1907. During all of this time, the area was alive with commercial enterprise—sailors in port from long voyages eager for activity and people who lived there going about their daily business.

In 1968 the Friends of South Street Seaport began planning for a new seaport, one that would depict the life of that area one hundred years ago. As you stroll through this walking village, away from traffic, you can feel some sensations from a century past.

Restored buildings house a gallery, stationer, book and chart store, boat building shop, and a children's center. During special programs children can learn how to furl a sail, sleep in a hammock, and observe other aspects of going to sea.

Head for the waterfront to see a fine collection of historic ships on display. The *Peking* is a four-masted bark built in 1911 in Hamburg, Germany; exhibits below decks depict life aboard this square-rigger. The *Ambrose Lightship* marked Ambrose Channel in New York harbor beginning in 1907. The *W.O. Decker* is a wooden tugboat that reminds us of "Little Toot." The *Lettie G. Howard* was built in 1893 in Essex, Massachusetts, as a Gloucester fishing schooner, typical of those bringing fish into the Fulton Fish Market. The *Pioneer* started life as a sloop in 1885, then changed into a gaff-rigged schooner in 1968. You can go for a sail on

Fulton Fish Market
200 Front Street
New York 10038
212–669–9416

Cloisters
Fort Tryon Park
New York 10040
212–923–3700

her during the summer. The *Wavertree* sailed from Liverpool during the 1880s on the jute trade between Europe and India. The *Major General William H. Hart* was built in 1925 as a New York City ferryboat.

The **Fulton Fish Market** is not easy to miss; if you like smells of the sea, you'll love it there. This market is the oldest continuously operating wholesale market in the United States, housed in the "Tin" building and "New Market." If you can arrive around 4:00 A.M., you will see lots of activity as fish are sold. A Fulton Fish Market tour is offered by reservation (see the number above).

The **Brooklyn Bridge** celebrated its centennial in 1983. It can be reached from Frankfort Street and Park Row. As the first suspension bridge and second-oldest bridge in New York, it has been called the "Eighth Wonder of the World." John Augustus Roebling was commissioned to draw up plans for the bridge in 1869. Unfortunately, he suffered a crushed foot before the bridge was completed, but his son, Washington Roebling, finished the bridge. Construction workers built caissons containing compressed air so that water would not disturb the work. The men went through a process of compression as they went down and decompression on the way back up, yet Washington Roebling suffered an attack of "the bends" and was partially paralyzed for the rest of his life. He continued to direct construction from a window overlooking the bridge. The bridge is 3,455 feet in length, and the central span is 1,595 feet. It cost $25 million and was completed in 1883. A series of legends, stories, jokes, and poems has arisen from this symbolic and beautiful bridge. Don't let anyone sell you the Brooklyn Bridge!—but if you could buy it, it would be worth a fortune.

Upper Manhattan

The New York City area has many other sights to see. Although we have concentrated on middle and lower Manhattan, we will suggest further possibilities for you to explore in upper Manhattan and the other boroughs.

The **Cloisters,** a branch of the Metropolitan Museum of Art devoted to medieval art, was built in 1934 through the generosity of John D. Rockefeller, Jr. The name comes from the open, rectangular courtyards with covered arcaded walks around the sides, or cloisters, found in medieval monasteries in Europe. European art dating from the twelfth century is exhibited in the gardens, arcades, cloisters, and galleries. The collections include wood carvings, furniture, religious statuary of alabaster and ivory, gems, stained-glass windows, and marble capitals. Don't miss the set of seven tapestries known as "Hunt of the Unicorn." The rich colors of the tapestries give vibrancy to life in the fifteenth century. Fort Tryon Park, where the museum is located, is between Broadway and Riverside Drive, from 192nd Street to Dyckman Street. **Riverside Church** is interdenominational. The Laura Spelman Rockefeller Carillon is the largest in the world, with seventy-four bells housed in a 400-foot tower. The church is especially known for its fine Gothic detail.

The **Ulysses S. Grant National Memorial** is between 120th and 124th streets on Riverside Drive. Both Grant and his wife are interred there. Colorful mosaic work around the tomb was created by schoolchildren.

Harlem

Nieuw Haarlem was settled in 1658 as a trading post and became a fashionable suburb after the railroad opened in 1837 and rapid transit lines emerged in 1880. The Harlem Renaissance of the 1920s produced a cultural center for black artists, writers, and performers. Now Harlem is undergoing a transition from abandoned buildings to luxury condominiums.

Visitors can take a Gray Line tour of Harlem (900 Fifth Avenue between 53rd and 54th streets; 800–669–0051) and leave the driving to someone else.

The **Cathedral of St. John the Divine** is the largest Gothic cathedral in the country. Stop by the fountain outside to see children's sculpture all around the edge of the fountain. Don't miss *Noah's Ark*. On the way to the cathedral, you'll pass Columbia University, Barnard College, Teacher's College/Columbia, Union Theological Seminary, City College of New York, and the Jewish Theological Seminary.

The **Apollo Theater** was where many black performers got their start, including Nat King Cole, Ella Fitzgerald, Pearl Bailey, Sarah Vaughn, Aretha Franklin, Sammy Davis, Jr., and Harry Belafonte.

Bronx

The **Bronx Zoo** is believed to be the largest zoo in the world. The

---

Riverside Church
Riverside Drive &
122nd Street
New York 10027
212–870–6828

Cathedral of St. John the Divine
Amsterdam Avenue at West 112th Street
New York 10026
212–932–7347

The Apollo Theater
253 West 125th Street
New York 10027
212–749–5838

Bronx Zoo
Bronx Park
185th Street &
Southern Boulevard
Bronx 10467
718–367–1010

New York Botanical Garden
Southern Boulevard
Bronx 10458
718–817–8700

American Museum of the Moving Image
35th Avenue at 36th Street
Astoria 11106
718–784–0077

Brooklyn Museum
200 Eastern Parkway
Brooklyn 11238
718–638–5000

animals are housed in environments that include the African Plains, Wild Asia, Aquatic Bird House, World of Darkness, and a special Children's Zoo. You can take the Sky Ferry Aerial Tramway or the Safari Train for an overview of the zoo.

The **New York Botanical Garden** in the Bronx Park grows a changing display of plants and trees on 250 acres. The Lorillard Snuff Mill, dating from 1840, produced snuff during the nineteenth century, and fields of roses growing nearby contributed petals to blend with the snuff for a pleasant fragrance. The Crystal Palace, an 1851 building constructed in Hyde Park, London, for the international exposition, was the inspiration for the Enid Haupt Conservatory building. The 90-foot-high glass dome shields a variety of palms, ferns, and tropical plants inside.

Queens

The **American Museum of the Moving Image** explores motion pictures, television, video, and digital media. Visitors are invited to film and video screenings, exhibitions, and displays of artifacts. More than 70,000 pieces are displayed, including costumes, props, set models, photographs, posters, and fan magazines. The permanent collection includes "Behind the Screen: Producing, Promoting, and Exhibiting Motion Pictures and Television," which focuses on the people who make it work—actors, directors, and costume and production designers.

We particularly enjoyed the set for *The Glass Menagerie,* a costume Marlene Dietrich wore as Concha Perez in 1935, and one worn by Rudolph Valentino as Duc de Chartres in 1924. Paul Newman's Buffalo Bill from 1976 and Robin Williams's Mork from 1978 are there as well. You'll see Liza Minnelli's Pookie Adams from 1969 and Hedy Lamarr's Delilah from 1949.

If you're a camera buff, take a look at some of them—a 1919 Akeley, the 1926 Bell & Howell "Ladies Filmo" (which was more user-friendly), a 1923 Cine-Kodak, and a 1908 Pathe Studio Camera, to name a few.

Brooklyn

The **Brooklyn Museum** contains collections of Egyptian art, primitive artifacts from Africa, collections from the Middle East and the Orient, and Greek and Roman artifacts. Reconstructed rooms of a seventeenth-century Brooklyn house are on display, as well as paintings by both European and American artists. Don't miss the sculpture garden that displays articles from "lost New York," including a column base from the old Penn Station and a lion's head from Steeplechase Park at Coney Island.

The **Brooklyn Botanic Garden** is well known for its Japanese meditation gardens. The Cranford Rose Garden contains many varieties of roses, and a special "fragrance" garden has been developed for the blind.

The **Brooklyn Children's Museum** began in 1899. Today it is a participatory museum where you can explore ethnology, natural history, and technology. Children can see a windmill and learn how it works, study fossils, or take a field trip. Workshops, demonstrations, storytellers, and concerts are available.

> Brooklyn Botanic
> Garden
> 1000 Washington
> Avenue
> Brooklyn 11225
> 718–622–4433
>
> Brooklyn Children's
> Museum
> 145 Brooklyn Avenue
> Brooklyn 11213
> 212–735–4400;
> 212–735–4432
>
> The Hudson River
> Museum
> 511 Warburton
> Avenue
> Yonkers 10701
> 914–963–4550

Yonkers

The **Hudson River Museum** offers contemporary galleries housing a variety of exhibits and the John Bond Trevor Mansion, a Hudson River estate dating from 1876. Changing exhibits of art, architecture, design, and history fill the galleries. The permanent collection includes paintings, photographs, graphic art, and memorabilia relating to the Hudson River. Family programs include fun walks, gallery games, and hands-on workshops.

The Andrus Planetarium contains a Zeiss star machine that is unique in the northeast. Laser shows are sometimes given in the planetarium; call to get the schedule. School shows are designed to meet the needs of each grade level.

Glenview, the Trevor Mansion, reflects the lifestyle of the Trevor family. It was designed by architect Charles Clinton and built of locally quarried gray stone. You can explore rooms with beautifully carved woodwork, stenciled ceilings, and tile floors. With the aid of an auction list of the Trevors' furnishings, the museum staff was able to provide authentic furniture, paintings, and decorative objects.

These suggestions are only a few of the sightseeing possibilities in the New York City area. It would take a lifetime to make a dent in all New York has to offer.

≋ *Long Island* ≋

Call **Long Island Convention and Visitors Bureau** at (800) 441–4601 for information about what it has to offer. There are a number of ways to reach your destinations on Long Island from New York City, including the Long Island Expressway (Route 495) down the center; to the north, the Northern State Parkway connecting with Route 25; or to the south, the Southern State Parkway connecting with Route 27. The **Long Island Railroad** runs down the island all the way to Montauk (718–990–7498; for schedule call 718–217–LIRR). **Long Island Airlines** services Long Island from New York, as well as Boston and Newark (516–752–8300). If you are coming from Connecticut, you can take one of two ferries: **Cross Sound Ferry** from New London to Orient Point (860–443–5281 for car reservtions or 516–323–2525) or the **Bridgeport and Port Jefferson Steamboat Company** (888–44–FERRY or 516–473–0286).

Long Island has a fascinating geologic history. Thirty thousand years ago a glacier ground through New England, loosening rock, pulverizing it, and embedding it within glacial ice. When the glacier reached the coast, it was met by warm air, making it drop accumulated rocks and debris as it melted. These piles of rocks were pushed into ridges sometimes hundreds of feet high—glacial moraines that stretch the whole length of Long Island, from New York City to the tips of Orient Point and Montauk. The extension of the moraine from Orient Point surfaces on Cape Cod; the one from Montauk reappears on Block Island, Martha's Vineyard, and Nantucket. Residents can attest to the rocks and pebbles under the surface of their land. Large boulders, swept along without being ground up, were also left along the north shore by the glacier. As the glacier melted, many streams flowed, carrying rock and pebbles to build up extensive plains; potatoes and vegetables now grow on the plains of Long Island.

Another specific glacial remain is the "kettle-hole" pond; Lake Success and Lake Ronkonkoma were formed this way. The original shape was outlined by a hard ice deposit that stayed put while water flowed around it. As the ice melted, round holes were left, some deep enough to fill with water and become lakes. Along the south shore the barrier beaches were formed by wave action working on rocks over the years to produce fine sand. That sand was moved by waves from the shore onto bars that grew into spits and peninsulas. The barrier beach along most of the south shore of Long Island protects the coast proper from the worst ravages of wind and wave erosion, but the sea is still working at reclaiming the land, as those who build too close to it discover to their dismay after a fierce winter northeaster.

> Sands Point Park
> and Preserve
> Port Washington
> 516–571–7900 or
> 7902

Long Island offers a microcosm of a much larger region, with distinct areas, ranging from the mansions of the "Gold Coast," old whaling and fishing ports, and farms growing those famous "spuds," to the natural beauty of coastal spits of land, dunes, beaches, and small villages. Musical entertainment encompasses rock concerts and classical concerts. You can go to thoroughbred races, harness races, or auto races. There are many wineries for touring and tasting and a variety of seafood and ethnic restaurants. You can fish, sail, swim, or just relax on a summer holiday. Long Island, just 125 miles long and no more than 23 miles wide, packs in a lot of variety for visitors to enjoy.

We suggest beginning your tour on the north shore, heading for Orient and Montauk Points at the forked end, and then continuing west along the beaches of the south shore. The Gold Coast stretches along almost one-third of the Long Island Sound shore. East of the Gold Coast is a historic triangle from Centerport to Stony Brook. Farmlands make up another third of the island, leading to the small villages, ports, and wineries of the North Fork. As you continue this circuit, take the ferries across to Shelter Island and Sag Harbor and then head out to Montauk Point. The South Fork, also known as "the Hamptons," is another, newer Gold Coast of exurban villas and mansions that serve as a retreat from the city. Its beautiful ocean beaches merge with the barrier beaches that line the remaining two-thirds of the Atlantic shore of the island, creating sheltered bays, all the way to Brooklyn.

Port Washington

If you are driving out from New York City, you may want to take one of the faster highways to reach your first destination on the north shore. Take exit 36N from the Long Island Expressway for Port Washington and head north on Route 101 to **Sands Point Park and Preserve.** Captain Harry F. Guggenheim's **Falaise,** a twenty-six-room, Normandy-style manor house, is located on the property. The collection includes sixteenth- and seventeenth-century Spanish and French furnishings and Guggenheim's silver racing trophies. Outside, a panoramic view of Long Island Sound awaits you.

27

Garvies Point
Museum and
Nature Preserve
Barry Drive
Glen Cove 11542
516–571–8010

Sagamore Hill
Cove Neck Road
Oyster Bay 11771
516–922–4447

Roslyn

Retrace your way down Route 101 and take Route 25A east to Roslyn, once the home of William Cullen Bryant, who was an editor of the *New York Evening Post*. He lived there from 1843 to 1878, helping to name the town Roslyn because it looked like Roslyn Castle in Scotland. Christopher Morley also lived there on Searington Road, now in Christopher Morley Park. If you tour the house, look for the "dymaxion bathroom," which has all bathroom plumbing formed into one unit.

Glen Cove

Follow signs to Glen Cove to **Garvies Point Museum and Nature Preserve,** which has prehistoric archaeological displays. There are 5 miles of nature trails within this sixty-two-acre park.

Picture yourself dining in a restaurant that houses a fine collection of marine exhibits, prepares memorable seafood, and has a view of Long Island Sound stretching beyond the graceful crescent of the beach. **Steve's Pier I** (33 Bayville Avenue, Bayville; 516–628–2153) is nautical throughout—from the decor outside the massive front doors to the bridge that crosses over a pool filled with milling lobsters, and into the spacious dining rooms filled with marine exhibits. Don't miss the collection of scrimshaw, ship models, a 200-pound bell from an Onassis ship, harpoons, a sponge-diver's suit, and a model of the USS *Constitution*. Ask about the forty-four-pound lobster, Charlie, who lived in the lobby pool for a year.

Oyster Bay

Continue on around Oyster Bay, which separates "West Egg" from "East Egg" in F. Scott Fitzgerald's *The Great Gatsby,* to **Sagamore Hill,** the home of President Theodore Roosevelt. Built in 1885, this house was named after Sagamore Mohanned, an Indian chief who lived in the area until the early eighteenth century. Outside, the house is painted red with green and yellow trim. It has a front porch, where the Roosevelts used to sit and rock, watching the sunset as well as the lights from passing vessels on the Sound. On this porch Roosevelt was notified of his nomination for governor of New York in 1898, for vice-president of the United States in 1900, and president in 1904. Walk around to the side to see "Speaker Cannon," playfully named for Speaker of the House Joe Cannon; it was fired every

Fourth of July, with Roosevelt on hand to see that the children "produced maximum noise with minimum risk of injury."

Inside the house most of the rooms are furnished as they were when Mrs. Roosevelt lived there, following her husband's death, until her own death in 1948. You can't miss all of the stuffed heads hanging in most of the rooms in the house, which, as a whole, resembles a hunting lodge more than an Oyster Bay mansion. The floors also display skins with heads from a white polar bear and several mountain lions.

> Old Orchard
> Cove Neck Road
> Oyster Bay 11771
> 516–922–4447
>
> Cold Spring Harbor
> Fish Hatchery and
> Aquarium
> Route 25A
> Cold Spring Harbor
> 11724
> 631–692–6768

In the downstairs hall hangs a framed buffalo robe given to Teddy after Custer's Last Stand. As a deputy sheriff he once found and returned two stolen horses to an Indian; the man took them and left without a word but later returned and gave this pictorial robe, which depicts the Battle of Little Big Horn in 1876, to Roosevelt.

The North Room has an eclectic collection of gifts received by Roosevelt—including a Samurai sword from the emperor of Japan, elephant tusks from the emperor of Abyssinia, an oriental rug from the sultan of Turkey, and books from the kaiser of Germany. The table in the family room is set for dinner; note the silver candelabra and exquisite silver platter.

The library was also Roosevelt's study and office during his presidency. This comfortable room has a fireplace with a wooden mantel, leather chairs, a collection of bronzes, a portrait of a moose, books, and, of course, lots of animal heads.

The Game Room replaced the nursery when the children became too old for it and needed a giant playroom. With its southern exposure, this room was warmer than most in the winter; it was chosen by Roosevelt during his last illness, and he died there in 1919.

You can also visit **Old Orchard,** which Theodore Roosevelt, Jr., built in 1937 because he and his wife wanted a home of their own after years of living in rented houses. He lived there for three years before he was killed following the D-Day Battle on Utah Beach, in Normandy; his widow lived there for the rest of her life, until 1960. The house has three permanent exhibits: one is based on Theodore Roosevelt's public life, another depicts the family life at Sagamore Hill, and the third contains memorabilia from the six children: Alice, Theodore Jr., Kermit, Ethel, Archibald, and Quentin. Old Orchard is located on the Sagamore Hill property, on the side opposite the parking lot.

Whaling Museum
Main Street
Cold Spring Harbor
11724
631–367–3418

Heckscher Museum
Route 25A & Prime
Avenue
Huntington 11743
631–351–3250

Walt Whitman House
246 Old Walt
 Whitman Road
Huntington Station
 11743
631–427–5240

Vanderbilt Museum
 and Planetarium
180 Little Neck Road
Centerport 11721
631–854–5555

Cold Spring Harbor

From Sagamore Hill head south to Route 25A and east to Cold Spring Harbor, an active whaling port during the middle of the eighteenth century. The **Cold Spring Harbor Fish Hatchery and Aquarium** is housed in what was a water-powered woolen mill more than a hundred years ago. The hatchery annually raises over forty thousand brook trout, rainbow trout, and brown trout; you can see them in stages from eggs to fingerlings to eight-pounders. The aquarium has both photographs and live fish to watch eyeball to eyeball through the glass. Don't miss the Turtle Room.

A little farther east along Route 25A is the **Whaling Museum.** The museum was developed around the gift of a whaleboat from the American Museum of Natural History. This whaleboat came from the brig *Daisy,* built just a few miles east of Cold Spring Harbor, in Setauket, in 1872. Many local residents gave or loaned whaling artifacts, which had been kept in their families, to the museum. The collection includes figureheads, ship models, scrimshaw, harpoons, maps, and tools; there is also a diorama depicting life in the village in the 1840s. Look for the skull of the killer whale. The museum holds workshops, such as a "Ship in a Bottle" session and a whaling-log session; shows films; and conducts walking tours of the village.

Huntington

Huntington is located just a few miles east along Route 25A. Did you know that Nathan Hale was betrayed by his cousin and captured in Huntington? Apparently he was fully aware of the risk involved when he was sent behind enemy lines; he was executed as an American spy on September 22, 1776. There is a monument to him on Huntington Bay.

Back in town the **Heckscher Museum** houses collections of American and European sculpture and painting from the sixteenth to the twentieth centuries. Also, Walt Whitman was born in this town, and you can visit his home. His desk, secretary, and some of his manuscripts and personal items are displayed.

Centerport

Sunken Meadow
State Park
Sunken Meadow
State Parkway
Kings Park 11754
631–269–4333

Just beyond Huntington, the **Vanderbilt Museum and Planetarium** is located a short distance north of Route 25A on Little Neck Road. William K. Vanderbilt II built the original structure as a Japanese-style, six-room home in 1907 and later expanded it into the mansion you see today; he lived there until 1944. As you approach the estate, you can't miss the white-stucco, Spanish-style wall surrounding the property; the twenty-four–room mansion also represents Spanish Revival architecture and interior decor. Wrought-iron windows and heavy carved doors and furniture accent the style. The dining room contains an 11-foot-long, seventeenth-century refectory table made of carved walnut. Don't miss the "Organ Room" on the second floor, where the chairs are covered with French petit point and needlepoint.

Outside, concerts are given in the mansion courtyard. Walk down the path to the planetarium, which offers a program of shows throughout the year; it is considered among the dozen largest and best equipped in the country. The grounds overlook Northport Bay; take a stroll down to the boathouse for another view. Retrace your steps back to the main house and head to the right to reach the Hall of Fishes, once known as the Vanderbilt Marine Museum. Mr. Vanderbilt made a number of scientific explorations in the early 1930s, and many of the animal and marine-life specimens in the museum are a result of these trips. On the second floor you will see both vertebrates and invertebrates, and the habitat wing contains dioramas of animals in their natural surroundings. Don't miss the whale shark hanging from the ceiling. The Bird, Moth, and Butterfly rooms display more collections.

Follow signs to **Sunken Meadow State Park,** which offers picnicking, three nine-hole golf courses, a driving range, swimming, athletic fields, hiking, nature trails, fishing, bike path, beach, bridle paths, and cross-country skiing (in the winter). Here you will find the first total relief from the influence of the city and its outskirts in a landscape unaffected by economic development in any form. As you approach the park, you drive off the ridges left from glacial moraine and move closer to the Sound, first through woods and then along an extensive salt marsh before you reach the beach. The approach itself provides half the pleasure of the park. This is truly a perfect spot to escape from frenetic city life.

East of the park on Route 25A, as you pass through **Smithtown,** look for the large bronze statue of a bull. It was apparently found on the coat of arms of Richard Smith.

The Museums
1208 Route 25A
Stony Brook
631–751–0066

Cutchogue Free
Library
Main Road
Cutchogue 11935
631–734–5537;
631–734–6532

Stony Brook

Continue east on Route 25A to Stony Brook, where you will see several museums, including a village rebuilt in the 1940s using eighteenth- and nineteenth-century Federal architecture. The **Art Museum** contains paintings by William Sidney Mount, a nineteenth-century genre painter who caught the essence of rural life on Long Island. The **History Museum** houses collections of toys, dolls, costumes, decoys, and fifteen furnished miniature rooms. The **Carriage Museum** exhibits sporting rigs, pleasure vehicles, farm and trade wagons, sleighs, children's vehicles, coaches, and firefighting equipment.

The State University of New York at Stony Brook maintains a **Fine Arts Library** (631–246–5000), which sponsors a variety of cultural programs and gallery exhibitions.

Port Jefferson

Port Jefferson is the landing for the ferry from Bridgeport, Connecticut. (See earlier in the chapter for information.) Also in Port Jefferson you will find **Brookhaven National Laboratory.** This atomic research center offers films, computer games, and other exhibits.

North Fork

Stay on Route 25A and Route 25 to **Riverhead,** the town at the junction of the North Fork and the South Fork, which serves as a center for the surrounding potato-farming country. If you want to bypass the town and head out the North Fork, take Route 58 until Route 25 rejoins it and keep going east toward Cutchogue.

Cutchogue, meaning "principal place," is the site of **Old House,** built in 1649 on the Village Green. It is the oldest English house still standing in New York State. Look at the English Tudor construction that is made visible through exposed sections inside the house. The furniture was all handmade by the early settlers who lived in the area. The **Wickham Farmhouse** on the Village Green, built in 1700, contains period furnishings. The **Old Schoolhouse** was built in 1840 and now houses a collection of antiques donated by families whose ancestors lived in the area. The **Cutchogue Free Library** is now in the church built in 1862 by the Independent Congregational Church and Society in Cutchogue.

A **Guild House** for artists and craftsmen is another building you can visit in Cutchogue. During the summer the town hosts a variety of events, including the Antiques Flea Market, Antique Car Show, Firemen's Parade and Drill, Village Square Dance, and the Outdoor Art Show of the Old Town Arts and Crafts Guild.

Hargrave Vineyard
Cutchogue 11935
631–734–5111
Orient Point State Park
Orient Point 11957
631–323–2440

If you enjoy vineyards, don't miss **Hargrave Vineyard,** the first vineyard producing estate-grown and -bottled wines on Long Island since colonial times. Alexander and Louise Hargrave began their research for a good site in 1972 after first looking at the Finger Lakes area. The tasting room has an 8-foot stained-glass window entitled "The Sower" (adapted from the François Millet painting) by Louis Comfort Tiffany.

Other wineries on the North Fork include Bedell Cellars, Main Road, Cutchogue, 631–734–7537; Duck Walk Vineyards, 162 Montauk Highway, Water Mill, 631–726–7555; Gristina Vineyards, Main Road, Cutchogue, 631–734–7089; Jamesport Vineyards, Route 25, Jamesport, 631–722–5256; Laurel Lake Vineyards, Main Road, Laurel, 631–298–1420; Lenz Vineyards, Main Road, Peconic, 631–734–6010; Macari Vineyard, Bergen Avenue, Mattituck, 631–298–0100; Palmer Vineyards, North Road, Aquebogue, 631–722–4080; Paumanok Vineyards, Main Road, Aquebogue, 631–722–8800; Peconic Bay Vineyards, Main Road, Cutchogue, 631–734–7361; Pellegrini Vineyards, Main Road, Cutchogue, 613–734–4111; Pindar Vineyards, Main Road, Peconic, 631–734–6200; Pugliese Vineyards, Main Road, Cutchogue, 631–734–4051; Wolffer Sagpond Vineyards, Sag Road, at Montauk Highway, Bridgehampton, 631–537–5106. Some of them require an appointment; others welcome visitors at any time during opening hours.

Farther east on Route 25 is **Greenport,** a yachting center for the North Fork; the terminus for the Shelter Island Ferry is located here. Greenport had a somewhat notorious past during Prohibition days, when fast boats were in and out bringing liquor to their customers. Stop for a meal at **Chowder Pot Pub,** adjacent to the ferry for Shelter Island (631–477–1345).

Beyond Greenport, at the tip of the North Fork, is **Orient Point.** This is the terminus for the ferry from New London, Connecticut. **Orient Point State Park** is a 357-acre park on Gardiners Bay that is a favorite stop for migratory birds.

Shelter Island

From Greenport take the ferry to Shelter Island. Once the site of a Quaker settlement, Shelter Island is now a popular resort located between the North Fork and the South Fork. Shelter Island is popular with yachtsmen because it has three good harbors: **Dering** on the north, **West Neck Harbor** on the southwest, and **Coecles Inlet** on the east. Most of them have saltwater ponds with marshes and the attendant wildlife you might expect. The island is a great place for biking and walking.

During colonial days Quakers fled persecution in New England and found peaceful lives on Shelter Island. Determined to learn more about this heritage, we followed a map that was compiled by the **Shelter Island Chamber of Commerce** (Box 598, Shelter Island, New York 11964; 631–749–0399) and lists historic sites. The **Shelter Island Historical Society's Havens House Museum** and **Manhanset Chapel Museum** is open during the summer from Thursday through Sunday (as of this writing). The **Havens House,** on South Ferry Road, was the home of James Havens, a member of the provincial congress, who lived there from 1743. The pleasant white house, located on a curve in the road, was kept in the family until 1925. Turn left onto North Ferry Road to the 1890 **Manhanset Chapel.** A little farther along the road, you'll come to the site of the first meetinghouse, dating from 1743, next to the present Presbyterian church.

Continue north on North Ferry, and look carefully on the right for the little road leading to the **Quaker Cemetery.** A memorial sign at that point states that Nathaniel Sylvester and other Quakers came there to escape persecution. You can drive into the woods to the cemetery, which has a large stone table in the center and a number of grave markers surrounded by a fence. It was a poignant moment for us as we stood there remembering my husband's Quaker heritage. (His ancestors, Eleanor and Edward Foulke, had left Wales in 1698 to find freedom.)

Try the **Ram's Head Inn** (Ram Island Drive; 631–749–0811; fax: 631–749–0059). (See Inns appendix.) When you have finished exploring the island, take Route 114 to the ferry for North Haven and Sag Harbor.

Sag Harbor

Sag Harbor's first inhabitants, the Indians, settled on a site that is now the center of town. They called it "Wegwagonock," or "Foot of the Hill." Later, as the place became a port, there was opportunity to take advantage of commodities going in or out, and by 1707 the British Crown was concerned enough about rum-running to appoint an officer to monitor this illegal activity.

Sag Harbor became a major whaling center during the eighteenth and early nineteenth centuries. The town was second only to New Bedford in the whaling business. In 1871 the last whaler, the *Myra,* left the harbor.

The call "Ship in the bay!" almost rings in your ears as you reminisce about the old days of whaling in town. And you can take a walking tour beginning at the Whaling Museum to see the homes built by whale oil. Don't miss the variety of picket fences and also doorways, each with different detail.

Sag Harbor Whaling Museum
Main & Garden Streets
Sag Harbor 11963
631–725–0770

Custom House
Garden Street
Sag Harbor 11963
631–941–9444

The **Sag Harbor Whaling Museum** is the place to go to reminisce and to learn more about whaling and the people who spent their lives in that profession. The Greek Revival home was built by Minard Lafever for Benjamin Huntting II in 1846. Today a modernistic sculpture of a whaling ship with crew pulling on the oars stands on the front lawn. Inside you'll see rooms chock-full of cases of displays of items brought back or made by whalers, or enjoyed by their families. Two portraits of little girls are hung in the parlor—in those days itinerant painters brought along canvases with the body finished so only the head had to be added. Look for the barber pole dating from 1900, when haircuts were 15 cents. The barber, Mr. Battle, used to tell outrageous stories, such as the one about watermelon seeds (giant-size watermelons are grown locally) being used to roof a barn. Don't miss the unusual washing machine and also the "Mammy Rocker" in the kitchen.

Both Sag Harbor and Nantucket inhabitants tried beach whaling, taught to them by Native Americans, before they ventured with their equipment onto ships. You'll see a collection of harpoons, samples of whale oil (the darker the color, the cooler the climate where the whale lived), ships' logs, and lots of scrimshaw. Mr. and Mrs. Walter Pharr donated a Narwhal tusk that is second in size to one in the Smithsonian. We heard the story about the pilot who collected it in Alaska, flew it sticking out of his plane, then brought it on the train and finally the subway to Bayside, Queens—what a journey!

The **Custom House** was the home of Henry Packer Dering, who was a U.S. custom master, in addition to raising nine children in his home. The lean-to section on Church Street was also the post office, dating from 1794. The first law in the United States was passed here in 1789. The office contains a history of Sag Harbor as one of two ports of entry—the other was New York. The kitchen must have been warm, with a huge fireplace and an oven for baking bread; don't miss the "baby minder" to keep little ones safe from the fireplace. Upstairs the master bedroom has a stenciled border. Many of the pieces were original in the Dering family. Look in the child's room for a squirrel cage.

First Presbyterian Church Union Street Sag Harbor 11963 Montauk Point Lighthouse 631–668–2428

An early version of the **First Presbyterian Church,** built after 1766, was called "a wooden building of uncouth shape" or "Old Barn Church." By 1816 parishioners began to erect a proper church, which was dedicated in 1818, later becoming a community hall and theater; the building burned in 1924. The present church dates from 1844, was built by Minard Lafever, and is listed on the National Register of Historic Places. The style is Egyptian Revival, and inside Lafever decorated with Greek volutes, rosettes, and anthemia. The tower was requested by whalers to be tall enough to be seen easily by returning mariners. But in the 1938 hurricane, the steeple was lifted 30 feet into the air, landed on the ground, and then toppled into the cemetery, with its bell tolling once. You can see the original bell in the church entry. Look for the silver nameplates on the pews. Fluted Corinthian columns soar to the ceiling, and the trompe l'oeil panel behind gives an impression of majesty. Don't miss the replicas of the original whale-oil lamps in between lavender windows.

James Fenimore Cooper began writing one of his first sea stories in Sag Harbor in 1824. More recently the town was the scene for the filming of *Sweet Liberty* (with Alan Alda) at the American Hotel. Stop for a meal at the **American Hotel** (631–725–3535) or at **Spinnakers** (Main Street; 631–725–9353).

Montauk

Head south on Route 114 to Route 27, where you can turn east to **Montauk Point.** One of the most productive fishing spots anywhere is the "cod ledge" off Montauk. Go to the very end to enjoy the view of the ocean full of boats and to see the **Montauk Point Lighthouse,** which George Washington ordered built in 1795. Very wisely, he insisted that it be set almost 300 feet back from the coast to allow for erosion. In November 1797 Jacob Hand lit the thirteen whale-oil lamps for the first time; he was up all night making sure they were all burning. By 1987 the vigil was over; as three Coast Guard seamen left their posts to the automated areobeacon.

We climbed up the 137 steps to the top of the tower. Views outside extend along the coast to crashing waves on the beach. Inside visitors can climb up six steps to see the continuously rotating giant beacon, which is lit twenty-four hours a day with a 1,000-watt bulb. Downstairs you can see the Fresnel lens that was up there from 1904 until 1987. A TV monitor presents a twenty-minute tape on the history of the lighthouse.

On February 20, 1858, a second lighthouse was completed farther along on the Long Island shore. Mariners had for years trusted the only lighthouse on Montauk Point, but because the two lights looked the same, the Montauk light was changed into a flashing light. Since this was long before the era of radioed notices to mariners, captains who had been away for some time did not have any news of this change. The *John Milton,* a clipper ship of 1,445 tons, was on her way to New York from Peru when her captain saw the light during a storm. Thinking his landfall was the Montauk light, he continued on course, with the crew in fine spirits to be so near port. The cliffs were there to meet them head-on, crunching the hull, breaking spars, and scattering cargo. The lighthouse keeper and his assistant plowed through the snow to find the source of the ship's bell they had heard, only to find the wreck with timbers, cargo, sails, and bodies swathed in ice.

> Second House
> Museum
> Montauk 11954
> 631–668–5440

Part of the history of Montauk includes the visit by Theodore Roosevelt and his troops after the port of New York denied them landing (because of the possibility of disease) following the Spanish-American War. Also, Rudolph Valentino filmed *The Sheik* here in the 1920s, and during Prohibition the waters around the point were used for drops by rum-running boats.

During the 1880s it became popular to walk from New York City to the Montauk Lighthouse and back. New York newspapers played up each successful venture. Some of the walkers even stayed overnight with the lighthouse keeper. In 1890 J. O. Whittemore rode the route on his cycle. (When we were there, hundreds of cyclists were going to the lighthouse on a bike-a-thon.)

In 1908 William K. Remsen of Brooklyn led a group of friends, each in his own car, on a wild ride to the lighthouse. The noise and smoke from those belching machines must have been something to witness. After they reached East Hampton, the road deteriorated, and several of the autos had problems: One rode off into the sea, another exploded, and others had a plethora of minor problems. Twenty-eight autos finally arrived, carrying all of the original forty drivers; they roared around the lighthouse three times. While they were climbing out of their cars, the lighthouse keeper approached them to express regret that he did not have enough food. But they did! From the cars came hampers of food for a great feast.

When you're ready for lunch, a good place to stop is **The Harvest,** on South Emery Street (631–668–5574), or **Gosman's,** on West Lake Drive (631–668–5330).

In the town of Montauk, **Second House Museum** was built in 1746 and rebuilt in 1797. The "First House," built in 1744, burned in 1909. The

Hither Hills State
  Park
Route 27
Montauk 11954
631–668–2554

East Hampton
  Historical Society
101 Main Street
East Hampton 11937
631–324–6850

Montauk Historical Association maintains the existing house, which includes an eighteenth-century kitchen.

From Montauk head west on Route 27 to **Hither Hills State Park,** which offers nature trails, hiking trails, picnicking, swimming, fishing, and camping, all in a beautiful setting.

For more information about Montauk, call (631) 668–2428.

Amagansett

The next town, Amagansett, is the site of the landing of German saboteurs during World War II, in June 1942. They disembarked from a submarine, fooled a coastguardsman with their fluent English, then buried some incendiary bombs in the sand. These were uncovered, and the four Germans were captured after a fifteen-day chase.

East Hampton

As you head west along the south shore of the Island, East Hampton is the first of the "Hamptons" you will come to. It is an attractive village with a number of historic buildings on its shady streets. In 1648 settlers purchased East Hampton for "20 coats, 24 hatchets, 24 hoes, 24 looking glasses and 100 muxes [an early tool used for making wampum]" from the Shinnecock Indians. You can't miss seeing **Hook Mill,** a windmill located between North Main Street and Pantigo Road. Built in 1806, it has now been restored to serve as a landmark of the past.

The **East Hampton Historical Society** is housed in the **Osborn-Jackson House,** dating from 1735. The house contains eighteenth- and nineteenth-century furnishings. Some rooms are used as galleries for temporary exhibits, and quilting and weaving are featured during the summer.

Clinton Academy was the first chartered academy in New York State; it dates from 1784. Boys came from New York City to study for college there. In 1815, 156 students were enrolled in a curriculum that included mathematics, navigation, surveying, geometry, accounting, Greek, and Latin. The house now contains East Hampton exhibits from the past.

Across the Green stands **Mulford Farm,** dating from 1680. A costumed interpreter will take you around the house, telling stories about the people and the items displayed there. Look for the patch of eel grass protruding from a hole in the wall up near the ceiling; although it was handy for insulation, inhabitants found that little creatures from the woods would hunker down in it during the winter and then find it difficult to get out. Displays include one on the maritime triangular trade; a chart of cattle ear marks so villagers could find their own animals; and a collection of wine bottles, silver, a delft platter in blue and white, and a pewter platter. Look for the "ghosts" of missing parts of hinges where the outlines still reveal their original shape. The parlor is the place where the men entertained themselves; women chatted upstairs. Squared-off bottles fit into slots within a carrying case for travel; there's a case in the room. Clay pipes lie on the table—fastidious smokers broke off the tip before using a pipe. China in the cupboard was saved for special occasions. Look on the mantel above the fireplace for "spiles," which are curly wood shavings used to light the fire. The bedroom downstairs was used by the oldest and the youngest members of the family. The rope bed has straw on top and then a feather mattress. There's a twister to crank up the ropes on the bed—hence the phrase "sleep tight." Look for the "fleam," which was used to bleed people who became sick. They had to hold on to a pole tightly so the veins stood out for bleeding. Blood ran down the fabric wrapped around the pole, and the end result looked like a "barber pole." People used to congregate in the kitchen with its roaring fire to sew, weave on the loom, make candles in the mold, and cook in three-legged pots. Look for the "temse," a container covered with goatskin and pierced with nails, used as a sifter for hand-ground grain. And look for the unique waffle iron and toaster.

"Home Sweet Home"
14 James Lane
East Hampton 11937
631–324–0713
Guild Hall
158 Main Street
East Hampton 11937
631–324–0806
East Hampton Town Marine Museum
Bluff Road
East Hampton 11937
631–267–6544

Don't miss **"Home Sweet Home,"** the childhood home of John Howard Payne, who wrote the song of the same name. You can see an eighteenth-century windmill, herb garden, gallery, and collection of English lusterware and ceramics.

The **Guild Hall** has changing exhibits, some from local artists who summer in town. There are 200 works in the permanent collection. The **John Drew Theater** (631–324–4050) offers a number of concerts, plays, and films.

The **East Hampton Town Marine Museum** has displays of early whaling history, fishing exhibits, models of fishing boats, and information on shipwrecks. Photos of the bulwark of the *Alice Reed* are there. Spoils of the ships turned up in "shipwreck" dresses that soon appeared on a number of women in town. One shipment carried shoes with metal tips, and the women tapped their way around town as well.

The Historical
Museum
17 Meeting House
Lane
Southampton 11968
631–283–2494

The Old Halsey
South Main Street
Southampton 11968
631–283–3527

Elias Pelletreau
Silversmith Shop
Main Street
Southampton 11968

Upstairs you'll find two "discovery rooms" for children, split into two age-groups. Here the kids can play and learn with lots of pieces to handle. Look out the window to see the jungle-gym trawler, just made for children to climb on.

Displays include a wetlands focus (on the interdependency of all parts in the wetlands); shellfish and how they are harvested; cod trawling; dragging with cone-shaped nets; haulseining, wherein nets are set in boats and then hauled into shore with winches; harpooning by boat at sea; aquaculture, or fish farming; pound trapping as fish migrate; and a collection of lobster traps. Look for the underwater archaeological exhibit.

Southampton

Southampton is the oldest English settlement in the state; people arrived there in 1640 from Lynn, Massachusetts. The name was chosen by the Earl of Southampton to commemorate the colonization of our country. In 1898 the Southampton Colonial Society formed; it maintains many of the historical sites in town. We suggest a walking tour as the best way to see the center of this interesting old town; you can get a map from the **Southampton Chamber of Commerce** (76 Main Street; 631–283–0402).

The Historical Museum is housed in the home built by whaling captain Albert Rogers in 1843. It includes a bedroom and a living room, both decorated as they would have been in his day; a colonial bedroom; the Shinnecock Room of Indian artifacts; and a collection of quilts, toys, china, glass, and old documents. Nearby are a one-room schoolhouse with the desks still in place, a whaling collection, farm equipment, weaving and spinning exhibits in the Red Barn, a carriage shop, country store and post office, blacksmith shop, carpenter shop, and an early drugstore.

The Old Halsey was built in 1648 by Thomas Halsey, one of the town founders. It is now the oldest English frame house in the state. Phebe, the wife of Thomas, was murdered there by Connecticut Indians. The furniture is from the seventeenth and eighteenth centuries. Local garden clubs maintain the herb and border gardens.

The **Elias Pelletreau Silversmith Shop** was operated by a captain who was both a famous silversmith and a staunch Revolutionary War patriot. His silver is now very valuable and an expensive collector's item.

The **Parrish Art Museum** is the permanent home of the William Chase collection. There are special exhibitions of local artists as well as of internationally famous ones. The museum runs a series of workshops for children and concerts in the gardens

Parrish Art Museum
25 Jobs Lane
Southhampton 11968
631–283–2118

during the summer, and other special events all year. As you will see, **Jobs Lane** offers one boutique, restaurant, and shop after another, inviting you to while away some time.

Conscience Point, where the group from Lynn, Massachusetts, landed in June 1640, is off North Sea Road. There is a plaque attesting to their landing and subsequent founding of Southampton.

Take a drive out to the "estate" area along the shore. Some of the homes are weathered cedar shake, while others are brand-new. Most are large houses, with landscaping protecting them from the road and more landscaping protecting the dunes from beach erosion. The cedar-shake house used in the filming of one of Woody Allen's movies is along the row.

Have you heard about the "Money Wreck" or "Coin Beach"? If you happen to be on a beach in the Hamptons, look for gold coins in the sand. In November 1816 a ship mysteriously went aground on the bar opposite Shinnecock Bay. The ship was broken up and auctioned by local people; during the auction some gold coins were found. Two local whalers, Henry Green and Franklin Jagger, secretly searched on board at night, gathering as many coins as they could. Eventually the sea completed the job the wreckers had not finished, when one storm littered the beach for miles around with pieces of the hull. A number of years later, gold coins, dated between 1740 and 1790, began to surface on the beaches. Some farmers used their teams to plow the beaches; one found $60 in a day. Some local historians believe that this ship was one that was boarded off the Easthampton bar by a crew who murdered the men on board, removed what valuables they saw, lashed the wheel, hoisted sails, and pushed off as the ship headed for the beach.

Restaurants recommended to us include **Barrister's** (36 Main Street, 631–283–6206), **Basilico** (10 Windmill Lane; 631–283–7987), **Driver's Seat** (62 Jobs Lane; 631–283–6606), **John Duck Jr.** (15 Prospect Street; 631–283–0311), the **Southampton Public House** (Bowden Square; 631–283–2800), and the **Lobster Inn** (North Highway; 631–283–9828).

From the Shinnecock Canal we suggest an excursion to a stretch of the barrier beach via Lynn Avenue and the Ponquogue Bridge onto the spit at Shinnecock Inlet, where there is a county park. The beach community on the spit is housed between sand dunes and low pines. Drive along

41

Fire Island Visitors'
Center
Box 248
Sayville 11782
516–289–4810

Tiana Beach on Beach Road and Westhampton Beach on Dune Road and turn back inland at the Swordfish Beach Club. Wend your way back through residential areas to Route 27A by any way that pleases you, or by Route 31 if you want to be direct. Then take Route 27 west to Shirley, turn left onto Route 46, and head for Fire Island across the Smith Point bridge.

Fire Island

Fire Island National Seashore is a 32-mile-long barrier beach that is kept in its wild state. You can park your car just over the Smith Point bridge, camp in the campground there, and walk into the park with your gear for the day. You can also take ferries from Patchogue, Sayville, and Bay Shore to reach the more remote areas. The **Visitors' Center** provides information and the beginning of the nature trail. Fire Island offers fishing—including excellent surf fishing—clamming, swimming, and bird-watching, among other recreational activities.

Sailors have always been aware of the hazards—especially in storms—of this barrier beach enclosing the sheltered waters of Great South Bay. Added to natural hazards was the human element: Some residents misled ships by placing lamps in their windows, then salvaged the wreck that followed. One legend attributes the name "Fire Island" to these lamps; others say that it was originally "Five Islands" and that the name evolved from poor penmanship.

Jones Beach

If you are not through swimming or beachcombing, you may want to drive out to Jones Beach, which is actually a series of beaches extending for 6½ miles. To reach it from the east, take the Robert Moses State Parkway and Causeway from Route 27 to Captree State Park; then head west along Ocean Parkway until you reach **Jones Beach State Park.** If you prefer swimming in a pool to swimming in the ocean, there is one available. Don't miss the Water Tower, reminiscent of the Campanile at St. Mark's Cathedral in Venice. The **Jones Beach Theater** is also located in the park.

From Jones Beach you can take Meadowbrook State Parkway back to Southern State Parkway or the Long Island Expressway to New York City.

The next section of this itinerary follows the Hudson River to the north.

✒ *Hudson River Valley* ✒

The Hudson River was discovered when Giovanni da Verrazano sailed along the coast under the flag of France in 1524. Not much was made of this discovery. When, however, the Dutch East India Company hired Henry Hudson to find a northwest passage to reach the riches of Asia, the river found a place in history. This inventive and aggressive English navigator hoped that he would find the way to the Orient as he sailed up the river in 1609 on his ship, the *Half Moon*. He sailed as far as Albany and, while disappointed to be unsuccessful in his original search, returned with enthusiastic reports of the fertile valley. Dutch settlers and traders led the way for other immigrants to follow.

The beauty of the Hudson River, with its tremendous cliffs amid views around each bend, has a geologic history of at least seventy-five million years. During the Ice Age the glaciers ground out the riverbed. The Continental Shelf was exposed long ago. Today the Hudson River channel is below sea level from Albany to the ocean. Therefore the river is tidal and saline partway up the 150-mile stretch to the Albany area.

Before the Revolution, use of the river was blocked by the Iroquois Confederacy; even during the early 1800s, the Mohawk and Oneida Indians controlled the Mohawk pass. Surrounded by steep walls of the cliffs, travelers did not have a chance against Indians poised to attack. During the Revolution about one-third of the battles took place somewhere along the Hudson River, since it was the main channel of communication between Canada and the colonies. The important Battle of Saratoga, regarded by some historians as the turning point of the war, kept the British from grasping that essential water route.

The Hudson River School of painters, active in the early- to mid-nineteenth century, had vibrant and majestic subjects for their work. This group of painters was the first in the country to band together. Led by Thomas Doughty, Thomas Cole, Asher B. Durand, and William Cullen Bryant, they were instrumental in breaking away from the traditional American Academy of Fine Arts, run by John Trumbull.

A more liberal National Academy of Design was encouraged by Bryant, with Samuel Morse as president. As editor of the *New York Evening Post*, Bryant had the power to provide publicity through his paper. He was determined to see America develop an art of its own.

The early years of the nineteenth century also brought remarkable commercial significance to the Hudson. In 1807 Robert Fulton sailed his first steamboat, the *Clermont,* from New York City to Albany with remarkable speed, creating a new mode of transportation that would make development of the river possible. When the Erie Canal opened in 1825, the river really came into its own, because the Great Lakes and the West were finally accessible by water. Not until the railroads supplanted water transportation did the river begin to lose its central importance, and even that development began with Commodore Vanderbilt's water route, which is still one of the best ways to appreciate the beauty of the river.

Over the years a number of mansions were built along the Hudson, perched on hills or cliffs like the castles along the Rhine, yet in their opulence resembling more the collection of chateaus in the Loire Valley. Some of them are now in ruins, but others have been restored to the splendor of the past. You can also visit vineyards along the Hudson and taste their wines, as you can on the Rhine and the Loire. The Huguenots planted grapes in the seventeenth century; there are now many wineries to visit, mostly concentrated on the west side of the river in the section around Newburgh. If you take a cruise, you will catch glimpses of all of it at once—mansions, vineyards, cliffs—and perhaps add to your collection of lighthouses at the same time.

The mountains along the river are part of the Appalachian chain, consisting of several small ranges, including the **Highland, Taconic, Catskill, Shawangunk,** and **Helderberg mountains.** The Highlands extend from Poughkeepsie on the north to Peekskill and West Point on the south. There is a gorge between Cornwall-on-Hudson and Stony Point that is unusually deep, with peaks ranging up to 1,400 feet above the river. James Fenimore Cooper's Natty Bumpo (in *The Pioneers)* remarked, "You must have seen them [the mountains] on your left, as you followed the river up from York, looking as blue as a piece of clear sky, and holding the clouds on their tops." Look for names such as Storm King, Breakneck Ridge, and Anthony's Nose in this area.

The Taconics lie east of the Hudson River, reaching 1,200 feet in height. The Catskills lie in an area bounded by State Highway 17 on the south, State Highway 23 on the north, U.S. Highways 209 and 9W on the east, from Kingston to Catskill, and from State Highway 30 south from Grand Gorge to State Highway 17 at East Branch on the west. The Shawangunk Mountains lie south of the Catskills. The Helderbergs run along the southern section of the Mohawk Valley on the west side of the Hudson River.

The geology of the Catskill Mountains may have been easy for geologists to uncover, because many identifying features are exposed—cliff faces, flumes (streams flowing over bedrock), and bare bedrock—which eliminates the need to dig and remove vegetation. The rock is sedimentary and thus retains more glacial scratches and fossils than igneous and metamorphic rock. Many of the fossils are of marine organisms, because the sea once covered this area. For more than fifty million years, erosion carried debris from the Acadians to an area known as the Catskill Delta. The delta rose up gradually and began to suffer from erosion, mostly from streams leading into the Hudson River. Glaciers advanced, leaving scratches and gouges; streams flowed beneath the glaciers as they melted, producing landforms such as kames, drumlins, eskers, drift pedestals, and kettle holes. As the glaciers melted, the land, which had been crushed by their weight, began to rise again; streams reversed their courses and produced waterfalls, rapids, and gorges.

There are hundreds of waterfalls for you to explore and photograph along the tributaries leading into the Hudson. A short list includes **Kaaterskill Falls, Bastion Falls, Haines Falls, Palenville Falls, Shinglekill Falls, Woodstock Falls, Glen Falls,** and the **Falls at East Durham.** James Fenimore Cooper wrote in *Leatherstocking Tales:* "The first pitch is nigh 200 feet and the water looks like flakes of snow afore it touches the bottom; and there the stream gathers itself together again for a new start and maybe flutters over 50 feet of flat rock before it falls for another hundred, when it jumps about from shelf to shelf, first turning this-a-way and then turning that-a-way, striving to get out of the hollow til it finally comes to the plain."

In spite of their proximity to New York City, the Catskills are still considered a wilderness area, with peaks up to 4,000 feet, deep gorges, rocky crags, and impenetrable ravines. The Indians, believing that the Great Spirit lived there, did not choose to live in the mountains; Dutch settlers found the fertile valley more profitable. Thus the Catskills were never developed and are today still a haven of natural beauty, with many remote areas prized by hikers.

If you are coming from New York City, we suggest that you begin this section at Tarrytown.

Tarrytown and Sleepy Hollow

Tarrytown, dubbed so by Washington Irving after farmers' wives who apparently lingered when they went in to market, or after husbands who "tarried" at the tavern, is steeped in the legends of Sleepy Hollow. The town is located just north of The Tappan Zee Bridge at the widest section of the Hudson River.

Sunnyside, the home of Washington Irving, was described by him as

Sunnyside
Route 9
Tarrytown 10591
914–591–8763
Sleepy Hollow
Cemetery
Route 9
Tarrytown 10591

"a little old-fashioned stone mansion all made up of gable ends and as full of angles and corners as an old cocked hat." Born in 1783 in New York City, Irving was named after General George Washington, whom his Scottish immigrant parents greatly admired. He remembered being patted on the head by General Washington when he was a child. In 1809 he published *Knickerbocker's History of New York,* a mixture of humor and satire about the Dutch settlers. Although the main character, Diedrich Knickerbocker, was fictitious, New Yorkers were also called "Knickerbockers." *The Sketch Book,* finished in 1820, first presented some of the characters that Irving is remembered for: Ichabod Crane, the Headless Horseman, and Rip Van Winkle. Irving also lived in Spain inside the famous Alhambra, as a guest of the Moorish Monarch of Granada, and developed his storytelling powers with *Tales of the Alhambra,* published in 1832.

After extensive traveling Irving returned home and purchased Sunnyside in 1835 from a member of the Van Tassel family, also featured in his writing. As you approach the house, look at the southerly view of the Hudson; once there were a beach and a boat dock, but when the railroad came through in 1849, the pleasures of the river were a little diminished. Look at the wisteria vine beside the front door; it was planted by Irving. The iron benches on the porch were housewarming gifts. Irving loved planning innovations for his house and invented a number of refinements that other homes did not have for many years. For example, he created a water system for his house that was unknown to anyone else around.

The Life of George Washington was written in this house and completed the year Irving died. His desk and books are still in the study as he left them, as is a couch where he slept when there were too many living in the house. His brother Ebenezer and his five daughters came to live with him, and later two of the girls, Sarah and Catherine, ran the house for Irving. The house is completely furnished, with his favorite chair poised by a window for the view and the dining room table set for dinner.

Follow Route 9 north of Sunnyside for 4 miles to visit **Sleepy Hollow Cemetery,** where Washington Irving is buried, and to immerse yourself in visions of Ichabod Crane, his horse Gunpowder, and the Headless Horseman. According to the story, Ichabod Crane rode off on Gunpowder to visit Katrina Van Tassel and ask her to marry him. He was turned down, and, as he made his way home, "It was the very witching time of night that Ichabod, heavy-hearted, and crestfallen, pursued his travel homewards, along the sides of the lofty hills which rise above Tarry Town. . . . In the dark shadow of the grove, on the margin of the brook, he beheld something huge, misshapen, and mounted on a black horse of powerful frame. . . . Ichabod was horror-struck, on perceiving that he was headless! . . . If I can but reach that bridge, thought Ichabod, I am safe." He was, however, thrown from his horse by the "head" tossed at him by the headless horseman. In the morning Ichabod Crane was gone, his horse Gunpowder was there, and a pumpkin was lying in the road. The bridge where the climax of the story is set crosses the Pocantico River by the Old Dutch Church and the cemetery.

Backtrack a few miles to **Lyndhurst,** which really looks the way a castle should! This Gothic Revival gray-white marble mansion was designed by Alexander Jackson Davis in 1838 for William Paulding. The second owner, George Merritt, enlarged the house in 1865. The last owner was Jay Gould, who almost cornered the gold market and caused the Black Friday panic in 1869. Some of the original furnishings that Davis designed for the house remain there.

| Lyndhurst |
| Route 9 |
| Tarrytown 10591 |
| 914–631–4481 |
| |
| Philipsburg Manor |
| Route 9 |
| Sleepy Hollow 10591 |
| 914–631–3992 |
| |
| Historic Hudson Valley |
| 150 White Plains Road |
| Tarrytown 10591 |
| 914–631–8200 |
| |
| Union Church of Pocantico Hills |
| Route 448 |
| Tarrytown 10591 |
| 914–631–8200 |

Philipsburg Manor has been restored to re-create the period from 1720 to 1750. After you leave the visitors' center you will cross a bridge over the river into that earlier era. Ducks and geese float and dive in the pond, and a mill wheel turns with a splashing sound. The Dutch-style manor house was built for Frederick Philipse in the 1700s. His home was in Yonkers, but this house was used as headquarters for his business. The interior is quite spartan, with bare floors and no curtains. In the parlor is a Dutch cupboard with painted scenes on it. The bed in Adolph Philipse's bedroom can be folded when not in use—an early Murphy perhaps? Visit the gristmill for a demonstration.

Historic Hudson Valley, which operates Sunnyside, Philipsburg Manor, and Van Cortlandt Manor, offers a variety of programs throughout the year: candlelight tours, winter cookery, a flower festival, country dancing, sheepshearing, concerts, storytelling, and crafts. Write for a brochure of events.

The **Union Church of Pocantico Hills** features stained-glass windows by Henri Matisse and Marc Chagall. Matisse designed a neo-Gothic rose window—in memory of Abby Aldrich Rockefeller, wife of John D. Rockefeller, Jr.—that was installed in 1956. Chagall created the "Good

Kykuit
Sleepy Hollow 10591
914–631–8200 or
631–9491

Van Cortlandt Manor
South Riverside
Avenue
Croton-on-Hudson
10520
914–271–8981

Samaritan" window in 1965, as well as eight side windows, seven of which represent Old Testament prophets.

Kykuit, the Beaux Arts mansion of the Rockefellers, opened in May 1994. The word *kykuit* is Dutch for "lookout," and the mansion indeed commands a spectacular view of the Hudson River and the Palisades. John Davidson Rockefeller had the vision for his mansion in 1908, before World War I, but left it to his son, John D. Rockefeller, Jr., to come up with creative ideas and supervise the building. (JDR Jr. also bought the land and paid for the construction of The Cloisters. He purchased Washington Irving's Sunnyside, Philipsburg Manor, and Van Cortlandt Manor to preserve them. He also restored Williamsburg and founded Rockefeller Center in New York.)

The mansion rises five stories high, enough to hold the collection of antiques belonging to the family. John D. Rockefeller, Jr., and his wife, Abby Aldrich Rockefeller, lived there after his father died in 1937. Nelson and his wife Margaretta (Happy) Rockefeller lived in the house from 1960 until he died in 1979; they were the last of the Rockefellers to live at Kykuit. Nelson collected oriental porcelain and contemporary art of all kinds—tapestries, sculpture, and painting.

The gardens combine Italian, French, and English styles. Visitors can walk along paths to see scuplture created by both European and American artists, including Jean Arp, Constantin Brancusi, Alexander Calder, Alberto Giacometti, Henry Moore, Louise Nevelson, and David Smith. And the views of the river are striking.

Visitors first tour the main floor and the art galleries. Next they enter the terraced gardens and finally the coach barn, where there are carriages and automobiles.

Croton-on-Hudson

Head north on Route 9 to the sign for Croton Point Avenue, which will lead you to **Van Cortlandt Manor.** In 1697 Stephanus Van Cortlandt's land was chartered by Royal Patent as the Manor of Cortlandt. Philip Van Cortlandt, his son, received the manor house and one-tenth of the land. He added a gristmill, store, church, school, and the Ferry House, which was an inn at the ferry crossing. Travelers came on the Albany Post Road and crossed the river on a family-owned ferry; local inhabitants frequented the taproom in the inn to get news from peddlers and other travelers. Philip Van Cortlandt's son Pierre was the first lieutenant governor of the state.

Garrison

Boscobel
Garrison-on-Hudson
10524
845-265-3638

Continue north on Route 9 to Route 403 and head into Garrison. The **Bird and Bottle Inn** dates from 1761, when it was known as Warren's Tavern. It is now a favorite spot for a meal or an overnight stay. (Call 800–782–6837 or 845–423–3000; also see Inns appendix.)

Boscobel was begun in 1804 by States Morris Dyckman. The name Boscobel was taken from a home of the same name in Shropshire, England. Charles II had hidden inside an oak tree in the forest of Boscobel in 1651 following his defeat by Cromwell. Dyckman had two pieces of wood from the "Royal Oak" made into two snuff boxes, which are on display in the house. He died in 1806 and his wife, Elizabeth, finished the house.

In the early 1950s the house had fallen into disrepair and was slated for the wrecking crew when it was finally purchased for $35. People in the area dismantled the house and stored the pieces in their barns until it could be rebuilt. Lila Acheson Wallace of the *Reader's Digest* generously financed the reconstruction of the house. It was completely restored and refurnished with as much accuracy as could be obtained from old records. The dining room contains silver belonging to the Dyckman family. Note the unusual wine-glass coolers and the washstand that was available for travelers who wanted to wash up before dinner. The center hall of the house is so large that it was frequently used for dancing. The living room is set up for tea; afterward the tea table would be moved so the guests could play parlor games. The next room is a more casual living room; look for the barrel organ.

Downstairs in the museum area is a collection of decorative arts and memorabilia. Look for the snuff box in blue and gold. Lemonade or cider and cookies are offered at the end of the tour. Ask about Boscobel's special candlelit tours if you are going to be in the area during the evening.

Cold Spring

Follow Route 9D into Cold Spring, a historic nineteenth-century village. A number of houses and shops are within the National Historic District. The West Point Foundry provided employment for workers who lived in Cold Spring; the Parrott Cannon, which some say won the Civil War for the North, was manufactured there. The village lures strollers with its many shops and restaurants.

Van Wyck Home-
stead Museum
Route 9
Fishkill 10524
845–896–9560

Locust Grove
Route 9
Poughkeepsie 12602
845–454–4500

Bardavon 1869
Opera House
35 Market Street
Poughkeepsie 12602
845–473–2072

Riverboat Tours
310 Mill Street
Poughkeepsie 12601
845–473–5211

Fishkill

From Cold Spring follow Route 9D north to Beacon and Route 52 northeast to Fishkill. The **Van Wyck Homestead Museum** is in a restored Dutch Colonial home. In 1732 Cornelius Van Wyck bought 959 acres of land and built his home, adding another wing in 1757. Between 1776 and 1783 it was used by Washington's officers as a headquarters. James Fenimore Cooper used this house as a setting for his novel *The Spy.*

Poughkeepsie

From Fishkill continue north on 9 through Wappingers Falls to Poughkeepsie. The Young-Morse Site, called **Locust Grove,** was the home of Samuel F. B. Morse. The house was named for the black locust trees lining the drive; Morse bought it in 1847 and remodeled it into a Tuscan villa. Memorabilia from his inventions, including the telegraph, are on display. The property was sold to the Young family in 1901, and the furnishings and collections of china, glassware, fans, dolls, costumes, and books are mostly those of Martha Innis Young.

The **Hudson Valley Philharmonic** (845–454–1222) offers a concert series during the year, both in Poughkeepsie and in Kingston. The Philharmonic also sponsors an innovative fund-raising project called "Designer's Showhouse." Every year a house in the area that could use renovation is revamped by local designers and architects; each provides the construction materials and furnishings for one room. Visitors buy a ticket from the Philharmonic to visit the house, and the owners of the house then have the choice of buying the results of the reconstruction or not. In any case, structural changes, wallpaper, and paint have refreshed the room and stay in place even if the furnishings are removed.

The **Bardavon 1869 Opera House** presents a full season of performances, including chamber music, opera, jazz, choir, drama, special programs, and a Young People's Theater series.

Cruises on the Hudson River are available from **Riverboat Tours.** The *River Queen* schedules sightseeing cruises, some of which include lunch or dinner.

Hyde Park

From Poughkeepsie follow Route 9 north to the south fringes of Hyde Park. **Springwood,** the home of Franklin Delano Roosevelt, dates back to 1810; it was purchased by his father in 1867. FDR and his mother remodeled the house in 1915. As you stand in the entrance hall, look for the Dutch clock, purchased by James and Sara Roosevelt in the Netherlands in 1881, and the bust of Franklin D. Roosevelt, sculpted by Paul Troubetskoy. His mother called the little room to the left "the snuggery"—a place where she could write or talk with a friend.

During World War I a new living room/library was added; there are many portraits, including one by Gilbert Stuart; statues; books; and comfortable furnishings. Eleanor Roosevelt once told the story of the night the king and queen of England arrived. Franklin planned to give them a cocktail after their long journey, but Sara, FDR's mother, felt that they would prefer a cup of tea. After they arrived and were given their choice, the king remarked that his mother would have made the same offer, but, in fact, he preferred to have a cocktail.

The Dresden Room—the music room—is furnished with floral slipcovers, Dresden china, and many family photographs. The dining room table is set with family china and silver as if the family were about ready to gather together, and Franklin's chair is placed at an angle so he could move into it easily from his wheelchair.

As you approach the staircase, you can't miss the old Chinese temple bell, which was rung half an hour before meals and then again when everyone was to be seated. At the top of the stairs is the room Franklin used as a boy; each of his sons used that room as he became too old for the third-floor children's room. Once, when Jimmy Roosevelt was sleeping in that room, there was anxiety about burglars; Franklin sat on lookout by the window with a gun, and Jimmy remembers being scared to death.

The king and queen of England stayed in the Pink Room, where they felt at home with the English prints on the walls. FDR was born in the room over the snuggery, in the southeast corner of the tower. The furniture in the room is original to that period of time. Franklin's dressing room contains his campaign hat, Navy cape, wheelchair, photographs, and other memorabilia.

The porch holds special memories of its own; FDR and his mother met guests there, and friends arrived at the porch to congratulate him each time he was victorious in an election. The rose garden, where his mother picked roses until her death, is the burial site of both Franklin and Eleanor.

The **Franklin D. Roosevelt Library and Museum** was built on land

Franklin D. Roosevelt Library and Museum Route 9 Hyde Park 12538 845–229–9115 Culinary Institute of America Route 9 Hyde Park 12538 845–471–6608

given by FDR for this purpose. He knew that his papers could not be housed in his home, and he wished to provide a place where historians and others could work with documents from this important era in American history.

This stone building with shutters holds personal papers, prints, a collection of Hudson Valley history, books, ship models, FDR's collection of naval prints, gifts given to the Roosevelts, and much more—even two Hudson River iceboats. You can spend hours looking at a collection that includes FDR's christening dress, a Scottish Murray clan kilt that he hated to wear as a child, a lock of his blond hair cut just before his fifth birthday, a hobby horse, Harvard cap and gown, photographs of his honeymoon in Europe—including one of FDR changing a tire in France with Eleanor and Aunt Doe looking on—photographs of the Roosevelt children, and an entire room filled with political photos and documents. The last-named exhibit re-creates each phase of FDR's career and gives visitors a great deal of information on the extraordinary accomplishment of the hundred days of emergency legislation in 1933, as well as on each phase of World War II.

The **Eleanor Roosevelt Gallery** in the FDR Library and Museum is symbolized by the engraved crystal flame depicting the spirit with which she lived and acted. You can see Eleanor's christening dress, photos tracing her unhappy early childhood (when her parents were estranged and then died), her wedding veil with orange blossoms, jewelry made from things her father collected on lion hunts in Africa, gowns, an oriental evening coat, an honorary doctoral robe from Oxford, and many travel mementos.

Val-Kill, situated on a more remote part of the grounds on a separate site (take a shuttle bus or drive), was a retreat for Eleanor. She thought it a much cozier home than Springwood. She built a furniture factory there, which manufactured reproductions of early American furniture and provided jobs for local farmers during the winters. After FDR's death Eleanor lived at Val-Kill, considering Hyde Park her real home even though she had an apartment in New York. Many distinguished guests visited her there, including Khrushchev, Tito, Haile Selassie, and Nehru.

Make an advance reservation at the **Culinary Institute of America,** where 1,850 students are enrolled in a twenty-one-month culinary arts program. Students learn the fundamentals and refinements of cooking, baking, and charcuterie in American, oriental, and international cuisines. Ninety chefs and instructors from eighteen countries teach within a restaurant setting. Be sure to make a reservation because these extraordinary restaurants are sometimes booked ahead for several months, particularly on weekends.

Tours of the seventy-five–acre campus are available two days a week.

Just north of Hyde Park is the **Vanderbilt Mansion.** This fifty-four–room, Italian Renaissance mansion was built by Frederick William Vanderbilt just before the turn of the century. Stanford White and his partners designed the mansion; they were also the architects for the Boston Public Library, the Pierpont Morgan Library, Columbia University, and the Villard Houses (now the New York Palace Hotel) in New York City. Edith Wharton and Ogden Codman, Jr., authors of *The Decoration of Houses,* published in 1897, were instrumental in developing the mansion's interior design. The oval center hall features Italian marble, a mantel that came from a palace, and a tapestry bearing the coat of arms of the Medici family. The living room is paneled in walnut from Russia; it was often used for dancing to music provided by a small orchestra. The mansion was furnished with elegant, ornate period pieces, mostly from France and Italy. The dining room table could seat thirty persons in a luxurious setting. The Vanderbilts lived in the mansion from Easter to early July, spent the summer in Newport or Europe, then returned in the fall until it was time to go to New York City for the winter social season.

> Vanderbilt Mansion
> Route 9
> Hyde Park 12538
> 845-229-9115
>
> Mills Mansion
> Old Albany Post
>   Road, off Route 9
> Staatsburg 12580
> 845-889-8851

You can walk through the gardens among the forty varieties of trees. The grounds were developed as early as 1795 by previous owners. On your way out you can follow a road that leads down to the river, where the Vanderbilt yachts once docked.

Staatsburg

A few miles north of the Vanderbilt Mansion is the **Mills Mansion,** the setting of Edith Wharton's *The House of Mirth.* She described the grounds with all of their "opulent undulations," and she said: "The library was almost the only surviving portion of the old manor-house of Bellomont. The library at Bellomont was in fact never used for reading, though it had a certain popularity as a smoking-room or a quiet retreat for flirtation."

Morgan Lewis and his wife, the sister of Chancellor Robert Livingston, bought the land in 1792 and built their home. Here the Lewises entertained many famous people, including Joseph Bonaparte and the Marquis de Lafayette.

The house was destroyed by fire in 1832 and rebuilt in Greek Revival style by the Lewises. Ruth Livingston Mills inherited the house and enlarged it in 1896 by adding two wings, balustrades, pilasters, and floral swags on

53

Rhinebeck
Historical Society
Box 291
Rhinebeck 12572
845–876–4778

Old Rhinebeck
Aerodrome
Stone Church Road,
off Route 9
Rhinebeck 12572
845–758–8610

the facade. Inside, marble fireplaces, gilded ceilings, and oak paneling enhance the ornate, carved and gilded furnishings, tapestries, paintings, and many art objects. As with many of the other mansions along the Hudson, Mills Mansion was occupied only a few months of the year.

The estate is part of **Mills-Norrie State Park,** which offers boating, fishing, camping, golf, nature and hiking trails, and picnicking facilities. Norrie Point Marina is a state-operated boat basin with launching and mooring facilities. In the park the **Dutchess Community College Environmental Museum** offers an educational program on the natural history of the mid-Hudson area for both students and the public.

Rhinebeck

From Staatsburg continue north on Route 9 to Rhinebeck. Five Dutch settlers bought 2,200 acres from the Sepasco and Esopus Indians for "6 buffaloes, 4 blankets, 5 kettles, 4 guns, 5 axes, 10 cans of powder, 8 shirts, 40 fathoms of wampum, 2 drawing knives, 2 adzes, half an anker of rum and one frying pan." Although Rhinebeck was founded by the Dutch in 1686, a group of German settlers named it Rhinebeck because its setting reminded them of cliffs along the Rhine. Today you can stroll through the National Historic District, maintained as a nineteenth-century village, with a walking-tour map from the **Rhinebeck Historical Society.** The Beekman Arms dates from 1766, the Delameter House from 1844, and the Dutch Reformed Church from 1809.

The oldest hotel in America, the **Beekman Arms** (see Inns appendix) is still operating in Rhinebeck on Route 9 (845–876–7077). Built by Arent Traphagen, the inn has sturdy stone walls 2 and 3 feet thick, mammoth oak beams, and floor boards 14 inches wide. As you walk in, you will see that the original structure still has the ambience that greeted guests during colonial days.

Old Rhinebeck Aerodrome houses a collection of aircraft dating from 1908 to 1938. Instead of Muzak your ears will pick up the ballads of World War I. On weekends there are air shows.

Germantown

Continue north on Route 9G to Germantown. **Clermont State Historical Site** was the ancestral home of Chancellor Robert R. Livingston.

His great-great-grandfather was born in Scotland in 1654, spent years in Holland, and arrived in America in 1673. In 1686 Governor Dongan granted him a manor of 160,000 acres of land along the Hudson River. As lord of the manor, Livingston had full control of both the land and his tenants, and he also had a seat in the Colonial Legislature. The British burned the manor house in 1777, but it was rebuilt with the same Georgian architecture; in the 1870s a French-style roof was added. The house may be toured during the summer.

> Clermont State
> Historical Site
> Route 9G
> Germantown 12526
> 845–537–4240
>
> American Museum
> of Fire Fighting
> Harry Howard
> Avenue
> Hudson 12534
> 845–828–7695

Livingston and Robert Fulton became friends and then partners as they planned and built a steamboat, named the *Clermont* after the estate. Robert Fulton married Livingston's cousin, and the partnership was firmly established. The state park offers nature trails, hiking, cross-country skiing, picnic facilities, and fine river views. From the park continue north on Route 9G to Hudson.

Hudson

Shades of Nantucket! In 1783 Seth and Tom Jenkins, worrying that the British would vanquish Nantucket in another attempt to regain control of the colonies, moved west to find another home. They chose Hudson as a site and moved there lock, stock, and barrel in their whaling ships, with a number of other families. Some lived on board ship while their houses were being constructed. The new residents built up a number of the businesses they knew, including, of course, shipbuilding, a distillery, a sperm oilworks, and a sail loft. The War of 1812 demolished much of their industry, but by 1830 whaling was again in full swing. Many of the old buildings have been restored: the **Robert Jenkins House** (113 Warren Street), the **Cyrus Curtiss House** (32 Warren Street), and the **Bank of Hudson** (116 Warren Street).

The **American Museum of Fire Fighting** houses one of the oldest and largest collections of equipment in the country. You can't miss the statue of a fire chief with his handsome blue and red coat, carved in the 1850s. Currier and Ives prints are also on display. Stroll among the decorated nineteenth-century fire engines until you come to the Weiner Hose Company's carriage, which was used only for dress occasions such as parades and thus maintained its glistening appearance.

Olana, 5 miles south of Hudson, was the home of painter Frederic E. Church. Set on a bluff 500 feet above the Hudson River, this home looks out of place with its Persian-style exterior. Church, a member of the

Olana
Route 9G
Hudson 12534
845–828–0135

Lindenwald
Route 9H
Kinderhook 12106
845–758–9689

Van Alen House
Route 9H
Kinderhook 12106
845–758–9265

The Shaker Museum
Shaker Museum
 Road
Old Chatham 12136
845–794–9100

Hudson River School, studied with Thomas Cole and painted amazing landscapes with a fine depiction of light. The views he had from his home must have been inspiring indeed. He wrote: "About one hour this side of Albany is the center of the world. I own it."

Kinderhook

North on Route 9 is Kinderhook. Henry Hudson sailed his ship here in 1609, noticed the group of Mohican Indian children who had come to stare at his ship, and named the village Kinderhook ("Children's Corner").

Lindenwald was purchased by President Martin Van Buren in 1839, while he was in office. His youngest son had the house remodeled as an Italian villa with a four-story brick tower. Earlier, around 1800, Washington Irving had tutored the children who lived in the house. He was interested in local legends and eventually used some of them in his own writing. The **Van Alen House,** nearby, may have been inhabited by the model for one of Irving's characters, Katrina Van Tassel. The house, built of red brick, reflects typical Dutch architecture, with gables, separate outside doors for each room, and a steep roof. A collection of delft and Hudson Valley paintings is on display.

Old Chatham

Nearby in Old Chatham **The Shaker Museum** preserves the history of a community founded by Mother Ann Lee in 1774. Born in 1736 in Manchester, England, she joined a sect of Quakers who were distinguished from others by the peculiarity that they would be aroused with "a mighty shaking" during their meetings. Ann's group also believed that men and women should be equal and celibate. She had a vision instructing her to travel to America, so with eight others she arrived in Watervliet on August 6, 1774, and set up their society. "Do all your work as though you had a thousand years to live and as you would if you knew you must die tomorrow" sums up their attitude toward work. The Shakers lived by the Millennial Laws, which prescribed celibacy, required separate schools for boys and girls, restricted the clothing that could be worn, and prohibited ownership of property. The Shakers were respected by the surrounding communities for the high quality of the goods they produced and for their hard work. This museum has exhibits of Shaker furniture, a blacksmith shop, a schoolroom, a collection of tools, nine rooms containing furnishings of that time, and a craft gallery.

At this point, if you are traveling a circular route up and down the Hudson River, head back to Route 9, follow it south through Hudson, and cross over the river to Catskill. If you are heading for Albany and upstate New York, head west to pick up Route 9H north to its junction with I–90; follow I–90 into Albany.

New York State Capitol
Albany 12242
518–474–2418

Governor Nelson A. Rockefeller Empire State Plaza
Madison to State Streets
Albany
518–473–7521

Albany

The cities of Albany, Schenectady, and Troy are linked together at the junction of the Hudson and Mohawk rivers, forming the Capital District. The **Albany Convention and Visitors' Bureau** can be visited at 52 North Pearl Street, or call them (800–258–3582 or 518–434–1217). Albany is the site of the capitol, a building in French Renaissance style. It is now overshadowed by the Governor Nelson A. Rockefeller Empire State Plaza, which contains the Empire Center at the Egg, the State Museum, State Library, and the Corning Tower Building. The plaza is a showplace complete with sculpture, pools, and the ripple of fountains.

The **New York State Capitol** looks like a French château. It took more than thirty years to build, from 1867 to 1899. Look at the elaborate carving on the building, especially the head of "Liberty," which is surrounded by garlands, and "Plenty," a female with intertwining grapes. Don't miss the "million dollar staircase," where the stone carvers sculpted faces of relatives and friends. Search for faces!

West Capitol Park, right next to the capitol building, is a great place to buy an ethnic lunch from one of many vendors. Another park, looking down State Street hill, has formal gardens, fountains, and a statue of General Philip Sheridan.

Governor Nelson A. Rockefeller Empire State Plaza is a ninety-six–acre government office complex surrounded by shops, restaurants, and entertainment centers. Referred to as "the Mall," this marble complex was a gleam in Governor Rockefeller's eye in 1962—with an estimated cost of $350 million. Labor problems caused delays, however, and it was finally finished for more than $2 billion in 1978. The Mall contains sculptures created by contemporary artists, including David Smith, Alexander Calder, Françoise Stahly, Dimitri Hadji, Donald Judd, Alexander Liberman, Clement Meadmore, James Rosati, and George Rickey. Below the plaza is a long

57

Empire Center
Empire State Plaza
Albany 12220
518–473–1845
New York State
Museum
Empire State Plaza
Albany 12223
518–474–5877

hallway called "The Concourse." A contemporary art collection lines the walls of the hallway, leading to shops, restaurants, banks, and ticket offices.

The most striking building on the plaza is the **Empire Center.** Locally known as "The Egg" because of its shape, the center features drama, dance, and music performances. Empire State Youth Orchestra and Noon Concert Series call the building home. There are two theaters: one seats 950, and the other seats 450.

The **New York State Museum** contains exhibits on various themes: Man and Nature in New York State, the City of New York, and the Adirondack Wilderness. See the film, *The Chronicles of Change,* which will give you an introduction to the exhibits. The museum added a life-size Mohawk Iroquois longhouse in October 1992. It is 60 feet long, 19 feet high, and 20 feet wide. As you approach the longhouse you will see an Indian astride the beams working on the roof. To meet the fire code, the museum was not allowed a full roof so near the ceiling. As a result, they left much of it open, as if it were "under construction." This gives visitors a chance to see how it was made.

Pass under the bark-covered entrance and into an area where you can sit and contemplate this communal style of wilderness living, where everyone had a function. Farther inside, your eyes will become sufficiently accustomed to the dim light to distinguish a Mohawk family of children, teenagers, and adults who are engaged in various activities. Listen carefully to hear the elder clan mother telling stories; in between each story you will hear conversations between the families in the room. This museum uses a variety of techniques to bring history alive for the viewer, including life-size dioramas of lumberjacks maneuvering logs down wild rivers, fishermen in action, and the sounds of birds coming from realistic woodland settings. The Adirondack Wilderness section begins with "Prehistoric Wilderness" and includes lifelike groups of animals and hunters. The geologic history of the Adirondacks illustrates the evolution of the mountains, beginning with the collision of two continents over a billion years ago. The museum also has a section on gems found in New York and an antique fire engine exhibit.

For a complete change of scene, walk to the other side of the museum. New York Metropolis Hall traces development of our country's largest city from prehistory to the present. Here's the place to wander at will through groupings of exhibits designed to re-create various eras and neighborhoods. We especially liked the street scene of the Lower East Side, complete with peddler, knife sharpener, cloth cutter, milk deliverer, rag picker, and shoeshine boy. Don't miss the boy sitting on the fire escape surveying it all.

"Colonial Commerce from 1700–1800" focuses on the South Street Seaport, where boxes and barrels stand ready to be loaded on ships. Walk through the

> Albany Institute of
> History and Art
> 125 Washington
> Avenue
> Albany 12210
> 518–463–4478

park area and spot the sandbagger yacht *Sandy,* dating from 1854. These boats, with high masts and too much sail, were raced for cash prizes in New York Bay, and they attracted gamblers, like football teams today. They were kept upright by crew members who shifted sandbags from one side to the other. When the wind got light, sandbags and crew alike were jettisoned into the bay.

Hanging on a wall you'll also see period bicycles, which might have cycled through the park. The skeleton of a 32-foot right whale poses in the Long Island whaling area. If you associate whaling only with New England ports like Nantucket and New Bedford, you'll learn how important Sag Harbor was in the industry. After being buffeted by the Revolution and the War of 1812, many frustrated Nantucket whalers left Nantucket to establish a new home port in Hudson, New York, not many miles south of Albany.

If your children or grandchildren watch "Sesame Street," don't miss the copy of the brownstone set used in the New York–based television series. Some of the favorite characters are there as well.

Ellis Island dioramas bring back the trauma of those who wanted to enter our country. They waited in long lines for medical exams, and some were turned back. One of the most poignant displays deals with August 4, 1944, when 982 refugees escaped from the Nazi Holocaust and were brought to America. They lived for eighteen months in Oswego, saved but not yet free. Walls of photos include one of a family portrait where someone marked those who were killed—and those who survived. A permanent exhibit portraying the rich cultural influence of Harlem opened two years ago. Entitled "Black Capital: Harlem in the 1920s," it explores everyday life in Harlem; education; the arts; cultural icons such as the Cotton Club; and political activism.

Robinson Square, on nearby Hamilton Street, was once slated for destruction until it was saved by the efforts of local residents. These brownstone row houses from the 1850s now contain shops, apartments, and restaurants.

Albany Institute of History and Art dates back to 1791. Exhibits depict life in the upper Hudson River Valley through period furniture, silver, china, pewter, and paintings. The institute holds lectures, concerts, tours, workshops, and classes throughout the year.

Ten Broeck Mansion
9 Ten Broeck Place
Albany 12210
518-436-9826
Historic Cherry Hill
523½ South Pearl
Street
Albany 12202
518-434-4791

Ten Broeck Mansion was built for Abraham Ten Broeck in 1798. General Ten Broeck was a member of the Colonial Assembly, a delegate to the Continental Congress, brigadier general in the Revolutionary army, and mayor of Albany. The general and his wife were both sixty-three years old when they built the house. The Great Albany Fire of 1797 had destroyed their previous home, so Ten Broeck leased the land from his father-in-law, Patroon Stephen Van Rensselaer. Thomas Worth Olcott moved into the house in 1850, and his family lived there for the next hundred years. It is now maintained by the Albany County Historical Association. This Federal mansion contains Sheraton, Phyfe, Hepplewhite, and Italianate furniture. Recently, a valuable collection of wine was discovered in a cellar under the structure. Much of the wine had been bought many years before in Europe or New York City, and some of the original cases remained intact. Heublein auctioned the wine, and the money received was used for restoration of the mansion.

Historic Cherry Hill, a Georgian-style home lived in by five generations of the Van Rensselaer/Elmendorf/Rankin families until 1963, was built in 1787 for Philip Van Rensselaer. Fortunately, because the house had never been sold outside of the family, all of their personal belongings and clothing were saved. Visitors enter the house through an orientation room, where diagrams of the family tree outline the sequence of those who lived in the house. Philip and Maria Van Rensselaer were the first to do so, beginning in 1787. Philip was the grandson of Hendrick Van Rensselaer, whose brother Kilian was patroon at that time. Philip Schuyler, who built Schuyler Mansion, was his cousin; a portrait of their grandmother, Elsie Wendell Schuyler, is in the dining room. Maria was the granddaughter of Peter Schuyler, the first mayor of Albany. Philip and Maria were merchant farmers who also owned a town house on North Pearl Street; they had thirteen children. The last member of the family to live in the house was Emily Watkinson Rankin, who died in 1963.

Cherry Hill is an unusual preservation site because it shows the life of a family from the 1780s to the 1960s, rather than in just one era. Visitors can trace the changes in life through nearly two hundred years of American history by examining the personal belongings left in the house. The collection includes china, furniture, silver, textiles, portraits, and documents. As you walk through the house you will see a mixture of furniture styles, because each generation added new pieces to supplement the original Chippendale. Catherine Van Rensselaer Bonney, daughter of Solomon and

Harriet Van Rensselaer, was a missionary in the Orient. She sent home many oriental furnishings and decorations, including mirrors, prints, and ceramics in the camphorwood trunks used for shipping goods. At another time an Albany cabinetmaker by the name of Reed made some pieces for the house. Look for the

Schuyler Mansion
State Historic Site
32 Catherine Street
Albany 12202
518–434–0834

collection of "branded" furniture in the dining room. To enable recipients to identify their possessions in the eighteenth century, brands were placed on furniture when it was shipped at the docks.

The house also contains an extensive collection of women's clothing, most of it made by dressmakers. Two of the bedrooms contain examples of clothing that had been found carefully preserved in trunks in the attic.

You can trace the development of heating in this house, beginning with the fireplace, then a coal grate in the fireplace, stoves of various kinds, and finally a hot-air furnace leading to grated floor vents. Lighting also underwent a series of changes, from candles through oil, kerosene, and gas lamps to electricity. The first and second generations living in the house did not have indoor plumbing but were dependent on the outdoor "necessity" and chamber pots. Before you leave, ask about Jesse Strang's murder confession; apparently he shot the husband of his lover through a window of the house.

The **Schuyler Mansion** is also called "The Pastures"; the two acres of lawns and gardens affirm the name. As you approach this home from below you will see the large brick structure high on a hill, which originally had a fine view of the river. Lawns went all the way down to the river, and guests arriving by water were sure to be impressed. This Georgian home was built in 1761 by Philip Schuyler. Schuyler came from a prominent local family and distinguished himself during the French and Indian War. He received a captain's commission in 1755 as recognition for gathering enough men to accompany William Johnson in the Battle of Crown Point. He was involved in the preparations for the Battle of Lake George but was, in fact, attending his own wedding to Catharine Van Rensselaer on September 7, 1755, while the battle was in progress.

George Washington visited here, as did Benjamin Franklin, Benedict Arnold, Baron von Steuben, Comte de Rochambeau, and even General Burgoyne. This last guest may seem surprising because he had ordered Schuyler's country house in Saratoga to be burned during the crucial Battle of Saratoga; actually, the defeated British general was a prisoner/guest in the house.

Look for the gash on the stair rail, which may have been made by an Indian tomahawk. Tories tried to kidnap Schuyler during the Revolutionary

War, but he heard of their plot in advance and was able to hire guards to thwart the attack. Although records do not indicate that Indians were involved in that incident, there is a legend that one of his daughters had run downstairs to rescue her baby sister, somehow forgotten in her cradle in the living room. She was on her way back up with the baby in her arms when, reportedly, an Indian tomahawk was thrown at her and gashed the stair rail. The house is furnished with period furniture, including some from the Schuyler family; Chinese export porcelain; delftware; and English glassware.

Some good restaurant choices in Albany include **Cranberry Bog** (56 Wolf Road; 518–459–5110), **Desmond** (660 Albany Shaker Road; 518–869–8100), **Jacks Oyster House** (42–44 State Street; 518–465–8845), **La Serre** (14 Green Street; 518–463–6056), **Nicole's Bistro at Quackenbush House** (25 Q Street; 518–465–1111), and **Ogden's** (Howard at Lodge Street; 518–463–6605).

Schenectady

Algonquin Indians first lived on the land that is now Schenectady; then the Iroquois battled their way to the site. In 1661 Arendt Van Curler bought 128 square miles from the Indians and banded together with fifteen other families to form a patroonship, where they built homes within a stockade for protection against the French. By 1690 there were sixty houses and four hundred persons living in the stockade.

On February 8, 1690, the people in the stockade were unaware of imminent danger. During January 114 Frenchmen and 96 Indians began an arduous trek by snowshoe from Montreal to attack Albany. When they were within 6 miles of the stockade, they stopped and talked with four squaws living in a bark hut, who told them all they needed to know. Advance scouts found that there were only two sentries and . . . both of them were snowmen!

They reached the Stockade, found the gate open, and sneaked around the houses in silence until a "single hideous and horrendous warwhoop" broke the silence and began the slaughter of inhabitants. Sixty persons were killed, twenty-seven were taken captive, and many others fled into the woods and died from exposure to the cold after their homes had been burned.

The **Schenectady Urban Cultural Park** depicts three centuries of life, beginning with the seventeenth-century frontier village within the Stockade. Head for the Schenectady UCP visitor center, located in the **Schenectady Museum and Planetarium.** There you'll see exhibits ranging from the 1690 massacre to the development of GE and the American Locomotive Company.

Visitors will find an audiocassette, accompanying a map of a walking tour, to be the easiest way to see the Stockade. The cassette and a player are available from the center. Called "Colonial Schenectady: An American Crucible," the cassette opens with colonial-style music and actors playing the parts of local people. There are twelve stations; a bell is sounded at the end of each. The first one reminds visitors of the massacre, with stories of that terrible night told by three residents.

Schenectady Museum and Planetarium Nott Terrace Heights Schenectady 12308 518-382-7890
Schenectady County Historical Society 32 Washington Avenue Schenectady 12305 518-374-0263

The **Schenectady County Historical Society** maintains a collection of exhibits from the area, a library, a genealogical collection, and files of many historical documents. We were fascinated by the paintings of the Stockade hanging on the walls. Don't miss the "Senility cradle" used for John Sanders II, who was born in 1757. There's a "Liberty flag" and arms of the Revolutionary War upstairs. Indian artifacts include arrowheads, a 1720 axe head, Iroquois dolls, and a bead bag.

The society also conducts a "walkabout" of the Stockade every September. One house has a tablet inscribed as follows: "Oldest house in City built before 1700 by Hendrick Brouwer, a fur trader, who died here 1707. Sold 1799, to James Rosa, Superintendent of Mohawk and Hudson Railroad, 1831." Hendrick's wife was Maritie Borsboom, and they were married two years after the massacre. The house is not open except during special house tours, but you can enjoy the simple elegance of its facade. Now that we've told you the history of one home in the Stockade, see if you can find out about others!

Turn down Front Street to the **Governor Yates House** (17 Front Street), which dates from 1760. In 1825 Major General the Marquis de Lafayette stayed in the house as a guest of the governor. The next house is the **Jeremiah deGraaf House** (25–27 Front Street), now divided into two homes. Note the doorway of Number 25 with its elegant pilasters and the oval sunburst medallion. The **Johannes Teller House** (121 Front Street) dates from 1740. The gambrel roof continues as a shed roof on the other side.

At the juncture of Front, Green, and North Ferry streets stands the statue of an Indian that was placed there in 1887 as a symbol of friendship with the Mohawks. These were the Indians who encouraged the white men to stay and rebuild their town after the massacre of 1690. The **Old Public Market,** dating from 1795, is on one of the corners, and **St.**

Union College
Union & Nott
Streets
Schenectady 12308
518-388-6000

International Festival
of Chamber Music
Union Memorial
Chapel
Schenectady 12308
518-382-7890

Schenectady
Museum
and Planetarium
Nott Terrace Heights
Schenectady 12308
518-382-7890

George's Episcopal Church, from 1759, stands on another. The **First Presbyterian Church,** elegant in Greek Revival style, is around the corner on Union Street. Turn right on Union Street to the **Abraham Yates House** (109 Union Street), dating from 1700. It is the only house in the Stockade built with a steep gable on the street side and a brick wall as a parapet above the roof. Don't miss the "butterfly" brickwork on the gables. Across the street is the **Old County Court House,** in Greek Revival style. Next to the Yates House is the **First Reformed Church,** dating from 1863, standing as the sixth building on the site of the original church built by Dutch settlers in 1682.

Union College was founded in 1795. The first planned college campus in the United States, Union was also the first institute of higher learning in New York State chartered by the Board of Regents. On the Nott Street side of the campus, **Jackson's Garden,** with sixteen acres of formal and wild gardens, including an evergreen garden and an herb garden, surrounds a brook; students and alumni often hold weddings under a geiko tree there.

Nott Memorial, at the center of the campus, is also worth a visit. Originally a gallery for sculpture, then a library, and once a theater-in-the-round, this sixteen-sided structure built over nearly forty years in the middle of the nineteenth century marks the transition from stone-and-wood construction to framing with iron and steel; its thin dome is made possible by the use of steel. Around its base, in Hebrew, is a rabbinical teaching: "The day is short, the task is great, God is urgent."

The Schenectady Museum and Union College are joint hosts for an **International Festival of Chamber Music** in the **Union Memorial Chapel,** which has fine acoustics. Eleven concerts are presented during the year by groups from England, Czech Republic, Germany, and the United States.

The **Schenectady Museum and Planetarium** has long-range plans to offer exhibits capitalizing on the advanced technological industries that developed in Schenectady during the nineteenth century; exhibits will be partly displays and partly participatory. The museum now offers classes in art, crafts, and antiques; a planetarium; and exhibits on history, science, and industry. The museum also sponsors a number of popular annual events, including plant shows, a crafts festival, and a festival of nations.

Schenectady Museum began as a children's museum in the Schenectady City School District in 1934. It outgrew its classroom and moved into the former County Almshouse for a thirty-year stay, until the city decided to tear down the almshouse and build an elementary school on the site; then the present museum was built. Don't miss the clever hands-on exhibits for children. In the

Proctor's Theater
432 State Street
Schenectady 12305
518-382-3884

"Discovery Center" children will find a number of "discovery boxes" that may be checked out and taken home. A box may include a small student-type microscope, a button collection, old locks with keys, small and sturdy musical instruments, and other items of interest to children. Also notice a display of stuffed animals that came largely from local residents who had their pets stuffed, and a costume collection that stretches from the early eighteenth century into the twentieth.

Jay Street Market Place, just across State Street, is a continuation of shops, restaurants, antiques shops, and bookstores. The street is closed to traffic.

Proctor's Theater is a restored 1926 vaudeville movie house. This theater, one of a chain of theaters, was owned by F. F. Proctor and was completed in 1926 for $1.5 million. During the 1970s local residents banded together to restore Proctor's, and in 1979 the theater opened again with a full program of music, dance, and opera. Half the fun of going is looking at the elegant gilt and crystal chandeliers, the gold leaf on ceilings and walls, and the Louis XV marble fireplace.

Friendly Indians in the area convinced the few settlers who survived to stay on their land and rebuild, which they did. When the Erie Canal was completed in 1825, business began to boom in Schenectady. Engines were built by the Schenectady Locomotive Works beginning in 1851, and in 1886 General Electric was founded there by Thomas Edison, leading to one rather expansive sobriquet—"The City that Lights and Hauls the World."

Schenectady is part of the 23-mile **Mohawk-Hudson Greenway** hiking and biking path, which runs through Niskayuna, Schenectady, Glenville, Scotia, and Rotterdam. Along it you can watch canal activity at Locks 7, 8, and 9. Contact the Schenectady Chamber of Commerce for a map.

When it's time for a meal or an overnight, try the **Glen Sanders Mansion** just across the river in Scotia. Some sections of the mansion date from the 1680s, including the Deborah Glen Room, which has original woodwork, mantels, and door paneling. The Great Room, now the main dining room, was built in 1713. The menu is also memorable; call 518-374-7262 for reservations. (See Inns appendix.)

For more information about the area, contact the **Schenectady Chamber of Commerce** (234 Canal Square, Schenectady 12305;

65

Bronck House
Museum
Route 9W
Coxsackie 12051
518-731-6490

Thomas Cole House
218 Spring Street
Catskill 12414
518-943-6533

Catskill Game Farm
Off Route 32
Catskill 12414
518-678-9595

518-372-5656).

From Schenectady take Route 890 to I-90 east, then I-87 south to Catskill to continue the Hudson River route back to New York City. If you are linking with Itinerary B (Upstate New York), take I-87 north to Saratoga Springs.

Coxsackie

North of Catskill is the **Bronck House Museum.** Pieter Bronck built this house in 1663; other buildings on the property date from the same year, 1685, and 1738. Inside the house are paintings by Thomas Cole, John Frederick Kensett, Ezra Ames, Richard Hubbard, Benjamin Stone, and Ammi Phillips. Period furniture, china, and glass are exhibited. A Dutch barn, a Victorian horse barn, and an unusual thirteen-sided barn with center-pole construction are on the property.

Catskill

The **Thomas Cole House, or "Cedar Grove,"** was built in 1815; artist Thomas Cole lived there from 1836 to 1848. *The Voyage of Life,* a series of allegorical themes, was painted in 1849–50 and is in the Munson-Williams-Proctor Institute in Utica. In 1852 one of Cole's protégés, De Witt Clinton Boutelle, completed the series. Today the house is open during the summer.

The **Catskill Game Farm** is a large park showing wild animals in their natural settings. The African section features cheetahs, antelope, and rhinos; a train runs around a bird garden, offering views of rare mountain goats and sheep on the other side. You can see bears, baboons, giraffes, a pygmy hippo, kangaroos, prairie dogs, and many more species, as well as baby animals in the nursery. Bring a picnic, or have lunch in the cafeteria.

In case you aren't going to the Orient, you can see Buddhist temples in a very unlikely setting—the Catskills. South Cairo (on Route 23 west of Catskill) boasts three temples, the earliest constructed in 1971 as the first Buddhist pagoda in the United States. One of them contains an 18-foot golden statue known as the Buddha of Mercy. A seven-story pagoda was built in 1984 as a symbol of good luck.

One of the things that visitors like to do in winter is ski at one of the Catskill areas. It's nice to escape the winter doldrums by heading to the crisp air and falling snowflakes for cross-country or alpine skiing, snowboarding, or just looking at the view. Some of the areas also offer year-round activities, so you can indulge in tennis, golf, hiking, or simply enjoy the view when the slopes are green. All of the areas offer a nice escape from the city. **Ski Windham** has a large lodge with wraparound, picture-window views. Windham's 1,600-foot vertical drop is one of the highest in the Catskills, attracting skiers from New York City, the capital district, and points north. Snowmaking covers 97 percent of the two mountains, so skiers are likely to find great conditions. And if you ski for an hour and decide to call it quits, you can return your lift ticket for a "Snow Check" good for another day.

> Ski Windham
> Clarence D. Lane Road
> Windham 12496
> 800–754–9463 (snow conditions) or
> 518–734–4300
> fax: 518–734–5732
> www.skiwindham.com
>
> Belleayre Mountain
> 800–942–6904 (snow conditions)
> www.belleayre.com

Snow tubing at Mountain Top Adventure Park is available by a free shuttle service from the Ski Windham base lodge. It's fun and it's easy!

The "Senior Skier" program welcomes those fifty-five and up on Tuesdays with continental breakfast, four hours of skiing with an instructor, lift tickets, and workshops.

Children can learn to ski at Windham from age three and up. They have fun learning to walk in boots and to side-step up and ski down a carpeted ramp. By age four they can join the "Mogul Skiers," who ski out in the terrain garden and then head up on the lift. Children between the ages of eight and twelve are "Mogul Masters," and they range from beginner to expert.

The Disabled Ski Program at Ski Windham started in 1983 with thirty-five students. The program has grown and improved, but the basic idea remains the same: to have fun, to learn, and to do it safely. Disabled persons five years of age or older are welcome. If you could see the smiles on faces and hear the hoots of joy as they come down, you might feel a lump in your throat—we did. Lessons take place every day of the week and last from one and one half to two hours in length. Each student *can* learn to ski with the aid of one, two, three, or four instructors—all coaching encouragement. "I can do it" is really true. They feel self-confident, enjoy success, and experience the thrill of a lifetime. A parent said, "Both of my children are blind and are considered blind people wherever they go. At Windham, however, they are skiers who happen to be blind."

Belleayre Mountain is operated by New York State in the Catskill Forest Preserve. As you can imagine, its setting in the forest is peaceful. The two-mountain system includes thirty-three trails, nine lifts, and three day-use lodges. Skiers are offered a free beginner lesson, and those over seventy can ski free all day. Snowmaking covers 90 percent of the slopes. NASTAR races are held every day for those who want to test speed and skill.

Hunter Mountain Ski
  Bowl
Box 295
Hunter 12442
800–FOR–SNOW
  (snow conditions)
  or 518–263–4223
www.huntermtn.com

Opus 40
7480 Fite Road
Saugerties 12477
914–246–3400

Children from four to twelve may join the SKIwee program; that's the time to learn! The "Beast of Belleayre," an all-terrain vehicle, takes skiers to the remote Cathedral Glen Trail. Belleayre's two mountains are now connected.

Summer music festivals include jazz, folk, country, classical, rock nostalgia, Broadway, and opera. Fall is the time to visit for the craft festival, chairlift rides in the midst of fall color, and a popular ski-swap sale.

The vertical drop at **Hunter Mountain** is 1,600 feet and all of it is covered through snowmaking. They focus on three groups: those just starting out, youngsters who want a hip experience, and frequent skiers and snowboarders, especially families. Hunter One First Tracks is a popular place to begin either skiing or riding. The Snowtubing Park offers new chutes with dips and rollers.

Summer and fall festivals include such features as German Alps, Celtic, Native American Indian, Microbrew, Wine & Fine Foods, and Oktoberfest.

Pine Hill Lake, also run by Belleayre Mountain, offers swimming, fishing, boating, hiking, and tennis. Pavilions and play areas are there for your use.

Palenville (southwest of Catskill on Route 23A) is the legendary home of Rip Van Winkle because Washington Irving wrote *Rip Van Winkle* while living there. James Fenimore Cooper later wrote that Palenville was "the greatest wonder of American landscape." The arts colony, known as **Interarts,** was begun in 1979 by Kevin Kennedy. A full schedule of music, dance, and theater is available.

South of Catskill **Opus 40** was developed by one man, Harvey Fite, who originally bought the quarry as a source of stone for his sculpture. He built a house and studio there, began to clear the piles of rubble, and, using a quarryman's hand tools, hammers, chisels, drills, and a boom with a tray to move rocks, he made terraces, walks, and stone walls. Fite displayed his sculptures amid pools and fountains, and in 1962 he used only fulcrum-and-lever principles to raise a nine-ton stone into position in the center of his garden. He named his quarry Opus 40 because he thought it would take him forty years to finish it. During the summer months classical, folk, and jazz concerts are held there. The **Quarryman's Museum** contains Fite's collection of quarryman's tools.

Those who think of the Catskills as nothing but an extension of the crowds and bustle of New York City are mistaken. The forest primeval lures hikers all through the Catskills. Almost everywhere you can hike to a quiet mountain lake or enjoy an unspoiled view from the top of a peak. For example, the **Escarpment Trail** is one that provides hikers with one scenic view after another above the cliffs of Kaaterskill Cove. The route begins at the junction of Route 23A and Kaaterskill

Senate House
312 Fair Street
Kingston 12401
914–338–2786

Creek and winds for 24 miles to East Windham on Route 23. **North Lake** is pristine, and nearby, at the site of the **Catskill Mountain House** (long since burned), there are panoramic views of the Hudson Valley, the Taconics, and the Berkshires. And to top it all, you are in the vicinity of Kaaterskill Falls, which has a longer drop than that of Niagara. That is the particular appeal of the Catskills—many treats within a small compass. Hikers and backpackers can approach these pleasures through the Appalachian Trail, which winds over the Catskills on its way from Pennsylvania to Vermont. Read some of John Burroughs's works to catch the particular flavor of these mountains. His study is in West Park.

For a pamphlet entitled *Catskill Trails,* write to the **Department of Environmental Conservation,** Region 4 Subregion Office, 439 Main Street, Catskill, NY 12414. Or you may call 518–943–4030. Topographic maps may be obtained from the **U.S. Geological Survey,** 1200 South Eads Street, Arlington, VA 22202.

The Catskills claim to have been the site of the first fly fishing. Try for rainbow trout on the upper Kaaterskill, brown trout farther downstream, and finally bass and panfish below High Falls. The Catskill Creek, with its tributaries—Ten Mile Creek, Basic Creek, and Shingle Kill—contains brown trout; upstream from Oak Hill rainbow trout inhabit it.

Kingston

After your excursions into the Catskills, return to the scenic river road, Route 9W, and continue south to Kingston. The original settlement, called Esopus, was built within a stockade for protection from the Indians, but the thatched-roofed houses were easily burned by Indians in 1663. The next houses were built of natural local limestone between 1670 and 1750. The rural Flemish style, originally a single room with a grain storage loft above, is also found in New Paltz. Just before the Revolution the residents began to build square, two-story town houses. The area is still referred to as the Stockade District.

The **Senate House** was the site of the first New York state senate meeting. The house had been built by Wessel Ten Broeck and overlooked the Esopus Creek. Abraham Van Gaasbeek owned the house in 1777 when Kingston served as the capital of New York. The first meeting in his house was on September 9, 1777. By October 7, however, with the British

Hudson River Maritime Museum Roundout Landing Kingston 12401 914–338–0071

advancing up the Hudson, the senate was moved to Poughkeepsie. Visit the Senate House Museum; it contains the largest collection of paintings by John Vanderlyn, who was a native of Kingston. Vanderlyn studied under Gilbert Stuart and made copies of Stuart's famous George and Martha Washington portraits. Aaron Burr offered to become his patron and sent him to study in France. In the museum look for a painting entitled *Ariadne Asleep and Abandoned by Theseus on the Island of Naxos.* Another favorite of many viewers is the portrait of Mrs. John R. Livingston, in which a mirror catches her profile.

There are many stone houses to see in the Stockade District. You can take a tour using a map from the **Friends of Historic Kingston** (914–338–5100).

Head across town and down the hill to the **Roundout** area, a nineteenth-century waterfront district. Originally called Kingston Landing, it came into its own in 1828 when the Delaware and Hudson Canal opened. The shipping of Pennsylvania coal, Ulster County bluestone, and Kingston cement and brick was big business. Shipbuilders set up shop there, first in sailing vessels and then in steamboats, but the area went into a decline when river traffic became less efficient than railroads and highways. The area is now being revitalized; a number of shops are open, and work is continuing on others.

The **Hudson River Maritime Museum** opened in 1980 to preserve the maritime heritage of the Hudson River, especially in the form of historic vessels afloat and ashore. You will see the *Matilda,* an 1899 steam tug, sitting in her cradle. She was retired in 1969 by McAllister Towing Company of Montreal, Canada, as the last operating commercial steam tugboat in North America. She was on display at the South Street Seaport in New York City until she sank at her dock in 1976. She was then raised, repaired, and given to the maritime center in 1983. The *Rip Van Winkle* and other tour boats offer all-day tours and music cruises on Friday and Saturday nights.

The museum has exhibits from the *Mary Powell,* a Hudson River steamboat built in 1861. She steamed to Manhattan on a daily basis, and people up and down the Hudson enjoyed watching her come into view. You can have a tour through the boat-building shop to watch the restoration progress on recent acquisitions. Pete Seeger is featured in a video presentation on the river, including a favorite, "Sailing down My Golden River." The **Hudson River Chapter of the Antique and Classic Boat Society** has its headquarters in the museum.

Head south on I–87 to signs for New Paltz.

New Paltz

Huguenot Historical
Society
Box 339
New Paltz 12561
914–255–1660 or
914–255–1889

In 1677 the heads of twelve families signed a treaty with the Esopus Indians for 39,683 acres of land. Four months later Governor Andros issued a patent for the lands, which were named a township, and in 1678 the twelve families arrived to settle on their patent. These settlers had originally come from Lille and Calais, France. As refugees from Catholic persecution in France, they lived near Speyer and Mannheim, Germany, in the province of "Die Pfalz," and so named their new town New Paltz. They were of the French Huguenot faith; *Huguenot* means "French Protestant" and may have been derived either from the Swiss Protestant *Hugues* or from the Flemish *Huis genooten,* which means "house fellowship," since the people met in homes to study the Bible and pray.

Abraham Hasbrouck, as the leader, was able to obtain a large tract of land for his people. The group set up a unique form of government called the *Duzine,* or "Rule of the Elders." Later one representative from each of the twelve families was elected to the Duzine.

Indians advised the twelve families to build on high ground because the river sometimes flooded the valley; they settled on what is now Huguenot Street. The settlers lived in log cabins until 1692, when they had enough stone to build stone houses like their homes in France. Although the original homes had one room with a cellar kitchen and attic above, they added on other rooms to create the larger homes we see today. Descendants of each of the original twelve families still maintain an interest in the houses; they have contributed some of the original furniture passed down through their families to be put on display. The houses today are owned by the **Huguenot Historical Society.**

The **Jean Hasbrouck House** has his initials carved in stone to the left of the door. Inside is a long central hall with two rooms on each side. In the living room the table is covered with a rug or tapestry; a dulcimer is in the corner, and a snodnose lamp (a very early brass oil lamp) is on the desk. The kitchen contains furnishings that were in the family before 1700. A large Dutch *kaas* (cupboard) has several delft spice jars on top, and the Hudson Valley rush-bottom chairs are typical of the area. A collection of pewterware and a variety of cooking utensils are displayed. Upstairs in the attic you will see a beehive chimney, a loom, and an exhibit on the production of linen from flax. Don't miss the store in the house, which has a variety of goods common to the period. Another room contains a bar with what looks like a picket fence on top. Could it be so that patrons could not lean their elbows too long as they imbibed? No, it was used to dry clean glasses.

Locust Lawn
Route 32
Gardiner 12525
914–255–6070

Mohonk Mountain
House
1000 Mountain Rest
Road
New Paltz 12561
914–256–2056

Washington's
Headquarters
84 Liberty Street
Newburgh 12550
914–562–1195

A large stone monument in the street lists the names of the original twelve patentees; this boulder was brought down from the mountains on a sledge in 1899. The cemetery contains the graves of all of the patentees and their wives. Look for the stone with primitive angels done by a local stonecutter. One gives the first letter of each word in the epitaph. On another stone the cutter did not think ahead—several letters in the name are stuck in above the line.

Locust Lawn, southwest of New Paltz, was built in 1814 by Colonel Josiah Hasbrouck. This Federal mansion contains period furniture, china, books, and paintings by Ammi Phillips, Alden Weir, and John Vanderlyn. The marbleized plaster walls in the central hall were a specialty of the architect, Cromwell. Outside are a slaughterhouse, a wood house, a carriage house, and a smokehouse.

Mohonk Mountain House, located in the Shawangunk Mountains right on a clear glacial lake, offers Old World charm in a beautiful setting. Dating back to 1869, when twin brothers bought the existing building and land around it, Mohonk has been run by the same family through its expansion from ten rooms to three hundred. Antique furnishings enhance this castlelike escape from the real world.

Walkers and hikers enjoy the many trails through this 22,000-acre estate. We especially recommend a hike up to the tower at Sky Top, where you can savor the view. Along the way you will find gazebos built out over sheer drops, deep crevasses, and unusual rock formations. Advance reservations for lunch will allow day visitors in the gate, or you can pay for a day pass in order to hike on the grounds of the estate. (See Inns appendix.)

Take I–87 south to Newburgh.

Newburgh

Washington's Headquarters were in the Jonathan Hasbrouck house from April 1782 to August 1783. The army remained encamped at New Windsor while negotiations prior to the Treaty of Paris were in progress. In 1782 Washington turned down a proposal by some of his men to turn America into a monarchy and name him king. Did you know that Washington originated the Order of the Purple Heart here? On May 3, 1783, he awarded the first "Badge of Military Merit" for acts of bravery. There is a museum housing memorabilia from the Revolutionary War.

New Windsor Cantonment, just south of Newburgh, is the site of the last encampment of soldiers during the Revolution. Seven hundred log cabins once filled the area, but now only one of the original cabins remains. The site includes reconstructed buildings, and there are periodic reenactments portraying the life of the soldiers.

Cornwall-on-Hudson

The **Museum of the Hudson Highlands** contains live animals as well as natural-history exhibits. You can take a self-guided nature trail walk. The **Ogden Gallery** features changing art exhibits as well as films and lectures.

Nearby **Storm King Art Center,** southwest of Newburgh on Route 32, is a display of more than two hundred sculptures on two hundred acres of landscaped gardens. You will find sculptures by David Smith, Barbara Hepworth, Henry Moore, Isamu Noguchi, Alexander Calder, Alexander Liberman, Louise Nevelson, and more.

New Windsor
Cantonment
Temple Hill
Newburgh 12550
914-561-1765

Museum of the
  Hudson Highlands
The Boulevard
Cornwall-on-Hudson
  12520
914-534-7781

Storm King Art
  Center
Old Pleasant Hill
  Road
Mountainville 10953
914-534-3115

United States
  Military Academy
Information Center
West Point 10996
914-938-2638

Hudson Valley Wineries

From the seventeenth century, when the Huguenots planted grapes along the Hudson Highlands, to the present day, vineyards have flourished in the area. You can plan your own wine-tasting tour as you visit some of the vineyards: **Adair, Baldwin, Benmarl, Brimstone Hill, Brotherhood, Cascade Mountain, Clinton, Maganini Farm, Milbrook, North Salem, Royal Kedem, Walker Valley, West Park,** and **Windsor.** For more detailed information on each vineyard, get a current brochure on winery tours from one of the tourist offices in the area (Kingston, New Paltz, Newburgh, or Poughkeepsie).

West Point

From Cornwall-on-Hudson take Route 218 to West Point. The **United States Military Academy,** commonly referred to as West Point, was founded in 1802, although it had been in the planning stages since the Revolution. West Point was occupied from 1778 on; during that year the "Great Chain" was draped across the river to stop British ships. Benedict

Bear Mountain State
Park
Route 9W
Bear Mountain 10911
914-786-2701

Stony Point
Battlefield
Route 9W
Stony Point 10980

Arnold almost lost West Point to the British by betraying his country to Captain John André, an aide to General Sir Henry Clinton.

Stop in the Visitors' Information Center located just outside the south gate (Thayer Gate) for information on touring the grounds. The West Point Museum is located in Olmsted Hall at Pershing Center. A collection of military weapons and relics was begun in 1777, starting with British weapons used during the Battle of Saratoga. There are two chapels to visit. The Old Cadet Chapel dates from 1836 and stands in the West Point Cemetery. This Greek Revival–style building houses marble shields used as memorials for officers during the Revolutionary War. The Cadet Chapel is bright with stained-glass windows. One of the largest church organs in the world is in this chapel.

Route 9W will lead you to signs for Bear Mountain State Park.

Bear Mountain State Park

Bear Mountain State Park contained both Fort Clinton and Fort Montgomery during the Revolutionary War. British General Sir Henry Clinton was able to capture both forts in October 1777. The **Bear Mountain Historical Museum** stands on the original site of Fort Clinton; it contains exhibits on the history of the forts as well as mementos from the soldiers who fought there. Perkins Memorial Drive will take you to the top of the mountain. The park offers boat rentals, a swimming pool, a nature museum, hiking trails, and a roller-skating rink.

Routes 9W and 202 lead to Stony Point.

Stony Point

Stony Point Battlefield, north of Stony Point, was the scene of one of the most daring attacks of the Revolution. In July 1779 the British held the fortifications there. General Washington commanded General Anthony Wayne to capture Stony Point. Wayne had ordered his soldiers to attack with bayonets, so that an accidental shot would not alert the British; just after midnight the Americans completely surprised the British, easily taking the fortifications. Wayne, who suffered a head wound, continued to direct his soldiers; he earned a gold medal for this exploit and the name "Mad Anthony."

Continue on Route 9W south to the Tappan Zee Bridge back to New York City. Or take Route 202 to the Palisades Parkway to the city. This completes itinerary A, covering New York City, Long Island, and the Hudson River Valley.

ITINERARY B:

Upstate New York

BOLDT CASTLE

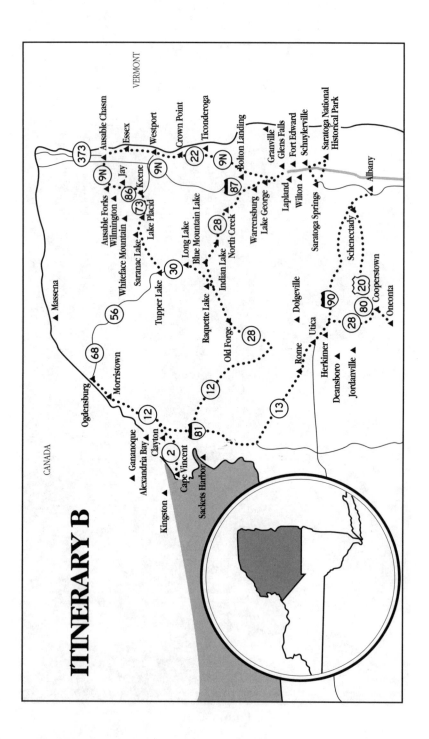

ITINERARY B

CANADA

VERMONT

Kingston ▲

Alexandria Bay ▲
Gananoque ▲

Clayton ▲

② Cape Vincent ▲

Sackets Harbor ▲

Ogdensburg ▲

Morristown ▲

⑫ 12

⑧ 81

⑬ 13

⑥ 68

⑤ 56

Massena ▲

Tupper Lake ▲

㉚ 30

Raquette Lake ▲

Old Forge ▲

㉘ 28

Rome ▲

Utica ▲

Dolgeville ▲

Herkimer ▲

Deansboro ▲

Jordanville ▲

㉘ 28

⑨ 90

⑳ 80

⑳ 20

Cooperstown ▲

Oneonta ▲

Schenectady ▲

Albany ▲

Saratoga Springs ▲

Saratoga National
Historical Park ▲

Schuylerville ▲

Wilton ▲

Fort Edward ▲

Lapland ▲

Glens Falls ▲

Granville ▲

Lake George ▲

Warrensburg ▲

Bolton Landing ▲

㊚ 87

North Creek ▲

Indian Lake ▲

㉘ 28

Blue Mountain Lake ▲

Long Lake ▲

Saranac Lake ▲

Lake Placid ▲

㊂ 73

㊏ 86

Whiteface Mountain ▲

Wilmington ▲

Ausable Forks ▲

⑨ 9N

Jay ▲

Keene ▲

⑨ 9N

Ticonderoga ▲

㉒ 22

⑨ 9N

Crown Point ▲

Westport ▲

Essex ▲

Ausable Chasm ▲

③ 373

Upstate New York

Saratoga Spa
State Park
Saratoga Springs
12866
518-584-2000

This itinerary begins in the pleasant town of Saratoga Springs, where visitors can discover intrigue among the Victorian personalities who once frequented the spa, bet on the horses at the track, bathe in the mineral waters, and attend concerts, ballet, and theater. To the north the Adirondacks beckon climbers, hikers, canoeists, sailors, and anyone else who enjoys the natural beauty of lakes and mountains. Lake Placid, the site of the 1932 and 1980 Winter Olympics, can be the jumping-off point for those who wish to explore the myriad lakes, rivers, and mountains in the wilderness area of the Adirondack Park. To the west is the St. Lawrence Seaway and the unique Thousand Islands area of New York State, where the confluence of five Great Lakes funnels into a single river that is used for both shipping and pleasure. At the conclusion of this tour, you can either head back to Albany and south on the Hudson River section of Itinerary A or continue west to join Itinerary C in the Finger Lakes region.

❧ *Saratoga Springs Area* ❧

Saratoga Springs, the "Queen of the Spas," is located on top of a liquid gold mine. During the glacial era streams deep in the earth picked up minerals that formed natural gases, which escaped in the form of springs and geysers. Iroquois Indians joined the forest animals in drinking from these bubbling, saline waters because they believed the waters had powerful medicinal effects. In 1767 the Iroquois carried Sir William Johnson, the British superintendent of Indian affairs, on a litter to Saratoga to cure his gout with the miraculous waters. George Washington was another who visited Saratoga Springs to partake of the waters.

Saratoga Springs

Today in Saratoga Springs you can drink the water from one of several fountains, buy bottled mineral water, or bathe in one of the bathhouses that are open to the public at **Saratoga Spa State Park.** Take it from us—the baths will relax you to the utmost. Each person has a private room for soaking in this soothing effervescence in a tub. You will find the tub quite long; for those of us under 6 feet, the tub has a little stool to hook your feet under so they won't float. The water is dark in color, hot, full of massaging bubbles, and conducive to a state of drowsiness until you are aroused by your personal attendant. You are wrapped in a hot sheet and allowed to continue your state of slumber. Eventually you will be awakened, and you must pull your renewed self together and return to the real world. Architecture in Saratoga Springs ranges from the Greek Revival style of the early 1800s, through the Gothic Revival style of 1830 through 1855, to the Victorian style. Although many of the grand hotels of

Saratoga Springs
Urban Cultural Park
Visitors' Center
465 Broadway
Saratoga Springs
12866
518–587–3241

the Victorian age burned during the first half of the twentieth century, when they were undervalued and unappreciated, much of the business district still retains the feel of its original Victorian architecture, with some modern structures sandwiched in between. **Franklin Square** contains a number of Greek Revival buildings; take a look at the house at 59 Franklin Street, with a facade resembling a Greek temple. Gothic Revival cottages, with steep roofs and decorated gables, usually had a porch like the one at 198 Regent Street. Victorian structures in Saratoga include a wide variety of styles: Italian Villa, Lombardian, Italian Palazzo, Mansard or French Renaissance, and Queen Anne. If you drive the length of North Broadway, Circular Street, Regent Street, and other streets on the east side of town, you will come across examples in all of these styles. Check at the **Saratoga Springs Urban Cultural Park Visitors' Center** in **Drink Hall,** across from Congress Park, for more detailed information about the historic homes in Saratoga Springs.

The **Saratoga County Chamber of Commerce** (28 Clinton Street, Saratoga Springs 12866; 518–584–3255) offers a series of booklets on accommodation, restaurants, antiques, shopping, and Saratoga Lake; it also provides a visitors' map and general information. Data are current so you can telephone a bed-and-breakfast, for example, and book a room easily. Be sure to plan ahead for the busy summer season when the New York City Ballet, the Philadelphia Orchestra, and the Race Track are all in full swing.

Drink Hall was originally a trolley station for the Hudson Valley Railroad. The arched windows and columns provide a neoclassical touch; if you are there in the spring, the flowering trees in front provide color and fragrance. Trolleys ran to Glens Falls, Schenectady, and Kaydeross Park at Saratoga Lake, and around the east side of Saratoga. Brass chandeliers, chestnut seats, and the trolley platform remain. The building was designed by the New York City architectural firm of Ludlow and Peabody in Beaux Arts style. On the facade two bas-relief murals show the surrender of British General John Burgoyne after the Battle of Saratoga in 1777 and Sir William Johnson at High Rock Spring.

By 1941 the name "Drink Hall" was a reality, as the state offered a choice of bottled mineral water. It was suggested to imbibe Hawthorn in

**Congress Park and
Canfield Casino**
Broadway
Saratoga Springs
12866
518–584–6920

**The Children's
Museum**
36 Phila Street
Saratoga Springs
12866
518–584–5540

the morning, Coesa before dinner, and Geyser during the evening.

The Saratoga Springs Urban Cultural Park (UCP) is one of fourteen in the state. Each is designed to trace the history and development of cities and towns. Six National Register Historic Districts are included in this park: Broadway; Canfield Casino, Congress Park, and Circular Street; East Side; Franklin Square; Union Avenue, Racetrack, and Yaddo; and Saratoga Spa State Park. You can take a guided tour or your own walking, biking, or driving tour. Pick up a brochure, which includes a map. UCP stocks a large number of brochures, tourist information, maps, books, posters, and postcards.

Stroll across the street into **Congress Park,** a thirty-three-acre landscaped garden complete with fountains and sculpture. Notice the *Spirit of Life,* which was designed by Daniel Chester French as a memorial for Spencer Trask. In 1870 the elegant **Canfield Casino** was constructed in Congress Park by John Morrissey to provide a setting for balls and gaming; large stained-glass windows decorate this Italianate building. Diamond Jim Brady and Lillian Russell were among the prominent visitors to Canfield Casino. Brady had one evening ensemble glittering with 2,548 diamonds, which must have intensified the illusion of wealth in the many mirrors of the casino. After you have admired the public rooms on the lower floor of the casino, be sure to visit the mementos of the grand era of Saratoga in the **Historical Society of Saratoga Springs Museum** (518–584–6920), on the second and third floors, and the **Ann Grey Gallery** (518–584–6920), which displays contemporary art. During the last quarter of the nineteenth century, when Broadway was filled with massive and elegant hotels, Saratoga was ranked in the world of fashion and wealth with Tuxedo Park, Newport, and Bar Harbor.

"I promise that we'll come back tomorrow!" said one mother as she coerced her two toddlers out the door of **The Children's Museum.** A number of children were obviously enjoying themselves when we were there. Learning was fun, to be sure. One little boy was putting his heart and soul into Karaoke, microphone in hand, as he belted out a song he knew. Several were playing in the store, which was stocked with a variety of food. Don't miss the preschool circus playhouse. Below a sign reading "People still come in many sizes," there was a size 22 shoe. Kids who want to be firefighters got to try on firefighters' clothing, including boots and a hat. One display on the history of grand hotels offered a phone to report an imaginary fire.

Programs include a live animal show, a book fair, and a drama workshop.

Do you enjoy listening to a concert or watching a ballet on a balmy summer evening? If so, you have come to the right place; the **Saratoga Performing Arts Center** provides pleasure for visitors and residents alike. In 1966 the shell amphitheater opened, seating 5,103. An additional 25,000 can relax on the lawn to enjoy the performances of the New York City Ballet in July and the Philadelphia Orchestra in August. You can buy tickets under the roof if you order in advance (and sometimes, with luck, on the day of a performance), or you can purchase lawn tickets for reasonable prices and bring your own blanket or lawn chair. Picnics on the grounds beforehand suit any style, from fast food to elegant gourmet treats. Have a meal in the **Hall of Springs Restaurant** (518–584–8000) on the grounds. **Scallions** (404 Broadway; 518–584–0192) packs picnic baskets. In addition to the ballet and the orchestra, the **Spa Little Theatre** is also on the grounds, staging performances year-round. Besides this extraordinary selection of cultural fixtures, specials at SPAC include popular singers, jazz ensembles, and a variety of other nationally recognized entertainers.

> Saratoga Performing
> Arts Center
> Saratoga Spa
> State Park
> Saratoga Springs
> 12866
> 518–584–9330 or
> 518–587–3330
> (during season)
>
> Saratoga Race
> Course
> Union Avenue
> Saratoga Springs
> 12866
> 212–641–4700 or
> 518–584–6200
> (during season)

Have you ever had breakfast at a Victorian racetrack? Try **Saratoga Race Course** (late July and August only), where you can combine the pleasures of the present and the past on a fresh, sunny morning when the dew is still clinging to the geraniums in the flower boxes. Make reservations and try to be at the track by 7:00 A.M. so you can get a ringside seat to watch the horses working out. An announcer calls out the name of each horse, stable, and trainer. Or come watch the thoroughbred racing in the afternoon. You'll have plenty of chances to admire the horses as they are being saddled in the tree-shaded paddock next to the track.

Open since 1863, Saratoga is the oldest track in the country, retaining its Victorian character not only in architecture but in ambience, by virtue of its exclusive right to run races in New York State during the summer. For these four weeks the track and the town revert to the customs of a century ago—with "boxes" at the track, "cottage" lists locating visitors published in the newspaper, and grand parties in the old style, with elaborate printed programs and ample newspaper reporting. Perhaps nowhere else does so much of the spirit of the old ways of high society survive, untrammeled by tourism, as here during these four weeks each year.

National Museum of
Racing and
Thoroughbred Hall
of Fame
Union Avenue
Saratoga Springs
12866
518–584–0400

Saratoga Harness
Raceway
Route 9
Saratoga Springs
12866
518–584–2110

Skidmore College
North Broadway
Saratoga Springs
12866
518–584–5000

If you are visiting during the second week of August, you can observe the annual **Fasig-Tipton Auction** of thoroughbred racehorses. Buyers sit inside the pavilion, signing their bids by such transparent signals as touching an ear or crooking a finger; the public is welcome to mill around outside the glass windows to watch the bidding and to stroll around the barns and paddocks, where some of the finest and most expensive derby winners of the future are waiting to be purchased. And as our young son once observed, there are few better places in the world to gaze at a collection of thoroughbred luxury cars; he found the Bentleys, Rolls-Royces, and Jaguars more fascinating than the horses.

Don't forget to visit the **National Museum of Racing and Thoroughbred Hall of Fame** opposite the race course. Visitors enter through starting gates and are immediately immersed in the world of horse racing. Full-size horses, jockeys, grooms, and patrons look almost real in their fiberglass bodies. Paintings, trophies, and racing silks compete with video presentations. A movie, *Race America,* begins with a truck tailgate opening at the track, the thundering as race horses jump right over the viewers, the roar of the crowds, and the excitement of the race.

And if you don't manage to get to Saratoga during the magic weeks of July and August, not all is lost. **Saratoga Harness Raceway** stages races ten months a year in the evening. You can have dinner there while watching your favorite trotter; television monitors guarantee your visibility all around the track. Though far younger than the flat track and less embellished with tradition, this track has established its own reputation for good racing and fine dining.

Skidmore College, once housed in some of the Victorian buildings along Union Avenue and adjoining streets, now has been in residence on the "New" Campus just off North Broadway for almost two decades. The red brick buildings, connected by covered walkways, are nestled in 800 acres of woods that are ablaze with color in the fall. This site, once filled with more than a dozen summer estates, was Lucy Skidmore Scribner's original choice for the campus, but it could not be acquired until 1965, when the college began developing a campus of forty-five new buildings that serve more than 2,000 students. If you want to take a look at this elegant new campus, drive up North Broadway to the entrance and follow the signs on the directory.

If you're interested in dance, take a trip to the **National Museum of Dance,** housed in a historic bath pavilion, the Washington Bathhouse, out on Route 9. The Mr. and Mrs. Cornelius Vanderbilt Whitney Hall of Fame resides in a lovely Beaux Arts foyer. Exhibits include costumes worn in Hollywood and Broadway productions, photos of dancers, and videos celebrating the lives of famous dancers.

The museum covers all styles of American dance, from George Balanchine's classical ballets to Katherine Dunham's ethnic dances. An increasing program of offerings, from exhibitions to master classes and dialogues with visiting dancers, attracts visitors. The educational component includes a library and resource center with videos, photographs, and publications on the Hall of Fame members.

National Museum of Dance
South Broadway
Saratoga Springs
12866
518–584–2225
Yaddo
Union Avenue
Saratoga Springs
12866
518–584–0746

The Lewis A. Swyer School for the Performing Arts is located adjacent to the museum. Visitors may watch dancers in action there through two-way mirrors. The New York State Summer School for the Arts is held there; 1,000 students try out and 100 are picked for the one-month session.

The rose gardens at **Yaddo,** on the eastern side of Saratoga Springs where Union Avenue joins I–87, are a pleasant retreat on a hot day. You can visit the gardens but not the buildings on the estate, for they are occupied by artists and writers in residence. Spencer and Katrina Trask bought the property in 1881, lived there with their children, and now are buried in the rose garden. Their little girl, Christina, called their residence, which was named "The Shadow," Yaddo, and the name stuck. The Trasks's wills left everything to a Yaddo foundation to provide a retreat and workplace for artists, writers, and musicians. Some of the literature and art that you enjoy may have been created in this peaceful setting. Each resident works all day in an individual house, studio, or room, having lunch there alone. In the evening the residents convene for dinner, relax, and perhaps attend a lecture or concert in town or at the college. Free of telephones and interruptions, these guests are able to compose, paint, or write more intensely than they could in less insulated surroundings—and this is the whole point of the Trasks's legacy.

Dining out in Saratoga can be a real treat, but it is a movable feast. We have tried almost all of the restaurants that seem to come and go each season and have returned to the old standbys time after time. A sampling includes **Eartha's Court Street Bistro** (60 Court Street; 518–583–0602), **43 Phila Bistro** (43 Phila Street; 518–584–2720), **Gideon Putnam** (Saratoga

Grant Cottage
Mount McGregor
Saratoga Springs
12866
518–587–8277

State Park; 518–584–3000), **Hattie's Chicken Shack** (45 Phila; 518–584–4790), **Inn at Saratoga** (231 Broadway; 518–583–1890), **Lillian's** (408 Broadway; 518–587–7766), **Olde Dater Tavern** (130 Meyer Road, Clifton Park; 518–877–7225), **Longfellows** (500 Union Avenue; 518–587–0108), **Olde Bryan Inn** (123 Maple; 518–587–2990), **High Rock Steakhouse and Pub** in the Sheraton (534 Broadway; 518–583–7625), **Maestro's** (371 Broadway; 518–580–0312), **Sperry's** (30½ Caroline Street; 518–584–9618), and **Spring Water Inn** (139 Union; 518–584–6440). For an evening of folk music, try **Caffe Lena** (47 Phila Street; 518–584–9789). Two more restaurants are located a few miles north in Wilton: **Chez Pierre** (Route 9; 518–793–3350), and **Wishing Well** (Route 9; 518–584–7640). Take a drive north on 9N to Hadley for a meal at **Saratoga Rose** (4174 Rockwell Street; 518–696–2861 or 800–942–5025).

Ulysses S. Grant fought his last battle in **Grant Cottage** on Mount McGregor, Wilton. It didn't involve swords and bullets—but throat cancer. The family had taken a cottage on Mount McGregor because Grant's doctors thought the mountain air would be beneficial.

One of his two last wishes was to die as a general instead of president; he wasn't happy with some of the details of his administration and preferred people to remember him in his military incarnation; so President Chester Arthur restored his status as general in 1885.

Grant's other wish was to finish his memoirs, necessary to provide cash for the family after his business partner had absconded with all of his money. Doctors told him that he did not have long to live, yet Grant plugged away and did finish just days before his death. He sat on the porch in his black silk top hat, a formal black coat with white silk ascot, and gray bedroom slippers, writing and writing.

In fact, his memoirs brought wealth to his widow through Mark Twain, who bought the finished manuscript for $450,000. Readers can envision the battle details written by a man who had excellent writing skills, even with morphine and cocaine in his body for pain.

Today the cottage is owned by New York State. After much research concerning the various colors used on the cottage over the years, the original colors were painted on clapboard and shutters. You can visit the cottage and find everything intact, just as Grant left it.

Inside, you can walk into the room where Grant died on July 23, 1885. The clock on the mantel was stopped after he died. His embalmed body was kept in an iced coffin until the funeral on August 4. The Grand Army of the Republic came up the mountain to keep order. An everlasting floral tribute with the note "Gateway to Heaven, given by Mr. and Mrs.

Leland Stanford" is still there.

Grant Cottage is located on the grounds of the Mount McGregor Correctional Facility, so visitors need to stop at the entrance before proceeding to the Cottage.

Schuylerville

You may want to take a side trip to **Saratoga National Historical Park,** located 12 miles southeast

Saratoga National
Historical Park
Routes 4 and 32
Schuylerville 12871
518-664-9821

Schuyler House
Route 4
Schuylerville 12871
518-664-9821

of Saratoga Springs and 8 miles south of Schuylerville. Drive south on Route 9 to Route 9P, where you turn east and drive around the south shore of Saratoga Lake. Turn right on Route 423, which is Battlefield Road, and meet Route 32, following signs to the battlefield. The visitors' center has an audiovisual presentation, a museum, and a special lecture series available on topics such as "Archaeology at the Saratoga Battlefield." From late spring to the fall, you can watch eighteenth-century crafts demonstrated by guides in period costumes.

The battles that are regarded as the "turning point of the Revolution" were fought here during the fall of 1777, when General Horatio Gates led the American troops on to victory over General John Burgoyne. The American commander, Horatio Gates, settled into position at Bemis Heights to wait for General John Burgoyne, the British commander. Benedict Arnold attacked the British at Freeman's Farm on September 19, 1777, and was relieved of his command by Gates for refusing to wait. He stayed near his troops, however, and reappeared in his general's uniform on October 7, riding his white horse at the head of his men. His courage enabled the Americans to take a redoubt located in an important position. Burgoyne's men were demoralized and hungry because the commissaries had not given them provisions. Having lost 1,200 men and surrendered 5,700 more, Burgoyne retreated to Schuylerville in a downpour, with his men slogging through the mud. When news of his defeat arrived in France, French military advisers decided to side with the Americans.

Take a self-guided tour of the battlefield on foot, by car, by bicycle, or on cross-country skis in winter. Along the route you will see markers for **Freeman Farm, American River Fortifications, Chatfield Farm, Barbers Wheatfield, Balcarres Redoubt, Breymann's Redoubt,** and **Burgoyne's Headquarters.**

Another Revolutionary War site lies nearby: **Schuyler House** is on the southern edge of Schuylerville. General Philip Schuyler lived in this pleasant estate setting; the original house was burned by the the British but rebuilt in

<table>
<tr><td>

Old Fort House
Museum
22 & 29 Lower
Broadway
Fort Edward 12828
581-747-9600

</td></tr>
</table>

1777 after the victory. The **Saratoga Battle Monument** is on Burgoyne Road near Route 29.

Fort Edward

The Fort Edward Historical Association, located in the **Old Fort House Museum,** has a collection of books containing information on Jane McCrea, who was scalped near Fort Edward on July 26, 1777, while on her way to meet her fiancé, a British officer.

There are many accounts of the death of Jane McCrea, who lived with her brother, John McCrea, on the west bank of the river several miles below Fort Edward. She was engaged to a British officer, David Jones, and went to the home of Mrs. McNeil in hopes of getting from there to the British camp. Some say that the two women were sewing outside near the house when a group of American soldiers went by. Then musket shots were heard and the Americans ran by with Indians right behind them.

The women went into the house and down a trapdoor into the cellar, along with a young man. Indians raised the trapdoor and hauled everyone out by their hair. Miss McCrea was placed on a horse (sent for her by David Jones) by Indians who thought they would get a reward for bringing her to the camp. Another group of Indians came along, and in a tussle over the bridle of her horse, one of the Indians shot her.

The museum has a piece of her shawl, a number of objects made from wood of the tree near where she died, an 1834 print of her scalping, and a large painting of the scene of her death.

The Old Fort House was built in 1772 and is one of the oldest frame buildings in this area. During the Revolutionary War, both sides used the house as headquarters. Benedict Arnold, Henry Knox, and John Burgoyne all lived in the house at different times, and George Washington had dinner there in July 1783.

The museum, which stands on four acres, contains nine buildings— four of them open to the public. The Toll House, dating from 1840, was saved from demolition and moved from Moreau to Fort Edward. The law office was used by A. Dallas Wait from 1853 to 1910. Inside are two portraits of the judge and one of his wife, Celina.

The Baldwin Barn contains artifacts from the colonial period that were unearthed in the early 1900s by people building new homes. Cases contain spades, hinges, axes, cannonballs, a bullet mold, buckshot, a French musket, lock flints, a powder horn, a compass case, ice creepers, and more.

Granville

Slate Valley Museum
17 Water Street
Granville 12832
518–642–1417

Slate was first discovered in this area in 1839, when many immigrants arrived from Wales and other countries in Europe and opened and worked slate quarries. This slate, including very rare red slate, is unusual in its multicolored appearance. The museum displays mementoes of the Welsh workers, including accordians, fiddles, harps, wooden shoes, clothing, and photographs. Tools used in the trade include trimming machines, block cutters, splitters, and punchers.

❧ *The Adirondacks* ❧

The Northway (I–87), one of the most scenic highways in America, will take you from Saratoga to the Adirondacks—8,900 square miles of lakes, forests, mountains, and wildlife. The **Adirondack Park** is the largest forest preserve in the United States, larger than Glacier, Olympic, Yosemite, and Yellowstone parks put together. There are forty-six peaks that spire over 4,000 feet above sea level, and nine of these have rocky alpine summits. Mount Marcy reaches 5,344 feet and Mount McIntyre is 5,112 feet. Whiteface is 4,867 feet high. For orientation you may think of the Adirondacks in terms of four sections: the High Peaks in the northeastern region; the lake and river area in the center; Lake George and other lakes in the southeast region; and flat woodland leading to the St. Lawrence valley in the west.

The Adirondacks contain some of the oldest exposed rocks on earth; the mountains were probably formed by pressure inside the earth that pushed older rocks up to the surface. Geologists feel that these rocks are an extension of the same landscape covering the whole Labrador Peninsula and part of the Laurentians of Canada. Hard, crystalline rocks, shot through with colored mineral streaks, were not washed by the sea or buried in sediment but remained pure. They still contain valuable ores; iron deposits in the area can be strong enough to affect compasses. The last glacial ice scraped the rocks bare, inscribing its path as it moved.

Altogether, the northern section of New York State is remarkable for its natural beauty, much of it unknown to people from other regions, who associate the whole state with New York City. The Adirondacks provide a wonderful getaway from the bustle of cities, a place where you can find peace and quiet while enjoying sports or simply looking at the view. You can count on finding wilderness in the Adirondacks because the state of

New York has declared about a third of the area to be "forever wild," a condition that has attracted visitors for many years. Teddy Roosevelt came for hunting, Robert Louis Stevenson spoke of the region as "Little Switzerland," and millionaires built elegant "camps" around the turn of the century.

The "Great Camps," as they were called, were not primitive in the least—nothing like tents beside a campfire. As word was passed about the scenery, fishing, hunting, and mountain hiking available in the Adirondacks, wealthy businessmen came for privacy while they relaxed and enjoyed their favorite sports. They built retreats surrounded by many acres of land so that each family could bring nannies, maids, guides, chefs, and other personnel to run their camps efficiently and yet not be bothered by neighbors. The architectural style that developed came to be known as the Great Camp style of the Adirondacks. Each "camp" contained a main lodge, guest lodges, dining room, social hall, kitchen, laundry, carpentry shop, blacksmith shop, boathouse, and other buildings as needed. The buildings were often linked by a covered walkway. Building materials consisted of logs, either peeled or unpeeled, and fieldstone common to the area. Other special features included bay windows, loggias, turrets, lintels, and porches. Most of the Great Camps are not open to the public; however, Sagamore Lodge and Conference Center, a former Vanderbilt camp, is open to the public in the summer (see the section about Lake George, later in this chapter).

History buffs will find in the Adirondacks relics and stories from the French and Indian War and the American Revolution, as well as from later eras of mining and lumbering.

If you have not visited the Adirondacks yet, you may have seen pictures or read literary accounts of the area. Winslow Homer spent time in Keene Valley and at the North Woods Club, near Minerva, where he painted extensively during the 1870s and sporadically until 1908. Other artists who have worked in the area include Asher Durand, Homer Martin, J. F. Kensett, Frederick Rondel, Arthur Fitzwilliam, James Smillie, and James E. Buttersworth.

A short list of writings about the Adirondacks would include James Fenimore Cooper's *The Last of the Mohicans;* Richard Henry Dana's "How We Met John Brown," in the *Atlantic Monthly;* Ralph Waldo Emerson's "The Adirondacks"; Kate Field's many magazine and newspaper articles during the nineteenth century; Hugh Fosburgh's *One Man's Pleasure;* Anne LaBastille's *Woodswoman, Beyond Black Bear Lake,* and *Assignment: Wildlife;* William H. H. Murray's *Adventures in the Wilderness;* Francis Parkman's *France and England in North America;* Jean Rikhoff's *Buttes*

Landing, Where Were You in '76, Sweetwater, and
One of the Raymonds; Theodore Roosevelt's *Outdoor
Pastimes of an American Hunter;* George Washington
Sears's (Nessmuk) *Woodcraft;* Robert Louis
Stevenson's *The Master of Ballantrae* and *The Letters
of Robert Louis Stevenson to His Family;* Seneca Ray Stoddard's *The
Adirondacks;* and Sloan Wilson's *All the Best People* and *Small Town, N.Y.*

| Hyde Collection |
| 161 Warren Street |
| Glens Falls 12801 |
| 518-792-1761 |

Hikers can obtain trail guides and topographical maps from the
Adirondack Mountain Club (818 Goggins Road, Lake George, NY 12845;
518–668–4447) or the **Department of Environmental Conservation**
(Hudson Avenue, Warrensburg, NY 12885; 518–623–3671).

Glens Falls

Exit 18 from the Northway will take you into Glens Falls, the site of
battles during the Indian Tribal Wars as well as the Revolutionary War.
Long ago Indians used the name "Chepontuc," which means "a hard place
to get around," to describe this place on the Hudson where they had to
carry canoes around the rushing waters. During high-water times the 60-
foot fall provides a refreshing swish of water; it has powered the paper
mills and other industries that are the economic basis of the city. **Cooper's
Cave** (now closed) on Hudson River Island, located under the bridge to
South Glens Falls, was an important setting in James Fenimore Cooper's
The Last of the Mohicans.

The **Hyde Collection** is housed in the former home of Louis and
Charlotte Hyde. Charlotte was the eldest daughter of Samuel Pruyn, a pros-
perous Glens Falls industrialist involved in mining, lumbering, canal trans-
portation, and paper manufacturing. While attending a finishing school in
Boston, Charlotte met Louis Fiske Hyde, a student at Harvard Law School.
They married in 1901 and began collecting art. The Hydes returned to
Glens Falls and built their Florentine Renaissance home in 1912 with plenty
of room to display their art collection. Perhaps they were inspired by
Isabella Stewart Gardner, who had her Venetian Renaissance home,
Fenway Court, built to house her growing art collection. They traveled to
Europe to collect furniture in the sixteenth-century Italian and seventeenth-
and eighteenth-century French styles. Tapestries, Aubusson rugs, and velvet
draperies completed the warm and pleasant appearance of their home.

An interior courtyard is filled with plants, sculpture, and fountains.
Windows on the second-story level open onto the courtyard. A new addition opened in November 1989, providing gallery space for contemporary
exhibits, concerts, and programs.

Chapman Historical
  Museum
348 Glen Street
Glens Falls 12801
518-793-2826

The Great Escape
Route 9
Queensbury 12804
518-792-3500

West Mountain Ski
  Area
West Mountain Road
Glens Falls 12804
518-793-6606
www.westmountain.com

The **Chapman Historical Museum** illustrates the development of the area in an 1841 home. Zopher Isaac and Catherine Scott DeLong bought the house in 1860 and lived there with their eight children. In 1923 their granddaughter married Frederick Braydon Chapman. Juliet Goodman Chapman gave the home to the Historical Association in 1966. The museum has been developed to depict the home of a Victorian family.

The Chapman is well known for its extensive collection of Seneca Ray Stoddard's photographs, paintings, and manuscripts. The toy and doll collection appeals to visiting children. A new wing has been added to house the gallery and gift shop. If you are there at Christmas, you will enjoy the special Victorian Christmas decorations in the museum.

If you're in the area during the latter part of September, you can attend the annual **Adirondack Balloon Festival.** Balloons have been coming here for the past fifteen years, and every year is better than the one before. Depending on wind and weather conditions, balloonists fly a couple of times a day over a four-day period.

Glens Falls restaurants include **Carl R's** (exit 18; 518-793-7676), **Crocke & Boule at the Queensbury Hotel** (88 Ridge; 518-792-1121), **Davidson Brothers** (184 Glen Street; 518-743-9026), **Fiddleheads** (21 Ridge; 518-793-5789), **Hilander** (Haviland Road; 518-793-6363), **Log Jam** (Lake George Road; 518-798-1155), **Montcalm** (Lake George Road; 518-793-6601), and the **Adirondack Coach House** (Lake George Road; 518-743-1575).

More food is available right on the canal in Whitehall: **The Liberty Eatery** (16 N. William Street; 518-499-0301) and **Finch & Chubb** (82 William Street; 518-499-2049).

The Great Escape fun park becomes more elaborate every year. Started many years ago as "Storytown" by entrepreneur Charles Wood, its change of names reflects both growth and a wider range of interests. Try "The Comet," a classic roller coaster rated among the top ten in the world by the American Coasters Enthusiasts.

As you drive along the Northway, you'll see **West Mountain Ski Area** stretching its trails up into the woods. Twenty-one trails range from easy to difficult, and the longest run is 1½ miles. One of the nicest features is that you can buy a lift ticket for four or eight hours—the clock begins ticking when you get there, so don't rush. Night skiing is a real favorite with locals who want to unwind after a day on the job. From Glens Falls take either I–87 or Route 9 to Lake George.

Lake George

Lake George is, without comparison, the most beautiful water I ever saw; formed by a contour of mountains into a basin thirty-five miles long, and from two to four miles broad, finely interspersed with islands, its water limpid as crystal and the mountain sides covered with rich groves of thuja, silver fir, white pine, aspen and paper birch down to the water edge, here and there precipices of rock to checker the scene and save it from monotony. An abundance of speckled trout, salmon trout, bass, and other fish with which it is stocked, have added to our other amusements the sport of taking them.

—Thomas Jefferson (A letter to his daughter, 1791)

The best way to see Lake George is from the water. Step on board one of the cruise ships in the village for a journey through pellucid blue water so clean you can drink it; past mountainsides covered with hemlock and pine, clumps of rocky outcroppings at the shore, mansions and a grand hotel from the nineteenth century; and finally into the wilderness area of the lake toward Paradise Bay. You're in for a surprise there. Keep your eye out for some of the sleek classic antique boats such as *Hackers* or *Fay and Bowens;* their owners enjoy taking them across the lake for a spin, and you will be able to recognize them by their mahogany brightwork and sharp bows, which cut easily through the chop. In the nineteenth century, steamboats like these were the primary mode of transportation up and down the 32 miles of the lake surrounded by mountains, which had only a few primitive roads along parts of its shores and still has none in its middle section.

Keep a watchful eye as your ship steams along the west shore. The first mansion along **"Millionaires' Row"** is a half-timbered English Tudor building, enclosed within a wrought-iron fence, with broad green lawns and a view of the lake you won't believe. It was built by William J. Price and later owned by Charles J. Peabody. As you continue down the lake, look for a series of large docks and boathouses left over from the days when steamers plied the waters with passengers, supplies, and mail.

As you continue along the west shore, on one side of Green Harbor you will see a forty-two–room Italian Renaissance mansion; the estate is perched on a peninsula of craggy rocks and evergreens, with a terrace providing an endless view of lake and mountains. Harold Pitcairn gave the

91

land to his wife and built the mansion as a birthday present many years ago; it is still used as a private home, but yachtsmen keep boats there in slips or at anchor all around the harbor.

Offshore to the north **Canoe Island** is really two islands with a passage in between; the smaller is in private hands and the larger belongs to Canoe Island Lodge, which brings guests to it for barbecues and swimming on a natural sand beach. The American Canoe Association, founded in 1880 at Crosbyside and dedicated to setting standards and establishing competitions for a popular and growing sport, held its first sailing and paddling regatta at Canoe Island, thereby creating the name.

A mile farther north along the west shore, the **Lake George Club,** built in 1909, is housed in a wooden Victorian structure, with an octagonal peaked roof perched over the dance floor. The terrace is perfect for those who want to watch sailboat races or savor the view of the mountains on the east side. (The club is private.)

Just beyond Basin Bay, north of the Lake George Club, Spencer and Katrina Trask, whose summer home, Yaddo, was at the edge of Saratoga Springs, built a retreat on a series of three islands. They called it **Triuna.** It is a private island. You will see a belfry and Gothic arch attached to one of the colonnaded bridges and walkways connecting the islands, with many guest rooms above the other bridge. Window boxes filled with flowers flourish all summer to complete this idyllic getaway spot.

Long before reaching Bolton Landing, you will see the gigantic white **Sagamore Hotel,** the scene of an international meeting with President Roosevelt during the thirties. The original developers bought Green Island for $30,000, built the hotel, and opened it in 1883. In 1893 the building went up in smoke, and its successor was completed the next year. In 1914 the Sagamore again burned to the ground. The current structure was completed in 1930 and refurbished several times—once again providing a luxurious haven for visitors as well as a new convention center.

For a special evening make reservations for the dinner cruise aboard *The Morgan,* which is docked at the Sagamore. She is a nineteenth-century replica touring boat with modern amenities. Guests enjoy cocktail hour on the upper deck as the vessel slides away from her dock and heads for scenic shores both south and then north of the Sagamore. She passes Fourteen-Mile Island and then steams up into the Narrows where campers wave from their campsites under pine trees. *The Morgan* is skillfully piloted almost within touching distance of rocky shores; you feel you're right in the midst of the forest as you glide along. Dinner is served below and the large windows look out on beautiful Lake George.

George Reis stayed with his parents at the Sagamore in the early

1900s. He was fascinated by the Gold Challenge Cup Race of 1914, when Count Mankowski raised hopes of a local winner but unfortunately struck a floating log. George bought a boat named *El Lagarto*, or "the lizard," which you can see in the Adirondack Museum at Blue Mountain Lake; he won the Gold Challenge Cup Race in 1933 in Detroit and in 1934 and 1935 on Lake George in *El Lagarto*.

As you steam in between pine islands, you will notice that some of them consist only of rock and a few trees—great for a private picnic. Others are larger, with several picnic tables and facilities for camping. Your surprise is coming! Watch carefully as you steam into the very narrow channel behind **Sarah Island** and then into **Paradise Bay.** Campers wave as you go by, and everyone waits for the proper maneuvering of your ship in the bay. Slowly she begins to back and fill, turning around, as if on a dime, within a few yards of shore. Boats toot their horns as she expertly completes her rotation without touching the shore or any boats, and everyone waves as she blithely departs through another narrow passage and heads off into the main lake again. Once while anchored in Paradise Bay, we were circled by an ancient but immaculate *Fay and Bowen* loaded to the gunwales with lovely young girls; suddenly they attacked us, laughing, with a barrage of water-filled balloons and then, like the steamer, sailed out through the channel and were seen no more. We might have been in the Greek isles or fairyland—of such stuff are the idylls of a timeless summer afternoon made.

As you enter the channel inside Fourteen Mile Island, on the east shore heading back south, you will see part of the **Knapp Estate.** In 1894 George Knapp bought the Hundred Island House, which had been a well-known hotel earlier in the century on a great deal of land. Later he built another home on the steep slope below the cliffs of Shelving Rock. This area contains some of the oldest exposed rock in the East—from the pre-Cambrian era. Just south of Red Rock Bay, you can still see marks made by the stone cutters as they quarried rock for the terraces and walls of the house. A cable-car railway was constructed to run from the shore into the cellar. In 1917 a fire started in the railway electrical system, spread into the house, and demolished it, but the chimneys and stone walls remain to this day. New York State bought much of the property and will preserve it as part of the wild forest that lines much of the eastern shore of the lake.

The return trip along the east side of the lake will take you past a wilderness area where there are no roads. Wildlife abounds, and you may be lucky enough to see a doe and her fawn, even from the water. While you cruise along, you may decide you would like to return to the area to explore this marvelous yet accessible wilderness at a slower pace; there are

> Department of
> Environmental
> Conservation
> P.O. Box 220
> Warrensburg 12855
> 518–623–3671

two ways to do so. The first is by hiking or backpacking, depending on whether you prefer daytrips or longer excursions into the woods and mountains along the lake. There is an extensive, marked trail system on the east side of the lake beginning at an EnCon parking lot off Pilot Knob Road. (Call the Department of Environmental Conservation for trail information or write for maps.) The trails lead to **Pilot Knob, Buck Mountain, Sleeping Beauty, Black Mountain, Shelving Rock,** and several isolated mountain ponds. All of the mountains have extensive views of Lake George, beating anything that can be reached by road, which is as it should be for dedicated hikers. None of the climbs is too arduous for a day's hike, if that is your preference.

Black Mountain, the highest in the Lake George region, may also be reached in a more interesting way by taking a boat to Black Mountain Point and climbing a spectacularly beautiful trail to the summit, where there is an old fire tower (now abandoned, since helicopters cover fire watches in the forest preserve). From the top of Black on a clear day, you can see the high peaks of the Adirondacks to the northwest, Mount Mansfield in Vermont to the north-northeast, Mount Washington and the Presidential Range in New Hampshire to the northeast, Killington Mountain in Vermont to the east, and Mount Monadnock in New Hampshire to the southeast. Meanwhile, the whole panorama of the northern two-thirds of Lake George is laid out below you. It's a view worth the climb.

The second way to explore the wilderness is by camping on one of the 179 state-owned islands in Lake George, all of which have beautifully maintained lakeside campsites with docks, tent sites, tables, barbecue pits, and outhouses. In some sites you have a small island all to yourself; in others your area, though generous, is contiguous to other campsites. Aficionados of the islands have their own favorites, based on a special view or unusual privacy, but to newcomers, especially those who have camped elsewhere, all sites seem extraordinarily beautiful. The islands fall into three groups, with those in the **Southern Basin** administered by an EnCon Headquarters on Long Island (518–656–9426); those in the **Narrows,** the middle section loaded with islands, from Glen Island (518–644–9696); and those in the **Northern Basin** from Narrow Island off Hulett's Landing (518–499–1288). (For general information on all sections of the lake, call 518–623–3671.) During busy times in the high season (July and August), it may be wise to make advance reservations for a site by calling 800–456–CAMP (2267) or by mailing forms available from **State Parks,** Albany, NY 12238 (518–474–0456). At less busy times simply go, take your boat to the island headquarters in the part of the lake you wish to stay in, and choose your island! In the spring and fall, local residents go where they please.

Out of the wilderness area, civilization returns with the sight of homes and sailboats patiently bobbing as they wait for someone to unfurl their sails. Around the next point you will see **Camp Chingachgook,** the Schenectady YMCA camp.

Lake George
Historical
Association
Museum
Canada Street at
Amherst
Lake George 12845
518–668–5044

Children from all over New York State have learned to swim, sail, and water-ski there. The camp now has a fleet of 24-foot Rainbow sloops— once the Lake George Sailing School. You will pass many private homes along **Pilot Knob, Cleverdale Point,** and **Assembly Point,** because this section of the lake is mostly residential. Land and homes command fantastic prices all along Lake George, and this shore is no exception. **Dunham's Bay,** another lovely, narrow bay, is filled with summer "camps."

As you return to the village, you will realize that of all the different views you have seen around the lake, none can be said to be choicer than the others. Residents feel that each view is unique, and as they visit one another they savor Lake George and the mountains from yet another perspective. The deep-blue water filled with islands, fringed by craggy gray-and-brown rocks and set against dark green mountains, has to be seen (or painted!) to be believed. Not all blue water is salt! For a cruise contact **Shoreline Cruises** (2 James Street; 518–668–4644) or **Lake George Steamboat Company** (Steel Pier; 800–553–BOAT or 518–668–5777). In Bolton Landing *The Morgan* is moored at the Sagamore (518–644–9400). Call for schedules. All offer dinner cruises. Cruise routes vary.

After you've gotten your bearings on a cruise, you may want to stop in at the **Lake George Historical Association Museum.** Dating back to 1895, when it was housed in a spare classroom in the Union School building, the museum now resides in the **Old Court House and Jail.** The mid-nineteenth-century building is interesting, as it displays architecture from three periods—1845, 1878, and 1900—and there are few jailhouse sites still standing.

The museum displays historical information concerning Lake George, including artifacts collected from the wars fought in this area. Look for the French and Indian War twelve-pound cannonball with a fleur-de-lis on it; the discovery of this cannonball indicates that Montcalm's artillery trench was on the present site of the Historical Association. An anchor from the steamship *Minnehaha* found on Meadow Point is also on display. Look for the large mural, *Lake George,* by David Cunningham Lithgow. The museum

Lake George
Battlefield Park
Lake George 12845

Fort William Henry
Route 9
Lake George 12845
518–668–5471

has an extensive collection of Stoddard prints from the nineteenth century and Thatcher works from the late nineteenth century to the mid-twentieth century.

Lake George Battlefield Park, located between the lake and Route 9 near the **"Million Dollar Beach,"** contains ruins of **Fort George,** which replaced Fort William Henry two years after it had been burned by the French, in 1759. The park has a collection of valuable bronze monuments depicting the historical past of Lake George. There is a statue of Father Isaac Jogues, the first white man to see Lake George, when he was a prisoner of the Indians. He was the one who created its more poetic French name, *Lac du San Sacrement.* Another statue of an Indian with the mythical name *Horicon* is in the park. On September 8, 1903, Theodore Roosevelt was present for the dedication of a monument portraying William Johnson and Prince Hendrick, commemorating the importance of Fort William Henry during the French and Indian War.

The Battle of Lake George was actually a series of three conflicts that took place in September 1755. Both the British and the French wanted control of a water route to Canada. The French built Fort St. Frederic at Crown Point, which threatened the British stronghold at Ticonderoga. General William Johnson left Albany in August 1755 and slashed out a military road from Fort Lyman (later called Fort Edward) toward Lake George, on his way to Crown Point. French Commander in Chief Baron Dieskau heard about Johnson's plan to attack Crown Point and set out to meet the British, but General Johnson, General Lyman, and the Mohawk Indian chief, King Hendrik, were already encamped on Lake George. Colonel Ephraim Williams and King Hendrik led their men north to meet Dieskau; King Hendrik was killed by bayonet and Colonel Williams was shot. (You can see the marker where Williams was slain on Route 9. A gray rock inscribed E.E. 1755 marks his grave near Bloody Pond.) Dieskau chased the Provincials to the area now called Bloody Pond, and then to Fort William Henry. A battle was fought at the fort, and Dieskau was taken prisoner. Johnson was incapacitated with a leg wound, and his command was taken by General Lyman.

Bloody Pond received its name after a contingent traveled from Fort Lyman along the military road and surprised 300 Frenchmen there. Two hundred French soldiers were thrown into it, coloring the water red for weeks afterward.

A reconstruction of **Fort William Henry** can be seen on Route 9, overlooking the southern end of Lake George. The original fort had been built by William Johnson after the Battle of Lake George and named after one of King George's grandsons.

By June 1757 the Marquis de Montcalm's troops had begun to journey south, by land and on Lake George. As Montcalm began to bombard the fort, Colonel George Munro realized that explosions within the fort had ruined his northwest bastion and that he had lost a lot of guns. He did not receive the expected reinforcements and therefore chose to surrender to Montcalm. Munro's men had permission to leave with "honors of war" and their personal possessions and head for Fort Edward.

What happened next, the infamous massacre of Lake George, has been detailed by all sides. Rum may have been at the heart of the matter, but what the Indians were really thinking is conjectural. They were also eager to capture prisoners and to take what they could for themselves. They felt they had a right to pillage the fort and the entrenched camp. After all, they had paddled a thousand miles to fight for trophies that were their only pay, trophies that supported their sense of manhood and self-esteem.

A war whoop became their signal to attack. They forced open locked trunks left by the soldiers and put on British uniforms. Then (unfortunately for them) they dug up recent graves in the military cemetery to scalp those who had died of smallpox. They later paid the price for their greed.

A French escort was provided for the surviving women, children, and British soldiers as they walked to Fort Edward, but the bloodthirsty Indians attacked them as well, scalping all who could not escape.

Today, visitors to the reconstructed Fort William Henry can witness four demonstrations that make it come alive, then wander in the courtyard where there is a well, perhaps containing a payroll of gold and silver—or the bodies of soldiers. Who knows? A crypt once held the bones of soldiers, most of whom died of diseases such as smallpox. A number of skeletons that had been displayed for years were reinterred in a respectful ceremony in 1994.

Walk down to the dungeon, where soldiers were imprisoned. There's a model of a prisoner in a tiny cell, a pillory, and a guard room. A fireplace from 1755 is still there. A long ramp leads from the courtyard down to the underground powder magazine, where kegs of black powder were stored. Curtains made of leather were hung there and kept wet with water to defuse sparks.

The reconstruction has stockades, dungeons, musket-firing demonstrations, exhibits, and an audiovisual program. James Fenimore Cooper wrote about the retreat of the survivors in *The Last of the Mohicans*.

To get a bird's-eye view of the lake and the islands, you can drive up the **Veterans Memorial Highway;** its entrance is located on Route 9 across from the battleground campsite, just north of Howard Johnson's.

97

You also can climb up a trail to the top of **Prospect Mountain.** The mountain once had a cog railway to the summit to provide the same advantage for nineteenth-century tourists. Today's trail uses the right-of-way for the old cog railway; it begins behind the high school and crosses the Northway on a footbridge. The view from the top is one you'll remember—panoramic to say the least. During the winter the Memorial Highway is open for snowmobiles and connects with a number of other trails in the region.

Other tourist attractions in the village of Lake George include **Magic Forest,** horse-drawn carriage rides, **Waterslide World,** golf, tennis, fishing, and boating. If you are here any weekend in February, you can attend the **Lake George Winter Carnival,** which has been held for a quarter of a century. Events include a polar bear swim, snowmobile races, motorcycle races, iceboat races, ice-fishing, parachute jumps, sleigh rides, snow sculpture, ice skating, snowshoe races, and canoe jousting.

There are so many good restaurants in the Lake George area that it is hard to choose among them; we will list some we have enjoyed. In Lake George: **East Cove** (Route 9L; 518–668–5265), **Boardwalk** (Amherst Street; 518–668–5324), **George's** (Route 9L; 518–668–5482; seasonal), **Grist Mill** (100 River, Warrensburg; 518–623–8005), **Log Jam** (Routes 9 & 149; 518–798–1155 or 800–672–0666), **Mario's** (469 Canada Street; 518–668–2665); and **Shoreline** (4 James Street; 518–668–2875). In Bolton Landing: the **Algonquin** (Lake Shore Drive; 518–644–9442); and **Villa Napoli** (Lake Shore Drive; 518–644–9750 or 518–644–9047).

For a weekend getaway or special night out, try one of the following for superb cuisine:

At exit 23 turn toward Warrensburg and the **Merrill Magee House** (at the Bandstand, Warrensburg, NY, 12885; 518–623–2449), which is very popular for lunch, brunch, or dinner among residents of the Glens Falls/Lake George area. The present tavern room was part of the original house dating from 1839; a Greek Revival section was built in front around 1850, and another section was added to the rear in the early 1900s. The house is filled with antiques, china, an 1864 rosewood piano, some original wallpaper, stenciled walls and . . . a surprise in the ladies' room. (For those of you who can't visit as soon as your curiosity would wish—there is a "lady in the tub" complete with satin shower cap and jewelry visible above the permanent bubbles!) (See Inns appendix.)

Bolton Landing is the site of the renovated resort hotel described earlier in this section. The **Sagamore** (Lake Shore Drive; 518–644–9400) offers meals in several restaurants and a spectacular view of Lake George.

The **Friend's Lake Inn** began life in the 1860s and has been completely renovated following a number of years when the only inhabitants were a contingent of raccoons. The owners, ski instructors at Gore Mountain, did much of the renovation work themselves, then turned their attention to providing fine dining. Their wine cellar is famous. (See Inns appendix.) In fact, their Nordic Ski Center is popular for cross-country skiers. With 32 kilometers of trails skiers can enjoy both the traditional track and also ski-skating terrain. More trails are marked for snowshoers who enjoy a great aerobic workout. The challenging "Cardiac Hill" attracts experts.

The **Copperfield Inn** (224 Main Street, North Creek; 518–251–2500) offers **Gardens Fine Dining,** as well as the more casual **Trappers Tavern.**

Lapland

Lapland Lake Cross Country Ski Center was created by Olympian Olavi Hirvonen within the Adirondack Forest Preserve. His Finnish background permeates the area, along with the flags of all of the Scandinavian countries flying outside the center. Reindeer are also on the site along with a REINDEER XING sign. Grooming provides in-track and skate skiing. The trail system winds through a pine forest.

Friends Lake Inn
   Nordic Ski Center
963 Friends Lake
   Road
Chestertown 12817
518–494–4751
www.friendslake.com

Lapland Lake Cross
   Country Ski Center
139 Lapland Lake
   Road
Northville 12134
800–453–SNOW or
518–863–4974
www.laplandlake.com

Marcella Sembrich
   Opera Museum
Lake Shore Drive
Bolton Landing
   12814
518–644–2492

Historical Museum
   of Bolton Landing
Main Street
Bolton Landing
   12814
518–644–9960

Bolton Landing

Take Route 9N out of Lake George Village and drive up the west shore to Bolton Landing to the **Marcella Sembrich Opera Museum.** Marcella Sembrich, the famous opera singer, spent summers there, teaching and encouraging students in their study of opera. She performed in the great opera houses of Europe and was a member of the Metropolitan Opera Company. Visitors can see her musical scores and opera costumes and her personal collection of paintings and art objects. The setting of this stucco house on Lake George is very pleasant.

Also in Bolton Landing is the home of sculptor David Smith on Edgecomb Pond. His statuary is positioned on the grounds. Stop in the **Historical Museum of Bolton Landing** to see clippings and information on Smith.

Up Yonda Farm Environmental Education Center opened in June

<table>
<tr><td>Up Yonda Farm
Route 9N
Bolton Landing
12812
518–644–9767</td></tr>
</table>

1997. The home of John and Alice Scott includes seventy-eight acres. Two barns were renovated to hold a museum and an audiovisual center. The memorial flower garden was created and planted by the Garden Club of Lake George. There's a nature trail to follow, a spectacular view of Lake George, and a butterfly house to visit. Naturalists conduct programs as well as guided tours of the property.

From Bolton Landing continue north on Route 9N over **Tongue Mountain,** where you can stop for a hike up to many outlooks for sweeping views of the narrows of Lake George. The whole Tongue Mountain range, east of Route 9N, is forever wild; it includes 16 miles of trails over five peaks to Montcalm Point and back along the shore of Northwest Bay. Don't underestimate the rigor of the full circuit, as we once did; that 16 miles is mostly up and down the five peaks, 500 or 600 feet up and down each way, much of it slow climbing or descending. Wear boots and watch where you put your hands, because timber rattlesnakes may be snoozing in the rocks. There are dens of them on Tongue Mountain; they are an endangered species, so just try to let them sleep. They are not at all eager to see you either, but if startled they could react. Professor William Brown of Skidmore College, an expert on the species and the area, suggests two simple rules: Don't disturb them (walk around), and don't put your hands or feet anywhere you can't see. Don't, though, let fear of the snakes keep you from the hike, which is magnificent on a clear day; we have done it in the fall during leaf season and on snowshoes in the winter, and the view of the narrows 2,000 feet below changes its aspect every minute of the trail. If you start at the summit of Tongue Mountain (marked parking lot on Route 9N), you will come to a spur trail to Deer Leap after 0.6 mile; this leads to a cliff overlooking the narrows where Indian lovers were supposed to have jumped off the edge to avoid separation. Then follows the series of five peaks, each with its own distinctive view, down the chain to the southernmost point 10 miles south, where the trail finally becomes easy and flat along the bay. If you want a shorter version of the hike, start at Clay Meadows (marked parking lot), which has a spur trail leading up to the main ridge trail.

From the ridge of Tongue Mountain, continue north on Route 9N through a long, lovely descent to **Sabbath Day Point,** the spot where General Amherst arrived in 1759 with 12,000 soldiers on the Sabbath and ordered religious services to be held. He was on his way to capture Fort Ticonderoga and Crown Point. Farther along this scenic drive, 4 miles north of Hague, you will come to **Roger's Slide,** which is famous for the legend of the snowshoes. During the French and Indian War, Captain Robert Rogers and his Rangers outfoxed the Indians who were chasing them by walking to the cliff's edge, tossing their packs down the cliff onto the frozen lake, then walking backward in their footprints in the snow to leave the impression that they had been forced to jump off the cliff. Fooled by this ruse, the Indians did not pursue them.

| Fort Ticonderoga |
| Ticonderoga 12883 |
| 518–585–2821 |

Continue north on Route 9N to Ticonderoga.

Ticonderoga

Samuel de Champlain discovered Lake Champlain and the future site of Fort Ticonderoga in 1609. He was impressed with the beautiful islands, wild game, rivers, and especially by the huge fish—up to 10 feet long.

Champlain journeyed with eleven Frenchmen and a group of Indians, arriving at a site northeast of the present fort, where they encountered the Iroquois. "When I saw them preparing to shoot at us, I raised my arquebus, and aiming directly at one of the three Chiefs, two of them fell to the ground by this shot and one of their companions received a wound of which he died afterwards . . . the Iroquois were greatly astonished seeing two men killed so instantaneously . . . they lost courage, took flight, and abandoned the field and their fort." The Indians had not seen firearms before and were eager to escape the "hurler of thunderbolts."

For the next 146 years, only traders, explorers, and Indians walked through this land. Of course, both French and English thought they owned the region, which was valuable because of its timber and fur.

Fort Ticonderoga was built in 1755 by the French during the French and Indian War. Originally named Fort Carillon, its position on Lake Champlain at the outlet from Lake George gave it control of the water route between New York and Canada. General Montcalm successfully defended the fort against the attacking force led by General Abercrombie in 1758, but the British captured it a year later. It remained in their hands until May 1775, when Ethan Allen, Benedict Arnold, and eighty-three Green Mountain Boys appeared without warning and easily captured it. "My party who followed me into the fort, I formed on the parade in such a manner as to face the two barracks which faced each other. The garrison being asleep (except the sentries), we gave three huzzas which greatly surprised them." Allen then ran up the steps and pounded on the door of the commanding officer, Captain Delaplace, ordering him to surrender his fort. Some say that he yelled, "Come out, you damned old rat."

Reconstruction of the fort began in 1908, and President Taft, along with the ambassadors of France and England, the governors of New York and Vermont, and other distinguished guests, visited for the opening of the museum in 1909.

Excavation took place carefully as artifacts such as firearms, buttons, pottery, china, cutlery, cannonballs, grapeshot, tomahawks, axes, sword blades, keys, and more were found. Visitors may walk through the museum to see priceless relics such as the breastplate of a French suit of armor from the eighteenth century and a blunderbuss used by Ethan Allen.

A colorful diorama features the Black Watch at Ticonderoga, with their red jackets and Black Watch kilts. The Black Watch collection includes a sporran, clay pipes, a broadsword, a highland pistol, buttons, bagpipe ferrules, which go around the pipes, and a camp axe.

Visitors can also see George Washington's spurs; swords belonging to Israel Putnam, Arthur St. Clair, and Alexander Hamilton; Benjamin Warner's knapsack; miniature toy soldiers belonging to Montcalm as a child; and a punch bowl belonging to Sir William Johnson. An original American flag, possibly made by Betsy Ross, is also on display, as is a needlework picture made by Sarah van Vechten in 1801 of Fort Ticonderoga with fishermen in Lake Champlain. The library contains letters, diaries, papers, and books from the period.

From the Place d'Armes, or central parade ground, visitors can walk into the cellar of the East Barracks to see two gigantic ovens that once baked bread for the entire fort. The West Barracks contains an armory in its cellar. Guns are displayed according to the time periods of their use. The collection also includes swords.

Crown Point

Continue north on Route 9N and Route 22 to Crown Point. The visitors' center (Route 9; 518–597–3666) has displays on the French **Fort St. Frederic,** built in 1731, and the British **Fort Crown Point,** dating from 1759. The Green Mountain Boys, led by Colonel Seth Warner, captured Fort Crown Point in 1776, lost control, gained the fort back, and finally left for the last time in 1777 as General Burgoyne entered New York. There are self-guided tours and an orientation film. Special programs are planned during the year, including reenactments of battles, an encampment of soldiers demonstrating life at the fort during the period of the French and Indian War, and an archaeological program that winds up the season with an especially popular "Archaeology Day." Take a walk outside and climb up to the bastions for a wonderful view of the lake as well as the fort. You can walk through the barracks where men slept up to eighteen in a room.

The **Champlain Memorial Lighthouse** stands just south of the Champlain Bridge. It is a memorial to Samuel de Champlain, who took two of his men and left with Algonquian-speaking Native Americans to head up Lake Champlain from the St. Lawrence River area. They engaged in battle, probably near the lighthouse site, were victorious, and Champlain named the lake for himself.

Although there are two ways to leave Crown Point to go to the next stop on the itinerary, our favorite is to backtrack from Crown Point to Ticonderoga and head west past Paradox Lake until you meet I–87 to go north. This part of the interstate is rated one of the most scenic stretches of interstate highway in the United States.

High Peaks Region

Along I–87 you will catch occasional glimpses of the "High Peaks" on your left, with the tallest, **Mount Marcy,** named for William Learned Marcy, onetime governor of New York. If you climb to the top of Mount Marcy, you will see **Tear-of-the-Clouds** below, the mountain pond that is the source of the Hudson River; it was named by Verplanck Colvin in 1872. Almost thirty years later, Theodore Roosevelt stood on that very summit when President William McKinley was close to death from the shots of an assassin. By the time he arrived back in North Creek, the nearest railroad terminal, he was president of the United States.

Do you have aspirations to become one of the Forty-Sixers? The original three persons to lay claim to this physical feat climbed all forty-six high peaks in the Adirondacks (those at or above 4,000 feet) by August 1921. Their six-year quest to bag them all set the permanent standard for climbing in the Adirondacks. Sometimes they would knock off more than a few peaks in a single day, even though at that time only fourteen of the mountains had trails to follow. This tradition has continued over the years, giving pleasure to many hikers. Age is not a factor; in 1983 five-year-old twins became the youngest to achieve Forty-Sixer status. It is very difficult to recommend a starting point—some peaks are easy, some are difficult, and some have more views than others on the way up.

If you're ready to begin climbing, continue on I–87 north to Route 73, then go west to Keene, the center of the region. Before you go, get a copy of *Guide to Adirondack Trails: High Peaks Region,* published by the **Adirondack Mountain Club** (818 Goggins Road, Lake George, NY 12845). You can stay overnight at one of the two lodges owned by the club: **Adirondack Loj,** located 9 miles by car from Lake Placid, and **Johns Brook Lodge,** accessible by foot on the trail system surrounding Mount Marcy; both make excellent bases for climbing Marcy and surrounding peaks.

Whiteface Mountain
Ski Area
Wilmington 12997
518–946–2223 or
800–462–6236
www.whiteface.com

A number of hikers feel that the High Peaks are becoming much too crowded and that the trails and foliage are suffering from the tread of too many feet. They recommend that hikers try some of the less-well-known mountain peaks. Others suggest climbing mountains that have more open terrain, for terrific views much of the way up. The **Department of Environmental Conservation** has trail guides and maps available for a variety of destinations. You will also need a topographical map for accurate trail-finding. Within the High Peaks region, some rewarding alternatives to the overcrowded Marcy climb are **Cascade, Porter, Basin** (difficult), **Haystack, Giant, Owls Head,** and the **Crows.**

Ausable Chasm

If you are interested in walking through a spectacular river gorge and then visiting Whiteface Mountain and High Falls Gorge, continue north on I–87 to Ausable Chasm (518–834–7454), formed over 500 million years ago by the layering of "Potsdam Sandstone." These cliffs rise to several hundred feet on both sides of the river, which continually carves a deeper and deeper chasm as it drops from the eastern fringe of the Adirondacks into Lake Champlain. Bring comfortable shoes to take a hike along walkways past Pulpit Rock, Elephant's Head, Jacob's Ladder, Mystic Gorge, and the Cathedral. You can also take a boat ride from Table Rock in a bateau with experienced boatmen. You'll go through a flume and a whirlpool basin and down rapids.

Wilmington

From Ausable Chasm look for signs to Route 9N heading southwest toward Au Sable Forks and Jay, then turn onto Route 86 to **Whiteface Mountain,** in the town of Wilmington. The Whiteface Mountain Veterans Memorial Highway takes you near the top of the only one of the forty-six Adirondack High Peaks that is accessible by car. (If you see some hikers working on the forty-six, be prepared for some condescension!) President Franklin Roosevelt dedicated this highway to the men from New York who died in the two world wars. You will arrive within 500 feet of the top and can then walk or take an elevator to the **Summit House.** You can also take the chair lift at the **Whiteface Mountain Ski Area.** The cylindrical building at the summit is used for research by the **Atmospheric Science Research Center.** The view from the top includes nearby Adirondack peaks, Lake Champlain, the Green Mountains in Vermont, and the

Montreal area. A nature trail tells the tale of weather erosion, alpine flora and fauna, and the changes that take place in such an exposed setting.

The Olympic Regional Development Authority (ORDA) was established to create and administer a post-Olympic (1980) program for the Lake Placid facilities. Whiteface Mountain ski area was the site of all the alpine events during the 1980 Olympics. The aftereffects of that world competition show in the many carefully groomed trails. During the Olympics busloads of spectators climbed up the sides of the trails to watch the best skiers in the world compete. We particularly remember Stenmark, whose impeccable runs in the giant slalom won him the Olympic gold medal. The area is a delight for recreational skiers; its network of trails offers every degree of challenge to skiers of various abilities. The Cloudsplitter gondola offers a heated ride in an eight-passenger cabin. It reaches the summit of Little Whiteface in seven and a half minutes.

High Falls Gorge
Route 86
Wilmington 12997
518–946–2278;
518–946–2211,
off-season

Olympic Center
Lake Placid 12946
518–523–1655 or
800–462–6236

Southwest of Whiteface on Route 86 is **High Falls Gorge,** which may be seen from a series of paths and bridges. The Ausable River has been cutting its way down through the gorge for over a billion years, aided by wind and ice erosion. You can take a self-guided tour with stops at listening posts.

Lake Placid

Continue on Route 86 and Route 73 into Lake Placid. (Or follow Route 73 from Keene into the town.) This is a pleasant resort town located in a broad valley surrounded by mountains. As the last glacier melted 14,000 years ago, gravel formed dams to create glacial lakes such as Lake Placid. Whiteface Mountain, with an elevation of 4,867 feet, provides a perfect contrast for the 300-foot depth of Lake Placid. As you enter town, you will see Mirror Lake first, as it lies along Main Street. During the summer you can bring a blanket and sit in the park overlooking the lake while listening to a concert. Motorboats are prohibited on Mirror Lake, so you can be assured of peace and quiet as you canoe, row, sailboard, swim, or just relax on its shores. Continue on to Lake Placid for a variety of recreational activities, including boat cruises.

Lake Placid is a center for a number of tourist attractions, including the extensive facilities built for both the 1932 and 1980 Winter Olympics. Stop in the **Olympic Center** for information and a map on Olympic sites. The **Olympic Arena Complex** is the center for ice sports, where four ice surfaces are maintained under one roof. The rinks are used for ice shows, hockey competition, professional hockey training, figure skating, and a summertime skating school. The **Olympic Speed Skating Oval,** where Eric Heiden earned five gold medals in 1980, is adjacent to the Olympic Arena. It is used by athletes in training and by the public during the winter.

The bobsled experience is one we remember with a tingle. As with any new, possibly threatening adventure, we wondered what it would be like. Dressed warmly from head to toe, we added large plastic helmets for protection. Four of us packed ourselves like sardines behind our professional driver and brakeman, a hero of the moment who promised us a safe trip.

The sled started with a whoosh and took off, rocketing down the course and banging the sides a bit on the curves. Our bodies felt little taps against the snow as the sled swung up on the banks into a vertical position, leaving us extended horizontally over the track. The next curve reversed that position 180 degrees, so we slammed down the track with our heads and bodies tilting in rhythm. Almost before we had settled down to relax and enjoy it, the ride was over. This "champagne of thrills" makes roller coasters seem like *vin ordinaire.*

The Mount Van Hoevenberg bobsled run was opened in 1930 and was tested and ready for the Olympic Games in Lake Placid in 1932. Mount Van Hoevenberg hosted the World Championships in 1949, 1961, 1969, 1973, 1978, and 1983. The run is 1,400 meters long, but visitors begin their trips from the half-mile point. Luge became an Olympic sport in 1964, and Mount Van Hoevenberg's fifteen-curve luge run was in place for the 1980 Olympic Games.

Take a drive to the **Ski Jump Complex,** where you will see two towers next to each other. The 90-meter (225-foot) tower houses a glass-enclosed elevator, which you can take to the top for a view of the Adirondacks. You can't miss seeing the ski-jump tower on Route 73 at the edge of town. Take the glassed-in elevator to the top for a bird's-eye view of the town, lakes, and surrounding high peaks of the Adirondacks.

When we were there a group of young jumpers was practicing. They rode up in the elevator with us, long, wide jumping skis in hand, then put them on and inched out along a plank at the top of a ramp that looked too steep to hold snow. When they felt ready they pushed off, dived down the ramp, took off, and soared with arms outstretched, as if reaching for more air, before they landed with amazing grace near the bottom of the hill.

On a practice day like this one, spectators can enjoy three unmatched views of jumping—far closer to the action than you would ever get during formal competition. You can see the start at the top, then move to a position just below the lip of the ramp to look upward at flying skiers, and finally watch the landings close up at the bottom. And you can record it all with a camera, or better still, a camcorder. During the summer plastic matting permits ski jumping, and a snow-making system is used to ensure plenty of snow all winter. The stadium there holds 25,000 spectators, with an electronic scoreboard to register distance, style, and total points.

Mount Van Hoevenberg Recreation Area includes the Olympic bobsled and luge runs, an extensive network of Olympic cross-country ski trails, and a biathlon course. You can also rent skates there; call ahead for days and times when the ice is available to visitors. We have found cross-country skiing there to be pure delight on a clear, sunny morning after a fresh snowfall. The trails are wide and provide all varieties of terrain, from easy flats to difficult descents. If snow has not fallen recently, the trails are still kept in good shape and hold their snow much better than windswept mountaintops in the area. If you come on a weekend or in a holiday period, don't be put off by a crowded parking lot; the system of trails is big enough to swallow a lot of skiers and give them the sense of space they came for. Ski school for children is offered from age two and up on Friday afternoon, Saturday, Sunday, and during holiday periods. Join "Racoon Romp" for a one hour lesson for ages four and up or "Fox Frolic" for children four to six or seven to twelve. "Camp Chipmunks" stay for one hour in an indoor playroom for ages two and up.

The **Lake Placid Center for the Arts** offers a full program of performances, such as dance companies, the Syracuse Stage Theatre, the Lake Placid Sinfonietta, the Sennel Theatre Group, the Community Theatre Players, and a classic film series. The gallery of fine arts features the work of current artists. The **Adirondack North Country Crafts Center** (518–523–2062), located in the library, sells Adirondack crafts.

The **John Brown Farm and Grave,** a historic site of New York, is located on Route 73, 2 miles south of Lake Placid. In 1848 John Brown arrived in Lake Placid, where he continued to strive for the freedom of the Negro. The house has been restored, and his mementos are on display.

If you're looking for a place to lunch, there are many to choose from. Local friends recommend **Jimmy's 21** (21 Main Street; 518–523–2353), **The**

Mount Van Hoevenberg Recreation Area
Route 73
Lake Placid 12946
518–523–2811 (cross country),
523–4436 (bobsled and luge), or
800–462–6236
www.orda.org

Lake Placid Center for the Arts
Saranac Avenue
Lake Placid 12946
518–523–2512

John Brown Farm and Grave
Route 73
Lake Placid 12946
518–523–3900

Robert Louis
Stevenson
Memorial Cottage
11 Stevenson Lane
Saranac Lake 12983
800–347–1992 or
518–891–1990

Cottage (35 Mirror Lake Drive; 518–523–9845), and **Goldberries** (137 Main Street; 518–523–1799). For a special dinner (reservations suggested), try the **Lake Placid Lodge** (Whiteface Inn Road; 518–523–2700). The inn was built as an Adirondack camp in 1895 on the shore of Lake Placid, with a view of Whiteface Mountain. The rustic simplicity of the lodge itself will not prepare you for its superb cuisine. (See Inns appendix.)

Saranac Lake

Continue on Route 86 to Saranac Lake to visit the **Robert Louis Stevenson Memorial Cottage,** where he lived from 1887 to 1888, when he came for a rest cure in a clinic directed by Dr. Edward Livingston Trudeau. Stevenson enjoyed the natural beauty of Saranac Lake and found the isolation and purity of the forest and lake conducive to his writing. He wrote much of *The Master of Ballantrae* as well as many articles in that house, and his bedroom is now a museum filled with memorabilia. Other rooms contain the furniture he used, including a desk; you can still see burns on the mantel from cigarettes he left burning there. Trudeau had told him to stop smoking and to stay in Saranac, and the cure worked. There are photos of a cast of Stevenson's hands from 1893, his velvet coat and cap, and a pair of ice skates that he used with pleasure on the lake.

In 1855 Queen Victoria's maid of honor, Amelia M. Murray, went on a camping trip in the Saranac Lake area with Horatio Seymour, governor of New York State, his niece, another man, and three guides. Murray wrote about seeing a loon for the first time and listening to its mournful calls; having freshly caught trout for dinner and partridge for breakfast; making a difficult portage around Raquette Falls; and other details of her trip.

In 1858 Ralph Waldo Emerson, James Russell Lowell, and eight other writers lived in "Philosopher's Camp" near Saranac Lake. Emerson wrote a poem describing the beauty of the place. Mark Twain had a summer camp on Lower Saranac Lake. Artists arrived to capture the landscape on canvas, and the Currier and Ives lithographs of the Adirondacks became popular.

Before leaving the Saranac Lake area, you should decide whether to complete a short circuit back to Saratoga and Albany or continue westward from the Adirondacks to the Thousand Islands region of the St. Lawrence.

Blue Mountain Lake

If you choose the short circuit, continue southwest on Route 3 to Tupper Lake, and take Route 30 to Long Lake and Blue Mountain Lake for a visit to the **Adirondack Museum.** This museum is both indoors and outdoors. Its exhibits are arranged professionally (with just the right amount of information provided) and attractively (with plenty of space around them). We suggest heading first for the Conference Building to see an orientation film. Exhibits are housed in cottages and buildings that are scattered around the grounds.

> Adirondack
> Museum
> Route 28
> Blue Mountain Lake
> 12812
> 518–352–7311

The museum has a superb collection of Adirondack guideboats, first seen in the mid-1830s, with full explanations. Don't miss the audio-guide diorama featuring an Adirondack guideboat in a hunting camp with a deer hanging in the background. *El Lagarto,* George Reis's elegant Gold Cup winner, is on display in front of a colorful mural of lake and mountains. Walk around to the other side and head for the "Poor Man's Yacht" display, which focuses on a canoe in a woodland setting with a straw hat on its stern. A painting by W. A. Rogers, *Canoeing in the North Woods,* hangs nearby. It appeared in *Harpers* in 1888. There's a mock-up of a Rushton canoe-building shop and a display featuring Nessmuk (George Washington Sears) with his *Sairy Gamp,* a tiny canoe that he took on a cruise through the Adirondacks in 1883. He wrote about his adventures in the magazine *Field and Stream.*

"Sunset Cottage," was built for Camp Cedars, which was owned by Frederick Clark Durant. It is a spectacular piece of radiating mosaic twig work. Cornelius Vanderbilt Whitney slid it across Forked Lake in the early fifties to Camp Deerlands, where it stayed until it was presented to the museum.

Don't miss the logging exhibit. "Mining in the Adirondacks" is another exhibit. The Rising Schoolhouse dates from 1907. Outside, the steamboat *Osprey* and the excursion launch *Mountaineer* are moored in the boat pond. The exhibit on lumbering in the Adirondacks is a capsule history of the area's major industry. The diorama of Noah John Rondeau—who was something of a hermit—chopping wood will give you a sense of nineteenth-century life in the woods. If you press a button on the relief map, you will illuminate the lakes, rivers, and scenery of the Adirondacks. The "Oriental" is a private railroad car owned by August Belmont, representative of the way the wealthy reached their camps. It is an elegant car, paneled in mahogany.

Gore Mountain

Continuing the short circuit, follow Route 30 to Indian Lake and Route 28 through North River to **Gore Mountain** for a gondola ride up to

**Gore Mountain
Ski Center
Peaceful Valley Road
North Creek 12853
800–342–1234 (snow
conditions) or
518–251–2411**

**Hudson River
White-Water Derby
North Creek 12853**

the top. Looking down from a gondola is one of the best ways to enjoy fall colors. If you come in the winter, you will find a very fine major ski resort favored by local residents. It is run by the Olympic Regional Development Authority (ORDA), which also operates Whiteface Mountain.

Gore Mountain dates back to the 1930s, and some of the people who work there today remember their parents enjoying Gore. The vertical drop is more than 2,000 feet, rivaling some of New England's ski areas. The eight-passenger, high-speed, heated Northwoods gondola is very popular.

Never-ever skiers can give it a try with ski equipment, a lesson, and a lower-mountain lift ticket—all for free on certain days. Clinics are available for mogul skiing, racing, women-only skiing, cross-country skiing, telemark skiing, and backcountry nordic skiing. A program for disabled skiers was begun in 1994 and continues with dedicated staff and volunteers. Disabled skiers love to arrive and find they can do more than anyone thought they could. One-on-one instruction provides confidence and great pleasure. The skiers have a ball, and their chuckles and whoops bring smiles to faces. The J-bar pro of today will become a chair-lift rider next week.

The Junior development program, for children of all levels, offers a program that works. A special six-week program provides the same coach each week and the chance to make friends and enjoy learning to ski together. Soon they will be skiing the whole mountain with pleasure. Little Buckaroos, from three to six, both play and ski. They learn to walk in their ski boots, slide with skis on, and make a wedge turn. Parents will receive a certificate with skills marked for each child.

Follow Route 28 to North Creek.

North Creek

If you think of the Hudson as a stately, broad river flowing between palisades, which it is downstream, you'll get another vision of it during the springtime white-water season here. Come during the first weekend in May, as thousands do, and watch the **Hudson River White-Water Derby,** which holds a slalom competition on a wild section in North River and a 7-mile downriver race from North Creek to Riparius. Spectators bring picnics and sit along the shores to watch participants paddle madly as they try to choose the best route through haystacks (the standing waves at the bottom of rapids that can swamp an open canoe) and avoid wrapping their canoes around rocks. The "Dean of American Canoeing," Homer Dodge (president emeritus of Norwich University), was still running the derby in his eighties. Downstream the section to the Glen also has a set of rapids, and ardent canoeists can continue on to Warrensburg through some Class-4 drops. (From damp personal experience, we recommend using a closed canoe, kayak, or raft for anything above Class 3.) The tributaries of the Hudson also provide a variety of white-water conditions. One of our favorite rivers is the Schroon, which ranges from flat water through the roughest water that an open canoe can

> Adirondack
>   Mountain Club
> Route 9N
> Lake George, NY
>   12845
> 518–668–4447
>
> Garnet Hill Lodge
> 13th Lake Road
> North River 12856
> 518–251–2444 or
> 251–2821
> www.garnet-hill.com

handle. It has the advantage of also being available in the summer, because flow is controlled by a dam. Those who want wilder water can go to the Indian River or the Blue Ledges section of the upper Hudson, both of which require expert guides. You can investigate taking a Hudson River rafting trip at **Cunningham's Ski Barn** in North Creek (518–251–3215), or **Adirondack River Outfitters** in Old Forge (315–369–3536).

For more precise information on specific canoe routes—anyone with white-water experience knows that you need it—write to the **Adirondack Mountain Club** for *Adirondack Canoe Waters*. Another helpful guide is *No Two Rivers Alike—Canoeable Rivers in New York and Pennsylvania,* by Alec Proskine (write to the Crossing Press, Trumansburg, NY 14866). If you are interested in a flat-water canoe trip, contact the New York State **Department of Environmental Conservation** (50 Wolf Road, Albany, NY 12233, or 2 World Trade Center, Room 6126, New York, NY 10047; 212–488–2755) for information on canoe routes in the state. Ask for *Adirondack Canoe Routes: Lake Chains*. There are many choice circuits, including **Paul Smith's, Saranac Lake, Tupper Lake, Raquette Lake, Raquette River, Long Lake,** and the **Fulton Lakes Chain.** You can also go ski touring on the canoe portaging trails in this area. Although hiking trails are often steep, canoe trails tend to be flat and wide enough for maneuvering a canoe and thus make ideal cross-country trails.

Cross-country skiers come from miles around to sample the trails at **Garnet Hill.** They range from easy to quite difficult. Gliding through the woods with quiet thoughts is a nice way to spend a day. The 2000 foot elevation provides great natural snowfall. Of the 55 kilometers of trails, 2 kilometers are lighted for night skiing.

Garnet Hill is not just another romantic name for a resort but a direct reference to the garnets that provide the reddish color in the rocks of the area. They take their color from iron ore and are actually twelve-sided crys-

Sagamore Lodge
and Conference
Center
Raquette Lake 13436
315–354–5311

Enchanted Forest of
the Adirondacks
Fulton Lakes
315–369–6145

tals. In 1893 Frank Hooper discovered how to remove the garnet from the ore with liquid. By 1894 he had begun the North River Mining Company at Ruby Mountain, and in 1905 he moved his mining operation to Garnet Hill.

Garnet Hill Lodge is a four-season resort with tennis courts and a private lake. (See Inns appendix.) Guests can enjoy paddling in canoes, mountain biking, or hiking in spring, summer, and fall. Guided naturalist programs last about two hours. Ask for a copy of the *Garnet Hill Wilderness Nature Trail Guide Book,* which has a tree-identification guide and numbered stations with explanations along the trail.

To complete the short circuit, continue on Route 28 through Warrensburg, where you can pick up I–87 south to Saratoga Springs and Albany.

To continue the itinerary to the Thousand Islands area, either take Route 3 west from Tupper Lake to Route 21 west; Route 28 southwest from Blue Mountain Lake past Old Forge to Alder Creek, where you can pick up Route 12 northwest; or Route 30 north from Lake Clear Junction to Malone and pick up Route 37 west to Route 12. There are no direct, fast routes from east to west across this part of the state—the wildest and least developed in the Adirondack Park. Why should there be? There is, however, some virtue in the enforced slower pace through this section of the mountains, forests, and lake; appreciate them and remember that you are still in New York, not Montana.

Raquette Lake

If you choose the southernmost of the three routes to the Thousand Islands, you will pass Raquette Lake, much favored by canoeists. You can visit **Camp Sagamore,** built by William Durant in 1897 and owned by the Vanderbilts beginning in 1903. This Tyrolean estate is a splendid example of the "Great Camps" of the area. During the summer a guided tour and slide presentation are offered. (The Sagamore also offers a variety of programs all year.) When we were there, we were entranced by the animal heads on walking sticks carved by the carpenter-in-residence in the carpenter's shop. When you visit the blacksmith shop, look for the champagne case drawer that says w. w. DURANT on the bottom. The Wigwam guest cottage is the place to be if you like hearing the rushing water of a stream outside your door. In the Main Lodge look for the doorjamb where the Vanderbilt children marked their heights. Also don't miss the covered bowling alleys that are still in use today.

Philomena D.
Westport Marina
Washington Street
Westport 12993
518–962–4899

Fulton Lakes

Along the same route the Fulton Lakes Chain is very popular for canoe trips. Canoe liveries operating from Old Forge will help you plan your trip. They will pick you up at the conclusion of your route, perhaps the most important service one-way canoeists need. If you are there in the winter months, you will find alpine and cross-country skiing as well as snowmobiling trails. If you have children, you may want to head for **Enchanted Forest of the Adirondacks,** a theme park featuring make-believe, shows, and rides. It is open from June to September.

Westport

Westport dates from 1764 when William Gilliland was granted 2,300 acres, which he called Bessboro, for his daughter. Edward Raymond, one of the colonists, built a home in 1770, then a sawmill and a gristmill. His mill produced timber for Benedict Arnold's boats.

By 1790 ferries ran from Rock Harbor to Basin Harbor and from Barber's Point to Arnold's Bay. In 1808 the second steam-powered vessel in the world was launched on Lake Champlain. The Hudson Canal was finished in 1823, which connected Westport to Albany and New York City. In 1876 the Delaware and Hudson Railroad came to town, reducing some of the water transportation. This allowed for an increase in summer visitors.

Vacation for many people means water activity. Tours are available on the ***Philomena D.*** from Westport Marina. This fifty-one year-old vessel was named for Philomena Daniels, who was born in 1835. She married a stone mason from Vermont. At one point her husband needed another captain for his steamship line, and she became the first female licensed captain in the world. They say she could swear like a sailor and wore very imaginative hats, which she picked up in New York in the winter. Philomena outlived her husband, ran the company herself, and died in 1912.

Our tour led to a flat rock where another captain ran the *Champlain II* aground. He was addicted to opium and spent several days wandering in the woods before emerging. The wreck now has a buoy over it with a chain leading down, so divers can look but not touch.

We cruised by Barn Rock, which looked like an overturned barn roof. It is 40 feet deep there. The grandson of the man who owned Fitch sham-

High Peaks Touring
1 Main Street
Essex 12936
518–963–7028

poo dove in there and died. His body was never found.

Next we cruised very close to shore to try to spot a family of eagles. The cliff is 110 feet at that spot and the rock walls head straight up for hundreds of feet. Lichen has been growing there and it has taken a long time to establish itself. Visitors are requested not to touch it.

We headed for Orebed Bay, also called "Snake Den" after the rattlesnakes who live there. From the mine over the crest of the hill men used to tip iron ore over the top and into a waiting barge. At one point 300 people lived up there, using a series of lattice ladders to get up.

There are many stories about Benedict Arnold, who went back and forth across the lake. At one time, after both the British and the Americans had stopped action for the night, Arnold decided to set sail, muffled the oars with clothing, and headed south. The British thought he had gone north and so headed in the wrong direction.

If you've been wondering about "Champ," there are a number of people who believe they have really seen the monster. Lake Champlain is located at the same latitude as Loch Ness in Scotland. Both were once connected to the sea and so could have sea creatures still lurking in the bottom. Some say it has a face like a horse, others that it is a giant sturgeon. After a lake tour you can have a meal in **The Galley,** located right on the dock (518–962–4899), or at **Westport Hotel** on Pleasant Street, (518–962–4501).

Essex

The country road from Westport to Essex is beautiful, with trees on each side, a curvaceous black-topped road, and few houses to mar the view.

The whole village of Essex is on the National Register of Historic Places. Homes were built in a variety of styles—Federal, Greek Revival, Carpenter Gothic, Italianate, and French Second Empire.

During the War of 1812 Essex was noted for ship building. Two hundred fifty bateaux and two sloops, the *Growler* and the *Eagle,* were created in Essex. Commodore Thomas MacDonough used them in his fleet in the War of 1812. Today you can arrive by boat—a ferry from Vermont. Or visit Vermont that way and return.

If you'd like to get out on the water in a kayak, head for **High Peaks Touring,** located on Main Street next to The Dock. You can take a course to learn the basic skills or head out on your own.

114

❧ *Thousand Islands Region* ❧

> Antique Boat
> Museum
> 750 Mary Street
> Clayton 13624
> 315–686–4104

Although you may not wish to leave the wilderness of the Adirondacks, other pleasures await you in the Thousand Islands of the St. Lawrence. There may be almost 2,000 islands, depending on what you count, but a French explorer gave the area its name. These "jewels" in the river provide a perfect environment for water sports, natural beauty of a very high order, and a variety of historical and culinary attractions. Although some islands are quite small, including those of one-rock size, others house a one-family home with space to spare, and some have the dimensions for a whole village. On them you will see large stone mansions, luxury hotels, colonial houses of historical significance, and even a castle. You can take any one of a number of boat trips or rent a houseboat for your holiday, but be sure you do get on the water; there is no other way to appreciate the extraordinary beauty of the region.

Clayton

Route 12 leads you to Clayton, where you can visit the **Antique Boat Museum.** This museum has collected a unique group of antique boats, including dugout and birchbark canoes, St. Lawrence skiffs, turn-of-the-century launches, and speedboats from the Gold Cup era. *Dixie II,* the 1908 to 1910 Gold Cup champion, resides here. *PDQ,* short for "Pretty Damn Quick," George Boldt's 39-foot boat, was built in Ogdensburg. *Ariel,* a naphtha launch owned by President Garfield, was built between 1880 and 1884, and *Anita,* another naphtha launch, looks like a surrey with a fringe on top. She has a brass steering wheel, mahogany seats, and an engine in the stern. Skiffs, bateaux, Adirondack guide boats, and canoes are displayed in a shed behind the main building. A 10-foot-long dugout canoe on display was found exposed in a creek bank after a heavy rain.

Cape Vincent

From Clayton continue west on Route 12 toward Cape Vincent, a harbor settled years ago by the French. Look for **"Stone House"** on Main Street, one of many historic homes. If you are fascinated by ocean-going vessels, this is the place to stretch out on the grass and watch. You can see Carleton Island 5 miles offshore and the ruins of Fort Haldemand. Tibbett's Point

Fort Henry
Kingston, Canada
613–542–7388
Hockey Hall of Fame
Alfred & Pine Streets
Kingston, Canada
613–544–2355
Marine Museum of the Great Lakes at Kingston
55 Ontario Street
Kingston, Canada
613–542–2261

Lighthouse is located at the junction of the St. Lawrence and Lake Ontario. Fishermen regard Cape Vincent as the black-bass center of the area, and you can visit the **Cape Vincent Fisheries Station** to see its displays on the conservation of fish. If you are there in the middle of July, you can be involved in the **French Festival,** which brings the history of the area to life.

Kingston, Canada

Since you are this close, you may want to make a side trip into Canada. You will need to go through Customs both ways, which does not take long. Check current regulations before you go. For example, we once came through with our dog and did not have her vaccination certificate with us, which caused some delay.

You can travel by ferry from Cape Vincent to Wolfe Island and by another ferry to Kingston, Ontario. Kingston, an early fur-trading center, was in a strategic location for military operations. **Fort Henry** was built in the years following the War of 1812; it has been restored and provides presentations during the summer season. The **Hockey Hall of Fame** is located in town. You can also take cruises to the Thousand Islands from Kingston.

The **Marine Museum of the Great Lakes** at Kingston has a variety of exhibits, including a blacksmith shop where the supplies necessary for shipbuilding were made, a steamboat display, a shipwreck chart, a display of half-models, a mast-step from a frigate used during the War of 1812, and a display on deep-sea diving. Signs invite visitors to hear a ship's whistle, rotate the dial on a radio direction-finder until the signals disappear, or pick up the telephone to hear the voice of the Coast Guard reciting weather conditions to mariners.

Stop in at the old **Prince George Hotel** (200 Ontario Street; 613–549–5440) for a Guinness or something else. It's right across the street from the **Visitor and Convention Bureau** (209 Ontario Street, Kingston, Canada K7L 2Z1), within sight of the waterfront.

If you drive northeast from Kingston on Route 2, you will come to the **St. Lawrence Island National Park,** where there is a visitors' center; check on the many activities available, such as hikes and interpretive programs.

Gananoque

Boldt Castle
Heart Island
Alexandria Bay
13607
315–482–9724
or 800–847–5263

From Kingston Route 2 will take you to the village of Gananoque, where you can shop endlessly for British china, woolens, and silver. This resort center has many water sports and various other activities for the visitor. During the summer season you can attend church services held from a rocky pulpit on the edge of a natural amphitheater at Halfmoon Bay. The congregation arrives by boat and views the service from the boats; canoe-paddling ushers distribute hymnals and collect offerings. Many Thousand Island boat trips begin at Gananoque.

The **Thousand Islands Bridge** is located east of Gananoque. This 7-mile crossing, dedicated in 1938 as a symbol of peace between Canada and the United States, provides magnificent views of the beautiful area. Park your car in the parking lot. A sky deck between spans of the bridge has an elevator to whisk you to a view ranging up to 40 miles. Ships flying different foreign flags thread through Seaway channels below as you look down from the top of the tower, and the vista of islands is spread before you. Don't miss it on a clear day.

Alexandria Bay

Heading northeast on Route 12 from the I–81 junction will take you to Alexandria Bay. Look out in the river to see **Boldt Castle** on Heart Island. George Boldt, the owner of the Waldorf–Astoria in New York City, blasted the island into the shape of a heart and built this dream castle for his wife, but she died in 1902, four years after construction had begun. As a result, the castle was never occupied. This 300-room building was designed to look like a castle on the Rhine. There is a legend that Thousand Island dressing was first served aboard George Boldt's yacht during a cruise in the Thousand Islands. Boldt's steward served him a new dressing that he liked so much that he decided to serve it in his hotel, naming it after his favorite vacation area. The steward was promoted and rose to fame as Oscar of the Waldorf. **Boldt Yacht House** is now open on Wellesley Island.

A boat trip is the only way to explore the intricacies of the islands. **Uncle Sam Boat Tours** (800–ALEXBAY or 315–482–2611) runs a variety of tours, including those on a new boat, the *Alexandria Bell*. You will pass through "Millionaires Colony," past the Devil's Oven, stop at Boldt Castle, then continue into Canada to cruise under the International Bridge, through Whirlpool Channel and Lost Channel, and past Fiddler's Elbow. Don't miss seeing the shortest international bridge in the world between two adjoining

Red Barn Museum
River Road
Morristown 13664
315–375–6390

Stone Windmill
Chapman Village
  Park
Morristown 13664
315–375–6390

Remington Art
  Museum
303 Washington
  Street
Ogdensburg 13669
315–393–2425

islands—one in Canada and one in the United States. Smugglers Cove was notorious as a meeting place for rum-runners; its seven entrances gave them a chance to get out without having to sink their bottles if the Coast Guard appeared.

Restaurants abound in Alexandria Bay: **Admiral's Inn** (33 James Street; 315–482–2781), **Pine Tree Point** (Outer Anthony Street; 315–482–9911), **Riveredge** (17 Holland Street; 315–482–9917), **Edgewood Resort** (Edgewood Road; 315–482–9922), and **Bonnie Castle** (Holland Street; 315–482–4511) are some possibilities. Bonnie Castle is one of the old mansions on the river, dating from 1877. **Caps Landing** (315–482–7777) is a floating restaurant.

Morristown

As you continue northeast (downriver) from Alexandria Bay on Route 12, you will find a number of state parks for leisurely stops. Route 12 merges with Route 37 near Morristown.

The **Red Barn Museum** has displays of some of the village's early residents, a blacksmith shop, and an icehouse. The **Stone Schoolhouse** in the museum dates from 1824. Typical desks, benches, and the schoolmaster's desk hold a collection of maps and books. As you might imagine, an old wood stove is in a prominent spot. The **Stone Windmill** was built in 1825 as a gristmill. Once it was used as a jail, and it saw action during World War II as an air-warning observation post.

Ogdensburg

Farther downstream, Ogdensburg has had a couple of forts in its history, including Fort Oswegatchie, which was built by the British in the late 1700s. The **Ogdensburg-Prescott International Bridge,** the eighteenth-largest suspension bridge in the world, arches 125 feet above the river at the center.

The **Remington Art Museum** contains more of Frederic Remington's work than any other museum. The priceless collection includes 14 bronzes, 140 watercolors, 70 oil paintings, and many sketches. The gallery displays a selection of his work and features new acquisitions as they are received. Mementos from his travels also grace this museum. Educational programs for students are held throughout the year. Frederic Remington lived on

Hamilton Street in Ogdensburg for eight years. He grew up during the time when horses were used all over town—horses and buggies, horses and carriages, work horses and wagons, racing horses, saddle horses, and fire horses. No wonder he chose to draw and sculpt horses.

Massena

Continue on Route 37 to Massena to **Robert Moses State Park,** where you can get information on the St. Lawrence Seaway as well as view some of the locks. Look for the original wooden map showing the adventures of Jacques Cartier as he discovered the St. Lawrence River. There is a 90-foot drop in the river here, which provides power for the Moses-Saunders Power Dam. The **FDR Project** on Barnhart Island has exhibits on river power developments.

Robert Moses
State Park
Barnhart Island
Massena 13662
315–769–8663

Sackets Harbor
Battlefield State
Historic Site
Sackets Harbor
13685
315–646–3634

Pickering Beach
Historical Museum
503 West Main
Street
Sackets Harbor
13685

After your tour of the Thousand Islands area, head south again on I–81 through Watertown.

Sackets Harbor

You may want to take a side trip from Watertown on Route 3 West to Sackets Harbor, a scene of fighting during the War of 1812. Some accounts claim that one American ship defeated five British ships, even returning the one ball that landed on shore to splinter the mast of the British flagship. General Zebulon Pike, who discovered Pike's Peak and also distinguished himself in the War of 1812, is buried in a military cemetery there.

Sackets Harbor Battlefield State Historic Site contains a visitors' center in the Union Hotel. There are lots of exhibits, dioramas, lectures, and special programs available. The site is right on the water, attractively landscaped with lawns and large maples. **Pickering Beach Historical Museum** is a historic home dating back to 1817. It contains items from the War of 1812, an antique doll collection, period furniture, silver, china, and other memorabilia. **Madison Barracks** on Pike Street was the site of training for a number of our most prestigious military leaders.

The remainder of this itinerary heads east to the Mohawk Valley and back to Albany. Take I–81 south from Watertown to Pulaski, then Route 13 and Route 69 to Rome. Alternatively, you can head south to join the Finger Lakes Itinerary.

☙ *The Central Leatherstocking Region* ☙

Sometimes regarded as the heartland of New York State, the Mohawk Valley has been called the "Leatherstocking" region because James Fenimore Cooper's book *Leatherstocking Tales* was set in this area. The name comes from the dress of woodsmen, who wore leather leggings to protect their legs from branches and thorns when blazing trails through the forest.

The Mohawk Valley was formed by the melting of glacial ice, which produced a wide river valley. The landscape is varied with rock groupings and precipices, forests, cataracts, and waterfalls dropping into jagged gorges. The Mohawk River begins just north of Rome and cuts a path through the Alleghany Plateau. This "river flowing through the mountains" is located between the Adirondacks and the Catskills, connecting the Great Lakes with the Hudson River. It flows for 150 miles until it dashes over the falls at Cohoes and into the Hudson.

Mohawk Indians lived there as "Keepers of the Eastern Door." These aggressive members of the Iroquois Confederacy protected the central part of New York State. Many of them prospered by farming their fertile land. As the fur trade grew, the valley absorbed increasing numbers of men transporting pelts by canoes, bateaux, and barges. German settlers arrived in the 1720s, building sturdy stone houses as a deterrent against fire during Indian raids. In 1755 the British built a series of forts to interrupt trade along this crucial route.

Rome

Rome was originally called "the carrying place" by the Indians; there is a portage right in the center of town. Stop in the information center located in City Hall (315–336–6000) if you have some time to spend in this interesting small city.

Fort Stanwix, in the center of town, was built in 1758 during the French and Indian War, then abandoned until 1776, when American soldiers rebuilt it. As you look at this star-shaped structure, you can imagine those inside using a pattern of crossfire to mow down attackers. A sentry from the Third New York Regiment, which was a colonial unit, is stationed at the drawbridge where visitors enter. At the visitors' center you can watch a film recounting the twenty-one-day siege by the British, in August 1777. By withstanding the siege, the defenders, under Colonel Peter Gansevoort, delayed the British General Barry St. Leger and prevented him from reinforcing General John Burgoyne at the Battle of Saratoga. You can walk inside the fort to see the officer's quarters; the men's quarters, where as many as ten men would sleep in a platform bed; the Surgeon's Day Room, where soldiers would go for possible amputation, bleeding, or quarantine; and the museum, which houses a number of artifacts found during the archaeological dig. You will hear the cannons boom on weekends.

Fort Stanwix
Rome 13440
315–336–2090
Erie Canal Village
Route 49W
Rome 13440
315–337–3999 or
888–ERIECON
Oriskany Battlefield
Route 69
Rome 13440
315–768–7224

When it's time for a meal try **The Savoy** (255 East Dominick Street; 315–339–3166) or **Michelina's** in The Beeches (Turin Road; 315–336–1700).

Erie Canal Village is an 1840s canal village complete with a train station, school, church, tavern, houses, shops, an icehouse, a steam-engine train, and a packet boat. The structures were taken apart and rebuilt in this location. You can walk along nature trails in the area, or take a boat, the *Independence,* pulled by Belgian horses. As you visit the buildings, you can watch blacksmiths, gardeners, weavers, and musicians at work, to name just a few of the trades and crafts practiced.

For a scenic drive in the area, take Route 46 north to North Western and continue along the gorge to Boonville. The **Black River Canal** is visible along part of this drive.

Or you can head southeast on Route 69 to **Oriskany Battlefield,** where a monument honors a group of colonial militiamen who were able to withstand an attack by Indians and Loyalists in 1777. There the "bloodiest battle of the Revolution" was fought during a period of six hours. The British had planned a three-part invasion to take control of New York State from the north, west, and south. General Barry St. Leger, who was to travel from Oswego down the Mohawk Valley to Albany, found a strong opposing force when he got to Fort Stanwix. When the resulting siege continued without resolution, Herkimer gathered 800 Tryon County militia and set off to Fort Stanwix. St. Leger sent troops, including some Mohawk Indians, to ambush Herkimer. General Nicholas Herkimer, commander of the militia, unknowingly led his men into an ambush in a ravine just south of the Mohawk. Herkimer was shot in the leg but refused to leave the battle. He sat on a log, with his

Munson-Williams-
Proctor Institute
310 Genesee Street
Utica 13503
315-797-0000

Children's Museum
of History, Natural
History, and
Science
311 Main Street
Utica 13503
315-724-6129

Utica Zoo
Steele Hill Road
Utica 13503
315-738-0472

F. X. Matt Brewery
Court and Varick
Streets
Utica 13502
315-732-0022

Stanley Performing
Arts Center
259 Genesee Street
Utica 13501
315-724-4000

Remington Firearms
Museum
Route 5S
Ilion 13357
315-895-3301 or
800-562-0897

sword drawn and his leg bleeding, and continued to direct his soldiers. When it was over, he was carried down the valley to his home, where his leg was amputated in an effort to save his life, but he died eleven days later.

Utica

Utica saw its real growth after the Erie Canal was completed in 1825. The **Munson-Williams-Proctor Institute** exhibits American and European art from colonial times to the present. The building was designed by Philip Johnson. Don't miss Thomas Cole's *The Voyage of Life,* which moves from childhood through youth and adulthood to old age. Next door is **Fountain Elms,** a decorative arts collection.

The **Children's Museum of History, Natural History, and Science** features a hands-on series of exhibits and has a variety of programs scheduled throughout the year. The **Utica Zoo** houses more than 300 animals, including reptiles, birds, mammals, and cats. Don't miss the special Children's Zoo, where your youngsters may pet the animals.

The **F. X. Matt Brewery** offers tours, including a trolley ride to an 1888 tavern for tasting.

The **Stanley Performing Arts Center** is a restored movie palace, now on the National Register of Historic Places. The building is shared by the Utica Symphony, the Central New York Community Arts Council Theater, and the Munson-Williams-Proctor Institute's great artists series.

From Utica take Route 5S to the **Remington Firearms Museum** to see antique and modern firearms. The first flintlock was designed by Eliphalet Remington in 1816. He soon switched to using a percussion cap that fired faster than the flintlock. In 1857 he produced his first revolver pistol, a .31 caliber "pocket" gun. Annie Oakley used Remington rifles.

Just on the edge of Utica you'll find **Hook, Line, and Sinker** (90 Seneca Turnpike, New Hartford; 315-732-3636), which is known for seafood, pasta, and steak.

Herkimer

From Ilion take Routes 28 and 5 to Herkimer. If you have always wanted to dig for gems, try **Herkimer Diamond Mines**. Silica deposits dating from Cambrian times grew into quartz crystals. You can use a two- or three-pound crack hammer and a bullpoint chisel to find your gems.

If you've read Theodore Dreiser's *An American Tragedy*, you'll find that the murder trial depicted there took place in Herkimer between 1906 and 1908. It seems that Chester Gillette may have murdered Grace Brown, pregnant with his child, on a trip to Big Moose Lake in 1906. He said that she committed suicide; others say that he drowned her in Punkey Bay.

Herkimer Diamond Mines
Route 28
Herkimer 13350
315–891–7355
Herkimer Home
Route 169
Little Falls 13365
315–823–0398
Florence Jones Reineman Wildlife Sanctuary
Off Route 29
Dolgeville 13329
518–568–7101

If General Herkimer interests you, **Herkimer Home,** located beyond Herkimer and Utica, just east of Little Falls, is open to the public. It contains period furnishings and personal items belonging to General Herkimer. Maple sugaring and sheepshearing are demonstrated during the appropriate seasons. Don't miss the colonial garden.

Dolgeville

Then head north on Route 167 to Dolgeville and the **Florence Jones Reineman Wildlife Sanctuary** for programs from the end of May through mid-August. Dorothy and Al Richard were given a pair of beavers by the State Department of Environmental Protection many years ago. The beavers, Samson and Delilah, made a dam at Middlesprite, where the Richards lived. They produced many litters of kits and grew tame enough to accept apples from a hand. At one point another beaver, Lilah, was caught in a trap and nursed back to health in the spare room at the Richards's.

African-violet lovers will want to head for **Lyndon Lyon Greenhouses** at 14 Mutchler Street in Dolgeville, where table after table of pink, purple, white, and variegated violets bloom. We couldn't resist bringing home a large boxful.

If you're heading into the Capital District, stop for a meal at the **Poplars Inn** (Riverside Drive, opposite exit 28; 518–853–4511) for dining on the Mohawk and a ride on the *Poplar Mist.*

Holy Trinity Russian
Orthodox Monastery
Route 167
Jordanville 13361

National Baseball
  Hall of Fame
Main Street
Cooperstown 13326
607–547–7200

American Baseball
  Experience
99 Main Street
Cooperstown 13326
607–547–1273

Farmers' Museum
  and Village
  Crossroads
Route 80
Cooperstown 13326
607–547–1450

Jordanville

If you're on the way to Cooperstown, head south on Route 167 to Jordanville to see the **Holy Trinity Russian Orthodox Monastery.** Begun by two young Russian immigrants in 1930, the cathedral, with its gold onion tops, was completed in 1950; the main monastery building, which houses the printing press, refectory, and cells of the monks, was constructed later. The inside of the cathedral is beautiful, with icons and frescoes on the walls and ceilings. Women must cover their heads and wear a skirt, as slacks or shorts are not allowed.

Cooperstown

If you're starting from Utica, take I–90 east and Route 28 south to Cooperstown, a lovely town at the foot of Otsego Lake, with many attractions for visitors. It is the home of the **National Baseball Hall of Fame.** Fans can peruse the photographs, displays, artifacts, and memorabilia associated with baseball's greatest players. New interactive exhibits have been added, as well as the Hall of Fame Library and a theater. A life-size wooden sculpture of Babe Ruth greets visitors at the entrance. Look for the bat used by Mickey Mantle to hit a 565-foot homer; the scorecard from the first World Series in 1903; a cornerstone from Ebbets Field; Jackie Robinson's uniform; the first catcher's mask, dated 1876; and Joe DiMaggio's bronze plaque. On display is Babe Ruth's locker, with his uniform and personal items, such as his shaving brush. As you enter the third floor, you'll hear baseball music playing from an old Philco radio. One side of the hall is lined with baseball sheet music; the other, with baseball cards.

American Baseball Experience is a new museum on Main Street. Visitors will see wax models of many baseball favorites including Babe Ruth, Ty Cobb, Lou Gehrig, Mickey Mantle, and Jackie Robinson.

The **Farmers' Museum and Village Crossroads** is a re-creation of a typical village during the period of 1790 to 1860. The village consists of twelve buildings. You'll begin your tour in the main barn, where there are displays depicting the hardships of families as they struggled to plant and reap crops. In contrast, they also had fun on skates, sleds, and even carousel horses. The Cardiff Giant, a 10-foot-long gypsum statue found in 1869, was originally thought to be a petrified prehistoric man.

The hoax was created by George Hull. Upstairs in the textile loft, you can watch spinning and weaving. As you walk around the village, you'll notice wonderful aromas, which probably come from the kitchen at Lippitt Homestead, where guides are preparing food.

Fenimore House
Route 80
Cooperstown 13326
607-547-1450

Cooperstown was named for Judge William Cooper, who founded the town in 1786. His son, James Fenimore Cooper, became a major American novelist and drew heavily on central New York for such work as *The Last of the Mohicans* and *Leatherstocking Tales*. **Fenimore House** contains James Fenimore Cooper memorabilia, a fine collection of American folk art, and life masks of prominent Americans molded by John Browere from 1817 to 1833. You'll see folk portraits, including "Who is it?" and "Who did it?" quizzes with three different doors to open to find the answer. Don't miss the portrait of the little girl with the defiant look on her face, entitled *One Shoe Off,* and *The Mariner* with spyglass in his hand. Nineteenth-century landscape paintings include *Escape of General Israel Putnam* from the Indians by Asher Durand and *Sugaring Off* by Grandma Moses, featuring vividly dressed people out in the white snow.

James Fenimore Cooper memorabilia include a pocketbook with adjustable calendar, inkstand, incense burner, and razor. There are photos of Otsega Hall, where Cooper grew up, and Fenimore College, which once stood on the site of the present ballroom.

As of July 15, 1995, a new lake level was added to Fenimore House. It houses the Eugene and Clare Thaw Collection, which contains more than 600 American Indian artifacts. Walk down the grand stairway and peek out the windows above to see the hills, then descend into the lower level.

The Great Hall, a preamble to the gallery, houses a number of examples of Indian cultures. Each section in the gallery offers special pieces of the American Indian communities from the Northwest Coast, Alaska, California, the Southwest, Plains and Prairies, and Northeastern Woodlands. Visitors can walk around the glass cases and view each object from all directions. You'll see animal effigy pieces, including a bowl with the head of a woman and perhaps the tail of a rooster. A red horse mask is colorful with decoration and a flowing mane. A shell gorget dates from between 1200 and 1350; it has a kneeling Indian in the center. Don't miss the ledger drawing by Black Hawk, which dates from 1880. You'll see beaded moccasins, pouches, clothing, and more.

The North Gallery contains works that depict the three primary

National Soccer Hall
of Fame
11 Ford Avenue
Ononta 13829
607–432–3351

realms of Creation: the Sky World, the Surface World, and the Under World. As you enter you will see a large hide with symbolic painting on it. Both celestial and winged beings, such as the sun, stars, birds, and butterflies, figure prominently in Native belief. Birds and insects provide continuity between humans and the Creator of the spirit world. Look for examples of eagles, bears, and turtles.

Just a few miles north on Canadarago Lake in Richfield Springs **The Lakehouse** (315–858–2058) offers dining with a view. In Cooperstown try **The Otesaga Hotel** (607–547–9931) for a meal in a grand old hotel.

Glimmerglass Opera House (Route 80; 607–547–2255) offers opera from June through September. The woodland setting on Lake Otsega is lovely.

If you're ready for a hike, go to **Glimmerglass State Park,** which is 4 miles south of Route 20 (607–547–8662). There is a beaver pond to explore and plenty of hiking trails to follow.

Oneonta

For a side trip to Oneonta, take Route 28S and Route 88W to Oneonta to visit the **National Soccer Hall of Fame.** TV monitors show national and international matches. Pro games and local soccer games are also held there. Visitors will see lots of historic balls and shoes on display. The family of Jim Brown is one where several generations played soccer; photos are on display.

The Wright National Soccer Campus was dedicated in 1989, and the fields are active with one match after another. Future plans call for a new 27,000-square-foot museum, a 10,000-seat stadium, more playing fields, and training facilities.

Oneonta is also the home of **Hartwick College** (800–828–2288, in state; 800–828–2200, out of state). The **Yager Museum** offers a collection of American Indian artifacts dating from 1000 B.C.

When you're ready for a meal, head for **Cathedral Farms** (Routes 23 and 205W; 607–432–7483) on the summer estate of millionaire Henry Buckley, who raised a prize herd of "Bigger and Better Guernsey Cows." Don't miss "Memory Forest," where 200 trees from friends were planted for his seventy-fifth birthday. If you're heading west, try two other restaurants run by the same group: **Christopher's** (607–432–2444) and **Sabbatinias** (607–432–3000)—both at exits 14 and 15, Routes 23 and 28—and **The Farmhouse** (Exit 16, Route 7; 607–432–7374).

I–88 East will take you to exit 22, the turnoff for **Howe Caverns**. Lester Howe discovered the caverns in 1842. With only the light from his oil lamp, Howe forced himself to crawl and slide farther in on each visit until he finally reached a large underground lake. Undaunted, he carried in materials to build a raft. On the other side of the lake, he found stalactites, stalagmites, and a variety of grotesque stone shapes. Today visitors take an elevator down and then walk on brick paths to view the sights of the cavern. You can also take a boat trip to see even more wonders.

> Howe Caverns
> Route 7
> Howes Cave 12092
> 518–296–8900
>
> Caverns Creek Grist Mill
> Caverns Rd.
> Howes Cave 12092
> 518–296–8448
>
> Iroquois Indian Museum
> Caverns Road
> Howes Cave 12092
> 518–296–8949

Caverns Creek Grist Mill dates from 1816 and is one of the most complete grist mills left east of the Mississippi. You'll see the 12-foot waterwheel turning as you walk to the building. A sluiceway moves the water from the lake above to the wheel.

Inside there are three floors to explore. First you will see a French Buhr stone, which has quilted segments held together with a wrought-iron band. Grinding takes place between the stones. There are bins where the grain was stored and a cleaning machine that removed all of the extraneous material. On the third floor there are spools wrapped with silk, which turn and sift the flour. An auger with cherry paddles still stands ready for work. After touring the mill you can take a ¾-mile nature trail into the woods. A picnic area is provided under the shady trees.

The **Iroquois Indian Museum** is housed in a modern structure that depicts the Great Longhouses of the Iroquois. Inside visitors will find out about the religion, government, and life of the Iroquois. Displays include an eagle pipe, wampum beads, corn-husk dolls, a Mohawk pot from the 1600s, and gourd rattles.

The archaeology collection of tools displays points that were sharp and used for arrows, darts, or spears. In the Early Iroquois Period, from 900 to 1300, you'll see an effigy pipe, points, mortars and pestles, and pottery. After contact with Europeans, the Eastern Iroquois Nations acquired an English musket from 1787, brass pots, shot, and powder horns.

Downstairs, children can make corn-husk dolls, match furs, identify points, create songs, play games, and engage in myriad activities.

From Oneonta take I–88 East back to Albany (in Itinerary A) or Route 28 back into the Catskills.

ITINERARY C:

Western and Central New York

Niagara Falls

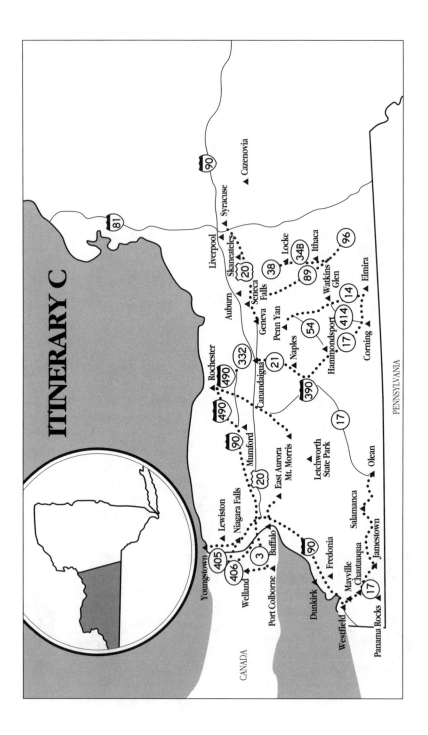

Western and Central New York

This itinerary can be the continuation of Itinerary B from the Thousand Islands section. It also links with Itinerary E: Western Pennsylvania.

❧ *Finger Lakes Region* ❧

The Finger Lakes region is one of wine and water—vineyards and eleven long, slender, and deep lakes left by departing glaciers. Waterfalls and gorges complete a water ambience of scenic splendor. The Iroquois believed that the Great Spirit placed his hand on this region and left behind his fingerprints. Other legends claim that the Creator reached to bless the land and left his fingerprints in the form of water-filled imprints. In fact, geologists report that the unique topographical contours of this area are the result of at least two Ice Age glaciers burrowing and grinding out long narrow lakes, gorges, and valleys. The earliest inhabitants were probably the Mound Builders. When Jesuit missionaries arrived from Europe, they found Cayuga, Seneca, and Onondaga Indians in residence. Many of the lakes bear Indian names, including Canandaigua, Keuka, Seneca, Cayuga, Owasco, and Skaneateles.

You can choose to tour some of the lakes on their northern side on Routes 5 and 20 with forays south at whim; along their southern side on Routes 13, 17, and 390 with jaunts north; or via several slalomlike sweeps around the lakes. For the purpose of this itinerary, we will move from one lake to the next in a westerly direction along a suggested route with side trips and options, leaving the final choice of route to be determined by your time and interests. You can also choose to cycle around the area if you are up to tackling the hills. For information on the Finger Lakes, call 800–228–2760.

Syracuse

Syracuse, a gateway to the Finger Lakes, on the shore of Onondaga Lake, was first inhabited by Indians as early as 1570. Hiawatha selected this location as the capital of the Iroquois Confederacy. The Indians discovered salt on this site; in the seventeenth century Father LeMoyne discovered a salt spring south of Fort Sainte Marie de Gannentaha, which eventually led to the development of the salt industry in Syracuse. The fort was founded in 1656 but later succumbed to Indian attacks.

Visit the **Salt Museum** in Onondaga Lake Park. A salt-boiling block is on display there.

Sainte Marie among the Iroquois is a living-history museum on the site of a 1657 French mission located north of Syracuse in Liverpool. In 1639 Jesuits came from Quebec to the area, but their first mission burned. By 1656 fifty Frenchmen had left Quebec for Onondaga, where they built another mission. They had been invited by the Iroquois nation to found a permanent settlement there, which would enable them to travel to nearby villages and teach Christianity. In July the chief men of Onondaga came to Ste. Marie to "unite us so closely that we might be hereafter but one people and to warn us not to place any confidence in the Mohawk." August was a busy month, with teaching and building.

> Salt Museum
> Onondaga Lake Park
> Liverpool 13088
> 315-453-6715
>
> Sainte Marie among
> the Iroquois
> Onondaga Lake
> Parkway (Rte.
> 370W)
> Liverpool 13088
> 315-453-6767

In June 1657 a second group of French left Quebec bound for Ste. Marie. Included in the party were six soldiers, eighty Iroquois, one hundred Huron women, and ten to twelve Huron men. In August the Iroquois in the group killed seven of the Huron men. The group arrived in Ste. Marie on September 1, but some of them came down with fever because of the change of climate.

They worked for about two years, building a stockade, chapel, workhouse, garden, and barn. Within twenty months it was abandoned after the Onondagas warned them to leave. They traveled in four canoes of Algonquin pattern and four of Iroquois, plus two other boats for shooting the rapids.

Today, visitors will see a reconstructed mission depicting the year 1656. Costumed interpreters from the seventeenth century speak to visitors. One of them told us that they expected to serve in the mission for life; they worked very hard and were tired enough to sleep when the sun went down. One said that he became ordained two years ago and then came to the New World. He admitted that he had a lot to learn, including the Iroquois language.

The blacksmith was at work with his bellows; he described his difficult journey along the St. Lawrence River, down small rivers, and across the portages before he arrived at the mission. The carpenter was making a wooden shoe called a *sabot,* as well as wooden nails and tunnels.

Someone was cooking over the fire in the huge fireplace; he told us he especially liked eating the flesh of beaver, which swam like a fish. The mercenary soldier enjoyed hunting and fishing as well as woodworking and did not believe in being idle. He hunted deer, elk, wild cows (moose), squirrels, rabbits, and beaver. Some of the inhabitants talked about leaving

Erie Canal Museum
Erie Boulevard East
  at Montgomery
  Street
Syracuse 13202
315–471–0593

Museum of
  Science and
  Technology
321 South Clinton
  Street
Syracuse 13201
315–425–9068

because they felt uneasy. The mission presents special programs throughout the year.

The Erie Canal also contributed to the growth of Syracuse. The **Erie Canal Museum** is housed in the only remaining weighlock of the original seven on the canal. This Greek Revival building contains a reconstruction of the west gates of the weighlock. In order to determine the toll owed by a canal boat, it was necessary to weigh the barge. After the water was drained from the lock, the barge remained on a giant scale that measured its weight. Tolls were abolished in 1883, and the building was used for administration; it was placed on the National Register of Historic Places in 1972. A replica of a typical canal boat lies inside the lock chamber. This museum is the only one in the United States concerned entirely with canal history and memorabilia. Special exhibits are featured at the museum, including a recent display on the canals of England.

The Erie Canal, dubbed "Clinton's Ditch" by those who doubted the value of Governor DeWitt Clinton's project, was dug by farmers and immigrant workers, who made 50 cents a day for very hard work. The canal was built 40 feet wide at ground level, 28 feet wide at the bottom, and 4 feet deep. A 10-foot-wide towpath ran along the bank; today the path is used for hiking and cycling. In 1836 the Erie Canal was deepened to 7 feet for boats carrying 240 tons, and in 1917 it was modernized. Eventually the paths along the canals will connect all the way from Buffalo to Albany. If you are interested in more extensive information on the canal system and its recreational opportunities, call 800–422–6234 for a recording of events, sail-ins, and traffic information along the canal system. Mid-Lakes Navigation Company offers canal cruises on the *City of Syracuse* as well as canal charters. Call 800–545–4318 or 315–685–8500. (See also under Skaneateles later in this chapter.)

The **Museum of Science and Technology** encourages participation by visitors in many of its exhibits. You can get your hands into exhibits on electricity, computers, energy, light, color, perception, sound, and the life sciences. Press a button and a special light will seemingly take the color out of you and your clothing. If you would like to see your hair stand on end, look for the static-electricity globe. The planetarium is open daily for star shows.

The **Everson Museum of Art** is considered to be one of the ten most architecturally interesting museums in the United States. It looks like a pinwheel with its cantilevered blocks around a central court. The collection includes both traditional and contemporary art from the nineteenth and twentieth centuries.

The **Landmark Theatre** was originally a Loew's theater and has been restored to all its glittering glory. Built in 1927, the interior features Persian and Moorish design. Programs include classic films, concerts, drama, and touring companies from Broadway.

Salt City Center for the Performing Arts (601 South Crouse Avenue; 315–474–1122) is open year-round for a series of musicals, comedies, and other dramatic performances. The **Civic Center of Onondaga County** (411 Montgomery Street; 315–424–8200) is the home of the Syracuse Symphony Orchestra, the Syracuse Symphony of Famous Artists, and the Syracuse Opera Company.

Everson Museum
of Art
401 Harrison Street
Syracuse 13201
315–474–6064

Landmark Theatre
362 South Salina
Street
Syracuse 13201
315–475–7979

Burnet Park Zoo
Wilbur and Coleridge
Avenues
Syracuse 13201
315–435–8511

The **New York State Fair** opened in Syracuse in 1841. It holds the record for being the longest-running state fair in the United States; it is open eleven days preceding Labor Day every year. Did you know that the first Ferris wheel was built in Syracuse? In 1848 two canalmen with time to spare during the winter freeze constructed a four-car wheel that would hold twenty persons.

The **Burnet Park Zoo** offers nine exhibit areas in this "new breed of zoo." You can walk into a semidark replica of a prehistoric cave to view fish, amphibians, and reptiles whose ancestors have been here for millions of years. You can compare those that have changed a great deal from their earliest ancestors to those that have not changed at all. A multilevel walkway provides views of the collection of birds. Another area illustrates how animals adapt in order to survive in various environments. Exhibits on extinct and endangered animals are displayed.

For more information about Syracuse, call the **Syracuse Convention and Visitors' Bureau** at 315–470–1800 or 800–234–4SYR.

Cazenovia

A side trip from Syracuse can take you to the pretty town of Cazenovia. Located right on Cazenovia Lake, the town is full of elegant old homes. After the Civil War the town was discovered by wealthy families who wanted a cool, attractive summer residence. Stop for lunch at **Brae Loch Inn** (Route 20; 315–655–3431). When you open the door, you are greeted by bagpipe music; it's a wonderful way to set the mood. The inn is family-run, and everyone wears kilts. (See Inns appendix.)

Greek Peak Resort
2000 New York
  Street
Route 392
Cortland 13045
800–955–2754 or
800–365–7669 (for ski
  conditions)

Seward House
33 South Street
Auburn 13021
315–252–1283

Cortland

Greek Peak Resort is located within easy access of Syracuse, Binghamton, Ithaca, and the Finger Lakes. Snowmaking covers 85 percent of the area, so don't worry about thin snowcover on the way in—the slopes will be covered with a good base. Ask about the resort's "Guarantee Learn to Ski" program, wherein skiers can go to the red flag at the bottom of Chair II or III to meet an instructor who will offer instruction and encouragement until they can ski from the top to the bottom of the Alpha Slope.

Skaneateles

William Seward, secretary of state during Lincoln's administration, called Skaneateles Lake "the most beautiful body of water in the world." The 18-mile-long lake is the highest of the region, at 863 feet above sea level. Hills green with forests converge into mountains at the head of the lake. The village of Skaneateles contains handsome homes, including **Roosevelt Hall,** which belonged to a cousin of President Theodore Roosevelt; this Greek Revival home overlooks the lake.

The *Mail Boat* brings mail, news, and guests to people living along the shore. You can ride on a "mail cruise" or take a luncheon or dinner cruise with **Mid-Lakes Navigation Company** (P.O. Box 61, 11 Jordan Street, Skaneateles, NY 13152; 315–685–8500). In fact, anyone fascinated by canal trips should look into this company's cruises, which head west to Buffalo, east to Albany, and continue north to Whitehall, lasting several days. Traveling on the canals has been popular in Europe for years; now you can cruise leisurely closer to home.

Lunch or dinner at the handsomely restored **Sherwood Inn** (Route 20; 315–685–3405) takes you back in time. (See Inns appendix.)

Local inhabitants recommend **Doug's Fish Fry** (8 Jordan Street) for fish—it has no atmosphere but terrific food; in fact, its logo is "Tourists Beware . . ." It is open seven days a week. **The Krebs** (53 West Genesee; 315–685–5714) has been in operation since 1899.

Owasco Lake, Auburn

Follow Route 20 to Auburn, on Owasco Lake. This town contains a number of stately homes, including that of William Seward. **Seward House** displays many family furnishings, letters from Lincoln to Seward, gifts given to him from friends around the world, antique toys, and paintings. In fact, this museum has an unusually complete collection of original family belongings, because they stored a great deal in the attic and never threw anything away. Gowns, including wedding dresses, were wrapped carefully in tissue paper, often identified, and stored. Careful records of purchases and placement of furniture provided authenticity when the museum was being developed.

> Harriet Tubman
> Home
> 180 South Street
> Auburn 13021
> 315–252–2081

Built in 1816 by Judge Elijah Miller, the house was home to William Henry Seward after he married Judge Miller's daughter, Frances. The Sewards lived in Washington, D.C., Albany, and Auburn for nearly fifty years during his career as governor of New York, United States senator, and secretary of state. Seward signed the treaty for the purchase of Alaska at 4:00 A.M. on March 30, 1867. Emanuel Leutze captured this signing in his oil painting *Signing the Alaska Treaty,* which hangs in the Diplomatic Gallery on the second floor of the house.

Every room in the house is furnished with elegant original furniture and is decorated with personal family mementos as well as gifts given by heads of state. The dining room is set with the family china, as if for a holiday dinner. The family owned several complete sets of china, including Meissen, Canton, and Sèvres. A large silver well-and-tree platter has a section underneath for hot water; it weighs over thirty pounds when empty. Thomas Cole's painting of Portage Falls, the largest canvas in the house, hangs in the drawing room. Also in the drawing room is a chair with a "musical message." Ask your guide to press the seat down, and you will hear a melody from the music box hidden underneath—that must have been a shock to guests!

Ten days before President Lincoln's assassination, Seward had a carriage accident that resulted in severe injuries to his jawbone, collarbone, shoulders, and arms. He was in bed at home the night John Wilkes Booth shot Lincoln. One of Booth's followers arrived at the Seward home and told the servant that he had medicine for Seward from his doctor. He went upstairs, where he met Frederick, Seward's son, who told him he could not see his father. The intruder aimed a revolver at Frederick that misfired, then clubbed him and ran into the room to attack the nurse and finally Seward. He slashed Seward's face and throat, but the leather neck brace used to hold his jawbones in place saved Seward's life. Mrs. Seward died two months later from the shock of this attempted assassination of her husband.

The **Harriet Tubman Home** was the site of the beginning of freedom for more than 300 slaves. The Underground Railroad was Harriet

Schweinfurth
Memorial Art
Center
205 Genesee Street
Auburn 13021
315–255–1553

Fillmore Glen
State Park
Route 38
Moravia 13118

Cornell Plantations
One Plantations
Road
Ithaca 14850
607–255–3020

Sapsucker Woods
159 South West Road
Ithaca 14850
607–254–BIRD

Tubman's prime concern during the Civil War. She also served as a spy and a scout for the Union army.

The **Schweinfurth Memorial Art Center** was opened in 1981. The center features exhibits of regional fine arts, photography, architecture, and children's art. There is a year-round series of workshops, concerts, and lectures.

A model of an Indian village depicting culture dating from A.D. 1100 is in **Emerson Park** on Owasco Lake. You can swim, fish, and go boating there as well. Follow Route 38 along the lake to **Moravia** and then to **Fillmore Glen State Park.** Five waterfalls enhance this limestone and shale glen; a swimming pool is available. Millard Fillmore, our thirteenth president, was born near Moravia.

Follow Route 38 to Locke, then Route 90 to Route 34B, and head south toward King Ferry and Ithaca.

Cayuga Lake, Aurora/Ithaca

Cayuga Lake, 43 miles long, boasts several colleges, including **Wells College** in Aurora, founded by Henry Wells, who also developed Wells Fargo and American Express. Ithaca has two colleges: **Ithaca College,** originally a conservatory of music, and **Cornell University,** founded by Ezra Cornell in 1865. You can visit **Cornell Plantations** to walk through the gardens, woodlands, swamps, and arboretum, all on 2,800 acres. The **Robinson York State Herb Garden** contains plants that have made a contribution to medicine or the culinary arts. For those who are interested in cultivating herbs to enhance cooking, this is the place to come. Don't miss the heritage garden that features plants popular in the 1700s and 1800s. All of the plants are labeled so you can identify them.

Sapsucker Woods is located 3 miles northeast of Cornell just off Route 13. In 1957 Cornell founded the **Laboratory of Ornithology** there as a research laboratory for the study of birds. The picture windows in the **Lyman K. Stuart Observatory** give the visitor a view of the pond, which is complete with microphones that transmit the sounds of birds as they feed. You can expect to see purple finches, downy woodpeckers, chickadees, and many waterfowl. Walking trails are open all year.

If you're in the mood for food, you will find many fine restaurants in the sophisticated college town of Ithaca. **Chef Yeppi's** (607–272–6484) and **John Thomas Steak House** (Route 96B; 607–273–3464) have been recommended by local residents.

Buttermilk Falls State Park (607–273–5761) was the site of the filming of *Perils of Pauline.* The falls here are spectacular because of the height of the cascades that can be seen from the bottom. Hikers, however, will find many more cascades as they climb up to the bridge and climb down the other side. We chose to head up on the right side and back down on the Rim Trail, which took less than an hour.

Enfield

Robert H. Treman Park is located on Route 13, 5 miles southwest of Ithaca near Enfield. A stone stairway will lead you down into the gorge for a series of vistas; cascades of water rather than a high waterfall provide the special beauty of this place. The park offers picnic tables, camping, swimming, hiking trails, and fishing.

Eight miles north of Ithaca, on Route 89 North along the west shore, is **Taughannock Falls State Park,** where there is a 215-foot drop into a mile-long glen. A great place for hiking, the park also offers camping, cabins, picnic shelters, a beach, biking trails, fishing, boat launching, and winter sports facilities.

The **Cayuga Wine Trail** consists of "estate" wineries where the owners grow their own special grapes for their wines. Vinifera grapes produce Chardonnay, Riesling, and Cabernet; French-American grapes produce Seyval, Cayuga White, Ravat, and Vidal; and native American grapes produce Concord and Niagara. As you taste wines along the wine trail, you will find that each has its own character.

Seneca Falls

Continue north along the lake on scenic Route 89 to Seneca Falls, famous as the birthplace of the women's rights movement. Both activist Amelia Bloomer and suffrage leader Elizabeth Cady Stanton lived there. The first Women's Rights Convention was held in Seneca Falls in 1848. A visitors' center is in the **Women's Rights National Historical Park.** The **Women's Hall of Fame** was established to pay homage to women who have devoted their lives to making life better in the United States. Women in art, athletics, business, education, government, humanities, philanthropy,

Robert H. Treman
  Park
Route 13
Ithaca 14850

Taughannock Falls
  State Park
Route 89
Ithaca 14850
607–387–6739

Women's Rights
  National Historical
  Park
116 Fall Street
Seneca Falls 13148
315–568–2991

Women's Hall of
  Fame
76 Fall Street
Seneca Falls 13148
315–568–2936 or
315–568–8060

Montezuma Wildlife
Refuge
Routes 20 & 5
Seneca Falls 13148
315–568–5987

Rose Hill
Route 96A
Geneva 14456
315–789–3848

Hobart and William
Smith Colleges
Geneva 14456
315–789–5000

and science have been honored. Exhibits include photographs and biographies of women such as Jane Addams, Marian Anderson, Susan B. Anthony, Clara Barton, Mary McLeod Bethune, Elizabeth Blackwell, Pearl S. Buck, Rachel Carson, Mary Cassatt, Emily Dickinson, Amelia Earhart, Alice Hamilton, Helen Hayes, Helen Keller, Eleanor Roosevelt, Florence Sabin, Margaret Chase Smith, Elizabeth Cady Stanton, Helen Brooke Taussig, and Harriet Tubman. Amelia Earhart's scarf was borrowed from the museum by Sally Ride and accompanied her aboard the space shuttle *Challenger*. It is displayed in a case along with other Amelia Earhart mementos.

Five miles north of Seneca Falls, the **Montezuma Wildlife Refuge** contains 6,432 acres as a habitat for birds, deer, and small animals. The refuge is also on the track for migrating geese and ducks.

Route 20 leads to Geneva.

Seneca Lake, Geneva

Geneva, at the northern end of Seneca Lake, contains a series of stately homes overlooking the lake. **Rose Hill** was built by William K. Strong in 1839. In 1850 Robert J. Swan received the house as a wedding gift from his father. In 1965 Swan's grandson, Waldo Hutchins, Jr., purchased Rose Hill, then in ruins, for $15,000 and gave it to the Geneva Historical Society. Restoration was begun, guided by the administrator and curator, H. Merrill Roenke. During the process each one of the columns in front of the house was taken down; one contained more than 200 pounds of honey and a swarm of angry bees!

This Greek Revival mansion contains furniture of the period around 1840. Some of the furniture belonged to the Swan family, including a pair of rosewood armchairs dating from 1845, a marquetry tilt-top table, and a mahogany sofa with the original cut-velvet upholstery. Some of the furnishings were donated by Geneva families, who are pleased to see their treasured heirlooms preserved in this elegant museum. Records and documents have made it possible to furnish the house authentically. Upstairs you will see a red bedroom with a colorful quilt, a green bedroom, and an elegant blue bedroom. The grounds include a carriage house and boxwood gardens. An earlier house, built by Robert S. Rose, a Virginian, is now used as a reception center.

Hobart and William Smith Colleges, now linked together as a single, coeducational institution, are also located at the northern end of Seneca Lake on adjoining campuses. The college owns a number of historic buildings; ask for a brochure of walking tours.

Seneca Lake wineries include **Prejean Winery, Four Chimneys Farm Winery, Hermann J.**

Watkins Glen State Park
Route 14
Watkins Glen 14891
607-535-4511

Wiemer Vineyard, Inc., Squaw Point Winery, Glenora Wine Cellars, Castle Grisch Winery, Chateau Lafayette Reneau, and **Hazlitt 1852 Vineyards.**

Watkins Glen

Head south on Route 14 and drive the length of the lake to **Watkins Glen State Park,** a site well known for its natural beauty. Nineteen waterfalls, cascades, and grottoes may be seen along the walkway through the gorge. Pick up a brochure at the park office for your self-guided tour. While standing on Sentry Bridge you can see a hole cut in the rock where water used to flow on its way to the waterwheel of a gristmill. You can walk behind Cavern Cascade, if you don't mind a little spray. A trail leads from Spiral Tunnel, up the Indian Trail, to the Suspension Bridge. As you enter the Cathedral area, you will see a large stone with a rippled surface; millions of years ago these ripples were in sand. Walk up through the Cathedral area to the Central Cascade, where you will see pools called "plunge pools." They were formed by waterfalls bombarding the same spot for centuries. Pools that are not caused by waterfalls are called "pot holes." Rainbow Falls is so named because there is sometimes a rainbow in the spray. Frowning Cliff and Pluto Falls are located in a narrow, dark gorge. (Pluto was the Greek god of the underworld.) At Mile Point Bridge you can walk up to Jacob's Ladder or return by one of the trails. You can also take a shuttle up and walk down.

Although the Grand Prix Racing Circuit pulled out in 1981, there is racing at Watkins Glen once more, under new management. (Phone 607-535-2481 for tickets.)

From Watkins Glen you can make a side trip to Elmira via Route 14, Corning via Route 414, or Keuka Lake via Route 23.

Elmira

Elmira is especially famous for its former summer resident, Samuel Clemens (Mark Twain), who wrote many of his best-known books there— *Tom Sawyer, The Adventures of Huckleberry Finn, The Prince and the Pauper, Life on the Mississippi, A Connecticut Yankee in King Arthur's*

Mark Twain Study
Elmira College
One Park Place
Elmira 14901
607-735-1941

Court, and *A Tramp Abroad.* His connection with Elmira stems from a trip he took on the Mediterranean. He met Charles Langdon while cruising, saw a miniature portrait of Olivia, Charles's sister, and fell for her. They were married in 1870 and continued to spend summer vacations in Elmira. Olivia's sister, Susan Crane, built an octagonal room that resembled a Mississippi steamboat pilot house for him to use as a study. Mark Twain was delighted with this surprise and wrote, "It is a cosy nest and when storms sweep down the valley and the lightning flashes behind the hills beyond, and the rain beats over my head, imagine the luxury of it." Each morning, after his favorite breakfast of steak and coffee, he went up to this study and worked all day, without lunch, until time for dinner. While living and writing in Elmira, Twain liked to try out his lectures in front of a live audience, and the Elmira Correction Facility provided a local captive audience. He felt that they laughed more readily than some of his other audiences.

> When I was a boy of fourteen, my father was so ignorant I could hardly stand to have the old man around. But when I got to be twenty-one I was astonished at how much the old man had learned in seven years. —Mark Twain

You can visit the **Mark Twain Study** at **Elmira College.** It was given to the college by his grandnephew, Jervis Langdon, Jr. The view from the study is pleasant, similar to the view at Quarry Farm (see below), with a pond and weeping willow to look at. Next to the study you will see a stone watering trough with his daughter Clara's name on it. He had four watering troughs made for the refreshment of horses on their way up the hill to Quarry Farm, each one carved with one of his children's names.

Quarry Farm was also given to Elmira College by Mark Twain's grandnephew. The **Center for Mark Twain Studies** is located there. Twain spent one last summer at the farm, in 1903. In 1904 he returned for Olivia's funeral, and in 1907 for the dedication of the organ in Park Church. He died in 1910 and is buried in Elmira's Woodlawn Cemetery. A monument was placed there as a memorial to Mark Twain and Ossip Gabrilowitsch, the first husband of his daughter Clara. Gabrilowitsch, a famous Russian pianist and conductor, wanted to be buried at the feet of Mark Twain.

If you've always had a yen to go soaring, you can do it here. **Harris Hill Soaring Corporation** (Harris Hill, near Elmira; 607-739-3219) offers you the chance to take off behind a tow plane and head up into the world of air currents, where you will soar silently over lakes, forests, and farms. An experienced pilot is at the controls, and you are free to take photos and enjoy the view.

The **National Soaring Museum** is at the end of the runway at Harris Hill. You'll see a 1911 Orville Wright glider, a 1933 Albatross, a 1936 model with gull-like wings, and lots of exhibits with explanations. You can also sit in the cockpit simulator and imagine yourself in flight.

National Soaring
  Museum
Harris Hill
Elmira 14902
607–734–3128

Corning

Route 17 will take you from Elmira into Corning. The **Corning Museum of Glass** encompasses the Museum of Glass, the Hall of Science and Industry, and the Steuben Glass Factory. It has had a major expansion into a new, innovative glass center. Begin your visit with a time-tunnel trip through the ages. Did you know that during the early thirteenth century, glass craftsmen were subject to death if they tried to leave the island of Murano, near Venice, with intent to use their knowledge elsewhere? These Murano craftsmen prized their fine filigree, diamond-etched, exquisite glass beads and vases. Don't miss the goblet made by Verzelini in 1577 for Queen Elizabeth I. The Hall of Science will provide you with hands-on experiences in the world of glass. You can light ninety-six different kinds of light bulbs, bend sheets of glass, use a glass insulator to break the flow of high-voltage electricity, and dip glass in acid. Whether or not you have children, don't miss the magic show.

Corning Museum of
  Glass
One Museum Way
Corning 14830
607–974–2000

Rockwell Museum
Old City Hall
Denison Parkway &
  Cedar Street
Corning 14830
607–937–5386

The **Rockwell Museum** contains the three collections of Robert Rockwell: western American art, Carder Steuben glass, and antique toys. Frederick Carder created his glass between 1903 and 1933 in Corning; 2,000 pieces are displayed in the museum. Paintings and bronzes by Frederic Remington, Charles Russell, Albert Bierstadt, and W. R. Leigh are also on display.

The **Market Street District** downtown has lots of shops and places to eat. During the summer you can ride around in an English double-decker bus.

Keuka Lake

At the southern end of Keuka Lake, you will find Hammondsport and wineries galore. **Bully Hill Vineyards, Hunt Country Vineyard, Dr. Frank's Vinifera Wine Cellars, Heron Hill Vineyards,** and **McGregor Vineyards** offer wine tasting.

The **Glenn H. Curtiss Museum of Local History** honors this native

Finger Lakes
  Association
309 Lake Street
Penn Yan 14527

Glenn H. Curtiss
  Museum of Local
  History
Route 54
Hammondsport
  14840
607–569–2160

Cumming Nature
  Center
Gulick Road
Naples 14512
716–374–6160

Sonnenberg Gardens
Gibson Street
Canandaigua 14424
716–394–4922 or
924–5420

son of Hammondsport in his role as "Father of Naval Aviation" with a collection of rare pieces from the early days of aviation. You can trace the development of aviation with models and photographs. In 1992 the collection was moved into a larger building on Route 54.

The Keuka Maid cruises around the lake for lunch, dinner, and Sunday brunch. Hills and vineyards make this lake especially attractive during the day, and the cottage lights are pretty at night. (Call 607–569–BOAT or 569–3631.)

For more information about the area, contact the **Finger Lakes Association** at 309 Lake Street, Penn Yan NY 14527; 800–548–4386 or 315–536–7488.

Naples

Follow the signs to I–390 to Cohocton, then Route 371 to Route 21 to Naples. The **Cumming Nature Center** is a division of the Rochester Museum and Science Center. This 900-acre center has nature trails, films, and an environmental education center. **Widmer's Wine Cellars** are located in Naples.

Canandaigua

Continue on Route 21 to Canandaigua. **Sonnenberg Gardens** is a fifty-acre Victorian garden estate located just north of town. In 1857 Frederick and Mary Thompson bought Sonnenberg for a summer home. In 1902 Mrs. Thompson began planning gardens as a memorial to her husband, who had died. She traveled to all parts of the globe visiting a variety of gardens and spent the next fourteen years designing gardens. There are eleven gardens, including the Japanese, Italian, Rose, Sub Rosa, Blue and White, Pansy, Moonlight, Conservatory, Colonial, South Lawn, and Rock gardens. The Rose Garden is planted in a design of arcs and interlocking circles, backed by a flawless green lawn. The Sub Rosa Garden is small and private; there are two cross-legged marble figures of Diana and Apollo beside the fountain. The blue and white garden, which Mrs. Thompson called her "Intimate Garden," contains peonies, phlox, snapdragons, vinca, delphinium, anchusa, salvia, and iris. The Victorians felt that pansies symbolized thought, so this garden is meant for meditation. As you see the multitude of pansies, check to see if their faces are smiling at you. The

Moonlight Garden is planted with white flowers that glow in the moonlight; this garden was lost for some time but has now been restored. The Colonial Garden contains all of the old favorites set into a symmetrical pattern. The Rock Garden encircles a tower from which you can survey the blossoms of the season.

> **Granger Homestead**
> **295 North Main Street**
> **Canandaigua 14424**
> **716–394–1472**

The mansion itself has eight restored rooms decorated with period furnishings. Special events such as a Victorian weekend, pageants, poetry readings, drama, concerts, and barbershop quartets are held during the year. A Festival of Lights is held in winter.

The **Granger Homestead** was the home of Postmaster General Gideon Granger, who served under Presidents Jefferson and Madison, and of Francis Granger, who served under Presidents Harrison and Tyler. Gideon Granger specialized in espionage work for the Jefferson administration; he discovered Federalist plots before they had been put into action. He retired from service in Washington in 1814 and began to build his mansion in Canandaigua, spending $10,098.11 on his house and $3,240 on the land, a large sum in those days. When it was complete, he sent for his wife, Mindwell, and their two sons. Although he had retired once, he was persuaded to stand for reelection to the state senate. Granger was also involved in the promotion of the Erie Canal. He died at age fifty-five, and his son, Francis, lived in the house for seventy-six years, until his death in 1868. During this time he added the north wing to the house. Francis's son, Gideon, was chairman of the war committee for raising troops during the Civil War.

This Federal mansion is furnished with period furniture, silver, and china. Note the extraordinarily high mantel in the South Parlour, with a portrait of Gideon Granger II over it. The three-part settee was constructed from three chairs; twenty matching single chairs are still in the house. The chandelier in the North Parlour was a gas fixture in use during the 1850s; later it was converted to electricity. The table in the dining room was originally in the White House; Gideon Granger purchased it after the executive mansion was burned by the British during the War of 1812.

The **Carriage Museum** at Granger Homestead holds fifty horse-drawn vehicles. An ointment wagon that was used to deliver patent cures is on display, as is a hearse with unusual lamps that are silver on the outside and gold on the inside.

George Eastman
House
900 East Avenue
Rochester 14603
716–271–3361

❧ *Northwestern New York* ❧

In Northwestern New York—at least in this itinerary—you will visit the cities of Rochester and Buffalo.

Rochester

Take Route 332 to I–90 to I–490 to Rochester. Rochester, the third-largest city in New York, is also known as the "Flower City." If you are there in lilac time (mid-May), a treat is in store for you. Earlier it was called the "Flour City" because of its flour mills; waterfalls provided the power. Contact the **Rochester Convention and Visitors' Bureau** at 716–546–3070 or 800–677–7282.

Internationally known for its **Eastman School of Music** (George Eastman was the inventor of Kodak cameras and founder of Eastman Kodak), Rochester's calendar of events overflows with many excellent music series. In addition to those offered by Eastman, the **Rochester Philharmonic Orchestra** offers a full program. There is also a theatrical season at the **Eastman Theater,** as well as performances by touring Broadway groups.

The **George Eastman House** reopened in January 1990 after being renovated and brought back to life as it was when Eastman lived there. He built the house between 1902 and 1905 using the finest materials, including plaster relief ceilings, carved woodwork, hand-painted window glass, and marble floors. He decorated his house with oriental rugs and appropriate furnishings to make fifty rooms seem homelike. Eastman and his mother lived in the house with a staff who provided fresh flowers from the greenhouses. After Eastman's death in 1932, the house was bequeathed to the University of Rochester, whose presidents lived in it for the next ten years.

Visitors may enter by the front door, which leads into a large hall and oriental-carpeted stairway leading upstairs. To the right is the living room, handsome with its plaster ceiling, done in an ornate pattern depicting the four seasons in medallions up in the corners. A grand piano is open and ready for a concert, with violins resting on music stands nearby. Period furniture, fresh flowers, and bookcases lining the walls give this room a comfortable touch.

Across the hall the library uses the Eastman system for cataloging books, with letters at the top of each case corresponding to a letter and

146

shelf number inside each book. The bookplates portray Eastman, shown from the back reading in his chair. A collection of ivory miniatures is displayed in a glass case on one wall.

The teak-paneled billiard room contains a green-felt-covered table, as well as a sofa on a raised platform that has room under its step for billiard and

> Rochester Museum
> and Science Center
> and Strasenburgh
> Planetarium
> 657 East Avenue
> Rochester 14603
> 716–271–1880

game equipment, in addition to providing a birds'-eye view for those watching the game. A cylinder phonograph and a classic radio blend in with family photographs.

The conservatory is a bright room with a two-story-high ceiling, lots of plants, and an organ. Eastman had a favorite group of women for lunch here every week—called the "Lobster Quartet" because they had lobster for lunch. These four younger women enjoyed his company and he theirs. The head of a life-size trophy is mounted high on the wall.

Visitors can walk back through the house, past the Dryden Theatre, solarium, galleries, and views of the garden outside the windows. The new wing at the back houses the **International Museum of Photography,** offering changing exhibits and demonstrations.

The **Rochester Museum and Science Center and Strasenburgh Planetarium** produces elaborate space shows geared for all ages. *The Space Shuttle: An American Adventure* is the first film designed to be projected on a planetarium's dome. You might see Bob McGrath of "Sesame Street" conducting preschool-age children through introductory astronomy on film.

One of the permanent exhibits features the Seneca Iroquois collection. Demonstrations are given on the process involved in making cornhusk Indian dolls. The computerized planetarium offers both futuristic space programs and a glimpse of the sky in prehistoric times.

Also under the aegis of the RMSC is the **Cumming Nature Center,** located 35 miles south of Rochester on 900 acres. It is located 7 miles south of Honeoye and 7 miles north of Naples in the Bristol Hills, at 6472 Gulick Road. The Beaver Trail leads to an observation tower that has a view of a thirty-five-acre beaver pond. You'll have a bird's-eye view of the habitat of the beavers—maybe a slapping tail or two to warn the young. The Conservation Trail leads to a sawmill that is actually running.

An outdoor art gallery features paintings by Jerry Czech along the Helen Gordon Trail. Don't miss the Iroquois Trail, which portrays the history of the Indians through the eyes of painter Ernest Smith. Programs there include hikes on the 8 miles of trails, cross-country skiing in winter, maple sugaring, and a host of other seasonal programs.

The **Seneca Park Zoo** may be another stop on your itinerary, espe-

Seneca Park Zoo
2222 St. Paul Street
Rochester 14603
716–467–9453

Susan B. Anthony
Home
17 Madison Street
Rochester 14603
716–235–6124

Strong Museum
1 Manhattan Square
Rochester 14603
716–263–2700

cially if you have children with you. Aim for feeding time, which is usually around 3:00 P.M.

The **Susan B. Anthony Home** was the headquarters for the women's crusade leading to passage of the Nineteenth Amendment. Her home contains the furnishings that were there when she entertained Elizabeth Cady Stanton and Frederick Douglass. It was here that Anthony was arrested in 1872—for voting. Walk up to the third floor to see her study and a collection of items that include a horsehair couch, a black hat on a wighead, an evening wrap, and a black dress. The Museum Room on the second floor details the development of the woman's suffrage movement. The desk Anthony used is there too.

The **Strong Museum** contains toys, silver, furnishings, and glassware of the period 1820 to 1930. An extensive doll collection, including miniatures and dollhouses, is sure to delight the "little girl" in most of us.

This is one of our favorite museums, with its attractive displays that are not overdone but tastefully arranged to give pleasure to the viewer. There is a clue to the exhibits: As you walk from one area to another, notice the floor—it changes style and material to fit each era about every 20 feet.

The first floor begins with a portrait of Margaret Woodbury Strong, a Kodak heiress who bought up the contents of whole houses in order to get what she wanted for her collection. Her father had been in the buggy whip business, until Henry Ford came along and put an end to that. The Orient was then the obvious place to conduct his business, and some of the collection was purchased there.

Margaret's wedding shoes from 1920, with white silk stockings to match, stand next to a wood carving of Barbara, done in 1930.

Margaret Strong's first love was dolls, and her collection is said to be the largest in the world. Upstairs they are standing in one case after another, carefully grouped and cataloged. You can even look up the details on any doll in the collection in the card catalog found beside each case. From wood, cloth, gesso, and bisque to felt, wax, and papier-mâché—they are all there. Dolls of all sizes, with plain or elegant clothing, stand ready to be played with. Perhaps at night they have a ball!

Toys include a cast-iron "burning building," a horse-drawn trolley, mechanical banks, battleships, automobiles, and much more.

When it's time for a meal, head for **The Spring House Restaurant,** dating from 1829 (3001 Monroe Avenue; 716–586–2300); **Erie Grill,** where you can dine in a restored railway car or station house (41 North Main Street, Pittsford; 716–381–9900); or **Rooney's** (90 Henrietta; 716–442–0444).

Rochester has a number of fine recreational areas, including **Cobb's Hill Park** between Highland Avenue and Culver Road; **Upper Falls Park** on the Genesee River off St. Paul Street; **Manhattan Square Park** at Chestnut and Broad streets; **Mendon Ponds Park** at Clover Street and Pond Road; and the **Barge Canal Trail,** which connects Perinto Park, Pittsford Park, Lock 32 Canal Park, and Genesee Valley Park. (For information on the Barge Canal Trail, call 716–442–8550.)

Route 383 will take you southwest to Mumford.

Mumford

The **Genesee Country Museum** is a nineteenth-century village containing more than fifty homes, shops, and other buildings. An Iroquois word meaning "Pleasant Valley" brought us "Genesee." After the Revolutionary War soldiers who had fought under George Washington against the Iroquois in the valley chose to settle there.

The **Hamilton House** appeals to visitors, with its Victorian Italianate architecture. Built in 1870 by J. D. Hamilton, the house has fifteen rooms and a tower in the center on the front side of the building.

The **Octagon House** has a surprise for the visitor; look up into the cupola, which was specially designed to accommodate the belief that the spirit ascended directly into heaven when one died.

The **Jones Farm House** has stenciled walls in remarkable condition. In the kitchen the farmer's wife would make cheese to store excess milk; shelves are designed to hold this cheese. The kitchen always smells warm and fragrant because the guide does a great deal of baking and cooking. Farm animals are in the yard.

Livingston Manor is an elegant "city" house in style. One winter when the house was closed, the lovely gilt harp was almost destroyed by a raccoon that knocked it over. Apparently the raccoon came in through the chimney, which is four stories up. A harpsichord is displayed in the same room with the harp. The house is furnished with typical furniture of the 1827 to 1840 period. A beehive oven in the kitchen is used for baking during the tourist season. The formal garden beside the house has been planted in nineteenth-century–style patterns.

Genesee Country Museum schedules many special events, such as Fiddler's Fair, Salute to Autumn, Battle of Gettysburg, Fire Muster, Dressage

Letchworth State Park
Route 36, off Route 19A
Castile 14427
716–493–2611

and Carriage Drive Competition, Black Powder Shoot, and Independence Day.

Letchworth State Park

You may want to make a side trip to Letchworth State Park, located just 35 miles southwest of Rochester. Take Route 390 south until you see signs for Mount Morris and the park. This 14,350-acre park is noted for the rushing Genesee River, which tumbles over three major waterfalls; the highest is 107 feet. Genesee Gorge is 600 feet in height; if you are an aficionado of gorge scenery, don't miss this one. Middle Falls are lighted at night. A restored **Seneca Indian Council House** and the **William Pryor Letchworth Museum** are also worth visiting.

Buffalo

From Rochester take I–490 to I–90 to Buffalo. This city was not really named after the animal of the same name; some think it came from a mispronunciation of the French *Beau Fleuve,* or "Beautiful River." The Niagara River connects Lakes Ontario and Erie. In 1825, when the Erie Canal opened, Governor DeWitt Clinton carried a barrel of fresh water from Lake Erie on the first trip along the canal until he reached the Atlantic, where he poured it into salt water. The Erie Canal had finally joined the Great Lakes with the Atlantic Ocean.

Buffalo has a number of distinct areas to explore. The downtown area contains some architectural treasures as well as modern structures. **City Hall** was built in 1932; the frieze on the front of the building characterizes workers of the 1930s. This Art Deco building has colorful mosaics. Take the elevator to the twenty-eighth-floor Observation Deck for a view. The statues on either side of the entrance are of Millard Fillmore, the thirteenth president of the United States, and Grover Cleveland, the twenty-second president. The monument across from City Hall honors William McKinley, who was assassinated in 1901 while attending the Pan-American Exposition in town. The **Old Post Office** building is Flemish Gothic, with lots of gargoyles, bison heads, and eagles on the facade. A 244-foot tower and skylight are situated above the inner court area. Erie Community College uses the building. **St. Paul's Episcopal Church** was built between 1888 and 1890, following a fire. The style is Gothic Revival; look for the Tiffany windows over the altar. The **Prudential/Guaranty Building** was among the first skyscrapers when it was built in 1896. The architect was

Louis Sullivan, Frank Lloyd Wright's teacher and mentor. The terra-cotta exterior is in contrast to the mosaics inside. You can't miss the **Goldome Bank,** built in Beaux Arts Classical style in 1889. Someone figured out how to keep birds from spoiling the gold; fake rubber snakes strewn around up there seem to keep them away.

The Theater District is highlighted by **Shea's Buffalo Theatre.** This ornate gilt interior is bright with mirrors, marble, and crystal chandeliers. Paintings and sculpture complete an elegant atmosphere. Performances include ballet, musicals, rock concerts, and special galas.

Allentown is an area that has come down through the years from the 1850s almost intact. It is on the National Register of Historic Places; many homes have been restored to their previous appearance. Look for the row of "painted ladies"—San Francisco has nothing on Buffalo!

Delaware Avenue is the epitome of the proverbial "Millionaire's Row." You will see one huge mansion after another. Some of them are still privately owned; others have been taken over by corporations.

The **Theodore Roosevelt Inaugural National Historic Site** was the home of Ansley Wilcox and his wife, Mary, beginning in 1883. On September 5, 1901, President William McKinley came to Buffalo for the Pan-American Exposition. During a reception Leon Czologoz shot him twice at close range. Vice-President Theodore Roosevelt arrived in Buffalo and stayed with his friend Ansley Wilcox. When it appeared likely that McKinley would recover, Roosevelt went on vacation in the Adirondacks. Fortunately, he left his itinerary and addresses with Wilcox. When Roosevelt arrived at the cottage near Mount Tahawus, he and his family canoed to the upper end of Colden Lake, where they set up camp for the night. In the morning Roosevelt climbed Mount Marcy, the highest peak in the Adirondacks. As he was returning, he saw a man hurrying up the trail with a telegram informing him of the worsening condition of President McKinley. Roosevelt found a wagon with driver and set off for the railway station in North Creek. The 50-mile ride was difficult in the middle of the night, but with changes of horses they made it to the station. As he boarded the waiting train, he received the news that McKinley was dead. When the train reached Buffalo, Wilcox met Roosevelt, loaned him some clothes, and took him to his own home for the inaugural ceremony.

One of the most famous landscape architects of the time, Frederick

Shea's Buffalo Theatre
646 Main Street
Buffalo 14240
716–847–1410
Allentown
45 Elmwood
Buffalo 14240
716–881–1024
Theodore Roosevelt Inaugural National Historic Site
641 Delaware Avenue
Buffalo 14240
716–884–0095

Buffalo Museum of
   Science
Humboldt Parkway
Buffalo 14240
716–896–5200

Albright-Knox Art
   Gallery
1285 Elmwood
   Avenue
Buffalo 14240
716–882–8700

Buffalo and Erie
   County Historical
   Society
25 Nottingham Court
Buffalo 14240
716–873–9644

Buffalo Zoological
   Gardens
Delaware Park
Buffalo 14240
716–837–3900

Buffalo and Erie
   County Botanical
   Gardens
2655 South Park
   Avenue
Buffalo 14218
716–696–3555

Law Olmsted, designed five of Buffalo's city parks and a number of parkways. He also designed Central Park in New York. Frank Lloyd Wright designed several houses in Buffalo. One was built in 1904 with long, low lines reflecting Wright's prairie style.

A number of literary and musical figures have lived and worked in Buffalo. Mark Twain lived there in the 1870s when he edited the *Buffalo Express*. Taylor Caldwell is a present resident, and Edwin P. Christy began his Christy Minstrel show there.

Buffalo has a number of museums for you to visit. The **Buffalo Museum of Science** contains dinosaurs, mummies, Chinese jade, anthropological artifacts, and a variety of natural history exhibits. Don't miss the special "Discovery Room" for children; they can touch everything there. The museum has an observatory, a research library, a lecture series, and a nature preserve 3 miles out of town.

The **Albright-Knox Art Gallery** contains a collection of contemporary art that includes works by Jackson Pollock, Clyfford Still, Willem de Kooning, Frank Stella, Henry Moore, Jean Dubuffet, Robert Rauschenberg, and Roy Lichtenstein.

The **Buffalo and Erie County Historical Society** reproduces an 1870 street on the lower level of the museum. This street has a "company store," a bank, a dime store, a sporting goods store, a drugstore, a theater, a cigar shop, and several more stores. Another display, entitled "People of the Longhouse," depicts Indian life inside the longhouse and in the village. It includes some of the sports enjoyed by the Iroquois, such as lacrosse, hoop and javelin, and snow snake. The Canal Exhibit offers artifacts, a replica of a canal boat, and the history of the Erie Canal. The Pioneer Life Exhibit concentrates on life along the Niagara Frontier during the early 1800s.

The **Buffalo Zoological Gardens** house more than 680 animals in their natural settings. An Asian forest, a rain forest, a gorilla section, and a children's zoo are among the areas to see.

The **Buffalo and Erie County Botanical Gardens** contain twelve greenhouses growing exotic plants, palms, fruit trees, and flowers. Frederick Law Olmsted designed the gardens. When we were there, four bridal parties were smiling for photos among the plants.

Our Lady of Victory Basilica and National Shrine is an ornate Italian Renaissance cathedral. Inside, the stations of the cross are sculpted life-size from white Italian marble.

The **Naval and Servicemen's Park** has a collection of World War II vessels, including the USS *The Sullivans* and the USS *Little Rock*. The museum contains seafaring memorabilia, including models of Benedict Arnold's fleet on Lake Champlain in 1776 and a display of painted flags, such as the 1620 *Mayflower*, 1775 Bunker Hill, and first Navy Jack flags. The section on John Paul Jones contains photos of the chapel in Annapolis where his tomb lies, models of ships he served on, and Jones memorabilia.

The "new kid on the dock" is the SS *Croaker*. If you've always wanted to visualize life at sea on a sub you can walk through this one from stem to stern. Living quarters were cramped to say the least, and some men shared sleeping space with torpedoes. When we were there, one of her men from World War II days in the Pacific was on hand to talk with us. You can also take a cruise for a couple of hours or an evening on *Miss Buffalo,* docked at Naval and Servicemen's Park; 716–847–1773.

Our Lady of Victory Basilica and National Shrine South Park Avenue & Ridge Road Lackawanna 14218 716–823–2490
Naval and Servicemen's Park 1 Naval Park Cove Buffalo 14240 716–847–1773
Herschell Carousel Factory Museum 180 Thompson Street North Tonawanda 14120 716–693–1885
Amherst Museum 3755 Tonawanda Creek Road Amherst 14228 716–689–1440

If you're wild about carousels, visit the **Herschell Carousel Factory Museum.** In the first room, journeymen carvers cut out carousel animals, and the smell of freshly cut wood is fragrant. You can wander through the paint shop, machine shop, blacksmith shop, and print shop, and on to the roundhouse. Along the way you'll be tempted to stop to ogle the carousel animals standing ready for a ride.

Your ride is coming—on the 1916 carousel. Choose the animal you'd like to ride on from the thirty-six ready to go round and round. The outer row has the "new and improved" 1916 horses; the inner two rows date from the 1890s. There's also a smaller carousel for little children called the "Kiddie Carousel."

The **Amherst Museum** consists of nine historic buildings that were moved to the site when threatened with demolition. You'll probably begin with the area entitled "Early 1800s–1900s." There's an 1866 map of the town, an oxen yoke, a hair picker for horse hair, and a frame loom with multicolored woven material. The facade of the 1835 Hopkins House is next, along with two rooms to visit.

Move on to collections of food-preparation equipment such as a coffee grinder and nut chopper, fireplace tools, crocheted textiles, a crimper, needlepoint, an antique wringer, and a 1905 doctor's buggy. The children's museum includes a puppet stage, toys, dolls, a plate collection of fairy tales, books, puzzles, and try-on clothes.

One of the buildings houses a Cunningham Hall plane, a pressurized flight suit, a parachute, and a helicopter. Don't miss the 1909 Wright flyer and a display of women in aviation, featuring Amelia Earhart.

Buffalo's many recommended restaurants include **Chef's** (291 Seneca at Chicago; 716–856–9187), **Anchor Bar** (1047 Main; 716–886–8920), **Towne Restaurant** (186 Allen at Elmwood; 716–884–5128), and **Lord Chumley's** (481 Delaware; 716–886–2220).

For more information on the area call the **Buffalo Niagara Partnership** at 800–283–3256.

➣ *Niagara Falls Area* ➣

Over 450 million years ago, a shallow, saltwater sea covered the Niagara Frontier area. Primitive marine plants and animals lived in this tropical climate. Gradually, sediments washed down from the mountains and the sea disappeared. These sediments buried plant and animal remains that became fossilized as the layers turned to rock. You can see four different types of sedimentary rock in the Niagara gorge. The top layer is Lockport Dolostone, which contains highly compacted materials as well as animal and plant remains. The second layer consists of Rochester shale, which is much less resistant to erosion. The third layer is limestone, and the fourth and lowest is sandstone. Glaciers carved through the land and made it sag with their tremendous weight. As the melted basins were filled, the Great Lakes were created, and water continued to seek an outlet to the sea. The Niagara River flowed north from Lake Erie to Lake Ontario, at Lewiston met the escarpment, a 300-foot cliff, and plunged over it. Thus Niagara Falls was born 12,000 years ago.

Because water freezes and expands, cracks and joints built up hydrostatic pressure, widening the gaps and causing the less sturdy Rochester shale in the second layer to weaken and wash away. The top layer, the Lockport Dolostone, was left hanging and finally broke off and fell, time after time. In 1931, 185,000 tons fell near the American Falls; later another fall took out the Schoellkopf Power Plant. Geologists dammed the river and stopped enough of the flow to study the rock. Cracks were analyzed, and several overhangs were removed. The Niagara Escarpment has receded 7½ miles since its birth, at a rate of 1 to 4 feet per year.

The falls have provided energy since 1895, when the world's first hydroelectric plant was constructed. While building that plant, experts realized that less water flowing over the falls would mean less erosion as well as more power for eastern states. For once, industry and ecology were in perfect agreement. Because of the rapid erosion of the falls, both Canada and the United States have been controlling the flow of water above the cascades by the use of gates. Water is diverted into generating plants instead of wearing away the rock. In 1950 Canada and the United States signed an international treaty that determined the amount of flow over the falls. They were able to leave enough for scenic beauty and yet divert 50 to 75 percent of the flow for use in the power plants downstream. During the tourist season there is still a minimum flow of 100,000 cubic feet per second, yet in 1961 the Niagara Power Plant opened with a staggering total output of 2.19 million kilowatts.

That figure is not surprising when one thinks of the sources of so much hydroelectric power. All of the Great Lakes flow into the Niagara River and drop 326 feet, which produces tremendous force. The Niagara River at the Great Gorge Rapids is understandably the most turbulent in the country. There is one offspring of this marriage of convenience between industry and ecology: The daily change of flow influences the whirlpool 3 miles below the falls. The whirlpool was formed 75,000 years ago when the river collided with another river and began scouring out rock down below the surface. The whirlpool normally swirls counterclockwise, but when the flow is decreased, the lower level of water redirects the flow and slowly reverses its direction.

Awe and wonder have always attended human perception of the unimaginable power of the falls and the turbulence of the river below. In 1678 a Franciscan missionary, Father Louis Hennepin, was the first white man to see Niagara Falls. The view of this gigantic, roaring waterfall brought him to his knees. Earlier the falls had figured in Indian legends. There are several versions of the "Maid of the Mist" story. One has been attributed to the Seneca Indians, who reportedly sent a maiden over the falls, as Maid of the Mist, for thanks after a good harvest. According to one version, the custom was terminated after a chief died trying to save his only daughter as she paddled to certain death. Another legend tells of a young girl who, after several misfortunes in her young life, despaired and decided to paddle her canoe over the falls to end her life. As she fell, her

Prospect Point
Observation Tower
Niagara Falls 14302
716–278–1770

Maid of the Mist
Niagara Falls 14302
716–284–8897 (U.S.);
416–358–5781
(Canada)

canoe was guided gently down under the falls, where she met the "Thunder Beings." They helped her to recover her confidence and, in fact, cured her so that she could go back to her people. Apparently, a small snake had hidden in her dress before her bad luck began and was released under the falls, crawling away and out of her life.

In more recent times the falls have been associated with those who would like to be legendary. You must have heard about the Niagara Falls daredevils who risked life and limb to perform various stunts over the falls. Sam Patch was the first to dive, not once but twice, from Goat Island. Jean François Gravelet walked a tightrope over the falls in 1859 and 1860. Can you imagine turning a somersault up there? Well, he did! Annie Taylor, the first woman among these daredevils, went over the falls in a barrel in 1901, but several men died trying to duplicate her successful trip; the last persons to survive the episode were Peter De Bernard and Jeffrey Petkovich in 1989. Such publicity stunts are now illegal.

Niagara Falls

There are actually three falls: the **American Falls** at 184 feet, **Horseshoe** (Canadian) **Falls** at 176 feet, and **Bridal Veil,** the smallest of all. Part of the fun of a trip to Niagara Falls is to see how many different ways you can view these dashing wonders. For a variety of vantage points, try some of the state parks, such as **Devil's Hole, Whirlpool, Upper Rapids,** and **Goat Island.** For a new perspective, be sure to see the falls at night when they are illuminated for several hours. You can also join escorted groups to view the falls by bus, boat, or helicopter. Niagara Reservation State Park Visitor Center (716–278–1796) offers electronic exhibits.

The elevator at **Prospect Point Observation Tower,** enclosed in a steel and glass structure, will take you to the base of the falls as well as 282 feet above them. The view from the top is actually 100 feet above the cliff, a bird's-eye treat. At the bottom you will have a closer look at the falls. If you're eager for a really close look, take a trip on the *Maid of the Mist,* which leaves from the base of the Observation Tower. You don foul-weather gear and your boat chugs over to each of the falls and into the Horseshoe Basin; the boat bounces increasingly as you draw nearer to the tumbling water. The roar of the water and the spray on your face (and the rest of you) enhances your perception of the power of this plunging natural wonder. (You can also take the *Maid of the Mist* from the Canadian side, boarding at the Incline Railway at the foot of Clifton Hill.)

Goat Island is located in the middle of the falls; you can reach it by a bridge either on foot or by car. Many people come to Goat Island to run, hike, and cycle, and you can see both the Canadian and American falls from the island. You may wonder how the island got its name. During the winter of 1770, John Stedman placed a number of his animals on the island to protect them from wolves and bears. Because the winter was very severe, all of the animals died but one—a goat. Soon after crossing the bridge onto Goat Island, you can follow a path up the hill to the right beside a branch of the American rapids that flow over Bridal Veil Falls. Walk down the steps onto Luna Island, where you can see the crest of the Bridal Veil Falls. As you might imagine, Luna Island was named for the moon; around the time of a full moon you can stand on Luna Island and see a rainbow, or "Lunar Bow." The spray from the falls reacts with the refraction of moonlight to produce this sight. Back on Goat Island again, you will come to the **Cave-of-the-Winds** building. You can take a walking tour, dressed in foul-weather gear, to within 25 feet of the base of the falls. On the far side of Goat Island you will see the Three Sister Islands. Cross the first bridge onto Asenath Island, the second onto Angelina Island, and the third to Celinda-Eliza Island. **Niagara Viewmobiles** (716–282–0028), which are sightseeing trains, run around Goat Island and Prospect Point. Commentary is available; you can also get out for a better view and hop onto another train later.

Farther downstream **Whirlpool State Park** overlooks the whirlpool from a high bluff. Hiking and nature trails are well marked.

If you want to find out more about how it all began, stop in the **Schoellkopf Geological Museum** for the history of the falls area for more than 500 million years. An audiovisual presentation tells the tale of the development of the falls, and a variety of other exhibits are there for you to see. The museum runs an extensive program of trips and hikes in the area. It also has a full schedule for schools and groups.

Niagara Falls, Ontario

If you cross over into Canada, you will have more views of the falls. (Don't forget, you'll have to go through Customs.) A **Great Gorge** trip,

Cave-of-the-Winds
Goat Island
Box 1132
Niagara Falls
14303
716–278–1770

Whirlpool State Park
Robert Moses
 Parkway
Box 1132
Niagara Falls
716–278–1770

Schoellkopf
 Geological Museum
Main Street near
 Rainbow Bridge
Niagara Falls 14303
716–278–1780

Table Rock Scenic
  Tunnels
Niagara Falls,
  Ontario
416–358–3268

Horseshoe Falls
  Incline Railway
Niagara Falls,
  Ontario
416–356–0943

Niagara Power
  Project Visitors'
  Center
5777 Lewiston Road
Lewiston 14092
716–285–3211

Shaw Festival
Niagara-on-the-Lake
800–724–2934
  (from U.S.) and
800–267–4759
  (from Canada)

beginning with an elevator descent to the level of the river, is available. You can see the rapids of the Lower Niagara River from the boardwalk below. **Table Rock Scenic Tunnels,** reached by elevator, give you a chance to see both the Canadian Horseshoe Falls and the Niagara River.

The Canadian side offers many other attractions, as well as magnificent public gardens full of beautiful plantings. The **Horseshoe Falls Incline Railway,** located next to Table Rock House, gives you a ride between Table Rock and the Minolta Tower. **Skylon Tower** (5200 Robinson Street) rises 160 meters (525 feet) above the ground and a total of 263 meters (863 feet) above the falls. On a clear day the view from the top is well worth the admission fee. The **Daredevil Gallery** (416–356–0943) includes exhibits showing the exploits of those who sought to challenge the falls. And don't miss the **Rainbow Carillon Tower** (416–354–5641) at Rainbow Bridge. Concerts are played on its fifty-five–bell set during the season.

The **Niagara Power Project,** one of the largest hydroelectric facilities in the world, has a capacity of 2.4 million kilowatts. Seven other plants contribute to the hydropower supply for New York State. The Visitors' Center has a view of the gorge with thirteen large turbines on the left. Inside, displays include a robotic arm, a 1920 telephone, and a huge model of the Niagara Falls area with the river winding over the falls and continuing around the city.

Downstairs take a historical tour from the white-water rapids and falls, ranging from 10,224 B.C., the time of the last glacier; to the falls in 2024 B.C., when the Egyptian pyramids were built; to the falls at the birth of Christ; to the separation of the falls in A.D. 900; to the falls seen by Father Louis Hennepin in 1678; to today. Questions are posed and answers discovered by way of hands-on computers. A movie, *Niagara Then and Now,* presents quotes from presidents and poets, including Abraham Lincoln, Mark Twain (who said that the fish don't bite near the falls), Oscar Wilde, and Walt Whitman.

Niagara-on-the-Lake, Ontario

From Niagara Falls, Ontario, you can take a side trip to Niagara-on-the-Lake, the home of the **Shaw Festival.** This theatrical company produces the works of George Bernard Shaw and his contemporaries, and its season runs from early May through mid-October.

Fort George National Historic Park dates from 1797. It changed hands several times until it was finally abandoned in the early 1820s. The reconstructed fort is open to the public.

Welland Canal, Ontario

For a side trip to the Welland Canal from Niagara Falls, Ontario, take Route 405 to signs for the Welland Canal. (From Buffalo take Queen Elizabeth Way to St. Catharines.) The canal was built to connect Lake Ontario with Lake Erie, avoiding the insurmountable barrier of the Niagara escarpment. It was designed for vessels needing deep water and safe passage into the interior of our continent. There are seven locks to negotiate, and it takes about twelve hours to complete the trip. Each lock is 859 feet in length and 80 feet in width; the entire canal is 27 feet deep. Locks are filled or emptied by gravity. A vessel going upstream enters the lock, valves are opened, and water flows in; the vessel rises, gates are opened, and the vessel moves out. Lock 1 is on Canal Road north of Lakeshore Road in St. Catharines. Lock 2, located just north of Carleton Street, has picnic areas along the banks. The **Welland Canal Viewing Centre,** a large elevated platform, provides views of the lock procedures at Lock 3. Tourist information, a picnic area, and a snack bar are also available there. Locks 4, 5, and 6 offer simultaneous locking of ships going upstream and downstream. Lock 7, in Thorold, is the last lift over the Niagara escarpment.

An abandoned channel in Welland is now used for recreational purposes, such as picnicking, boating, and water-skiing. **Merritt Island,** on a strip of land between the Welland River and Welland Recreational Waterway, offers hiking, biking, and cross-country skiing. A lighthouse, a tourist information center, and a park are located at Lock 8 in Port Colborne, very close to Lake Erie. The elevated observation deck provides a view of lock operations.

> Fort George National
>   Historic Park
> Niagara-on-the-Lake
> 416–468–2187
>
> Welland Canal
>   Viewing Centre
> Canal Road
> St. Catharines
>
> Fort Niagara
> Youngstown 14174
> 716–745–7611

Youngstown

Back on the American side, take I–190 and the Robert Moses Parkway to Youngstown. In 1726 **Fort Niagara** was built by the French; you can visit the fort on the state park grounds. It has been restored, and special reenactments are held to take you back into history. This fort was

159

Artpark
Lewiston 14092
716-745-3377 or
800-659-PARK

very active during the French and Indian War, the American Revolution, and the War of 1812.

A self-guided tour takes you to the Provisions Storehouse, Powder Magazine, Dauphin Battery, Gate of the Five Nations (a good place from which to view the mist above Niagara Falls on a clear day), the South Redoubt, 18-Pounder Battery, Land Defenses, North Redoubt, and around to the "French Castle." The castle, restored to its mid-eighteenth–century style, shows how the officers and men lived in those days. Rooms include storerooms, a powder magazine, chapel, guardhouse, and bakery. Stop to see the well that was used from 1726 until 1812. It was sealed at that time and reopened in 1927. You can hear the story of the headless ghost of a murdered French officer who still searches for his head. Some say that he sits on the edge of the well at midnight and rises when the moon is full to continue his search. Major Robert Rogers (of Rogers's Rangers fame) was imprisoned in the castle for several weeks in 1768.

For a number of summers, archaeologists have conducted scientific excavations on the site. Each six-week dig takes place during July and August, and visitors are welcome to watch.

Lewiston

On the way back from Fort Niagara, you may want to stop in Lewiston to stroll among buildings dating back to the War of 1812. Thirty-five thousand years ago Niagara Falls was located there. Later, Indians landed at this spot to begin their portage around the falls. Father Hennepin, the first white man to see the falls, stopped in Lewiston in 1678.

Lewiston was located in a strategic position on the Niagara River, with access to the Great Lakes, so Indians, French, and British fought for control in this area. The first railroad in America was constructed by the British there as a tramway to carry supplies up the steep cliffs. American control was in force during the Revolution, and the town became a successful center for transportation as well as for trade.

Did you know that the first cocktail was created in Lewiston? Catherine Hustler, who owned a tavern on Center Street, mixed gin and herbed wine in a tankard and stirred it with a pheasant feather.

Artpark is a theater and art complex in a 200-acre state park. Visitors can walk around the park to see the sculptures made of wood, steel, masonry, and other materials. There are workshops for children and adults. Artists-in-residence create their works in open-air studios so everyone can watch the process. Performing artists include musicians, mimes, actors, clowns, dancers, and storytellers. You can buy tickets for performances ranging from jazz to classical music. If you want to buy lawn tickets at a very reasonable price, plan to arrive early to stake your claim to one of the few flat pieces of grass on the hillside outside the stage; otherwise you may find yourself sliding downhill during the performance.

Lewiston is a great place to stay if you want to be out of the mainstream of the Niagara area, but close enough for convenient touring. A popular bakery in town is **DeCamillo Baking Co.** (535 Center; 716–754–2218). For lunch or dinner head for **Carmelo's Coat of Arms** (425 Center; 716–754–2311), which has a variety of continental dishes to offer, or the **Riverside Inn** (115 South Water Street; 716–754–8206), located right on the water.

From Lewistown retrace I–190 to Buffalo and take I–90 along the south shore of Lake Erie.

❧ *Southwestern New York* ❧

This part of New York State includes Dunkirk and Fredonia down to Salamanca and Olean.

Dunkirk

Dunkirk is the largest city in Chautauqua County on Lake Erie. A revitalization program to restore the charm of this lakeside setting is under way. The natural harbor has lots of yachting activity because it is an easy sail to Canada from Dunkirk. Beaches, launching sites, and fishing piers are available for anglers interested in coho salmon, black bass, walleye pike, and pan fish.

Dunkirk is in the heart of the grape-growing area along the Erie shore. There is a 3- to 5-mile-wide strip of lowland bordering on Lake Erie that is perfect for raising grapes. The low altitude and the warmth of the lake provide a long growing season with delayed frost. The first grapes were raised in the country in 1818, and by 1859 the Concord grape became an important product. A dentist, Dr. Thomas Welch, created unfermented grape juice.

The **Seaway Trail** was formally designated by the New York State Legislature in 1980. It was designed to commemorate the linking of the

161

Dunkirk Lighthouse
Point Gratiot
Dunkirk 14048
716–366–5050 or
716–366–5765

SUNY Fredonia
Fredonia, NY 14063
716–673–3111

Darwin R. Barker
Museum
20 East Main Street
Fredonia 14063
716–672–2114

Great Lakes coastlines with the St. Lawrence Seaway, from the Pennsylvania border to the gates of the Eisenhower Locks at the end of New York's northern border with the St. Lawrence. Dunkirk is one of the stops on the Seaway Trail.

The **Dunkirk Lighthouse** dates from 1827. Originally, the light coordinated with a pier-head beacon to guide ships safely into Dunkirk Harbor; it was the first oil-burning lighthouse on Lake Erie. The original tower and a brick lighthouse-keeper's house were replaced in 1875. The last lighthouse keeper lived there until 1951, when the light became automatic. A **Veterans' Museum,** containing artifacts, uniforms, and memorabilia from each of the armed services, has been opened in the lighthouse. Photographs detail the International Iceberg Patrol, formed after the sinking of the *Titanic*. Photos of the original lighthouse show the amazing height of ice formations during one year; when lake ice moves under the force of strong northwesterly winds, it crunches everything in its path. As you go up the stairs, look at the lovely carved capstan on the staircase.

Fredonia

Follow Route 60 to Fredonia. This is a pleasant village with a number of stately homes dating from the 1830s to 1850s on the main streets. The **State University of New York College at Fredonia** is located in this town. The **Michael C. Rockefeller Arts Center** on campus offers a year-round program of drama, music, film, and dance. The art gallery mounts exhibits by students and faculty as well as changing traveling exhibits.

Fredonia and the area claim a number of firsts: the first naval skirmish of the War of 1812 at the mouth of the Canadaway Creek (located just off Point Gratiot); the first grange in the world; the first Women's Christian Temperance Union, organized at the Fredonia Baptist Church in 1873; and the first natural gas well in the United States.

The **Darwin R. Barker Museum** has exhibits depicting the evolution of the town from prehistory to the present. The house was originally built in 1821 by Leverett Barker, who was a tanner. It was the first brick house built in Chautauqua County. The museum holds period clothing, military uniforms, books, documents, period furnishings, and portraits. A genealogical-society reference library enables you to trace your ancestry in the region.

Continue south on I–90, a scenic route, to Westfield.

Westfield

In 1860 Grace Bedell, an eleven-year-old Westfield girl, sent a letter to President Lincoln suggesting that he grow a beard to improve his appearance. He replied by letter, and when his inaugural train stopped in Westfield on the way to Washington in 1861, Lincoln asked for her as he told her story to the assembled crowd. He alighted from the train, showed her his new whiskers, kissed her, and said, "You see, I have followed your advice." His letter brought $20,000 in 1966 when sold at auction in New York City.

Chautauqua County
Historical Society
Village Park
Westfield 14787
716–326–2977

Barcelona
Lighthouse
East Lake Drive
Westfield 14787

Chautauqua
Institution
Box 1095
Chautauqua 14722
716–357–6200 or
800–836–ARTS

The **Chatauqua County Historical Society** is housed in a mansion built in 1818 by James McClurg. The mansion is furnished with period pieces, including a bull's-eye gilt mirror dating from 1795, needlepoint chairs original to the house, a Hepplewhite secretary from 1820, and many portraits.

The **Barcelona Lighthouse,** a 35-foot-high lighthouse built of field-stone, cost $3,400 to build in 1828. It was the first building in this country to use natural gas for illumination. The light guided boats loaded with furs, logs, salt, and fish until 1859, when it was no longer useful because the railroad had garnered most of the transportation business.

Chautauqua

In Westfield pick up Route 394 to Chautauqua Lake. **Chautauqua Institution** was founded in 1874 on the western shore. Although its original purpose was to provide educational training for Sunday-school teachers, the institution developed a program of activities for all ages in the form of lectures and entertainment in the arts, religion, education, and recreation. You can take summer courses as well as attend an opera, symphony, ballet, or play in the evening.

In the early days Chautauqua was controlled by several hundred families, who passed on their heritage through the generations. After 111 years of self-governance, the trustees developed a land-use code in 1985. The goal now is to keep the old Chautauqua and yet allow realistic development in keeping with the old ideals. The typical wooden Victorian cottages with gingerbread on the porch eaves remain, and colorful displays of flowers enhance the homes. You must have a gate ticket to get into the grounds during the nine-week season.

You have probably heard about the Chautauqua tent shows that went from town to town, giving inspirational lectures. William Jennings Bryan was among the early traveling tent orators. Imitations spread rapidly, but of them all, only Chautauqua remains.

Among the famous visitors of the past were George Gershwin, who composed "Concerto in F" there in 1925, and Thomas Edison, who placed his new electric streetlights there in 1880. Leo Tolstoy came as a speaker, as did Henry Ford and Amelia Earhart. In 1936 Franklin Roosevelt gave his "I Hate War" speech there, and Teddy Roosevelt spoke of the Chautauqua Institution as "typical of America at its best."

Chautauquan fishermen know that the native muskellunge, or "muskie," lies in wait for unwary anglers who think it will be easy to land one. Try your luck at fishing. From Mayville you can cruise on the *Chautauqua Belle;* this replica of a nineteenth-century steamboat offers brunch and sunset cruises.

Panama Rocks

From Chautauqua Lake you might want to take a side trip to **Panama Rocks.** This site can be reached from Route 474, heading west from the lake. These rocks were formed more than 300 million years ago as sediment on an ocean floor. One million years ago the glaciers created this labyrinth of caves and passageways, twisting the rock as it moved. When the ice melted, crevices, cliffs, and caves remained; water and winds have further shaped and etched designs in the rock. The forest grew, with wildflowers, ferns, and mosses adding contrast to the rocks.

The rocks and caves were used for shelter in ancient times; part of a fireplace can still be seen near the top of one ridge. The Eriez Indians, sometimes known as the "Cat People," lived there until the Senecas conquered them. They sold lead ore, taken from a hidden spot on the ridge, to the settlers. During the 1800s the rocks were used by robbers as a perfect place to stash their loot. It has been reported that there is still some gold hidden deep in a cave or hole.

Jamestown

Jamestown is located on the southern tip of Chautauqua Lake. James Prendergast founded the town, and in 1811 he bought 1,000 acres, where he built a sawmill and dam. Jamestown is still known for its production of furniture and other wooden products.

The **Fenton Historical Center** is housed in a mansion built by Governor Reuben E. Fenton. The museum includes a library, genealogical center, Swedish and Italian heritage rooms, archives of early Jamestown, and articles from the Fenton family. It also offers a self-guided tour of the nineteenth-century historic area.

The **Art Gallery,** in the James Prendergast Library, contains collections of French, German, and American paintings, as well as a special collection of Scandinavian memorabilia.

The Jamestown Audubon Society sponsors the **Roger Tory Peterson Wildlife Sanctuary.** It offers special programs on natural topics and the environment, workshops, and tours.

Lucille Ball grew up in Jamestown. Roger Tory Peterson, author of *A Field Guide to Birds,* and Horace Greeley were residents of the town.

Conewango Valley

Northeast of Jamestown, in the Conewango Valley, is an area fairly recently settled by Amish families. Route 62 west from Ellington to Cowens Corners Road, to Route 241 north to North East Road to Chautauqua Road, will take you by bakeries, and shops selling handcrafted quilts, chairs, cheese, antiques, and fresh fruit.

Salamanca

Retrace your steps and take scenic Route 17 to Salamanca. It is the only city in the world right on an Indian reservation. The **Seneca-Iroquois National Museum** contains more than 300,000 items depicting the culture of these Indians. You will see displays from prehistory up to contemporary culture.

The **Salamanca Rail Museum** is housed in a 1912 passenger rail depot. Exhibits present the history of the western New York railroads. You can also take a scenic ride on a train during the summer.

Fenton Historical Center
67 Washington Street
Jamestown 14701
716–664–6256

Art Gallery
509 Cherry Street
Jamestown 14701
716–484–7135

Roger Tory Peterson Wildlife Sanctuary
Riverside Road
Frewsburg 14738
716–665–2473

Seneca-Iroquois National Museum
Broad Street Extension
Salamanca 14779
716–945–1738

Salamanca Rail Museum
170 Main Street
Salamanca 14779
716–945–3133

Allegany State Park
716–354–2535

Rock City Park
Route 16
Olean 14760
716–372–7790

Allegany State Park

Allegany State Park, located off Route 17, has 65,000 acres tucked against the Pennsylvania border. Open year-round, this park offers hunting, fishing, boating, swimming, tennis, and 75 miles of hiking trails. A nature education center is on the grounds.

Take Route 417 to Olean.

Olean

Rock City Park, with the remains of a prehistoric ocean bed, is dramatic. The world's largest deposit of quartz boulders is also on view. A mineral museum and a nature trail provide explanations for visitors.

This is the end of Itinerary C. You can continue south into the Allegany National Forest for more of the same beautiful scenery and vacation attractions; head west on I–90 to Erie (linking with Itinerary D); or drive back to the Finger Lakes area on Route 17.

ITINERARY D:

Northern Pennsylvania

KINZUA DAM

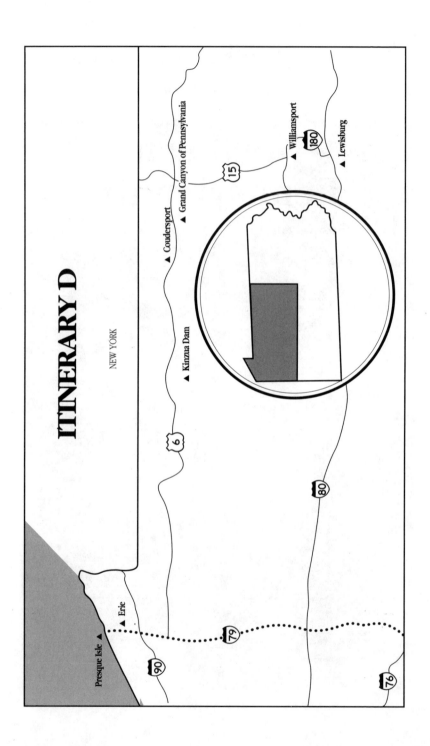

Northern Pennsylvania

This itinerary can be a continuation of Itinerary C, from Western New York, or it can be done in reverse from the South-Central area of Pennsylvania (Itinerary F). The routes include Erie, Presque Isle, and North-Central Pennsylvania.

≈ *Erie and Presque Isle* ≈

Did you know that at one time Erie was the scene of clandestine rum-running? Many of the local residents were in cahoots with one another, traveling in groups of two or three boats in case of trouble. Their boats were specially made for speed and built with heavier planking so that they could take the pounding the Coast Guard would inflict during the chase. They had aircraft engines, called Liberty engines, which were noted for their 500 horsepower. The boats were also built with a number of hatches to receive cases of liquor in a hurry. When the weather was favorable, they would cross the lake, sometimes managing to make it to land, where cars were waiting to receive the liquor. At other times the Coast Guard received a tip and were on hand to meet them, lobbing a one-pound shell across the bow or opening machine-gun fire to stop the smugglers. Close calls were a way of life for those who engaged in rum-running.

The romance of days gone by is present not only in stories about rum-running but also in legends based on historical fact from the early days of Erie. The Underground Railroad is depicted in one of the houses open to the public. And, of course, Commander Perry brought fame to Erie through his seafaring ventures during the War of 1812. On one occasion the Marquis de Lafayette was the guest of honor at a dinner held on a bridge under an awning of sails from captured British ships.

Erie

Erie was originally named for the Eriez Indians, a group 12,000 strong at the beginning of the seventeenth century. The Indian Wars in 1653 and a pestilence destroyed this tribe. In 1753 the French built Fort Presque Isle, but they abandoned it in 1759. The British were on the scene until an Indian uprising—Pontiac's Conspiracy—demolished their outpost. In 1794 General Anthony Wayne succeeded in vanquishing the Indians during the Battle of Fallen Timbers. An American settlement was begun the next year.

Commander Oliver Hazard Perry supervised the building of ships in Erie during the War of 1812. The keels of the *Niagara* and the *Lawrence* were laid in March 1813, and the vessels were launched in June. On

August 1 Perry undertook the task of floating the boats across the sandbar at the entrance to the bay with the aid of "camels," or empty tanks. On September 10 Perry and his men, on board the *Lawrence,* challenged the British and engaged them in battle. When the *Lawrence* was reduced to a hulk by British long guns, Perry and his remaining men dashed by boat to the *Niagara;* from this ship Perry reattacked the battered British fleet and decisively won the Battle of Lake Erie. He wrote: "We have met the enemy and they are ours: Two ships, two Brigs, one Schooner and one Sloop." Both the *Lawrence* and the *Niagara* were allowed to sink in Misery Bay after the battle. The *Lawrence* was raised in 1876 and, although she was not intact, was taken to Philadelphia for the country's Centennial and finally burned in a fire that consumed the Centennial build-

Niagara
164 E. Front Street
Erie 16507
814–871–4596

Erie Art Museum
Old Custom House
411 State Street
Erie 16502
814–459–5477

Erie County
Historical
Society
Cashier's House
417 State Street
Erie 16501
814–454–1813

ings. The *Niagara* was raised in 1913 for the centennial of the battle; she was towed by the *Wolverine* to various ports on Lake Erie during that summer. She was brought back to Erie and remained in the water until the 1930s, when she was put into her cradle. Until September 1987 visitors could climb aboard the *Niagara* and look up to see the flag flying from the shrouds: "Don't give up the ship."

In September 1987 the *Niagara* was completely dismantled, and salvageable pieces were stored. She has been rebuilt using some of the original 1813 timbers. She was launched on September 10, 1988, and now rocks at her mooring. The **Erie Maritime Museum** opened in 1998.

Nearby there's a reproduction of one of the yawl boats carried by Commodore Oliver Hazard Perry's flagship *Lawrence* and the *Niagara* during the 1813 Battle of Lake Erie. The yawl boat is built of Douglas fir and white oak in a lapstrake design (the planks overlap each other). She was used to ferry supplies between ships in the squadron and from the shore.

Walk up State Street to the **Old Custom House,** which was built in 1839 as a bank (with Andrew Jackson as president) and used as a custom house from 1849 to 1888. This Greek Doric structure, built of white Vermont marble, now houses the **Erie Art Museum.** The walls, doors, and windows of the original building are still intact, but the museum added an inner wall for the gallery. Look at the ceiling of plaster over lath that highlights elaborately decorated classic Greek motifs, such as acanthus leaves and Greek fret in a circular pattern.

Right next door is the home of the **Erie County Historical Society** in the **Cashier's House.** Also of Greek Revival design, this building was

171

| DicksonTavern/ |
| Perry Memorial |
| House |
| 201 French Street |
| Erie 16502 |

constructed in 1839 as a home for the cashier of the bank next door. Inside you will find a surprise if you try to open the doors along the right side of the hall: There is nothing but plaster on the other side! Some of the furniture in the hall came from the SS *Wolverine,* including the sofa and the campaign-style desk. Ask the guide to tell you stories about Captain Dobbin and some of the other people in portraits on the walls. There are collections of copper luster china used on the *Wolverine,* and a blue-and-white platter that was used at the banquet for Lafayette in 1825. Look for the furniture decorated with "feathering" (painted with a feather). The **Erie Society for Genealogical Research** is located in the museum, if you would like to look up your past in the region. You can do your own research or ask the staff to do it for you.

Walk around the corner to **Dickson Tavern/Perry Memorial House.** John Dickson built this house in 1815; at that time it was on the waterfront. Look out of one of the front windows toward the hospital, and you will see the site of a historic banquet. In June 1825 Lafayette toured the country he helped save. Tables were set on the 170-foot-long bridge on Second Avenue, which is now behind the hospital. Sails from British vessels vanquished by Perry provided an awning for diners, and flowers and greens decorated the banquet area. This grand feast cost $2.00 per person, according to the bill received by Giles Sanford.

You may hear local legends about the secret passages in the basement of this house, which were used by runaway slaves in the Underground Railroad. The theory was that they crawled down under the fireplace into a tunnel below, yet there is no structural evidence of an opening under the fireplace. It is known, however, that the Underground Railroad did exist in the area—in one residence or another. You can see an exhibit of two slaves in hiding as you peek into a basement window. The tavern taproom in the basement features two male mannequins drinking from pewter tankards. They may have been drinking "flip," which was a combination of beer, rum, and water stirred with a hot poker to give it a pungent flavor. Or it may have been punch made with a rum or tea base and flavored with lime or lemon juice. The building also has a diorama showing some of the vessels built in Erie, including the *Scorpion, Tigress, Porcupine, Ariel, Niagara, Somers, Lawrence, Caledonia,* and *Ohio.*

Next head to Sixth Street, where you will find **Perry Square.** Look for the statue of Perry erected for the two hundredth anniversary of his birthday on August 23, 1985. He is shown as he went aboard the *Niagara,* with the flag draped over his shoulder.

Continue on Sixth Street to the **Erie Historical Museum.** H. F. Watson built this Romanesque-style house in 1895; Felix Curtze bought the house in 1924. Look for the many stained-glass windows and friezes; some in the dining room have cherubs on them. The den has an Eastern look with its carved wooden trim and vaulted ceiling. Mr. Watson kept his insect collection in the rows of shallow drawers there. There is a peacock frieze in the gift shop and dolphins on the stained-glass windows. The striking fireplace in the hall displays gold, marble, and delicate carving, and there is a clock next to the staircase that belonged to the Watson family. Upstairs look for Winifred's bedroom—a perfect room for a little girl—with steps leading up to a balcony, shelves, and a three-dimensional window with pansies in soft shades of green, yellow, white, and blue. The museum contains exhibits on the Battle of Lake Erie, ship models, and the history of commercial fishing in Erie. Look in the carriage house for the planetarium, which offers classes in astronomy.

Erie Historical
Museum
356 West Sixth
Street
Erie 16507
814–871–5790

Firefighters'
Historical Museum
428 Chestnut
Erie 16502
814–456–5969

Presque Isle State
Park
P.O. Box 8510
Erie 16505-0510
814–833–7424

The **Firefighters' Historical Museum** is full of firefighting equipment, including fire extinguishers, fire alarm systems, uniforms, an 1830 hand-pumper, and an 1886 hand-pulled hose cart.

Stop for lunch or dinner in the **Pufferbelly Restaurant** (414 French Street; 814–454–1557), which is housed in the original Fire House Number 1. Various items from firefighting in the past decorate the restaurant.

Presque Isle State Park

Adjoining Erie on Route 832 is **Presque Isle State Park.** This 3,202-acre sandy peninsula extends into Lake Erie for 7 miles. As you drive out you will see Presque Isle Bay on your right and Lake Erie on your left. The bay provides shallow "nursery" waters where fish spawn and propagate. Among the fish you might catch in the lake are walleyes, smallmouth bass, largemouth bass, muskies, northern pike, blue gills, perch, carp, and bullfin. Fishermen and visitors alike have been delighted to see the lake coming back, after a murky period when it was polluted. A local fisherman remarked that previously he could see only about 10 feet down into the lake to spot his yellow downrigger balls, but now he can spot them at 40 feet. The quality of the water is improving every year.

Besides fishing, you can swim along the 7-mile stretch of sandy beach on Lake Erie, hike, jog, or cycle, and picnic at the many tables.

There are six launching ramps, a marina, and a boat livery where you can rent canoes, rowboats, and motorboats. During the winter cross-country skiing, ice skating, and ice-fishing are popular. A nature center provides exhibits and special programs. Because hundreds of species of birds, ducks, geese, and several kinds of cranes live in the park, ecologists come to study plant and animal life in the ponds, bay, and lakeshore areas. While you are in the park, look for the Perry monument; it is a memorial to those who died during the Battle of Lake Erie.

≈ *North-Central Pennsylvania* ≈

An alternative route if you want to head east instead of south to Pittsburgh is to take Route 19, then Route 97 to Route 6. This Grand Army of the Republic Highway was named to honor the veterans of 1861 and 1865. Earlier it was known as a forbidden Indian trail; the Seneca Indians denied the white man passage. It has been named one of the top ten scenic routes in the United States.

Kinzua Dam

From Warren take Route 59 for 6 miles to **Kinzua Dam** and the **Allegheny Reservoir.** During the summer visitors can enjoy swimming, boating, fishing, and hiking in the area. Kinzua Dam and the Allegheny Reservoir were designed in 1936 as a flood control measure; the dam was completed in 1965. Hydroelectric power is another result of the project; the **Big Bend Visitor Center** demonstrates this process. The word *Kinzua* means "land of Many and Big Fishes." Look upstream of the dam to see a "trash boom," which is a line of floating timbers to catch debris before it enters the sluiceway. Rim Rock provides a scenic view of Wolf Run.

Back on Route 6 you'll pass Kane, then Mount Jewett, and finally the **Kinzua Bridge,** built in 1882. At that time it was the highest railroad bridge in the world, at 301 feet. The Pittsburgh, Bradford, and Buffalo Railroad ran from Knox, Pennsylvania, to Marienville, Pennsylvania, by 1881 and continued on to Kane in 1882. A legend dating back to 1893 has sent people to look for $50,000 buried somewhere within sight of the bridge. A gunman robbed the company store in Palmerville and made off with his loot. Later, searchers found a young man who was delirious with fever—he kept muttering something about "the money," "see the bridge," "glass bottles," and "three-cornered stone" before he died.

Continue on Route 6 past Coudersport for 10 miles to the **Pennsylvania Lumber Museum.** Much white pine and hemlock lumber came from the state of Pennsylvania, and two of the largest sawmills in the world were located in the area. Here's the place to see how the "woodhicks," or lumbermen, lived in camps. Conditions were terrible, and, even into the early 1900s, the pay was as low as $1.50 a day. Visitors walk from building to building to see the engine house, loader shed, logging cars, stable, filer's shack (where the men sharpened their tools), blacksmith-carpenter shop, bunkhouse, mess hall, kitchen, and sawmill.

Pennsylvania's Grand Canyon is located west of Wellsboro. The canyon is 50 miles long and 1,000 feet deep. Overlooks provide spectacular views. Visitors can cruise the canyon by canoe and raft. **Leonard Harrison** and **Colton Point State Parks** lie within the Grand Canyon.

Pennsylvania
Lumber Museum
5560 US 6 West
P.O. Box 239
Galeton 16922
814–435–2652

Little League
Baseball Museum
Route 15
Williamsport 17701
717–326–3607

Lycoming County
Historical Museum
858 West Fourth
Street
Williamsport 17701
717–326–3326

Williamsport

Turn south on Route 15 to reach Williamsport, the home of the **Little League Baseball Museum.** Here's a museum hands-on enough to delight any youngster. The kids can swing bats, throw balls, and push buttons. A video replay captures each participant's actions and plays back the results. Don't miss the World Series Room to see forty years of Little League World Series Championship on film. A special room of memorabilia contains the collection of George Bebble, one of the founders of the program.

The **Lycoming County Historical Museum** offers Indian artifacts collected in the area. Exhibits trace the history of life for the first settlers until the present day. You'll see a one-room country school of 1900, the inside of a home from the frontier era, a blacksmith shop, a carpenter shop, and a Victorian parlor. Don't miss the displays of children's toys, including a doll's house. The train collection is one to delight all ages.

Lewisburg

Continue south on Route 15 to Lewisburg, which contains a lot of Victorian and Federal-style homes. The **Packwood House** began as a 1796 log cabin and ended up a three-story building used as a hotel and tavern.

John and Edith Fetherston bought the house during the 1930s, named it Packwood House after the Fetherston mansion in Warwickshire, England, and furnished it with their personal collection of art objects. One of the original log walls remains in the "log wall room." Edith became a painter, and there is a gallery displaying her work. She also established a Chinese garden, complete with bronze statues.

ITINERARY E:

Western Pennsylvania

INCLINE RAILWAY, PITTSBURGH

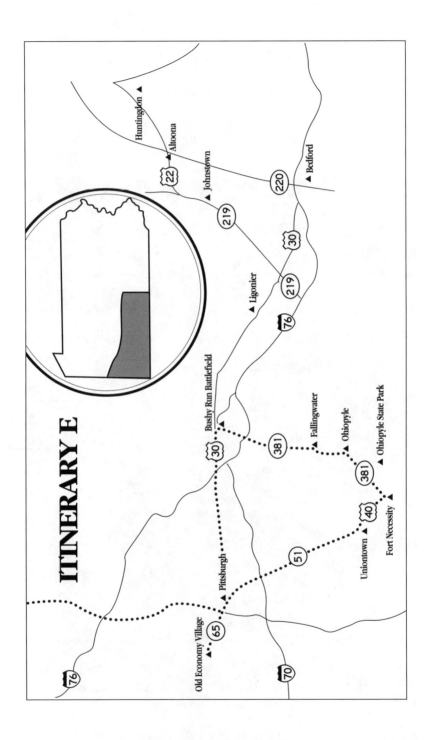

ITINERARY E

Huntingdon ▲
Altoona ▲
Johnstown ▲
22
219
Bedford ▲
220
30
Ligonier ▲
219
76
Bushy Run Battlefield ▲
30
381
Fallingwater ▲
Ohiopyle ▲
Ohiopyle State Park ▲
381
Uniontown ▲
40
Fort Necessity ▲
51
Pittsburgh ▲
Old Economy Village ▲
65
76
70

Western Pennsylvania

Pittsburgh Area

❧ *Pittsburgh Area* ❧

Where was your town on the list when Pittsburgh was rated Number 1 as a place to live by Rand-McNally? In spite of the grousing by those of us who live elsewhere, let's give Pittsburgh a chance! It was once a grimy, smoky city, but in the late 1940s a countywide smoke-control program began to clear the air. In the 1950s Gateway Center and Point State Park were developed over the rubble of downtown gloom. Since then a number of skyscrapers and new stores and restaurants have been added to the scene. Visually you will be amazed to discover the Gothic influence in the city—gargoyles, stained glass, arches, turrets, and pinnacles.

Fort Pitt Blockhouse
Point State Park
Pittsburgh 15222
412–471–1764

Fort Pitt Museum
Point State Park
101 Commonwealth
Place
Pittsburgh 15222
412–281–9285

Pittsburgh

George Washington was responsible for the choice of the "Golden Triangle"—where the Ohio, Allegheny, and Monongahela rivers meet—as the location for a fort. Fort Prince George was in the process of construction when a flotilla of bateaux and canoes arrived, carrying both French and Indians. Surrender was inevitable, with only forty men available to defend the new fort. The French disassembled the stockade and made use of the beams as they built Fort Duquesne. In 1758 General John Forbes took the fort from the French, but they blew it up as they retreated. He began construction again and changed the name to Fort Pitt, named for William Pitt, the prime minister of England, who was respected by the colonists. The blockhouse was built in 1764, with two rows of holes for firing on attackers. You can visit the **Fort Pitt Blockhouse,** the only remaining structure of Fort Pitt, located in **Point State Park.** Walk around in the park to see some of the bastions and earthworks of the old fort. The **Fort Pitt Museum,** located near the blockhouse, has exhibits, models, a reconstructed trader's cabin, displays of frontier life, and materials on early Pittsburgh. If you're there in June, the **Three Rivers Arts Festival** will be in full swing.

As Pittsburgh developed industrially, its position at the junction of three rivers was very advantageous. Coal dug locally, a glassworks, and a blast furnace were the forerunners of the tremendous steel and iron industry. During the late nineteenth century, Andrew Mellon, Henry Heinz, Andrew Carnegie, and Henry Clay Frick developed their empires. The names "Iron City" and then "Smoky City" were not without claims to truth.

Theodore Dreiser lived in Pittsburgh in 1894 as a newspaper reporter. In *A Book About Myself,* he describes arriving by the Monongahela River and seeing the rosy glow from the stacks pouring forth an orange-red flame. He goes on to mention the pounding and cracking noises, which sounded as if they emerged from subterranean depths.

Monongahela Incline
Carson Street
Pittsburgh 15219
Duquesne Incline
Fort Pitt Bridge
Pittsburgh 15211
412–381–1665

During both world wars Pittsburgh's industries were able to produce the materials needed for the war effort. After World War II Richard King Mellon was largely responsible for the antismoke campaign, the clearing of outmoded downtown areas, the construction of architecturally interesting buildings, and the creation of **Mellon Square Park** as a beauty spot. Although coal and steel still play a major role in the life of the city, their presence is unobtrusive and controlled. The renaissance of Pittsburgh is a transformation much admired by old and new visitors alike.

Our first impulse when traveling to a city new to us in Europe or the United States is to climb centuries-old worn steps up to the steeple of a cathedral, to shoot up to the top of a skyscraper in an outside elevator, or to take a funicular or cog railway to the peak of a mountain for the view. In Pittsburgh you can take one of the two remaining incline railways (simply called "inclines") to the top of Mount Washington for a view of the city across the river. The **Monongahela Incline** was built in 1870 so that people who lived on top of Mount Washington could travel down to their jobs easily. It has been renovated several times and now has new cars that carry twenty-five persons up the 635 feet of vertical rise. You can catch the "Mon" at the Carson Street Station Square and ride up to Grandview Avenue. The **Duquesne Incline** travels from Fort Pitt Bridge up 400 feet to an area of several restaurants. These cars have handsome, carved cherry panels with bird's-eye maple trim and amber glass transoms. Take a look at the large collection of postcards that depict cable cars and cog railways from all over the world in the waiting room. For a spectacular evening, have dinner on the top of **Le Mont** (1114 Grandview Avenue; 412–431–3100), where you can watch the sunset reflecting in clouds, lights turning on, the 200-foot fountain spraying in Point Park, and lights glinting on the sparkling glass skyline of Pittsburgh.

Among the downtown buildings you can't help but admire is **PPG Place,** which looks like a crystal castle complete with spires, towers, turrets, and a real fairyland ambience. The forty-story office tower shimmers and reflects everything around it. Pay particular attention to the inside Wintergarden, with its great profusion of greenery.

Gateway Clipper
 Fleet
Station Square Dock
Pittsburgh 15219
412–355–7980

Station Square
One Station Square
Pittsburgh 15219

Westin William Penn
 Hotel
William Penn Place
Pittsburgh 15219
412–281–7100 or
800–228–3000

The Carnegie
4400 Forbes Avenue
Pittsburgh 15213
412–622–3131,
 exhibitions;
412–622–3289, tours

The **National Steel Center** in downtown Pittsburgh is shaped in the form of a triangle. Its restaurant, located sixty-four stories up, has a view that is worth the trip. We were told that the columns in this building have water in them as protection against fire.

Gateway Clipper Fleet offers visitors views from the river, complete with narration. You can choose a dinner cruise, a sightseeing cruise, or one on the *Good Ship Lollipop* with Lolli the clown, if you are traveling with children.

Station Square, located right on the Monongahela River across the Smithfield Bridge, is a restored historic site with boutiques and restaurants. The **Grand Concourse Restaurant** (412–261–1717) offers a fine view of the busy river, which has a constant stream of tugs and barges going up or down; a train whizzed by in front of us as we were having lunch. This restaurant is in the terminal building, which was built around the turn of the century. Look up at the domed roof with its yellow stained-glass windows, carved woodwork, and marble columns. Complete renovation has made these rooms a romantic reminder of the Golden Age of Rail.

Another historic building in Pittsburgh is the **Westin William Penn Hotel,** built in 1916 by Henry Clay Frick. If you have a chance to see the Ballroom, on the seventeenth floor, don't miss it. This two-story room has a gilded balcony, crystal chandeliers, and elegant furnishings. (See Inns appendix.)

Pittsburgh has more colleges and museums than you may have time to explore, so we will describe a sampling of them. Andrew Carnegie is a name you can't miss as you visit Pittsburgh. He was intensely interested in many of the arts and built everything on a large scale. The **Carnegie** contains both the **Museum of Art** and the **Museum of Natural History.** Within the Museum of Art you can see the permanent American art collection in the Sarah Mellon Scaife Gallery. Silver, furniture, and porcelain from England, France, and Germany are in the Ailsa Mellon Bruce Collection. The Museum of Natural History has more than 10,000 items on exhibit, including Dinosaur Hall, Polar World, Hillman Hall of Minerals and Gems, Indian relics, wildlife, anthropology, and the Walton Hall of Ancient Egypt. The Benedum Hall of Geology opened in 1988. The **Carnegie Library,** at the same address, is gigantic, with more than four million entries in the catalog.

Our favorite tower is located right on the campus of the University of Pittsburgh. **The Cathedral of Learning** is a forty-two–story Gothic structure containing "nationality classrooms"—rooms decorated and designed by artists from each of the ethnic groups that settled in Pittsburgh. The design of each room reflects cultural and aesthetic influence, and the emphasis is on the roots of the people prior to 1787, the date of the U.S. Constitution. The authenticity of each room has been ensured by the expertise of the designers, many of whom were born and educated in the respective country. Studying in these rooms creates an appreciation and understanding of America's heterogeneous cultural heritage; nationality committees promote that understanding by sponsoring scholarships, lectures, exhibits, and programs for visitors from abroad.

Cathedral of Learning
University of Pittsburgh
Pittsburgh 15260
412–624–6000

Heinz Memorial Chapel
University of Pittsburgh
Pittsburgh 15260
412–624–4157

Phipps Conservatory
Schenley Park
Pittsburgh 15213
412–622–6914

Civic Arena
Auditorium Place
Pittsburgh 15219
412–642–2062

The center of the building is magnificent, with its four-story Gothic columns and vaulted ceiling. The classrooms line up on all four sides of this central Commons Room. The Chinese Classroom exhibits an ornate painted ceiling with a golden dragon in the center. In the English Classroom you can see items saved from the House of Commons after bombings in 1941, including a fireplace with a monogram of Queen Victoria on it. Coats of arms from a number of English cities are set into stained-glass windows. The German Classroom will please children with its scenes from Grimms' fairytales on stained-glass windows. In the Norwegian Classroom look for the tapestry done in reds and blues; the theme is the biblical story of the five wise and the five foolish virgins. If you are there during December, you will find the rooms decorated to represent each nationality's celebration of Christmas.

Walk across the lawn to the **Heinz Memorial Chapel,** which was fashioned after Sainte Chapelle in France. This French Gothic interdenominational chapel has 73-foot-high stained-glass windows. You can spot hundreds of historical and religious figures in the windows. Special concerts and programs are held in the chapel.

The **Phipps Conservatory** is a two-and-one-half-acre conservatory under glass. A variety of different plant species may be seen in the thirteen sections of the conservatory.

Sports fans will enjoy the $22 million, circular **Civic Arena,** located downtown at Chatham Square. The stainless-steel dome is partly

183

Three Rivers
Stadium
North Shore Drive
Pittsburgh 15212
412–323–5000

Children's Museum
1 Landmarks Square
Allegheny Center
Pittsburgh 15212
412–322–5058

Carnegie Science
Center
One Allegheny
Avenue (North
Side)
Pittsburgh 15212
412–237–3400

Benedum Center
719 Liberty Avenue
Pittsburgh 15222
412–456–2600

Clayton
7227 Reynolds
Pittsburgh 15208
412–371–0606

retractable. The arena houses the Pittsburgh Penguins hockey team. **Three Rivers Stadium** is home to the Pittsburgh Pirates and the Pittsburgh Steelers.

If you have children with you, don't miss the **Children's Museum,** located in the Old Post Office Building. Six areas have been built to encourage hands-on learning for young children.

The newest building in town is quite dramatic; it features a very modern design and is located right on the water. The **Carnegie Science Center** includes four theaters, over 250 hands-on (or feet-on) exhibits swarming with children, a planetarium, and the Omnimax theater. Plan to spend many hours there; your children won't want to leave. There are learning centers for children ages three to six and seven to thirteen, with a limited number allowed inside at one time. Children can pet live animals, work with computers, engage in water play, and avail themselves of a variety of educational toys.

Outside, the USS *Requin,* which was commissioned in 1945, was rebuilt as the first U.S. Navy Radar Picket Submarine in 1946, and saw duty in the Arctic Circle, Atlantic, Caribbean, Mediterranean, and South America, arrived on the scene in September 1990. Visitors can go aboard for a tour to see how men lived and worked there.

You may not be able to keep your mind on the performance when you sit beneath the glittering chandelier set in the gilded, domed ceiling of the **Benedum Center.** The old Stanley Theater, dating from 1928, has become the Benedum, home of the Pittsburgh Ballet Theater, the Pittsburgh Opera, the Civic Light Opera, and the Pittsburgh Dance Council.

Clayton is the Henry Clay Frick estate, which was renovated over a six-year period to the tune of $6 million and opened to the public in September of 1990. Inside the Victorian mansion, where President Theodore Roosevelt lunched in 1902, visitors will see original pieces kept in the family over the years. Visitors walk first into the Carriage House Museum, which has a 1931 Lincoln, a 1902 Spider phaeton, a 1903 country omnibus with white wool seats to protect evening clothes, an 1888 Victoria (which is open and used only in summer), and an 1880 Brougham with mirrors, a shade, map pocket, and bell. The Carriage House Museum houses many automobiles and carriages belonging to the family; our favorite is a handsome 1914 Rolls-Royce Silver Ghost.

Gardeners will want to visit the Greenhouse and stroll through the landscaped grounds. The **Frick Art & Historical Center** is located on six acres within the Henry Clay Frick Estate.

The **Frick Art Museum** is located in an Italian Renaissance building on the estate. The collection includes Flemish, Italian, and French paintings and furnishings. Several paintings dating from the thirteenth century are on display. Look for the Savonnerie rug made for Marie Antoinette and furniture owned by Marie Antoinette and Madame Adelaide, Princess of Orléans. Italian Renaissance bronzes, Russian silver from the seventeenth century, and a Florentine fifteenth-century plaque from the atelier of Andrea della Robbia are in the collection.

> Frick Art & Historical Center
> 7227 Reynolds Street
> Pittsburgh 15208
> 412–371–0606
>
> Fourteenth & Church Streets
> Ambridge
> 412–266–4500

Nearby **Frick Park** offers nature trails, a nature museum, tennis courts, picnic facilities, and a parcourse fitness circuit. Other parks in the city include **Schenley Park,** which has a lake, walking trails, golf, roller skating, ice skating, cross-country skiing, tennis, and baseball. Pittsburgh supports numerous free concerts, as well as drama and special programs in the parks. Ask for a copy of *The Citiparks Guide,* published by the Department of Parks and Recreation, which lists all the performances and special events. For example, the Three Rivers Regatta, Renaissance Fair, Grand Prix boat racing, sternwheeler competitions, skydiving show, hot-air balloon races, and more are held each August.

There are a number of side trips to take from Pittsburgh. Some of them are on the way to Gettysburg, the first stop on Itinerary F.

Old Economy Village

Route 65 heading northwest from Pittsburgh will take you to **Fourteenth & Church Streets.** This village was once the home of a Christian communal society called the Harmonists. Eighteen buildings, dating from 1824, are open and are furnished with pieces belonging to the Harmony Society. Guides are dressed in the period costume worn by the sect. The community was once very prosperous, producing wool, cotton, silk, textiles, and shoes. Its Great House, originally owned and occupied by George Rapp, who was the founder of the village, is a thirty-five–room mansion.

Fort Necessity

Fort Necessity (take Route 51 to Uniontown and Route 40 to the fort)

Fort Necessity
  National Battlefield
Route 40
Farmington 15437
412–329–5512

Ohiopyle State Park
P.O. Box 105
Ohiopyle 15470
724–329–8591

Fallingwater
Route 381
Mill Run 15464
412–329–8501

was the scene of George Washington's first military action in 1754. Virginia's Governor Dinwiddie sent Washington on a difficult assignment, with poor supplies of food, equipment, and weapons. His men were inexperienced and discouraged. The battle at the fort marked the beginning of the French and Indian War. Visitors can tour a reconstructed stockade that encloses a storehouse. **Mount Washington Tavern** is a restored inn, which was frequented by stagecoaches during the nineteenth century. Look for the "coachman's horn," which the driver blew to announce his arrival. He could alert the innkeeper to prepare a hot meal and have drinks waiting on the bar.

Ohiopyle

From Fort Necessity take Route 381 to Ohiopyle and the **Ohiopyle State Park.** The name comes from an Indian name meaning "White Frothy Water." The Youghiogheny River flows through the area, providing whitewater canoeing, a scenic gorge, and Cucumber Falls. Outfitters offer group rafting trips, which include transportation to the river and a promise to hold your car keys safely in case you inadvertently take a swim. The park offers picnicking, a nature center, fishing, boat launching, hiking, and camping. Ohiopyle is also the jumping-off point for the **Laurel Highlands,** a region of Pennsylvania noted for its great natural beauty. Visitors are attracted to this area for hiking and for other recreational pleasures. Ohiopyle State Park is the southern end of the 70-mile **Laurel Highlands Hiking Trail,** which is accessible in a number of places.

Continue on Route 381 to **Fallingwater,** one of Frank Lloyd Wright's spectacular homes. Did you think that the name "Fallingwater" refers only to the waterfall under the home Frank Lloyd Wright designed for Edgar J. Kaufmann? Recently an architectural historian, in writing about the way architects "sign" their work, proposed that Wright used words instead of the usual red tile bearing his initials. The word *Fallingwater* contains his initials—F, L, and W—as well (as the vowel A, the double LL, and the final strong consonant T. Very clever indeed!)

This sandstone house has balconies cantilevered from gigantic boulders and a waterfall below the main terrace. Inside the living room is a glass hatch that may be lifted to reveal a set of steps leading down to the rushing water, thereby cooling the room. As you move up through the house, you will feel drawn out to each terrace, to savor the views and wonderful sounds as the water dances downward.

To the northeast of Falling Water is **Seven Springs**. This year-round resort offers a variety of activities, including golf, tennis, swimming, hiking, and skiing. Skiers of all ages will find hours of fun here. Although it's in a natural snowbowl, Seven Springs also has snowmaking on 95 percent of its slopes. Night skiing is popular on 80 percent of the trails.

Seven Springs
  Mountain Resort
Champion 15622
800–452–2223

Fort Ligonier
Route 30
Ligonier 15658
412–238–9701

Old Bedford Village
Route 220
Bedford 15522
800–622–8055

Ligonier

Fort Ligonier can be reached by following Route 381 and turning west on Route 30. (From Pittsburgh take I–76 to Route 30.) General John Forbes built Fort Ligonier to stand as a base in the attack against the French. Today's full reconstruction of the 1758 to 1766 fort contains barracks and a museum. The parlor of General Arthur St. Clair, a local resident who was very helpful during the war, is in the museum. There are mannequins in the Officer's Mess Building, the Officer's Quarters, and the Supply Room. The town of Ligonier has been restored in eighteenth-century Georgian style. There are Sunday-evening concerts in the bandstand on the square during the summer.

When it's time for a meal, head west on Route 30 to the **Mountain View Inn** (Greensburg; 412–834–5300). (See Inns appendix.)

From Ligonier you can take Route 30 to Bedford for a visit to Old Bedford Village.

Bedford

Old Bedford Village is the reproduction of a village as it would have evolved from 1750 to 1850. Original log cabins, one-room schools, and other structures were moved from their sites and brought here to establish the village. The oldest building is the Biddle House, dating from 1762. It has a double fireplace, with one side for cooking and the other for heat and light. Don't miss the eight-sided school, which was used by Quakers around 1850. Visitors may smell freshly baked cookies from the oven and watch a weaver, blacksmith, broom maker, or carpenter work. Special programs are held throughout the year, including Militia Days in early June.

Bushy Run Battlefield

Johnstown Flood
Museum
Washington &
Walnut Streets
Johnstown 15907
814–539–1889

Community Arts
Center of Cambria
County
1217 Menoher
Boulevard, Route 271
Johnstown 15905
814–255–6513

If you enjoy seeing historic battlefields, take a side trip to **Bushy Run Battlefield.** Take Route 30 west to Jeanette, turn north at Lowry Avenue, then take Route 130 west to Route 993 east. The battlefield (412–527–5584) is 1 mile east of Harrison City. Bushy Run Battlefield was the location of a battle in August 1763 between the Indians and the British, led by Colonel Henry Bouquet. Through careful strategy, Bouquet diverted the Indians, who had stronger forces than he did. This victory prevented the Indians from driving out the British and from capturing Fort Pitt. It marked the turning point in Pontiac's war and decided the territorial fate of the frontier. It also reopened the line of communication and supplies. The museum contains exhibits relating the details of the battle. You may picnic on 183 acres.

Johnstown

For another side trip from Ligonier, take Route 271 into Johnstown for a ride on the **Inclined Plane** (814–536–1816). Look up the unbelievably steep tracks to the top; then drive your car onto the platform and move on up! The structure was built in 1891, after the Great Flood of 1889, as a "lifesaver," to carry people to safety during future floods (which included the 1936 and 1977 devastations).

The **Johnstown Flood Museum,** housed in the former Carnegie Library, tells the tale of the 1889 flood with exhibits, including a giant animated model that shows the path of the flood. You will feel as if you were there on that fateful day in 1889 as the dam broke. Don't miss the collection of articles recovered from the flood. You will see a pinwheel-design quilt that became a lifeline used to pull people from the water into a house. There is also a handkerchief that was found in the pocket of a man who did not survive.

Before you leave Johnstown, stop by the **Community Arts Center of Cambria County,** which is in an 1834 log house. You can stroll through arts and handicraft galleries and attend classes, concerts, and craft fairs there.

Huntingdon

What kind of ears does a train have? (Engineers.) You might hear more of these jokes if you catch an Amtrak train from Johnstown to Altoona. Our jovial conductor kept us entertained during the trip.

Or you can drive from Johnstown to Altoona on Route 219 north and Route 22 east. Then continue east to Huntingdon to see **Lincoln Caverns** and the adjoining Whisper Rocks. The stalactites gleam with crystals, and the formations look like a fairy castle.

| Lincoln Caverns |
| Route 22 |
| Huntingdon 16652 |
| 814–643–0268 |

From Huntingdon take Route 22 to Mount Union, Route 522 to Route 30, and head into Gettysburg. If you are coming from Pittsburgh, take I–70/76 to Route 30 to Gettysburg.

189

ITINERARY F:

South-Central Pennsylvania

VALLEY FORGE NATIONAL HISTORICAL PARK

ITINERARY F

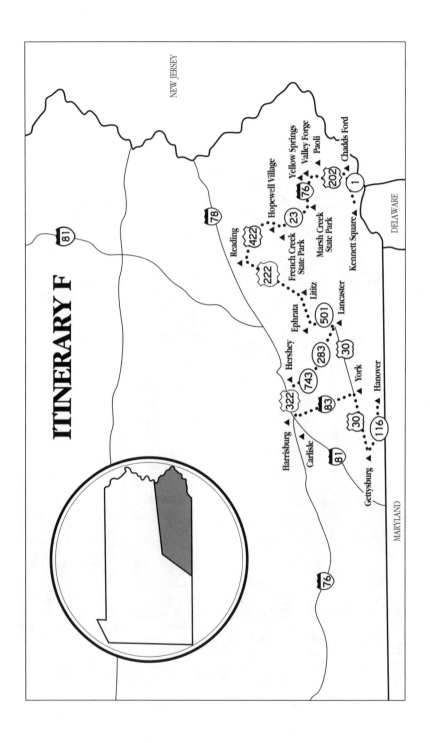

South-Central Pennsylvania

This itinerary can be traveled from the end of Itinerary E eastward or done in reverse from the Philadelphia area westward. The route includes Gettysburg, York, Harrisburg, Hershey, Lancaster, Lititz, Ephrata, Reading, Hopewell Village, Valley Forge, Chadds Ford, and Kennett Square.

❧ *Gettysburg Area* ❧

The Civil War had been waged for two years when Confederate General Robert E. Lee marched into Pennsylvania on June 3, 1863, with 75,000 soldiers from the Army of Northern Virginia. General George G. Meade had 97,000 men ready under the Union flag of the Army of the Potomac. The greatest battle of the Civil War—at Gettysburg—came about by accident.

Before the battle Gettysburg was a peaceful little town, known to few except those who chose to live there. At that time Lee's troops straggled out in a lengthy line running from Chambersburg almost all the way to Gettysburg. He decided to move his soldiers together; Gettysburg seemed to be a convenient location to consolidate them. During this time his soldiers had been garnering supplies from around the area; on July 1, 1863, a group led by General Harry Heth started out toward Gettysburg to find shoes, which they badly needed. On the way they encountered John Buford's cavalry just by chance, and so the battle began.

Eyewitness Billy Bayly and two other young boys were picking raspberries when they were surprised to hear the sound of cannon. They ran to the blacksmith shop and straddled the fence there to watch the fight. As they watched, the Yankee cavalry dismounted and fought hand to hand with the Confederates; then reinforcements arrived, and, when the action got too close for comfort, the boys "skedaddled" out of there.

Much of the fighting on the first day took place around McPherson's barn on McPherson Ridge. John Burns, a Scotsman who lived in Gettysburg, had earlier tried to enlist but was turned away because of his age. At age seventy-two he was still determined to fight, so when the fighting broke out, he took his musket and joined the soldiers heading for the McPherson Farm. When he arrived on the line, some of the soldiers in the 150th Pennsylvania Volunteers gave him one of their more modern muskets in place of his antique firearm. He was wounded several times but kept on fighting—an inspiration to the younger men around him. You can see a statue of John Burns, musket in hand, standing on a boulder on the site of that day's fighting.

By July 2 the armies were a mile apart on parallel ridges. Lee and his Confederate forces were on Seminary Ridge, while Meade and the Union army had dug into Cemetery Ridge. Amazing as it may seem, these two generals who were about to fight each other with such vigor remained on friendly

> Gettysburg National
> Military Park
> Visitors' Center
> Route 134
> Gettysburg 17325

terms after the war. At one point Lee asked Meade why his beard was so gray. Meade replied, "You have to answer for most of it."

Lee advanced first and pushed the Union forces back through Devil's Den, Little Round Top, the Wheatfield, the Peach Orchard, and finally back to Cemetery Ridge. On the second night of battle, the Union army had decided neither to advance nor retreat—but watched preparations for the final assault they knew would come. In fact, they were a perfect target; artillery shells and rifle fire ravished the advancing line. Fewer than 5,000 Confederate soldiers reached Cemetery Ridge.

The Battle of Gettysburg took a tremendous toll on the young men of America—51,000 casualties were recorded. Although the Civil War continued for another two years, the Confederacy never fully reconstituted its army after the mangling at Gettysburg. "The world will little note, nor long remember, what we say here; but it can never forget what they did here." Abraham Lincoln solemnly spoke ten sentences that said it all. On November 19, 1863, the cemetery at Gettysburg was dedicated.

Lincoln's Gettysburg Address

"Fourscore and seven years ago our fathers brought forth upon this continent a new nation . . ."

Gettysburg National Military Park

When you visit Gettysburg National Military Park, be sure to look for the visitors' center entrance. You can get information on both self-guided and guided tours there. Allow two to three hours for a trip around the park by automobile. There are also hiking trails of varying lengths. The well-organized center has many displays and presentations to enhance your visit. Don't miss the electric map, which pinpoints each section of the three-day battle with colored lights. A short walk from the visitors' center, the **Cyclorama Center** features a painting of Pickett's charge by Paul Philippoteaux that is accompanied by a sound and light program in the circular auditorium. You can also see a ten-minute film, *From These Honored Dead,* and view a number of exhibits.

Eisenhower National
Historic Site
Gettysburg 17325
717–334–1124

Lincoln Room
Museum
12 Lincoln Square
Gettysburg 17325
717–334–8188

Lee's Headquarters
401 Buford Avenue
Gettysburg 17325
717–334–3141

While you are in the visitors' center, you can buy bus tickets for the **Eisenhower National Historic Site.** (The tour starts and finishes at the visitors' center.) The tour itself is free; you pay only a nominal sum for the bus. This 230-acre farm was owned by Dwight and Mamie Eisenhower; it was given to the U.S. government in 1967, effective upon their deaths. As you walk through the house, you will see their paintings, gifts given to President Eisenhower, photographs, and their furniture. Look for the ornate marble fireplace in the living room, which was given to them by the White House staff. The Eisenhowers rarely used the living room; they spent their time on the porch, which has one wall of glass and is especially bright and cheerful. The white chairs are contrasted by touches of red; memorabilia from their travels fit into the decor. Ike's easel stands ready for a painting of the view, the card table for a relaxing game, and the television for Mamie's favorite "soaps." You may walk through all of the rooms on the first floor, then proceed to the second floor along the hall to look into the bedrooms and sitting room. Look for oil paintings created by Eisenhower; there are seven in the house.

Take a look at the "bank barn." The cattle and horses lived on the bottom floor; the top floor was a hayloft accessible from the outside by a sloping bank. Don't miss seeing the attractive barbecue area, where Ike loved to grill steaks for his guests. In the garden you will see the "Frisco Bell," which was given to him by the St. Louis–San Francisco Railway Company, and a putting green presented to him by the Professional Golfers Association. Peek into the garage to see the "Surrey with the Fringe on Top," their favorite means of getting around the farm with their guests.

The **Lincoln Room Museum** has a collection of Lincoln memorabilia. Lincoln stayed there in 1863, working on his famous Gettysburg Address in the house. There is a presentation of the Gettysburg Address in stereophonic sound.

Lee's Headquarters is the site of Lee's development of strategy for the battle. Although he usually slept in his tent, just like his men, he slept in this house just before the battle. There are exhibits of both Confederate and Union clothing, and military equipment. The house dates from the 1700s.

The Conflict is a four-section documentary produced by six projectors and stereo soundtracks to reproduce the sights and sounds of the Civil War. During the summer you can also see a fifth film, entitled *Three Days at Gettysburg.*

Gettysburg has a heroine named Jennie Wade. The **Jennie Wade House** was actually the home of her sister, Mrs. Georgia McClellan. Jennie had chosen to stay with her sister, who had had a baby a few days before the battle began. She was baking bread for the family as well as for Union soldiers when a Confederate cannonball zoomed through two doors in the house and hit Jennie in the back. At the time of her death, twenty-year-old Jennie had in her dress over her heart a picture of her childhood sweetheart, Jack Skelly, and a letter confirming his wish to marry her. She never knew that he too had been killed in battle. Jennie was the only Gettysburg civilian to die in the battle; her grave in **Evergreen Cemetery** is marked by a statue and a Union standard that flies around the clock by Congressional Proclamation.

The Conflict
213 Steinwehr Avenue
Gettysburg 17325
717–334–8003

Jennie Wade House
Route 97, Baltimore Street
Gettysburg 17325
717–334–4100

Gettysburg Travel Council
35 Carlisle Street
Gettysburg 17325
717–334–6274

If you are interested in a walking tour of downtown Gettysburg, stop in the **Gettysburg Travel Council** office. You will receive a map with historical data on the Civil War period, and you can pick up a calendar of annual events.

For a special dinner try the historic **Dobbin House** (89 Steinwehr Avenue; 717–334–2100). Reverend Alexander Dobbin built this house in 1776 on 300 acres of land. He established a classical school in his home, where a number of prominent men were educated. Later, in the mid-1800s, runaway slaves hid in a secret crawlspace behind sliding shelves. After the Battle of Gettysburg, the house was used as a hospital for soldiers from both armies. This stone house has 2-foot-thick walls and seven fireplaces. It is furnished with antiques, including four-poster beds with canopies. Diners sit "in bed" for dinner. Waitresses in colonial dress will bring you a "compleat" dinner.

The **Farnsworth House** (401 Baltimore Street; 717–334–8838) dates back to 1810. Some people believe that Jennie Wade was shot from the garret on the top floor. You can dine in a restored dining room or in the garden beside a stream.

The area around Gettysburg is attractive, with farmland and gently rolling hills. You can continue to explore more of the many museums and attractions in Gettysburg or spend time in the country cycling, hiking, or driving on a scenic tour, perhaps to **Mount Newman.** The Gettysburg Travel Council will provide you with details.

Route 30 east will take you right into York. Or you can first take a

Hanover Shoe Farms
Route 116
Hanover 17331
717-637-8931

Historical Society of York County
250 East Market Street
York 17405
717-848-1587

Bonham House
152 East Market Street
York 17405

Golden Plough Tavern
157 West Market Street
York 17405
717-845-2951

side trip to Hanover on Route 116. A third alternative is to skip Hanover and York and go directly to Harrisburg, via Route 15.

Hanover

Hanover Shoe Farms, 2 to 3 miles east of Hanover, claims to be the finest standardbred horse farm in the world because it produces record-breaking trotters and pacers. Several large stallion barns are open. If you can go in April, May, or June, you may be on hand when some of the foals are born.

There is a battle monument in Hanover Square dating from the Battle of Hanover in 1863, just prior to the Battle of Gettysburg.

York

During the fall of 1777, British troops were on the march to Philadelphia, inspiring members of the Continental Congress to flee toward the west to a more secure place for conducting their affairs. They crossed the Susquehanna River and took lodgings in York. From September 30, 1777, to June 27, 1778, York was the national capital. There the Continental Congress adopted the Articles of Confederation that provided a legal national government.

Visit the **Historical Society of York County** to see a museum featuring daily life in York County in a village square; exhibits from the War of 1812 and the Revolutionary War; and a library of books, manuscripts, and historic newspapers. The society sponsors several historic houses. **Bonham House** is decorated in several different periods, including Federal and Victorian. The **Golden Plough Tavern** was built in the 1740s and retains a German style of architecture with William-and-Mary-period furniture. It has now been combined with the **General Gates House,** so you can walk from one to the other. As you walk through the tavern, look for sections exposed to show the original construction. A settee from 1710 still has its original hide. The fireplace has a hole where hot coals could be pushed through to heat the next room. You will see the taproom, where the men sat smoking their pipes and drinking ale.

In this house, where General and Mrs. Gates lived in 1778, Lafayette was instrumental in preventing the ousting of George Washington as chief of the army. The toast he gave to Washington was the signal for the end of the plots to remove him. The guide will tell you about the "soul hole," which Germans believed was important to have in a house; should someone die, the soul could escape quickly and not be trapped in the house. Note the short bed that must have forced sleeping in a semi-sitting position; perhaps the prevalence of respiratory problems caused by dampness and cold made this position more comfortable.

Next door you will see the **Barnett Bobb House,** which contains furniture decorated with a quill dipped in paint. Look for the chest that looks as if it was painted with a corncob.

York is known for its markets, where farm families sell their farm produce as well as Pennsylvania Dutch and German foods. **Central Market House** (34 West Philadelphia Street), **Farmers Market** (380 West Market Street), and **New Eastern Market** (201 Memory Lane) are three to visit.

York Little Theater 27 South Belmont York 17405 717–854–3894
Strand-Capitol Performing Arts Center 50 North George York 17405 717–846–1111
York Symphony Orchestra 13 East Market York 17405 717–852–0550

Cultural offerings include the **York Little Theater,** which presents six drama productions each year, five productions especially for children, and five "Studio Five" productions. The **Strand-Capitol Performing Arts Center** presents a variety of live entertainment, including comedy, big bands, drama, and children's theater. You can also see classic movies there. The **York Symphony Orchestra** is a community orchestra that plays five to seven concerts every year.

Special events in York include a St. Patrick's Day parade, a street fair in May, a Bavarian festival in August, an art festival in August, an agricultural fair in September, an oyster festival in October, a Halloween parade, and a Yuletide festival.

From York I–83 will take you north to Harrisburg.

Carlisle

As a side trip you might want to drive to Carlisle, near the junction of I–81 and I–76, to visit the Carlisle Barracks, located on U.S. 11, 1 mile north of the city. It was once a Revolutionary War forge. In 1777 Hessian soldiers built the magazine and used it to store gunpowder, cannon shot, and small arms. General J.E.B. Stuart's troops burned it just before the Battle of Gettysburg. It was reconstructed and served as the first Indian school in the United States located off the reservation. Today the **Hessian Powder Magazine Museum** offers displays in chronological order, begin-

Carlisle Barracks
U.S. 11
Carlisle 17604
717–245–3152

State Museum of
Pennsylvania
Third & North
Streets
Harrisburg 17105
717–787–4978

Governor's Home
Front & Maclay
Streets
Harrisburg 17105
717–787–1192

ning with the Revolutionary War and including the Civil War and the period when it was used as a school (1879–1918).

⮿ *Harrisburg and Hershey* ⮿

Harrisburg and Hershey offer you glimpses of two eras in the historic development of South-Central Pennsylvania.

Harrisburg

Etienne Brulé first spotted this location in 1615 as he was traveling on the Susquehanna River. In 1710 John Harris opened his trading post there; John Harris, Jr., provided ferry service across the river in 1753. He insisted that the name of the town be changed from Louisbourg to Harrisburg, contingent on selling land to the legislature. Harrisburg became the state capital in 1812, and the **Capitol Building** was begun in 1819. (The State Capitol complex is between North and Walnut Streets, and Third and Sixth Streets.) This Italian Renaissance structure is a work of art, with a dome very much like that of St. Peter's in Rome. The marble staircase imitates the staircase at the Paris Opera. Don't miss the bronze doors and stained-glass windows. George Grey Barnard sculpted the two groups at the central entrance area.

The **State Museum of Pennsylvania** is housed in a circular six-story building, adjacent to the Capitol building. There are exhibits on Indian life, natural history, archaeology, geology, military history, antique cars and carriages, and period furnishings. Don't miss the painting by Rothermel entitled *The Battle of Gettysburg,* which is among the largest framed paintings in the world. A planetarium has scheduled shows.

The **Governor's Home,** planned in Georgian style, was completed in 1968. In 1972 Hurricane Agnes flooded the basement and first floor; the house was then remodeled. It is furnished with period Pennsylvania antiques, including a mahogany cylinder Hepplewhite desk.

In addition to the State Museum, Harrisburg features a number of free attractions, including the Planetarium, the Harrisburg Area Community College Friday Night Film Series, band concerts at Italian Lake, lunchtime concerts at Market Square, and a downtown walking tour.

Special events include the Pennsylvania Farm Show in January, Pennsylvania Relief Show and Sale (featuring crafts and foods) in April, Harrisburg Arts Festival in May, July Fourth Regatta on the Susquehanna, Antique Auto Club of America Fall Meet in October, and several flea markets throughout the year. The Kipona Celebration on Labor Day weekend (*Kipona* means "Summer's End") includes water sports and boating on the Susquehanna, with daily events such as water-skiing and boat and canoe races. There are craft demonstrations and art shows in Riverfront Park, magicians, concerts, a 10-kilometer run, a bicycle race, and more.

Go east to Hershey via Route 322/422.

> Hersheypark
> Information Center
> Hersheypark Drive
> Hershey 17033
> 717-534-3005
>
> Hershey's Chocolate
> World
> Hersheypark Drive
> Hershey 17033
> 717-534-4900

Hershey

Hershey was founded and developed by Milton S. Hershey as a planned community. He built his chocolate factory in 1903, and the town grew around it. If you loved *Charlie and the Chocolate Factory* or if you are a confirmed "chocoholic," you will feel at home in Hershey. The streets have names like Chocolate Avenue and Cocoa Avenue, and the streetlights are shaped like candy kisses. On the other hand, if all of this turns you off, with images of modern "fun" parks and artificial tourist traps, take a second look. We first entered Hershey with some skepticism and emerged with a great deal of respect for the vision of the founder and the institutions his ideas created. Here is a "new town" with its own stamp and integrity, dreamt and built long before the end of the Second World War spawned many other "fun" parks in America and Europe.

Stop in the information center at the entrance to Hersheypark, where you can pick up a map of the area to plan your day. Right next door is **Hershey's Chocolate World,** which is free of charge. In plush automatic vehicles you will ride by artistic exhibits of typical Pennsylvania Dutch farms and cacao tree plantations in Africa and watch the process of turning the raw material into chocolate bars. Don't panic as you begin the journey through a roasting oven—it gets warm but not roasting temperature. And just see if you can resist buying a gigantic chocolate chip cookie after you emerge!

Hersheypark offers areas depicting themes from Pennsylvania Dutch, German, and English origins. Anglophiles will enjoy Tudor Square, where buildings imitate that architectural style right down to the leaded-glass windows. Carousel Circle features an antique carousel, built in 1919,

Hersheypark
Herseypark Drive
Hershey 17033
717–534–3916

Hershey Museum
Hersheypark
Hershey 17033
717–534–3439

ZooAmerica
Hersheypark
Hershey 17033
717–534–3860

where music is provided by the original Wurlitzer band organ. The Pennsylvania Dutch place contains crafts such as pottery, candle-making, and leather-work, silversmiths, and a blacksmith. Typical Pennsylvania Dutch foods and gifts are sold by staff in costume.

How would your children like to engage in "ball crawling"? An area called Kid Stuff has 40,000 balls to crawl in, a tubular sliding board, teeter-totter horses, a fairly-tale teller, and a Hound Dog Jamboree. A dolphin and sea lion show is presented in a circular theater around a water tank. For the feeling of being in Germany, visit Rhine Lane, where painted walls, geraniums flowing from window boxes, and guides in German costume enhance the shops.

The **Hershey Museum,** near the visitors' center, has remarkable collections. For a peek into a typical Pennsylvania German household, look at the reconstructed home of Adam Danner, who was both a weaver and a farmer. This house was built inside the museum from lists of his household belongings and includes a weaver's loom and various kinds of equipment used in the early 1800s. The Apostolic Clock is one of the most popular exhibits in the museum. This 1878 clock shows the procession of the apostles before Christ; he comes out of one door and they all file by, turning to him, except for Judas. Time, Manhood, Old Age, and Death are also represented here.

ZooAmerica houses more than 200 mammals, reptiles, fowl, and fish within five distinctive regions. The evergreen forests planted in "North Woods" feature three peregrine falcons, a great horned owl, a black bear, and a timber wolf. "Gentle Woodlands" duplicates the fields and wooded areas of Eastern North America with raccoon, otters, wild turkey, bobcats, and deer roaming among wildflowers, flowering dogwood, mountain laurel, hemlock, and red oak. The Southern Florida Everglades are represented in "Grassy Waters," where you can see alligators, long-legged birds, and fish. "Big Sky Country" has been landscaped to represent the Western Grasslands and Rocky Mountains. Don't miss the antics of the prairie dogs, who are on constant show; you also will see a bison, a puma, and a golden eagle. In the "Cactus Community" you will enter a semidark corridor to see nocturnal animals awake and active. These creatures include tarantulas, gila monsters, sidewinders, ringtails, and spotted skunk.

Hersheypark Arena is home to the Hershey Bears of the American Hockey League. Basketball games are played there; ice-skating shows and entertainers come on tour. The **Hersheypark Stadium** hosts college and high-school football, rodeos, concerts, and special sports events. Golf is very popular in Hershey; there are seventy-two holes on five courses, and three of them are championship-level courses.

Milton Hershey
School
Route 322
Hershey 17033
717–534–3500

Hershey Gardens
Hersheypark Drive
Hershey 17033
717–534–3439

The **Milton Hershey School,** founded in 1909, provides education for children who have lost one or both parents. Hershey believed that all students should learn a vocational skill before graduation, that they should have religious training, and that they should have experience working on a farm. He also insisted that every graduate should be given $100 as he or she left school. This may be related to the story told about his own experience as a young man. He was trying to find a job in Denver when he saw a sign, BOY WANTED. After he had entered the room, he realized that the boys there were being "railroaded" to a mining camp as captives. He pulled out a gun, demanded to be released from the locked room, and was lucky enough to escape. Because he had $100 in his pocket, he was not destitute; he felt both relieved for himself and disturbed about the captives inside, who were down on their luck without any means of remedy.

Don't miss the **Hershey Gardens,** which opened in 1937 with just roses and now display thousands of flowers on twenty-three rolling acres. Follow the path through twelve areas, which bloom at different times of the year. There are six theme gardens: English Formal Garden, Italian Garden, Fountain Garden (don't miss the statue of the little boy holding a boot with water spurting from a hole in it), Colonial Perennial Garden, Japanese Garden, and Rock Garden. The Colonial Garden is especially attractive; much of the information about plant species for this garden was discovered in the garden records kept by Thomas Jefferson. The garden maintains collections of many different trees and shrubs all year. If you come during spring, summer, or fall, you can expect to see tulips, dogwood, azaleas, magnolias, and flowering cherries in April and May; rhododendrons, viburnum, irises, and peonies in late May and June; roses from June to October; daylilies, herbs, and annuals in July and August; and chrysanthemums in September and October. Bird-watchers will see a variety of birds, including warblers and hummingbirds, among the more than forty species that have been spotted there.

Hotel Hershey (800–533–3131), an elegant, Mediterranean-style building, was built in 1932 from a picture on a postcard given to the architect by Mr. Hershey. Enjoy the reflecting pool and formal gardens, the fountain lobby, and the quiet elegance of this hotel on a hill. It has an ambience all its own, one that seems to hold its place without being pretentious in this town of unique institutions. You can enjoy lunch or dinner there, as well as spend the night. Both Hotel Hershey and **Hershey Lodge and Convention Center** (800–533–3131) offer special rates for getaway weekends. (See Inns appendix.)

From Hershey take Route 743 south and Route 283 to Lancaster, the first town to see in the Pennsylvania Dutch region.

⮞ *Pennsylvania Dutch Region* ⮞

Beginning in 1727 the Amish, also known as the "plain people," emigrated from Europe to find freedom from persecution. The Pennsylvania Dutch region is a fascinating place to visit because of what you can learn about the Amish people and their way of life.

Because the Amish were persecuted in Germany, they don't wear anything of a military nature. They do not wear buttons, because military uniforms have brass buttons. Pockets are removed from their shirts. They wear suspenders (belts are considered too modern), black shoes, and broad-brimmed hats. Men may wear a beard after they are married. Small girls can have buttons and dresses in blue, green, purple (or pink, under age six). Women wear the same-colored dresses with a black apron. Single girls wear a white apron on Sundays. Women's dresses are fastened with about thirty pins. When they marry, they take off the white aprons and do not wear them again until they die; when someone in the family dies, they wear black dresses. Women part their hair in the middle and pull it back into a bun, covering the hair with a white organdy prayer veil or a black bonnet. Children may play with dolls as long as certain restrictions are observed. In earlier days dolls did not have faces; now, commercially made dolls are acceptable if the original clothing is replaced by Amish clothing.

The Amish are well-known for their superior farming results; they work very hard to plan and produce their crops as well as keep up with new techniques of soil conservation. The typical farmer tills about sixty acres of grain, alfalfa, corn, and tobacco. (The usual cash crop is tobacco.) He uses horse-drawn equipment that he laboriously repairs and rebuilds. He grows almost everything the family needs. Dairy herds are found on most farms. Any profits are put right back into the farm, because frugality is a virtue. As you drive past their farms, you will see that there are no electric lines leading into their homes; they do not use electricity; nor do they own telephones. Yet the first-time visitor is likely to be amazed by the apparent prosperity of these small, "uneconomical" farms in splendid repair, with huge barns clustered together on tiny parcels of land like the houses of a village. Sixty acres would not support a single family in Iowa or Nebraska, but here they sustain extended families. Within each Amish house is a room reserved for church services. Amish families in the district take turns having services in their homes. The meal is provided by the host family and consists of sandwiches, salads, and hot coffee. Men and boys eat first; women and girls, afterward. Church services take place from 8:00 A.M. until noon, using the Martin Luther Bible as well as the King James version. Interpretation of the Bible is literal; they accept the words of the Bible by faith. The Amish do not believe in infant baptism. They wait until the child is at least fourteen to ensure that he understands the full meaning of commitment. Anyone may choose to leave the faith before that time, but if one chooses to leave after baptism, he is shunned for life by the community. The Amish believe in a close brotherhood and will gather to help each other when needed. In fact, they do not carry insurance against natural disasters; after tornadoes or floods, they will bring food to neighbors and get to work rebuilding their barns and houses.

Weddings are held in November on Tuesdays or Thursdays; November is the least busy month for the men, and Tuesdays or Thursdays are the least busy days for the women. The guests bring dishes of food to the wedding, but gifts are given later. The couple will spend the first night in the home of the bride's parents, then will honeymoon until March, spending one night with each of the wedding guests and receiving gifts at that time. They receive two gifts from each wedding guest: The man receives farming equipment or animals, and the woman gets something she can use in her home. In March they settle into their own house and farm, given to them by the groom's parents. The bride's parents give them furniture and perhaps a dairy herd.

No motorist can be unaware of the buggies in this part of Pennsylvania, because they have their own marked highway lane, but the uninitiated may miss the meaning of the type of black buggy they see. Unmarried Amish ride in an open "courting" buggy; no chaperone is needed, as anyone can see what is going on! Married couples have a closed buggy, designed in a rectangular shape with glass in front. Both types of buggies are graceful and well sprung, with contours fitted to the human body that no modern automobile can match.

Lancaster

Stop in the **Visitors' Information Center** located just off the Route

Visitors' Information Center
501 Greenfield Road
Lancaster 17604
717–299–8901 or
800–723–8824

Lancaster Walking Tour
100 South Queen Street
Lancaster 17604
717–392–1776

Heritage Center of Lancaster County
Penn Square
King & Queen Streets
Lancaster 17604
717–299–6440

Wheatland
1120 Marietta Avenue
Lancaster 17604
717–392–8721

Lancaster Central Market
Penn Square
Lancaster

30 bypass east of Lancaster. There you can see a film, *The Lancaster Experience,* that will give you information about the Amish people and their way of life.

Downtown Lancaster has enough historical buildings and cobblestone courtyards dating from the days of the Continental Congress to give the visitor a strong feeling of the past. The **Lancaster Walking Tour** includes an audiovisual presentation and a ninety-minute tour with costumed guide. The tour covers a 6-block area and fifty sites.

The **Heritage Center of Lancaster County** has a collection of household furnishings, clocks, pewter, silver, samplers, rifles, and various crafts typical of the area.

Wheatland was the residence of President James Buchanan. He bought the mansion in 1848 and used it during his presidential campaign. Guests were entertained there by his niece and "First Lady" Harriet Lane. The building is Federal in style, with Empire pieces in the dining room and Victorian furniture in the parlor. Look for the large porcelain Japanese goldfish bowl and the zinc-lined tub.

Lancaster Central Market is the oldest operating market in the country. Andrew Hamilton arranged for land for a market in 1730, and in 1742 King George II proclaimed the site as the Central Market. You'll find fruits, vegetables, cheese, poultry, meat, seafood, and flowers—all ready to be taken home.

Did you know that the Conestoga wagon was first used on the turnpike between Lancaster and Philadelphia? This type of large, four-wheeled wagon was usually drawn by either four or six Conestoga horses. The wagon was a boat-shaped bedframe made from white oak, with poplar boards for the floor. It was made with a sag in the middle, which distributed the weight from the end gates—a useful feature for rolling hills. Hoops were attached to the side boards and then covered with a white canvas or homespun top. The axles, hubs, and wheels needed to be sturdy for use over rough roads. One of the most important items taken on a trip was an iron jack, capable of raising loads weighing many tons. The wagons carried a set of bells made of brass or iron. If you got stuck in the mud, you had to wait until someone came along to help; then you had to give him a set of bells. When you arrived in town "with bells on," it meant that you had not had trouble on the road; but if you came without bells, you were in disgrace. The drivers led a rough life, sometimes carrying brass knuckles or a blackjack to deal with problems. They often smoked "stogies," cigars that were supposed to keep the dust out of their throats. Sometimes the drivers would pick up a little boy to help, and he would run and hop onto the "running board." On these wagons there was actually a shoe on the brake—hence the name "brake shoe." You can see Conestoga wagons in various museums around the county.

Landis Valley
  Museum
2451 Kissel Hill Road
Lancaster 17604
717–569–0401

Hans Herr House
1849 Hans Herr Drive
Lancaster 17604
717–464–4438

Special events in the Lancaster area include an antiques show in March; sheepshearing in April; an old-fashioned country hoe-down in May; a woodcarving show in June; craft days and a country fair in July; a carriage, sleigh, and antique auction in August; Harvest Days and Octoberfest in October; and various events during the Christmas season.

Head north from Lancaster on Route 501 to Route 272 to the **Landis Valley Museum.** Henry and George Landis pulled together the implements, tools, and furnishings of various eras and established them in appropriate buildings to create this museum of rural life and culture. The museum is divided into three chronological areas, which cover the time span from the colonial period to the end of the nineteenth century. The first area centers on a settler's farmstead of 1750 to 1800. It is a treat to stroll into this peaceful setting on a sunny summer day and watch the animals walking around the yard. The farm has a typical Pennsylvania "bank barn"; you get to the top level by walking up a bank at the back; the livestock live in the lower level. Walk into the settler's cabin to see a costumed guide weaving a basket or engaged in some other task. The second area is built around a Federal farmstead depicting the 1815 period, with an adjoining "grandmother's" house. The third area has been designed as a typical village crossroads of the 1825 to 1900 period. It includes craft buildings, a tavern, and a hotel. Don't miss the museum and its variety of exhibits. A group of women were quilting when we were there. The museum hosts special programs, including the Harvest Festival in October; crafts, seminars, workshops, and an institute in June; a country picnic day in August; and a Christmas program with a candlelit tour in December.

The **Hans Herr House** dates from 1719. It is the oldest building in Lancaster County and also the oldest Mennonite meetinghouse in America. Andrew Wyeth is a descendant of Hans Herr, and you may have seen this medieval-style stone house in some of his paintings. The house has been restored and furnished. You'll find interpreters working at their tasks, such as cooking at the gigantic fireplace, where pots hang from an iron crane. You'll see a collection of various utensils standing on the hearth, including a toaster, a waffle iron, and a roaster that was turned with a crank. Or maybe the cook will have trussed a chicken and hung it over the fire, to be twirled around whenever she goes by.

Lititz

Return to Route 501 and head north to Lititz, settled in 1743 by Moravians who named the town for their hometown in Bohemia. Take a walk along Main Street to see eighteenth-century homes that are still lived in today. Although most of the buildings are not open to the public, the **Johannes Mueller House** is the home of the **Lititz Historical Foundation,** where you can get information on the town.

Across the street is the **Moravian Church Square;** you can visit the **Brethren's House,** by appointment, to see the collection of church archives. **Linden Hall,** one of the two oldest girls' schools in the country, is located in this square.

From Linden Hall cross the street again for a stop in the **Sturgis Pretzel House,** where Julius Sturgis made the first pretzels. If you love soft pretzels, you won't want to miss this stop; you can even help twist some pretzels!

Ephrata

From Lititz take Route 772 and look for signs to Ephrata, where you can visit the **Ephrata Cloister.** This eighteenth-century German Protestant monastic group cultivated choral music known as *Vorspiel*—musical drama (presented today by performers) that will give you an idea of the way of life in this communal settlement. The **Pennsylvania Historical and Museum Commission** now runs the Ephrata Cloister; you can tour the grounds as well as buy tickets for the Vorspiel. The settlement was founded by Conrad Beissel, a German Seventh-Day Baptist. He led a hermit's life and then gathered a group of celibate recluses, both male and female. Besides a male order and a female order, there was a third order, that of householders. These married men and women lived in the community, worshiped there, and supported the work of the Cloisters. They believed in a life of simplicity and self-denial. Because they baptized converts in the river, they were sometimes called the "Seventh-Day Dunkers." These people were well-known for their art, music, and their calligraphy, called *Fraktur*. This term describes the printing on eighteenth- and nineteenth-century colorfully painted or printed watercolor documents common in their German community. The letters in these documents look "fractured." The collections include writing exercises, bookmarks, birth and baptismal certificates, marriage certificates, and valentines.

Ephrata Cloister
632 West Main Street
Ephrata 17522
717-733-6600

The Cloister Press published a great many books, including the *Martyrs Mirror* for the Mennonites in 1748. With 1,200 pages, this book was the largest to be printed in America during the colonial period. As you tour the cloister, you will have to bend your head to enter each room and move single-file through the very narrow halls. Don't miss seeing the narrow wooden beds with wooden blocks for pillows! The society was closed in 1934, partly as a result of diminished membership.

As you travel around Pennsylvania Dutch country, you will have the opportunity to taste wine at a number of wineries, sample wares from farmers' markets, and have a meal in one of the fine restaurants that feature typical food of the area. For family-style dining head for **Groff's Farm** (650 Pinkerton Road, Mount Joy; 717–653–2048).

Tucked back on a wooded hillside between Lititz and Ephrata you will find the **Log Cabin** (11 Lehoy Forest Drive, Leola; 717–626–1181). During Prohibition, liquor was hidden under the wooden booths in the front room. You will need local directions to find it because it once was a hideaway. On the way you will pass through the Rose Hill covered bridge; did you know that a kiss exchanged on the bridge will bring good luck? These "kissing bridges" are also called "wishing bridges," so if you are alone when you cross, just make a wish.

In case you have been wondering about the hex signs you have seen on barns in the Pennsylvania Dutch region, there seems to be a difference of opinion as to their significance. Some people stoutly claim that they were used just for decoration; others maintain that they would keep lightning from striking; and still others report that the signs were used as a fire mark for insurance purposes. No matter which theory you espouse, it is fun to look for new shapes and patterns as you travel around the area.

From Ephrata head north toward Reading via Route 222. Along the way you will pass many large barns with hex signs on them.

Reading

The area south of Reading is now "John Updike" country. There are no landmarks to guide you, but Updike set a number of his early novels in this area where he grew up. **Shillington** is 3 miles south of Reading, between it and Plowville; in Updike's books "Olinger" is between Alton (or

| Hopewell Furnace |
| National Historic |
| Site |
| Route 345 |
| Birdsboro 19508 |
| 610–582–8773 |

Brewer in the Rabbit novels) and Firetown. If you enjoyed *The Centaur,* you will probably recognize the high school where John's father, Wesley Updike, taught mathematics. John was editor of the high school newspaper; old copies of his teenage work are kept in a vault in the new high school across the road.

If you head south on Route 222 from Reading (this route is called Lancaster Avenue here), you will come to a building called **Mifflin Plaza.** The words *Shillington School* are engraved in the stone at the top; John Updike attended this elementary school. The **Town Hall,** a red-brick building, is also still there. From the Town Hall turn onto Route 724; 2 blocks down you will see **177 Philadelphia Avenue,** where Updike lived until he was thirteen years old. The Updikes planted the dogwood tree there when John was born. Head south on Route 10 to Plowville, where the **Robeson Lutheran Church** stands; it was built by Updike's grandfather, among others. His father and all of his grandparents are buried there.

Reading is a major center for factory outlet stores. As you enter town, you will see numerous signs for the factory outlets. Pick up a map and brochure in the first store you enter.

Hopewell Village

Take Route 422 and Route 345 from Reading to **Hopewell Furnace National Historic Site.** The National Park Service has completely restored the original village surrounding **Hopewell Furnace.** This village is an authentic example of eighteenth- and nineteenth-century iron-making villages.

Mark Bird developed Hopewell Furnace in 1771 on French Creek. Four essential natural resources made the location a good one for an iron furnace: fast-flowing water to turn the waterwheel and provide mechanical power for the bellows; a supply of limestone; many hardwood trees to be cut and burned into charcoal to fuel the furnace; and easily mined iron ore near the surface of the earth. Mr. Bird paid his employees good wages, and by the time of the American Revolution, the village was making skillets, pots, pans, stoves, and pig iron. During the Revolution Hopewell Furnace produced cannon, shot, and shells. Mark Bird commanded the second battalion of Berks County Militia and also bought uniforms, tents, and provisions for 300 men. In 1778 he sent a thousand barrels of flour down the Schuylkill River to Valley Forge to feed Washington's starving men. Unfortunately, Mark Bird fell deeper and deeper into debt during the war; in 1788 he lost Hopewell Furnace. A number of other owners tried to make the furnace prosper, but by 1808 the furnace was closed again. In

1816 it was fired once more because the iron industry was booming. By 1820 there were more than 150 employees, and the village was thriving. Five years later the Schuylkill Canal opened, so the wagons did not need to travel as far; the canal increased the range for Hopewell products to New York and Boston. In 1838 the Reading Railroad further increased the customers for Hopewell. Wagons brought in goods from Reading, Wilmington, and Philadelphia and took out iron products. But as the middle of the century approached, new technologies for iron-making began to make these older furnaces obsolete. In 1853 Hopewell built an anthracite furnace, but finally Hopewell closed in 1883.

The "Big House" was the center of activity for the village; sometimes thirty people lived there, along with the ironmaster and his family. Visiting businessmen came to sell or buy; because the village was so remote, they were always invited to stay overnight. The villagers gathered in the house for parties, marriages, deaths, and other occasions. The ironmaster himself was a key figure in the community; he had to be an expert in personnel, technology, production, and transportation control, as well as a salesman, expeditor, currency expert, marketing analyst, credit manager, bill collector, purchasing agent, investment counselor, and bookkeeper. This heavy load was shared with the company clerk, who also lived in the Big House. The clerk spent all of his time in the village store, where he was the storekeeper and the furnace paymaster. Most village workers were not paid in cash, but instead they charged their purchases against their earnings. Many of the men who worked in Hopewell were skilled workers, including the founder, who was responsible for producing high-quality iron; the molder, who poured the liquid iron into molds; and the blacksmith, who made mine and furnace tools and repaired the machinery. Unskilled labor included the woodcutters, colliers, and miners. Men worked in twelve-hour shifts to tend the furnace when it was in blast.

Stop in the visitors' center for an audiovisual program on iron making and the village during its heyday. As you walk around the village, you will see a demonstration of the charcoal-making process, which shows all of the layers added to the conical pile. It took almost four days to complete the process; a good collier would get thirty-five to forty bushels of charcoal per cord of wood. Walk into the furnace building, look at the giant waterwheel, and listen to its slap-slap-slap as it turns. You can visit tenant houses, barns, the blacksmith shop, the office store, and the Big House.

There are several state parks in the area where you can stop for recreation or for a picnic lunch. **French Creek** (adjacent to Hopewell Village) offers picnic facilities; swimming in a pool; a nature center and interpretive trails; fishing; boat mooring, launching, and rental; hiking trails;

| Gardens of Japan |
| Charlestown Road |
| Malvern 19355 |
| 610-933-6916 |

horseback riding trails; and camping. During the winter you can skate, ice-fish, cross-country ski, and use the snowmobile trails. **Marsh Creek** (south of French Creek near I–76) provides picnic facilities; swimming in a pool; fishing; boat mooring, launching, and rental; hiking trails; horseback riding trails; ice skating; and ice-fishing. **Ridley Creek** (east of West Chester) offers picnicking, a nature center and interpretive trails, hiking trails, horseback riding trails, cycling, and cross-country skiing.

Retrace your steps back to Route 23 and head for Phoenixville. From Phoenixville follow Nuff Road; turn at the light at Fountain Inn on Bridge Road, which becomes Charlestown Road, and continue until you reach **Swiss Pines,** to see the **Gardens of Japan.** The teahouse was designed by Katsuo Saito. Stone lanterns decorate the grounds, which include a stone garden, waterfalls, and a variety of trees and flowering shrubs.

Yellow Springs

You may want to drive along Yellow Springs Road to **The Yellow Springs Inn** (610–827–7477). We have friends who go there every Sunday night for dinner. The seafood entrees are a specialty. Once a colonial-period health resort, this building served as a Revolutionary War hospital, a Civil War hospital, an orphanage, and a summer campus for the Pennsylvania Academy of the Fine Arts.

Continue on Route 422 or Route 23 to signs for Valley Forge.

Valley Forge

Begin your tour at the visitors' center, where you can view an audiovisual presentation on the events of 1777 and 1778. And yes, George Washington really did sleep here! You will see his canvas tent, 53 feet in circumference, which was used as his office and his bedroom. Information on the park is available in the center; you can take a self-guided tour or a bus tour with a taped narration, which you can leave and rejoin as you wish.

Had Washington had his way, the troops would have spent that winter of 1777 to 1778 in Wilmington, Delaware, where equipment and supplies could be brought by water and the men could be housed comfortably. The Pennsylvania legislature, however, demanded that the troops remain out in the country to prevent British foraging parties from ransacking homes and villages. Washington responded to the legislature that it was easy from their vantage point, in their warm and comfortable homes, to send his men out into the cold, seemingly with little pity; Washington knew how miserable they would be and felt sorry for them.

Accounts written by men on the march describe the snow and cold, the lack of food, and their fatigue and utter despair. As Washington rode beside a group of men without shoes, he asked the colonel why he had not provided them; he was told that the supplies had run out. The outlook was bleak when the troops arrived at Valley Forge, with its few stone houses and the ruins of an old sawmill. They went to sleep by their campfires, too tired to put up tents. Ironically, the next day was proclaimed Thanksgiving; they received half a gill of rice with a little vinegar to ward off scurvy.

> Valley Forge Visitors' Center
> Route 23 & Outer Line Drive
> Valley Forge 19481
> 610-783-1077

The priorities of the winter encampment were to rest the troops, encourage them to stay the winter, and then train them. They built log houses 14 to 16 feet in length and half as wide, each with a fireplace and bunks. As the winter progressed, many men died and many more deserted and returned home. Other men learned, and what's more, gained confidence from their new skills, which raised their morale.

As you progress along your tour, you will first see **Muhlenberg Brigade,** where the militia defended the outer line of the area. The **Memorial Arch,** dedicated in 1917, will almost make you think you are in Paris viewing the Arc de Triomphe. General Anthony Wayne's statue is made of bronze; he is seated on a horse facing the direction of his own home. A local resident told us a story about Wayne, who was sometimes known as "Mad Anthony Wayne." On his way home from fighting Indians in the Northwest Territory, Wayne died in Erie (this is a very eerie story!); his son, Isaac, came about thirteen years later to recover his father's bones from Presque Isle. When they unearthed the body, it was completely intact. Isaac had the surgeon boil the body and bury the remains on the grounds; the bones were taken home. But because the roads were very bumpy, the bones kept falling out of the box. So every January 1 General Wayne gets on his horse Nancy and goes out looking for his bones.

Can you manage another Wayne story? Hannah Wayne, who lived in the Wayne mansion in the 1860s, went up to the attic to get something, carrying a candle with her to light the way. She got caught on the opening of the attic door; the flame ignited her clothing and set her on fire. She tried to kick out a window to get the attention of people outside the house. The women who were out in the garden heard her screams, but by the time they reached her it was too late. But the men in the fields never heard her at all. Later, during a dinner in the 1960s when the house was

Museum of the
Valley Forge
Historical
  Society
Valley Forge 19481
610–783–0535

Wharton Esherik
  Studio
P.O. Box 595
Paoli 19301
610–644–5822

being restored, both men and women were sitting around the dining table when the women heard screaming from the attic and the crashing of glass; the men did not hear a thing.

The **Isaac Potts House** was Washington's headquarters. The **Dewees House** and adjacent huts for his lifeguards are also in this particular group of buildings. Nearby Redoubt 3 and 4 are the sites of the earthenworks, where cannons were placed in the indentation in the center, with men behind to load and fire them. **Artillery Park** contains a concentration of cannon; artillery was stored there, ready for deployment where needed. **General James Varnum's Quarters** were in an early-eighteenth-century farmhouse that looks down on the **Grand Parade. Washington Memorial Chapel** contains stained-glass windows tracing the founding of our country. Look up to see forty-eight ceiling sections inscribed with the states' arms. The bell tower contains a fifty-eight-bell carillon. The **Museum of the Valley Forge Historical Society,** located adjacent to the chapel, contains a collection of articles saved from the terrible winter of 1777. William Trego's famous painting, *The March to Valley Forge,* is in the museum.

During the year Valley Forge holds four special events: one on Washington's Birthday weekend (he celebrated his forty-sixth birthday there), one on December 19 to honor the Continental army, one on May 6 when the French joined the American side, and one on June 19 to celebrate the climactic moment when the army broke camp and charged after the British. Free driving tours are available. Call 610–834–1550.

If you're ready for lunch or dinner, try the **Kennedy-Supplee Mansion** (Route 23; 610–337–3777), a restored 1852 mansion run by Valley Forge. It is elegant, with chandeliers, silver, and bone china.

Paoli

From Valley Forge head south on Route 252 to Paoli. The **Wharton Esherick Studio** is located in Esherick's home, in a lovely woodland setting up on a hill. Esherick was an artist, sculptor, and furniture craftsman who did his most notable work in the early 1900s. You can't help but notice the unusual lines of his garage (none are straight). The hexagonal building in three parts features dovetailed corners with a curved base, and the studio has to be seen to be believed. Inside the studio the visitor is confronted with a variety of Esherick's work—each piece distinctive and unusual. Favorites include a blue horse, a sandstone pelican, Winnie-the-Pooh, a dancer in two pieces, and a spiral pole. Although Esherick began as a painter, he quickly moved into making his own furniture as well. Two desks have slots for papers; a tog-

| Chaddsford Winery |
| Route 1 |
| Chadds Ford 19317 |
| 610–388–6221 |

gle "boomerang" mechanism to open the doors, drawers, and top, which pull out on runners; and a light that turns on when the desk is opened. His three-legged stool was very popular among his clients. The studio contains his own design for hinges, andirons, carved doors, copper sinks, steps, and a special row of coat pegs caricaturing each of the workmen. The stair rail going upstairs is really a mastodon tusk.

❧ *Brandywine Valley* ❧

The Brandywine Valley begins along the banks of the meandering Brandywine River in southeastern Pennsylvania and ends in confluence with the Delaware River at Wilmington. Rich in pleasant, rolling landscape, the valley attracted settlers in colonial times. Industrialists who wanted to use its water power, people who came later to build country estates, and painters who captured the charm of the valley on canvas have left their mark on this lovely valley.

Chadds Ford

From Valley Forge follow signs to Route 202 south and proceed to Route 1 to Chadds Ford. Shoppers will enjoy the village shops, which sell stained glass, antiques, china, bakery goods, Wyeth reproductions, carvings of bears, general-store goods, silver, dried flower arrangements, fudge, and pottery. The **Chadds Ford Inn** (610–388–7361) is a pleasant place for a meal. Built for Francis Chadsey in the early 1700s as a home, it was later used by his son, John, as a tavern. John's nephew, Joseph Davis, entertained American officers there just before the Battle of Chadds Ford on September 11, 1777.

Or try the gourmet **Pace One Restaurant and Inn** (Thornton and Gleus Mills Road; 610–459–3702). They offer imaginative cuisine for lunch, dinner, and Sunday brunch in a 1740 stone barn. (See Inns appendix.)

You can visit **Chaddsford Winery,** located across the river from the Brandywine River Museum. Watch the process of wine making from grape crushing through fermentation and bottling. The owner did careful

| Brandywine |
| Battlefield |
| Chadds Ford 19317 |
| 610–459–3342 |

research to find the right grapes to produce full-bodied and earthy serious reds and a light and fresh spring wine, like a Vouvray.

If you come during September, you can participate in Chadds Ford Days. This special weekend features colonial craftsmen, art, country rides and games, antiques, and lots of food. It is held in a meadow at the edge of town.

Brandywine Battlefield is the site of the battle between George Washington's soldiers and the British in September 1777. Stop in the visitors' center to see a slide narration and exhibits. You can visit the farmhouse, owned by Gideon Gilpin, that was used by General Marquis de Lafayette. It is half-timbered, with rubble construction. This is a typical Penn-plan house: two rooms on the first floor and two on the second. A carriage used by Lafayette is on display. Next door is the reconstructed house used by General Washington; it was owned by Benjamin Ring. Washington stayed there for two nights before the battle.

Before the battle Washington's men were stationed along the east side of Brandywine Creek from Pyle's Ford, south of Chadds Ford, to Buffington's Ford toward the north. Under cover of fog the British began marching toward the American troops, pausing for a wine party at Jeffery's Ford on the way. Unfortunately, Washington did not receive enough accurate information about troop movements, so the British had the advantage. The American militia fought valiantly and were able to slow the British advance—they pushed them back many times—but eventually had to admit defeat. Although victorious, British General William Howe was not able to crush the Americans completely. Washington told Congress, "Notwithstanding the misfortune of the day, I am happy to find the troops in good spirits; and I hope another time we shall compensate for the losses now sustained."

If you're ready for a day of canoeing on the lovely winding Brandywine, call **Northbrook Canoe Company** (610–793–2279 or 793–1553) and find out about the various places upstream where you can begin your paddle, ending up at Northbrook. It is also possible to paddle south from Northbrook and be picked up at the designated spot. You can canoe for an hour or all day if you wish.

The **Brandywine River Museum** is housed in Hoffman's Mill, a gristmill constructed in 1864. When it faced extinction at auction in 1967, local residents formed the Brandywine Conservancy, which bought the mill. The group then spearheaded a funding program in 1968 to restore the building and turn the interior into a sparkling new art gallery. This was a $3.6-million project. A new wing is striking, with its twin turrets and glass tower.

Large windows provide views of the river from several different angles. A restaurant takes up a floor of the glass-walled tower. Take a look at the remarkable lighting, which allows the natural light to focus on the paintings and statues in the gallery. If you are there during the Christmas season, you will see the model

<table>
<tr><td>Brandywine River Museum
Route 1, west of Route 100
Chadds Ford 19317
610–388–2700</td></tr>
</table>

railroad in one gallery: Five miniature trains zoom along the track, past villages and bridges and through farmlands. Christmas trees fill another gallery, complete with life-size animals.

The museum has a research library, which includes books, periodicals, letters, scrapbooks, and diaries. More important, the museum contains paintings by three famous American artists from a single family: N. C., Andrew, and Jamie Wyeth. The museum also includes works by John McCoy, Maxfield Parrish, Horace Pippin, Harvey Dunn, George Cope, and Howard Pyle. Although the museum contains much variety in its permanent collections and special exhibits, many visitors regard it as a place to study the development of artistic talent in a remarkable family.

N. C. Wyeth was noted as an illustrator. He painted the title page for *The Boy's King Arthur* in 1917, the cover for *The Mysterious Island* by Jules Verne, and the cover for the 1919 edition of *The Last of the Mohicans* by James Fenimore Cooper.

Look at his painting of *Blind Pew,* which focuses on a man wearing a huge, soaring cloak, feeling with his staff for his lost three-cornered hat. The moonlight lands on his tooth and his buckle with brillance. Also poignant is *Treacherous Trail,* which depicts snow blowing on a cliff and men struggling along through the drifts. Another N. C. Wyeth acquisition, *In a Dream,* depicts the artist standing on scaffolding talking to George Washington, who is asking directions. Rolling hills in the background reveal soldiers on a march and Andrew Wyeth, pictured on the left as a boy with his sketchpad.

There are two worlds of N. C.'s son, Andrew Wyeth: Chadds Ford and Maine. One of his favorite paintings, *Trodden Weed,* focuses on a pair of boots given to him by his wife, Betsy, as a Christmas present. He was supposed to use them in his paintings but instead put them on and found they fit beautifully.

The Andrew Wyeth Gallery contains many paintings, including *Widow's Walk,* which offers the contrast of his Chadds Ford house on Route 1 with Maine in the background. Portraits include *Maga's Daughter, Betsy,* and *Helga. Fast Lane* almost got Andrew in trouble as he stopped to sketch a dead squirrel on Route 1 near his home: A policeman was ready to write up a ticket, asking, "Who do you think you are, Andrew Wyeth?"

Christian C.
Sanderson Museum
Route 100, north of
Route 1
Chadds Ford 19317
610–388–6545

until he found out the truth.

Jamie Wyeth, following in his father's footsteps, is also revered as a fine artist. Look at his painting *Roots* for the feeling of intense detail. He was also very fond of pigs, and his portrait of one, Den-Den, is on display. *Pig* brings forth the rough texture of the fur, the smooth pink nose, and the curly tail. This nursing mother almost seems to smile.

Trompe l'oeil, or "fool the eye," paintings include one by DeScott Evans entitled *Free Sample—Try One,* which is painted on canvas that looks like wood with broken glass over it.

Besides the Brandywine River Museum, you can now visit N. C. Wyeth's studio. It has been restored to reflect the year of his death, 1945. His widow lived in the house and painted until she died in 1994. Visitors can take tours at specified times, departing from the museum on a shuttle bus.

Don't miss the wildflower gardens around the museum. For another Wyeth experience stop at the **Christian C. Sanderson Museum,** located across the river from the Brandywine River Museum. Chris Sanderson, always called "Sandy" by the Wyeths, was a close friend of the family. He was a teacher, musician, poet, actor, lecturer, humorist, writer, traveler, sportsman, radio commentator, historian, and—above all—collector. Chris began collecting at the age of ten, while living in Washington's headquarters near Chadds Ford. He moved into the house that is now his museum in 1937; he saved the front half for a museum and lived in the other half. After his death his friends, headed by Andrew Wyeth, formed a corporation to continue his collection, which now fills the whole house.

What is in the museum? Everything and anything. Besides his personal collection, there are items saved by his mother, artwork from the Wyeth family, and mementos sent to him by friends. A favorite painting is one painted by Andrew Wyeth in 1937—a portrait of Sandy. Most of the Wyeths signed his guest book many times, sometimes with a little sketch— don't miss the one of Den-Den by Jamie Wyeth. You can see a piece of bandage used on President Lincoln during his final moments; it was obtained from a physician who attended Lincoln. Look for "Jennie Wade's Pocketbook," which was given to Chris by Jennie's sister. This pocketbook was in her apron when she was killed in her sister's home during the Battle of Gettysburg. There is a sign made by N. C. Wyeth to hang outside the Sanderson home when Chris lived in Washington's headquarters. At one time Chris played Rip Van Winkle; he wanted an autograph of Joe Jefferson, who was the first to play Rip Van Winkle. Knowing that Joe was a close friend of President Grover Cleveland, Chris wrote the president to ask if he could get an autograph—which he received. Look for the upside-down sketch, which you can see in a mirror on the ceiling. Andrew Wyeth sketched on both sides of the paper, and Chris wanted to save both.

A few miles to the east on Route 1, you'll come to the **Franklin Mint Museum.** If you're a collector of sculpture, dolls, jewelry, antique car models, plates, or coins, you'll enjoy this museum. The Fabergé collection includes a mystery clock, a crown,

> Franklin Mint
>   Museum
> Franklin Center
>   19091
> 610–459–6168
>
> Longwood Gardens
> Route 1
> Kennet Square
>   19348
> 610–388–1000

eggs, flowers, butterflies, and an Egyptian necklace (the original is in the Louvre). Porcelain "songbirds of the world" feature a blue-winged warbler, among others. We were especially entranced with a 1909 Rolls-Royce, the "Silver Ghost." Commemorative medals include one of Columbus.

Kennett Square

Continue west on Route 1 to **Longwood Gardens.** William Penn originally sold this land to George Peirce in 1700. As this horticultural family passed the land down through the decades, the garden grew and an arboretum was developed. In 1906 Pierre S. du Pont bought the estate and 203 acres of the famous gardens. As the du Ponts traveled abroad, they developed ideas to use at home, including the special features of English, French, and Italian gardens. The outdoor gardens are set beside two lakes, with fountains bursting forth in formal gardens, and forests with tall trees for accent. You can stroll through 350 acres and see an astounding 14,000 varieties of species. Pierre du Pont took great pleasure in designing the system for the fountains and waterfalls, which are illuminated with colored lights and sometimes enhanced by fireworks as well. He was an MIT graduate with a penchant for putting his engineering expertise to work. The collection is continually being increased by horticulturists who travel around the world and bring back exotic plants for the gardens.

As you walk through the arboretum building, watch for automatic sprinklers that might give you a shower. A favorite area for many young visitors is the topiary display, in which animals are designed on metal frames, using Styrofoam and sphagnum moss. Plants used in this type of garden include fig, ivy, baby's tears, ferns, spider plants, and succulents. One room contains a large pool that is sometimes drained for a concert. The orchid room is a real treat, with many different colors in the various species; there may be as many as 25,000 species gathered from throughout the world. In tropical areas you will see the tropical pitcher plant, Spanish moss, pineapple, and the Panama hat plant. Medicinal plants used to make lotions, tonics, and healing ointments grow there; a strychnine plant is set back, away from visitors' hands. The rain-forest room has a walkway all around so you can view the palms from all angles.

Look for the cute scarecrow in the outdoor vegetable garden. Head for the bell tower and walk up the steps, past green shrubs and trees, to the "eye of water," which was built in 1968. It was inspired by a similar structure in Costa Rica. The eye sits above the reservoir for the main flower garden. Surplus water flows through the eye to the nearby waterfall. An initial morning surge of 8,000 gallons per minute begins the ripple and flows over the eye. The rate soon drops to a steady 5,000 gallons per minute for the rest of the day. The pattern of the flow changes as you watch the eye.

You can become a student at Longwood; courses in horticulture are offered, as well as a variety of lectures and programs. Stop in at the tourist information center at the entrance to Longwood Gardens (610–388–2900) for information.

The **Terrace Restaurant** at Longwood Gardens serves lunch. After lunch stop in **Phillips Mushroom Place** (610–388–6082), which has a museum and gift shop. The mushrooms in the cooler there are the most pristine we have ever seen—nary a bit of earth on them. Also in Kennett Square you will find the **Longwood Inn** (Route 1; 610–444–3515), which features mushroom specialties and seafood.

Itinerary F ends here. You can head into Philadelphia and go north to the Poconos and Delaware Water Gap (Itinerary G) or go south into Delaware (Itinerary H).

ITINERARY G:

Eastern Pennsylvania

PHILADELPHIA

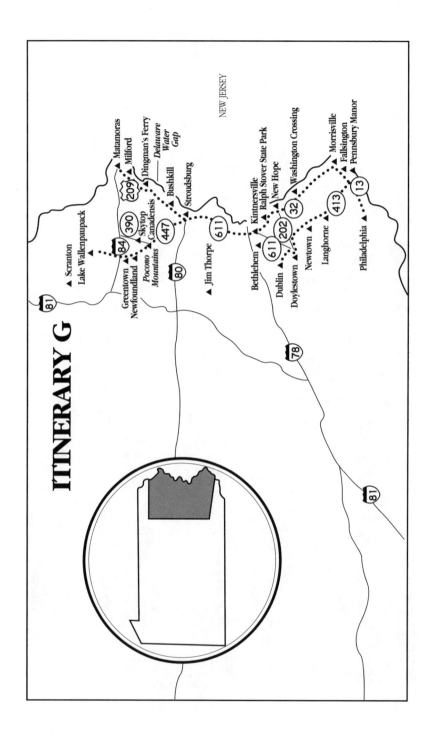

ITINERARY G

NEW JERSEY

Eastern Pennsylvania

This itinerary begins in Philadelphia and then heads north through Bucks County, the Delaware Water Gap, and the Poconos. It can also connect with Itinerary H to Delaware, the Delaware shore, the Jersey shore, and Princeton. Or it can link with Itinerary F at the Brandywine Valley for exploration of Valley Forge, Lancaster, Hershey, Harrisburg, York, and Gettysburg.

≈ *Philadelphia* ≈

The "City of Brotherly Love" was so proclaimed by William Penn, who believed that settlers should be free to live by their own laws and that no one should be "molested or prejudiced for his or her own conscientious persuasion or practice." As a wealthy Quaker, Penn was determined to develop a colony in the New World that would provide anyone with freedom to practice his own faith. He convinced King Charles II to provide him with a tract of land in payment for a debt owed by the Crown to his father, Admiral Sir William Penn. The charter he received for "Sylvania" gave him full authority to impose taxes "by act of Parliament." He arrived in 1682 and named the colony Pennsylvania, "Penn's Woods," in honor of his father. Then he named Philadelphia after a Christian city in Asia Minor.

Inaugurating one of the first attempts at city planning, Penn was determined to lay out the streets on a grid pattern. When Charles Dickens visited in 1842, he commented that Philadelphia was a "handsome city, but distractingly regular." Penn's surveyor, Captain Thomas Holmes, also planned five squares to provide the residents with greenery, fresh air, and sunshine. By 1776 Philadelphia had become the second-largest English-speaking city in the world.

In 1774 the First Continental Congress met at Carpenters' Hall in Philadelphia. The Second Continental Congress met at Independence Hall, then called the Pennsylvania State House. Thomas Jefferson worked arduously drafting the Declaration then gave it to his colleagues to approve, and it was signed. (You can see the inkwell used to sign the Declaration of Independence as you walk through Independence Hall.) The Declaration of Independence was read in the State House yard on July 8, 1776. In 1787 the Articles of Confederation were revised by the Constitutional Convention here. Philadelphia remained the capital of our nation until 1800.

We suggest beginning your adventure back into time with a walking tour of the "most historic square in America," **Independence National**

Historic Park. Several walking tours are available. Visit the **National Historical Park Visitor Center,** where you can watch the film *Independence,* consult with park rangers on your choice of tour, and buy one of several books on walking tours of the park. If you would like to capture historical Philadelphia with a guide, call **Historic Philadelphia** (800–76–HISTORY) for information on tours: The Liberty Tale, Tippler's Tale, Tory Story, and Betsy Ross of Philadelphia.

Philadelphia on Foot (800–340–9869) offers tours: Philadelphia on Foot, First City Tour, Hoof and Foot, Saints and Sinners, and Colonial V.I.P. Tour.

National Historical
Park Visitor Center
3rd & Chestnut
Streets
Philadelphia 19106
215–597–8974

Liberty Bell Pavilion
Independence
National Historical
Park
Market Street,
between 5th & 6th
Streets
Philadelphia

The **Liberty Bell Pavilion** in the Independence National Park is an appropriate place to begin your tour. The bell is now housed in a glass-enclosed structure so visitors can see it twenty-four hours a day. Records from January 1750 detail the need for a steeple superstructure as a "suitable place thereon for hanging a bell." The arrival of the bell was to coincide with the Fiftieth Anniversary of William Penn's Charter of Privileges, which ensured freedom of faith for the citizens of Pennsylvania Colony. The bell was ordered through the colonial agent of the province in London in November 1751. The specifications read, in part, "Get us a good bell, of about two thousand pounds weight, the cost of which we presume may amount to one hundred pounds sterling, or perhaps with the charges something more. . . Let the bell be cast by the best workmen, and examined carefully before it is shipped. . . ." The bell arrived aboard the vessel *Myrtilla,* sailed by Captain Richard Budden. But as luck would have it, the bell cracked the first time it was rung.

Two Philadelphia foundrymen, John Pass and John Stow, recast the bell in 1752; because the tone was not ideal, they recast it again, using an additional one and one-half ounces of copper per pound to change the tonal quality. The new bell was installed in June 1753 in the steeple of the State House, but it was fated to be peripatetic. During the Revolution the bell resided in Allentown from September 1777 to June 1778. After its return it was placed in the tower until 1846; in the Assembly Room until 1872; then in the hallway of Independence Hall. In 1875 it was moved into the Supreme Court Chamber; in 1877 it was suspended on a chain from the ceiling in the hall; it was moved back to the Assembly Room in 1878; then placed in a glass case and moved back to the tower in 1896. Finally, in 1915, the glass case was removed so visitors could touch the bell. During the Bicentennial year, 1976, the bell was moved to its final resting

225

Independence Hall
Independence
National Historical
Park
Chestnut Street
Philadelphia 19106

place in the new glass pavilion. With a history as unsettled as the country it represents, this movable bell deserves a rest! No one knows for sure how the bell got its name, but in 1839 a pamphlet dealing with antislavery referred to it as the "Liberty Bell." William Ross Wallace wrote, "That old bell is still seen by the patriot's eye, And he blesses it ever, when journeying by. . . ."

The bell was apparently rung too loudly and too often according to some of the neighbors; in 1772 there was a petition asking for moderation in the ringing of the bell. Apparently it was rung to call members into session both morning and afternoon, as well as for various public functions. Some of the more memorable ringings include 1753, rung for the first time to call the Pennsylvania Assembly together; 1757, Franklin left for England to solicit redress for grievances; 1761, King George III ascended to the throne; 1763, end of the French and Indian War; 1765 (with the bell muffled), when ships carrying stamps for Pennsylvania, New Jersey, and Maryland sailed up the Delaware River; 1771, calling the Assembly to petition the king for repeal of the tax on tea; 1774, news received on the closing of the port of Boston; 1775, news of the battle of Lexington; 1775, George Washington's acceptance of the appointment of commander in chief of the Continental army; 1776, proclamation of the Declaration of Independence; 1787, adoption of the Constitution of the United States; 1799, the death of George Washington; 1801, inauguration of Thomas Jefferson as third president of the United States; and 1824, welcome to General Lafayette to Philadelphia. In 1835 the bell cracked while it was being rung on Washington's birthday; later that year it cracked during the funeral for Chief Justice of the United States John Marshall. Since that time the bell has been tapped only for very special occasions.

Walk down the mall to **Independence Hall,** built in 1732, and the scene of a major portion of the history of our fight for freedom. In this building the Second Continental Congress met; George Washington was appointed commander in chief of the Continental army; the Declaration of Independence and the Articles of Confederation were adopted; the American flag was received as official; and Cornwallis's defeat in Yorktown and the end of the Revolutionary War were announced. Unfortunately, most of the original furniture was burned as firewood by the British in 1777. Look for the "Rising Sun" chair in the Assembly Room, which was used by George Washington during the Constitutional Convention in 1779. The silver inkstand on his desk was used by the signers of the Declaration of Independence and the Constitution. The Supreme Court Chamber did not have fireplaces, so little boxes of hot coals were provided to warm feet. Look for a 7-foot painting in the bell tower showing a view of early Philadelphia. The Long Gallery has served as a banquet room, a meeting room, a prison for American officers during the British occupation, and a museum. Look up to see the handsome brass chandeliers; the one in the center dates from 1740.

The man most frequently associated with Philadelphia during the Revolutionary era, Benjamin Franklin, was born in Boston in January 1706. Although his father, Josiah, wanted him to train as a minister of the Gospel, Franklin chose to train as a printer's apprentice and to teach himself a wide range of subjects. He went to New York in 1723 to find work but was not successful, so he went on to Philadelphia. There he landed, a seventeen-year-old youth who walked through the streets hungry, looking for work. In front of Franklin Field, the athletic stadium of the University of Pennsylvania, you can see a statue of him with his sack and a walking stick. Within five years Franklin had bought a printing business and a newspaper, *The Pennsylvania Gazette,* and, at the age of twenty-seven, he began to publish *Poor Richard's Almanac.* His desire was to become wealthy so that he could have free time to pursue his interests to further society; he was not interested in joining the aristocracy. Within twenty years he was able to retire and begin his career as statesman, politician, and diplomat. He was involved in the first firefighting company in America, a fire insurance company, an academy that grew to be the University of Pennsylvania, the local hospital, and a local militia. A creative genius, he developed experiments and inventions with electricity, lightning rods, and the "Franklin stove." He was made clerk of the Pennsylvania Assembly in 1736, a member in 1750, and deputy postmaster-general of America in 1753.

Franklin's house on Market Street between Third and Fourth streets was in the process of construction in 1764 when he was called back to London. His wife, Deborah, stayed behind to oversee the house construction, which progressed with many difficulties. Franklin did not return for ten years, and Deborah died just before he arrived. The next year he was sent by Congress to France, along with Silas Deane and Arthur Lee, to try to persuade the French to sign treaties with America. He settled into a house in Paris and was sought after by the court of Louis XVI and Marie Antoinette. In Philadelphia his house was confiscated for a while by British General Sir Charles Grey and his officers. In 1778 treaties between France and America were signed, and in 1785 Franklin returned home.

Franklin was honored with the title of President of the Pennsylvania State Council, even though he was in poor health and in his early eighties. Some politicians accused him of senility because he had chosen to take on such a demanding job; Franklin wrote: "I had not firmness enough to resist

Franklin Court
Market Street,
  between 3rd & 4th
  Streets
Philadelphia

Penn's Landing
Delaware Avenue
Philadelphia
215–923–8181

Independent Seaport
  Museum
211 S. Columbus
  Boulevard
Philadelphia
215–925–5439

the unanimous desire of my country-folks; and I find myself harnessed again in their service. They engrossed the prime of my life. They have eaten my flesh, and seem resolved now to pick my bones." In 1787, when the Constitutional Convention convened in Philadelphia, Franklin contributed his intellect and persuasive powers during the revision of the Articles of Confederation. He also entertained many members of the convention in his home, including George Washington. He died at age eighty-four. The house was razed in 1812; the National Park Service began archaeological excavations in 1953 to uncover the foundation as well as artifacts.

As you visit **Franklin Court,** the site of his home, you will find the restored office of the *Aurora and General Advertiser,* a newspaper published by Benjamin Franklin Bache, his grandson. Next door you can see demonstrations of eighteenth-century printing and bookbinding, reminiscent of his early trade. An exhibit of architectural interest promotes proper construction to prevent fire. A colonial post office where you can buy commemorative stamps is also on the site; letters are hand-canceled with a special Franklin postmark. The **U.S. Postal Service Museum** is next, with a variety of exhibits. From the courtyard take a ramp into an underground museum. Look for the telephone "hotline," where you can dial Franklin's friends both in America and Europe to hear them tell stories about him.

After you have visited some of the many other sites of interest in the park, you may want to have lunch at **City Tavern** (Second and Walnut streets; 215–413–1443). This reconstructed eighteenth-century tavern serves typical colonial food, and the waiters and waitresses are dressed in period costume. Originally built over 200 years ago, this site has seen the likes of John Adams, Paul Revere, Thomas Jefferson, and George Washington, to name but a few.

Walk down to Philadelphia's waterfront area, **Penn's Landing,** where you can stroll along the park through a sculpture garden and into an amphitheater area. There fountains play, and performances are given on a barge anchored in the river. The centerpiece of the **Independent Seaport Museum** is "Home Port: Philadelphia." In this exhibition you can climb bunks and pretend you're sailing steerage. There's an interactive computer program, and an extensive maritime collection. It contains ship models, figureheads, scrimshaw, paintings, and other marine exhibits. This museum also has **Workshop on the Water** at Penn's Landing in a converted 1935 barge, where you can see small-craft exhibits and attend classes to learn how to build boats.

Reading Terminal
Market
51 N. 12th Street
Philadelphia 19107
215–922–2317

You can visit a number of other interesting vessels moored at the Independent Seaport Museum's Historic Ship Zone, Penn's Landing. *Gazela of Philadelphia* (215–923–9030) is an 1883 Portuguese square-rigger used in conjunction with a fleet of small dory cod-fishing boats. Each year she sailed from Lisbon with a crew of fifty men to the fishing banks off Newfoundland. After the crew filled her hold with salted cod (sometimes taking as long as six months), she would return to port. Her spars, hull, and boom were cut from Portuguese pine originally planted by Henry the Navigator in 1460. Call to see when she is open, as this is not often. The USS *Becuna* (215–922–1898), a guppy-class submarine, was commissioned in 1944 to serve in the South Pacific. If you've always wanted to go below on a submarine, here's your chance! The USS *Olympia* was Admiral Dewey's flagship in the Spanish-American War. Models portray life on board. Look for the antique copper tub in the Commodore's Quarters.

For a dinner in the world's oldest and largest four-masted ship turned into a retaurant, head for **Moshulu** (215–923–2500) on Philadelphia's Pier 34. Dating from 1904, she survived fifty-four voyages around Cape Horn. She suffered a fire in 1989 and has now been completely renovated.

Society Hill is a historic district, near the river, that has been restored by its residents. Walk on the cobblestone streets past Georgian and Federal houses lighted by Franklin lamps. **Head House Square** was originally a marketplace dating back to 1745. Renovated in the 1970s, it is now a red-brick collection of shops and restaurants. Try **Dickens Inn** on Second Street between Pine and Lombard. The original **Harper House** (215–928–9307) dates from 1788. Nearby **South Street** is a sight to behold if you are there during the evening—people stroll around to be seen in outlandish dress and hair styles. There are many shops and ethnic restaurants in this area. **Downeys** (Front and South Streets; 215–629–0525) is a good choice for Irish specialties. Look for the unique collection of antique radios perched on high shelves in each room.

If you're hungry and want an unusual experience, head for the **Reading Terminal Market** for some taste treats. Merchants are there six days a week; on Thursday, Friday, and Saturday, Amish farmers bring in their produce and homemade products. In this large enclosed market, you can also have lunch while you listen to musicians.

Philadelphia has more extraordinary museums than you can visit in a day or two. Drive out Benjamin Franklin Parkway to the **Franklin Institute.** Four floors await you and your comfortably shod feet. Don't

Franklin Institute
20th Street &
 Benjamin Franklin
 Parkway
Philadelphia 19103
215–448–1200, taped
 message

Please Touch
 Museum
 for Children
210 North 21st Street
Philadelphia 19103
215–963–0667

Academy of Natural
 Sciences Museum
19th Street &
 Benjamin Franklin
 Parkway
Philadelphia 19103
215–299–1000

miss the walk-through heart, which is an interesting sensation. Anything you can think of in the realm of science and technology is on display. Much of the museum is available for hands-on exploration. The **Fels Planetarium** features seasonal constellation shows, among other programs.

One of the most charming museums we have seen is the **Please Touch Museum for Children.** Exhibits have been planned for children seven years of age and younger. If older children come along, they may spend time in an adjacent area working on computers. We were enchanted with the large elephant that greeted us at the top of the ramp. He is built with wire framework from a wooden base and is adorned with much-loved toys donated by hundreds of children. Every time they visit the museum, children can find and touch their favorite toys on the elephant. You and your child can interact with each other and the touchable exhibits as you progress from the rural area to the urban, the contemporary to the future. There are clothes to dress up in, dolls to play with, hopscotch and other street games to try, video presentations to look at, and live animals to watch. Children learn from their play, and there is more than enough here to keep them inspired and happy.

The **Academy of Natural Sciences Museum** welcomes you with a roaring dinosaur at the entrance. Don't miss "Outside-In," an outdoor exhibit indoors telescoped down to child's size. You can see a working beehive in a tree, safely enclosed in glass. You can crawl through a fossil cave to see the skull of a saber-toothed tiger. The saltwater aquarium has fish, and the salt marsh has miniature sand dunes. Have a look through a microscope at one of the creatures who live there.

Continue on out the Benjamin Franklin Parkway to the **Fairmount Park** area. This is the largest landscaped park in the world. You can walk, jog, cycle, ride horseback, canoe, sail, play tennis, golf, swim, or see one of a number of performances. You also can take the Fairmount Park Trolley Bus (215–879–4044) to view a number of sights, if only fleetingly: the **Horticulture Center and Arboretum, Japanese House and Garden, Fairmount Waterworks,** several eighteenth-century homes, and **Memorial Hall.**

Don't miss the **Philadelphia Zoo,** where more than 1,600 mammals, birds, and reptiles live. The highlight here is the Treehouse, where visitors can have the sensation of what it is like to be the animal. Look out through the eyes of a frog, hatch out of an egg in the Everglades Swamp, climb through a 35-foot-tall honeycomb to see what a bee's-eye view is like, and swing inside a cocoon. Don't forget to nudge Daisy, the 2,000-pound fiberglass dinosaur—she will roar for you. Ask for your magic ring so you can press yellow

> Philadelphia Zoo
> 34th Street & Girard Avenue
> Philadelphia 19104
> 215–243–1100

lights to make the action happen. You can also tour the park on the Safari Monorail.

Try to be in town on New Year's Day for the **Philadelphia Mummers Parade,** which is like nothing you've ever seen before. The parade brings out 20,000 costumed participants, who march for twelve hours. The lead mummers begin their march at 7:45 A.M., so don't oversleep. The first parade was sponsored by the city in 1901; however, local ethnic groups had been celebrating at that time of year a long time before. The origins of these customs include the shooting of guns by Swedes and Finns; Mumming plays by the English and Welsh; the celebration of Belsnickle (similar to Santa Claus) by the Germans; the carnival of horns and other noisemakers; and the theme song, "Oh, Dem Golden Slippers," by Southern blacks. Marchers include clowns, string bands, and brass bands. Many clubs make identical costumes for their members, some of them costing as much as several thousand dollars each. If you go, you may be drawn into the festivities along the route—or you can always watch the parade on television.

Now for a tour in the country.

❧ *Bucks County* ❧

A getaway to Bucks County will take you out of the city and into lush green rolling hills, past large farms with sleek horses and woods and meadows interlaced with many gushing creeks and meandering rivers. Peace and beauty abound in these 620 square miles.

For more than 300 years Bucks County has been significant in American history. You can stand on the spot where William Penn built his summer mansion or where our colonial forebears settled as they arrived from England, Sweden, Ireland, Wales, Holland, Germany, and many other countries. This area was known to be a haven to those who had been persecuted for their religious beliefs. Several men who signed the Declaration of Independence lived in the county. During the Revolutionary War George Washington crossed the Delaware to surprise the British on the other side. The Delaware Canal played a major role in developing commerce in the

> Pennsbury Manor
> Visitors' Center
> 400 Pennsbury
> Memorial Lane
> Morrisville 19067
> 215–946–0400

nineteenth century, by providing a more direct route for the transportation of goods. Later residents of the county have included Henry Chapman Mercer, Pearl Buck, James A. Michener, and Margaret Mead.

Pennsbury Manor

From Philadelphia take Route 13 to signs for **Pennsbury Manor,** magnificently situated on a bend of the Delaware River. (The manor's mailing address is Morrisville, but it is a distance from the town.) William Penn chose this location for his country home from the twenty-three million acres granted to him for the state of Pennsylvania. Although the land had been given by King Charles II of England, Penn instructed William Markham, his secretary, to buy it from King Sepassing of the Delaware Indians. William Penn met with three tribes—the Lenni-Lenape, the Mingoes, and the Shawnees—to consummate this "Great Treaty of Friendship" in 1682.

James Harrison directed the construction of this English manor house for Penn, beginning in 1683. The next year, when the house had not yet been completed, Penn was forced to return to England to oppose challenges to his proprietorship of Pennsylvania. He carried on a detailed correspondence with Harrison as the latter finished the house, constructed outbuildings, and developed the gardens. Penn returned from England in 1699. The family, which included his second wife, Hannah, newborn son, John, and twenty-one-year-old daughter, Letitia, moved into Pennsbury Manor in the spring of 1700.

The house required a large staff to provide a smoothly run household, to tend the gardens, and to operate the entire plantation. Crops included corn, wheat, barley, vegetables, and fruits, and the plantation made its own cider and beer. Like the streets of Philadelphia and English formal gardens, Penn's gardens were laid out in a geometric pattern. He encouraged his gardeners to transplant native plants from the woods into the gardens; seeds, roots, and trees were also imported from England.

Although the original house was destroyed, all of the buildings are reconstructions based on records. Inside the house rooms are furnished with period furnishings, but only one armchair belonged to William Penn. The outbuildings include a bake-and-brew house, smokehouse, plantation office, icehouse, stable, and barge house. The Penns traveled between Pennsbury Manor and Philadelphia on their own 27-foot river barge—a five-hour trip with six oarsmen, a coxswain, and a boatswain. A replica of the English river barge is on display. A number of domestic animals live on the plantation, just as they would have in Penn's day, and horticulturists maintain seventeenth-century gardens and orchards. Picnic facilities are available near the visitors' center.

Fallsington

Head back to Route 13 and turn right; you will see signs for **Historic Fallsington,** a village that has preserved 300 years of history—from log cabins to Victorian mansions. Some of them are inhabited by descendants of the first settlers. The **Burgess-Lippincott House** dates from 1780; its doorway is considered to be one of the most handsome in the county. Inside look for the matching parlor mantel and the second bannister on the stairway. The **Stage Coach Tavern** operated from the 1790s until the 1920s, when Prohibition forced it to close. The **Moon-Williamson House,** dating from 1685, is one of the oldest houses in Pennsylvania still on its original site. Two field-stones on the **Schoolmaster's House** bear the date 1758. William Penn traveled from Pennsbury Manor to attend the **Friends Meeting House.** Stop in the visitors' center for a walking-tour map and the audiovisual presentation.

From Fallsington continue on Route 13 to Morrisville, where you will meet Route 32 as it begins to wind along the Delaware Canal.

Historic Fallsington, Inc.
4 Yardley Avenue
Fallsington 19054
215-295-6567

Summerseat
Hillcrest & Legion Avenues
Morrisville 19067
215-295-7339

Washington Crossing Historic Park
Route 32
Washington Crossing 18977
215-493-4076

Morrisville

Morrisville was the home of two signers of the Declaration of Independence, Robert Morris and George Clymer. The house they each owned, at different times, is called **Summerseat.** It was built in the early 1770s by Thomas Barclay; George Washington slept here on December 8, 1776. Robert Morris bought it in 1791; George Clymer, in 1798. Each room in the mansion has a fireplace.

Washington Crossing

Continue on Route 32 to **Washington Crossing Historic Park,** which is in two sections. The first is **McConkey's Ferry;** the second is **Thompson's Mill.** During the winter of 1776, the campaigns of George Washington had not been successful; his men were near starvation, and many had deserted. He knew that a victory was needed more than ever before. Fortunately, Washington was experienced in handling riverboats;

McConkey's Ferry
Washington Crossing
Historic Park
Washington Crossing
18977

Thompson's Mill
Washington Crossing
Historic Park
Washington Crossing
18977

David Library
Route 32
Washington Crossing
18977

only the weather could defeat his daring plan to surprise the British at Trenton. If the river froze, all would be lost, for the ice would not be thick enough to support troops, horses, and heavy equipment. Meetings to prepare for the crossing were held in the **Keith House,** the **Merrick House,** and the **Thompson-Neeley House,** at the foot of Bowman's Hill.

On Christmas Day 1776 the password among the troops was "Victory or Death" as they prepared to advance into a dark, gray, ice-strewn river. As they walked toward the boats 200 yards north of McConkey's Ferry, men without adequate shoes left blood on the snow. They embarked at 6:00 P.M. to ensure that the six-hour crossing would be completed in the dark. The weather turned from snow to sleet, slowing their progress through the ice floes, but they made it! You can see the famous painting *Washington Crossing the Delaware,* by Emanuel Leutze, in the **Washington Crossing Memorial Building.** A nearby building, the **Durham Boat House,** has reproductions of eighteenth-century cargo boats and exhibits about transportation on the Delaware.

Three and one-half miles up the road, you will come to the Thompson's Mill section of the park, which includes **Thompson's Mill Barn,** a restored eighteenth-century barn. **Thompson's Grist Mill** is now an operating mill, rebuilt in the style of 1870. The **Thompson-Neeley House** dates from 1702; a number of crucial meetings took place there during the Revolution. **Bowman's Tower** was constructed in 1930 on the site of the Continental army's observation point. If you are interested in seeing a collection of original Revolutionary War manuscripts, stop in the **David Library,** located 1 mile north of Washington Crossing.

As you head north again on Route 32, you will pass a covered bridge, one of thirteen remaining of the original thirty-six in the county. The **Van Sant Bridge** is 86 feet long and was built in 1875. It is sometimes called Beaver Dam Bridge. For a brochure on the other twelve bridges in Bucks County, contact the Bucks County Tourist Commission (800–836–2825 or 215–345–4552).

New Hope

As you enter New Hope, you will see the barge landing on the towpath. Don't miss the one-hour trip on the canal, which will take you past one garden after another, the homes and studios of local residents, and railroad tracks with a number of restored coaches from the days of railroad prosperity. The canal was built between 1827 and 1832 to support the coal industry; barges also carried limestone, grain, lumber, and a multitude of other goods. The bargemen told us that the canal was dug by hand. Apparently there was considerable feeling between the "canalers" and the towpath strollers elegantly dressed in hoop skirts and tall top hats, since some canalers took delight in throwing coal to knock off those hats. Young boys at the tender age of eight or nine began training to act as guides for the mules that pulled the barges.

> New Hope Mule Barge
> New Hope 18938
> 215–862–2842
>
> Van Sant House
> Mechanic Street
> New Hope 18938
>
> Parry Mansion
> Main & Ferry Streets
> New Hope 18938
> 215–862–5652

Now the barges are pulled by two horses, which are led by a guide. We were treated to musical selections on a dulcimer, "bones," and a mouth organ. "Haul those barges up and down, Haul them up and down" was the refrain from the Delaware Canal Song. "Whiskey for Breakfast" came from an Irish folk song. As we leisurely drifted along, the fragrance of honeysuckle wafted over us; the sight of hemlock, sumac, and maples added spring-green color; and only ducks punctuated the stillness with their quacks to each other.

As you stroll around New Hope—a retreat for artists, writers, and visitors alike—you will have a choice of many shops and boutiques. The historic **Van Sant House,** dating from 1743, was damaged by British shelling in 1776. Grapeshot can still be seen in the attic walls. The **Parry Mansion** is a restored stone house that was built in 1784 by Benjamin Parry, a wealthy lumbermill owner. The New Hope Historical Society has furnished the rooms in different styles, including the 1775 to 1800 period; 1800 to 1825, or the American Empire period; the Victorian era; and the turn-of-the-century period. Look for the progression from candles to oil lamps as you view the rooms.

If you are in New Hope in the evening, you may want to attend the **Bucks County Playhouse** (215–862–2041) or the **S. J. Gerenser Theater** (215–862–2432), which overlooks the river and serves continental cuisine in elegant style.

The New Hope area makes a convenient and pleasant base for side trips in Bucks County. Besides the accommodations in town, you will find quite a few on Route 32 north. You can be refreshed and pampered in the elegance of years gone by. (Some of these inns are listed in the Inns appendix.)

Ringing Rocks
Route 32
Narrowsville

Ralph Stover
  State Park
State Park Road &
  Stump Road
Point Pleasant
610–982–5560

Fonthill
E. Court Street
Doylestown 18901
215–348–9461

For more information on attractions in Bucks County, contact the **Bucks County Tourist Commission** at P.O. Box 912, Doylestown, PA 18901; 800–836–2825 or 215–345–4552.

Excursion North of New Hope

Go north from New Hope on Route 32 to **Ringing Rocks,** found near Narrowsville, which really do ring when hit with a rock or hammer. Visitors enjoy hiking and picnicking in a number of parks all along the Delaware. You can also take canoe, raft, or tube trips on this section of the river. If you are there during the spring, the white-water season will be in full swing. Five covered bridges are located along this stretch or just inland.

The **Ralph Stover State Park** is located 2 miles north of Point Pleasant. If you are there during a period of high water, you can try canoeing, rubber-rafting, or tubing on Tohickon Creek in the park. The course is challenging, so closed-deck canoes are recommended. For a view of the horseshoe bend in the creek, head for the High Rocks section of the park. Hiking, fishing, and picnicking are available to visitors. You can also rent one of six cabins by the week; contact the park office, because they are booked by a lottery system prior to the opening of the season.

Excursion West of New Hope

From New Hope head west on Route 202 to visit the numerous antiques shops concentrated along this road. Lahaska is the site of several complexes of shops, boutiques, and restaurants. Don't miss **Peddler's Village,** with its ducks quacking and splashing in a pond set into landscaped gardens. The **Cock 'n' Bull Restaurant** (215–794–4010) is a convenient place for lunch.

Continue on Route 202 to **Doylestown** to visit the "Mercer Mile," where you will find an unusual medieval castle named **Fonthill,** built by Henry Chapman Mercer. Fonthill contains Mercer's collection of tiles, prints, and engravings. Next door is the **Moravian Pottery and Tile Works,** where you can watch tiles being made, see a slide presentation on all three Mercer sites, and browse in the gift shop, which has sconces, paperweights, hot plates, and tiles. In the summer Shakespearean plays are produced outdoors on the grounds. The **Mercer Museum** features an extensive collection of early American tools and folk art. If you are there at the right time in the spring, you will be surrounded by blooming forsythia. The **"Folk Fest"** held on the second weekend in May includes sheepshearing, folk dancing, wagon rides, woodcarving, folk art, tinsmithing, blacksmithing, and other eighteenth-century crafts. Across the street is the **James A. Michener Art Museum,** which is located in the beautiful stone building that was the Bucks County Jail in the 1800s.

Take Route 313 from Doylestown to **Dublin** and the home of Pearl S. Buck at **Green Hills Farm.** Her gravesite is on the left as you drive in. She lived in China from the age of three months, taught at Nankin University, married John Buck there, and had a child, Carol, before returning to the United States in 1935. This house was her home for many years with her growing number of children; she adopted Eurasian children, and her foundation still supports many children of mixed races. Pearl Buck received the Pulitzer Prize in 1932, the Nobel Prize in 1938, and the William Dean Howells Prize. The house is alive with memories of this intelligent, energetic, and caring woman. Look for her medals, the desk where she wrote some of her books, her exquisite ceremonial Chinese robes, interesting Chinese chests, and other furnishings, including Peking carpets. Among her books on display are *The Good Earth* and *This Proud Heart.* The grounds and flagstone patios were colorful with hanging pink plants when we were there.

Mercer Museum
Pine Street
Doylestown 18901
215–345–0210

James A. Michener
 Art Museum
Pine Street
Doylestown 18901
215–340–9800

Green Hills Farm
Dublin 18917
215–249–0100 or
800–220–BUCK

Sesame Place
Route 1
Langhorne 19047
215–752–7070

From this point you need to decide if you will return to Philadelphia via Newtown and Langhorne; drive north to Bethlehem via Routes 313, 212, and 412; or go north to the Delaware Water Gap and the Poconos. If you are going north, take Route 113 to Route 611 and I–80 north to Stroudsburg for more views along the Delaware River. For a faster trip to Stroudsburg, take Route 113 to Route 611 to Route 22 west to Route 33 north, to Route 209 east.

Newtown and Langhorne

For those heading back to Philadelphia, return to Doylestown and head south on Route 611. Or, you can take Route 423 south through Newtown, which contains a number of eighteenth- and nineteenth-century buildings, and then go on to Langhorne, the home of **Sesame Place.** This educational play-park, adjacent to Oxford Valley Mall, helps children

| Moravian Museum |
| 66 West Church |
| Street |
| Bethlehem 18016 |
| 610–867–0173 |

explore the worlds of science and technology; there is a computer gallery and a variety of exhibits. Physical skills are developed by climbing, jumping, bouncing, and sliding activities. Bring a change of clothing for the water activities.

Bethlehem

Bethlehem was founded on December 24, 1741, when Count Nicholas Ludwig von Zinzendorf celebrated a communion service with a group of newly arrived Moravian settlers in their first house. Their Protestant religion began with Jan Hus during the fifteenth century in Czechoslovakia, and they came to America to spread the Gospel to the Indians. The Moravians brought their traditions with them; advent stars with twenty-six points beam from almost every front porch. Their music is a highlight, as it combines voice, organs, woodwinds, strings, and brasses; we attended a concert we will long remember.

Moravian community *putzes,* or miniature nativity scenes, are assembled by volunteers, who arrange the tiny wooden and ceramic figures, gather pine boughs, and crawl under the stage to install the lighting prior to the Christmas season. The *putzes* include both sound and light. Visitors enter a darkened and quiet room, waiting for the first spotlight to appear on a scene. Voices describe the nativity story, and one scene after another is illuminated. It is a moving experience.

Traditionally, on December 1 the city is suddenly illuminated on the north side with thousands of white lights on trees and on the south side with colored lights. An 81-foot-high star gleams from the top of South Mountain. Guides in Moravian dress lead tours through the historic district.

The Gemein Haus, which is the oldest building in town, was built in 1742 and held all fifty-six settlers. The original concept of the church was its communal plan—all worked for the church and lived in separate "choirs" according to sex and age. By 1700 this plan was not needed, as families chose to build their own homes. The Gemein Haus is now the **Moravian Museum.** Saal Hall, which was the original place of worship, is within the house; services were conducted two or three times every day. A 1530 Nuremberg Bible is on display. The room that the count stayed in is there, complete with a brown leather chair and wrought-iron hinges on the door. Quilts, such as one by "Christine," were made from scratch—the Moravians sheared the sheep, carded and dyed the wool, and wove the cloth. The music room contains an old flute, trombones with their cases, and a serpentine-shaped wooden horn covered in leather, with fish skin in between.

The **Old Chapel,** the second place of worship in Bethlehem, dates from 1751. Movable wooden benches provided flexibility for the congregation. An open Bible stands on a table. Indians were baptized there. Our guide explained the significance of ribbons on caps: Red was for little girls, burgundy for teens, pink for those confirmed, blue for married women, and white for widowed women. Women wore a gray jacket, gray skirt, gray woolen cloak, and white apron.

> Asa Packer Mansion
> Jim Thorpe Lion's Club
> Jim Thorpe 18229
> 717–325–3229

The **Central Church** was completed in 1806, and the Bell House clock was placed in the belfry in 1824. Private residences include the Sisters' House, dating from 1744, which is where single women lived and worked, and the Widows' House. The Brethren's House, dating from 1748, was where single men lived. Now it is part of Moravian College's music department.

Jim Thorpe

Jim Thorpe was named for an athlete who never lived there—the American hero of the 1912 Olympics in Stockholm. If you'd like to visit the town, take Route 78 to Route 9 to Route 209. In the early 1950s two towns, Mauch Chunk and East Mauch Chunk, decided to merge. Mrs. Patricia Thorpe heard about the merger and was impressed with the community spirit, as citizens donated 5 cents a week to the economic development fund. Because the state of Oklahoma, where Jim Thorpe was born, would not provide a memorial for him, she offered his name and his body to the merging towns. A granite mausoleum was built to honor Jim Thorpe. In fact, the name change has meant an economic upswing for this community and its citizens. The **Carbon County Tourist Promotion Agency** at Railroad Station in Jim Thorpe may be reached at 717–325–3673.

The **Asa Packer Mansion,** dating from 1861, contains the original furnishings as the Packer family left them. This Victorian Italianate home gives visitors a glimpse into life in the late 1800s. The library has Mr. Packer's safe and a blue glass chandelier from the 1876 Centennial Exposition in Philadelphia. The parlor windows are hung with rose velvet draperies that were made for the Packers' fiftieth wedding anniversary. Don't miss the carved cameo-glass turquoise vase, which is worth $40,000. Two paintings by George Henry Boughton hang there; he also painted *First Thanksgiving.* A replica of the gasolier chandelier was used in the movie *Gone with the Wind.* Upstairs in the hallway stands a Welty Orchestrian—a Swiss roller organ, bought in 1903 for $500.

≈ *Delaware Water Gap* ≈ *and the Poconos*

The Middle Delaware River region, which stretches for 40 miles between Stroudsburg and Milford, Pennsylvania, is a recreational area for those who enjoy hiking, canoeing, swimming, photographing a series of views around each bend of the river, and exploring the many waterfalls on tributary streams along the way. Since the 1960s the government has been developing this area for recreation. The river runs through a narrow valley, with the Kittatinny Mountains on one side and the Poconos on the other, producing the gorge and the natural beauty of rushing waters at Delaware Water Gap. The name Pocono may have been derived from the Indian *Pocohanne,* which means "A River between Mountains."

Bushkill Falls
Route 209
Bushkill 18324
570–588–6682

The region is close to both New York City and Philadelphia, so it's easily accessible for daytrips and getaway weekends. There's an abundance of resorts to suit any taste or style.

Delaware Water Gap

Begin your exploration of the area with a stop in the **Kittatinny Point Information Station,** located just off I–80 west of the southern end of the Gap. For an overview of the river both north and south, climb to the top of **Mount Minsi.** The trail begins from the parking lot of the information station.

Bushkill Falls is located a few miles north of Stroudsburg. Be prepared to do some walking, unless you choose to stop at the lookout, situated a short distance from the parking lot. The main Bushkill Falls cascades down 100 feet over a series of rocks. You can also hike for 1 mile up the **Bridal Veil Falls Trail,** which has several waterfalls to photograph. There are a number of bridges over Little Bushkill Creek and Pond Run Creek and at the juncture of the two creeks.

A Bushkill legend involves a Lenni-Lanape Indian maiden named Winona and a young Dutchman named Hendrick van Allen. The couple fell in love and spent their time canoeing on the Delaware and climbing the mountains for the views. Whether he told her the news that he had to return to Holland or one of their families would not approve of their marriage is open to conjecture; in any event, they were found at the bottom of a cliff beside the waterfall. **Winona Falls,** several miles away, now bears her name; it is no longer open to the public.

Continue north on Route 209 to signs for the **Pocono Environmental Education Center,** a regional study center. From the center Keystone Junior College and the National Park Service explore the 200,000 acres of public land stretching through forests, across fields, beside ponds and waterfalls, and along a fossil slope—both to study and preserve it.

Dingmans Falls is a preserve along a streambed run by the National Park Service. A twenty-minute walk will take you through a forest of hemlocks and rhododendrons to Silver Thread and Dingmans Waterfalls. This is an extremely pleasant area, without any of the trappings of commercialization. The **Dingmans Falls Visitors' Center** focuses on the river, mountains, and area wildlife, such as black bears and bald eagles. Picnic facilities are available, and the park service offers a variety of trips all along the Delaware Water Gap.

Pocono
Environmental
Education Center
Route 209
Dingmans Ferry
18328
570–828–2319

Dingmans Falls
Visitors' Center
Route 739
Dingmans Ferry
18328
570–828–7802

Grey Towers
Route 6
Milford 18337
570–296–6401

Big Pocono State
Park
Box 173
Henryville 18332

If you're planning a vacation that includes canoeing on the Delaware, you may want to contact one of the following outfitters: **Shawnee Canoe Trips** (Box 189, Shawnee-on-Delaware, PA 18356; 800–SHAWNEE) or **Kittatinny Canoes** (Dingmans Ferry, PA 18328; 800–FLOAT–KC).

Milford can be reached by heading north once more on Route 209. Mary Pickford and Lillian Gish came to Milford to film *The Informer* in 1912. **Grey Towers** was originally built as a summer home for James W. Pinchot. This forty-room mansion in medieval style was designed by Richard Morris Hunt in 1886. Pinchot's son Gifford became governor of Pennsylvania and first chief of the U.S. Forest Service. The mansion is the home of the **Pinchot Institute for Conservation Studies.** Visitors may enjoy terraces, lawns, and hiking trails to nearby **Sawkill Falls.**

Pocono Mountains

A number of state parks lie to the west of the Delaware Water Gap. From Stroudsburg scenic I–80 will take you to **Big Pocono State Park,** one of the highest points in the Poconos. From the elevation of 2,131 feet you can see the Catskills of New York on a clear day. Park facilities

241

Hickory Run
State Park
RD1, Box 81
White Haven 18661
570–443–0400

Camelback Ski Area
Tannersville 18372
800–233–8100 or
570–629–1661
www.skicamelback.com

Big Boulder Ski Area
Lake Harmony 18624
800–468–2442 or
570–722–0101
www.big2resorts.com

Jack Frost
Blakeslee 18610
800–468–2442
570–443–8425
www.big2resorts.com

include picnicking, cross-country skiing, hiking, equestrian trails, and hunting.

Hickory Run State Park offers picnicking, swimming, a nature center, fishing, hiking, and camping. The area just north of Hickory Run contains a number of ski resorts, as does the area to the northeast surrounding Skytop. **Camelback Ski Area** is located in Tannersville. Take exit 45 from I–80. Camelback has a vertical drop of 800 feet.

Camelback transforms itself from a waterpark in the summer to a ski area in the winter. Within a three-month period the waterpark equipment is removed and a substantial snow base is built up on the golf course and the river. The same water system is in use year-round and there's 100 percent snowmaking on the trails. Night skiing is popular at Camelback. The snowtubing park has single and family tubes.

Instruction begins for "sugar bears," ages four through six, then moves into "ski/boarding bears," from ages seven to twelve. Children twelve months through four years spend time in the "teddy bears." Camelback has an Adaptive Skiing Program for persons with disabilities.

Summer activities include an alpine slide, bumper boats, a pool, and go carts.

Big Boulder Ski Area is located off exit 43 from I–80 in Lake Harmony. The vertical drop there is 475 feet. Big Boulder is a pleasant area consisting of a wealth of easy slopes leading up to a few black diamond runs on the left side looking up. Big Boulder has snow tubing facilities. Big Boulder has sixteen chutes and five lifts; night tubing is also popular.

Big Boulder attracts dirt bike riders from all over the country in March. Riders race uphill on very steep terrain for 2,000 feet—that must be a thrill! Big Boulder and Jack Frost are four-season resorts with year-round activities such as in-line skating, Traxx Motocross, and paintball games.

Jack Frost is located on Route 940, 4 miles east of the Pocono interchange of the N.E. Extension of the Pennsylvania Turnpike, near White Haven. Its vertical drop is 500 feet. Jack Frost added snow tubing to the Pocono Mountains in 1994. It's easy—just sit in the tube, let the tow take you to the top and pick your chute for a fast ride down. Night snow tubing is now available on Saturday nights. Try the Avalanche Mega Tube if you dare!

Shawnee Mountain, near Shawnee-on-Delaware, is accessible from exit 52 from I–80. The vertical drop of Shawnee is 700 feet. Kids get into skiing with the PreSKIwee program, which provides fun with learning, then move into SKIwee from ages five through twelve. Mountain Cruisers and Miniriders offer fun for kids ages eight to fifteen. Weekend training programs include the Development Race Program and the Junior Race group. Summer activities include golfing, canoeing, rafting, tubing, horseback riding, and tennis.

I–80 and I–380 lead to **Tobyhanna State Park,** which offers picnicking, swimming, a historical center, fishing boat rental, boat launching and mooring, hiking, bicycling, and camping.

Near Tobyhanna State Park the **Sterling Inn** (South Sterling, PA 18460; 570–676–3311 or toll-free from Connecticut, New York, New Jersey, Maryland, Delaware, and Washington, D.C., 800–523–8200) offers lunch and dinner in a cozy dining room. You may also want to stay overnight. (See Inns appendix.)

Perhaps you would like to head north from Stroudsburg. Take Route 447 along the Brodhead Creek past Canadensis and Route 390 past Skytop to **Promised Land State Park,** which offers picnicking, swimming, a nature center, fishing, boat rentals, boat launching and mooring, hiking, horseback riding, and camping.

Shawnee Mountain
Shawnee-on-
    Delaware 18356
800–SHAWNEE
    for reservations
800–233–4218
    for snow report
    or 570–421–7231
www.shawneemt.com

Tobyhanna State
    Park
Box 387
Tobyhanna 18466
570–894–8336

Promised Land
    State Park
RD1, Box 96
Greentown 18426
570–676–3428

Scranton Iron
    Furnaces
Between
    Lackawanna
    Avenue & Moosic
    Street
Scranton 18501
570–963–3208

Lake Wallenpaupack lies a few miles north of Promised Land; this man-made lake, 15 miles long, is a popular recreation area. During the summer visitors water-ski, sail, swim, scuba-dive, fish, play tennis or golf, and hike along marked trails at the Ledgedale and Shuman Point areas. Alpine and Nordic skiing are available during the winter.

Scranton

Route 84 leads westward to Scranton, a city we had not visited until a couple of years ago; since then we have been back three times, with pleasure. In the 1840s four anthracite blast furnaces were built. Molten iron flowed from the furnaces into forms, where they were cast into rectangular shapes called "pigs" and then formed into rails. The glowing furnaces lit the sky until 1902, when the company moved to Lake Erie. The **Scranton Iron Furnaces** can be visited in downtown Scranton.

Steamtown National
Historic Site
150 South
  Washington Avenue
Scranton 18503
570–961–2033 or
888–693–9391

Pennsylvania
  Anthracite Heritage
  Museum
RD1
Bald Mountain Road
  (McDade Park)
Scranton 18504
570–963–4804 or
570–963–4845

Lackawanna Coal
  Mine
Scranton 18504
570–963–MINE or
800–238–7245

Steamtown National Historic Site can be found a block west of the furnaces in the former Delaware, Lackawanna, and Western Railroad yards. Here's the place to see a great collection of locomotives and rolling stock. A park ranger will take you on a tour to see the Little Red Caboose, built in 1920; a 1926 baggage car that was once part of the Phoebe Snow train; a wrecking crane called Big Hook; and lots of locomotives.

Phoebe Snow was created by the DL&W Railroad as an advertising gimmick. Earlier, travel by train was dirty, as smokestacks spewed out soot. With the advent of anthracite, or hard coal, passengers were relieved to enjoy trips in comfort and cleanliness. Phoebe Snow wore a white gown, and ads portrayed her speaking in rhyme, such as "Says Phoebe Snow about to go, upon a trip to Buffalo, 'My gown stays white from morn to night upon the Road of Anthracite.'"

Visitors can take a short train ride within the yard or a three-hour trip from Scranton to Kingsley and back. Be sure to ask for the "hobo" handout before your trip so you can interpret the stick-figure signs used by real hobos.

The **Pennsylvania Anthracite Heritage Museum** offers displays on the lives of people living in this area. Visitors will see a collection of the tools used by the miners, displays of Indian lore and railroad transportation, and the textile mills where both women and children worked.

The **Lackawanna Coal Mine** is adjacent to the Heritage Museum. Visitors almost step inside a miner's boots as they get into a car for a ride down into the mine. The depth at the bottom where we got out was 250 feet; the temperature is about 50 degrees year-round, so wear a jacket. In the early days mules were taken down there, never to emerge into daylight, as their stables were at the bottom. Miners worked as laborers for three years, took a test, and finally received mining papers. The men spent every day drilling 8-foot-long holes, inserting dynamite, yelling "Fire" several times, setting off the blast, and removing the coal. Some of them had to work on their stomachs in areas a few feet high. As you walk through the mine, you'll see models of miners at work, wearing caps and looking grimy. One little boy with his donkey looked sad and vulnerable. Child labor laws were in fact initiated as a result of experience in the mines. As we passed an open office door, the "fire boss" was relaxing with his feet on his desk. Startlingly, two hands waved at us from the ground. At the end of the tour, we each received a "miner's certificate."

The **Everhart Museum** contains collections of nineteenth- and twentieth-century American art, folk art, Dorflinger glass, European art, Native American art, and science displays. A "dinosaur hall" houses a 20-foot skeleton of a stegosaurus; a tyrannosaurus head is also on display. The Environmental Gallery contains exhibits on acid rain, animal species that are now extinct, and a chronology of disasters such as the *Exxon Valdez* oil spill. The Spitz Planetarium is the oldest in the United States, and programs are given. Don't miss the beehive in the basement—you can watch the queen bee and all of her workers at work.

Montage Ski and Summer Recreation Area is located just outside of Scranton on Montage Mountain Road. The area offers skiing in the winter and both waterslides and an alpine slide in the summer. The adjacent stadium is very popular for sports events much of the year.

Everhart Museum
Nay Aug Park
Scranton 18510
570–346–7186

Montage Ski and
  Summer Recreation
  Area
1000 Montage
  Mountain Road
Scranton 18505
570–969–7669 or
800–GOT–SNOW
www.skimontage.com

Elk Mountain
RR 3
Box 3328
Union Dale 18470
570–679–4400 or
800–233–4131
www.elkskier.com

All twenty-two trails are covered by snowmaking and lighted at night. White Lightning is an awesome double diamond trail—it has a 70 percent pitch. A separate area contains the Tubing Park with its own tow and five chutes.

Elk Mountain is located on Route 374 off of I–81. Elk Mountain has a Quad chair lift on the north side and five double chairs. About half of its 1000 foot vertical drop has lighted trails for night skiing. Midweek skiing at Elk is popular, with less crowds and less cost. There's a "first-time skiers package" for anyone six years and older. It is available midweek as well as on weekends and holidays.

This is the end of Itinerary G. You can head northeast toward the Hudson Valley on I–84, drive east toward New York City on I–80, or return to Philadelphia on the N.E. Extension of the Pennsylvania Turnpike.

ITINERARY H:

Delaware

ZWAANENDAEL MUSEUM, LEWES

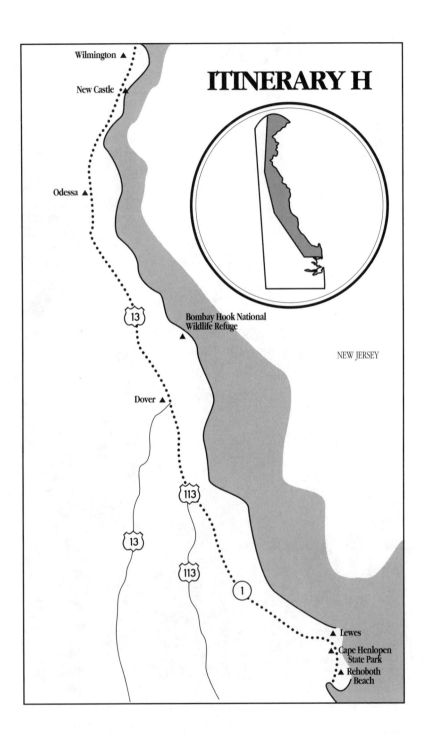

ITINERARY H

Wilmington ▲

New Castle ▲

Odessa ▲

13

Bombay Hook National
Wildlife Refuge
▲

NEW JERSEY

Dover ▲

113

13

113

1

▲ Lewes
▲ Cape Henlopen
State Park
▲ Rehoboth
Beach

Delaware

Holy Trinity Church
and Hendrickson
House Museum
606 Church Street
Wilmington 19801
302–652–5629

Kalmar Nyckel
1124 E. Seventh
Street (near Fort
Christiana Park)
Wilmington 19801
302–429–7447

This itinerary features Delaware. It links with Itinerary F (South-Central Pennsylvania) in the upper Brandywine Valley, with Itinerary G (Eastern Pennsylvania) in Bucks County, and with Itinerary I (New Jersey) along the Atlantic Ocean coastline.

Delaware

We begin our tour of Delaware in Wilmington, in the Brandywine Valley, then head south to Dover, Lewes, and Rehoboth Beach.

Wilmington

The *Half Moon,* with Henry Hudson at the helm, set out in 1609 to find a route through America to Asia. Hudson hoped that the shining, blue waters of Delaware Bay might lead all the way through the New World to Asia—but he was disappointed. Furthermore, the mouth of the river was shallow and he was leary of becoming shipwrecked along the shoals.

The next year Dutch ships arrived to trade with the Lenni Lenape Indians—fur was their focus. They knew about the shallow water but took soundings as they proceeded so as not to run aground.

In 1638 Peter Minuit brought two ships, the *Kalmar Nyckel* and the *Vogle Grip,* up Delaware Bay and came ashore. The fort they built was named for the twelve-year-old queen of Sweden, Christina.

The New Sweden Company founded Wilmington as Fort Christina in 1638; the name was changed by Quakers who developed the town a hundred years later. The **Fort Christina Monument** stands where Peter Minuit landed after his voyage from Sweden; the sculptor was none other than Carl Milles from Stockholm. **Holy Trinity Church,** sometimes called Old Swedes Church, is the oldest active Protestant church in North America. The building dates from 1698 and is still in use. Adjacent to the church is **Hendrickson House,** dating from 1690, which has a museum containing seventeenth- and eighteenth-century exhibits.

Those with a yen for wooden sailing ships will want to visit the **Kalmar Nyckel,** which was commissioned on May 9, 1998. The original vessel brough settlers from Sweden, Finland, Holland and Germany, landing at "The Rocks" in 1638. Unfortunately, she was lost during a naval battle in the seventeeth century. The three-masted pinnace replica was built by an international team of craftsmen. She is used as a tourist attraction as well as a training vessel. Delaware now has a tall ship ambassador of good will and you can expect to see her sailing in tall ship parades.

Brandywine Park follows the river between the Augustine and Market Street bridges. Frederick Law Olmsted designed the park; one of its highlights is the garden with 188 Japanese cherry trees. The zoo in the park has Siberian tigers, monkeys, lions, bears, and a number of other animals.

The **Delaware Art Museum** accents American art from the past 150 years. The Bancroft collection displays English Pre-Raphaelite paintings created by artists in the late nineteenth century. There are paintings by Howard Pyle, known as the father of the Brandywine School of painting, who immortalized legendary heroes like King Arthur, Sinbad, and Robin Hood. The museum also highlights the Phelps collection of Andrew Wyeth's paintings.

The Historical Society of Delaware operates the **Delaware History Museum,** which focuses on Delaware history and decorative arts. The 1941 Woolworth building has been renovated and is open to visitors. The Delaware History Museum is a good place to begin touring and learning the early history of Delaware. Early explorers such as Henry Hudson are featured. Models of Native Americans are shown in their everyday life. Interactive displays and games draw people of all ages. You can touch the models, sit in a long house, and put on furs. There's also a trivia game. The gift shop offers Delaware-handcrafted items and memorabilia.

Nearby, the **Delaware Museum of Natural History** has one of the most extensive shell collections in the country, thanks to the late John E. du Pont, a naturalist who collected shells for many years. The museum also leads you across Australia's Great Barrier Reef, a reconstruction placed under glass that you walk over. The Hall of Birds represents some extinct species, other exotic birds, and their eggs, including the large bird egg—that of the Elephant Bird, which weighs in at twenty-seven pounds.

The **Rockwood Museum** is housed on a nineteenth-century estate. Exhibits feature American, English, and continental decorative arts from the 1600s to the 1800s.

When it's time for a meal in Wilmington try one of these: **Deep Blue Bar and Grill** (111 W. 11th Street; 302–777–2040), **Garden Restaurant**

Delaware Art Museum
2301 Kentmere Parkway
Wilmington 19801
302–571–9590

Delaware History Museum
504 Market Street Mall
Wilmington 19801
302–656–0637

Delaware Museum of Natural History
Route 52
Greenville 19807
302–658–9111

Rockwood Museum
610 Shipley Road
Wilmington 19809
302–761–4340

Winterthur Museum,
Gardens, and
Library
Route 52
Wilmington 19735
302–888–4600 or
800–448–3883,
out-of-state

and Tea Room (Winterthur Museum; Route 52; 302–888–4826), **Green Room at the Hotel du Pont** (11th and Market Streets; 302–594–3154), or **Harry's Savoy Grill** (2020 Naamans Road; 302–475–3000).

Winterthur Museum, Gardens, and Library, one of the most remarkable museum complexes we have ever visited, emphasizes the decorative arts made or used in America between 1650 and 1850. This massive and comprehensive collection of furniture, silver, paintings, textiles, and art objects is displayed in a series of period rooms. The naturalistic garden extends over 200 acres; a tram ride with narration is a good way to get an overview of the property. Visitors need to make reservations for some guided tours of period rooms, but others are available without reservations, including the new galleries, with changing exhibits.

Winterthur took its name from the Swiss city of Winterthur, home of James Antoine Bidermann. In 1816, Evelina Gabrielle du Pont married Bidermann, and in 1837 they bought 450 acres north of Wilmington and built their home. Their son, James Irénée Bidermann, inherited the estate but lived in France; his uncle, Henry du Pont, bought the property in 1867.

The Bidermanns' great-nephew, Henry Francis du Pont, was the force behind the development of the museum to house his growing collection. He started with the purchase of a Pennsylvania-made chest dated 1737, studied and learned about American crafts at a time when little research had been done, and continued collecting. He was interested in the decorative art objects found in early American homes. Further, he collected interior woodwork, paneling, fireplace walls, and doors from houses built between 1640 and 1860. Interiors from houses all along the Eastern seaboard were dismantled and reassembled in his mansion. Du Pont gave his estate to the Winterthur Corporation in 1951, and the museum opened later that year.

The Montmorenci Stair Hall is one of the most striking exhibits in the museum. This free-hanging staircase flows upward in a graceful curve; it was removed from a North Carolina house and dates from 1822. The Commons Room from the Red Lion Inn is decorated with clay-pipe holders and political posters of the nineteenth century and has the decor of a taproom for men only. The du Pont Dining Room displays Federal furniture grouped around a mahogany dining table with an inlaid eagle in its center. The table is set with porcelain dessert dishes, including *glacières* to keep ice cream cold. On the sideboard are silver tankards made by Paul Revere. Visitors can see almost 175 different room settings within the museum, all furnished with period pieces.

Henry Francis du Pont was known as the "Head Gardener" because of his zealous interest in developing the gardens. He created pleasing combinations of color and texture, often moving large trees several times until they were just right. Du Pont's goal was to provide a different view for every turn of one's head, and he achieved it. Visitors can take a tram around the gardens or walk its many paths.

Hagley Museum
Route 141
Wilmington 19807
302–658–2400

The Winterthur shops and galleries sell an impressive line of Winterthur reproductions, including furniture, textiles, wall-coverings, silver, pewter, porcelain, glass, clocks, brass, and carpets. Books, plants, and garden statuary are also available.

Many special events are scheduled at Winterthur throughout the year. The Point-to-Point horse race takes place in May, when jockeys ride four 3-mile steeplechase races over post-and-rail fences. In December Yuletide decorations culminate in an 18-foot-tall Christmas tree. You can enroll in graduate programs in Early American Culture, Conservation of Artistic and Historic Objects, or the History of American Civilization through the University of Delaware.

Wilmington is well known for the du Pont family. E. I. du Pont arrived from France and founded a black powder plant, Hagley, and he gave buildings and money to Wilmington over the years.

The **Hotel du Pont** was created by Pierre S. du Pont, and in 1913 guests arrived in Pierce arrows, Stanley Steamers, and horse-drawn carriages to the new hotel. Many of the rooms have intricately carved ceilings, paneling, marble floors, and lavish chandeliers. The **Playhouse Theatre** dates from 1913 and still presents performances. Original art hangs on walls including that of Howard Pyle, Frank Schoonover, N. C. Wyeth, Andrew Wyeth, Jamie Wyeth, A. N. Wyeth, and many local artists.

The **Hagley Museum** is a 230-acre complex on the Brandywine River. Originally the site of the E. I. du Pont black powder works, the museum was developed in 1952 to portray American industrial growth during the eighteenth and nineteenth centuries. To get an overview of the site, stop in the museum first for background on the development of the valley; dioramas, films, and exhibits provide clear explanations of both the technological and economic aspects of the industries clustered along the river. At this stage of industrial development, you could tell what a man did by looking at his hands: The man who worked on stone wheels in the mill had little chips of stone embedded in his hands; the man who tanned leather had brown hands from the tannin in the leather; the man who worked in an office had smooth hands; and the farmer had hands full of calluses.

In 1802 Eleuthère Irénée du Pont bought land in the area. He constructed a powder yard at Hagley because two necessary ingredients were there: water and willow trees to make charcoal. He built his home, named Eleutherian Mills, on the hill above the powder mill at Hagley; with a speaking trumpet he could direct the operation of the mill from his balcony. On the second floor of the museum is a statue of Don Pedro, the prize ram purchased by Irénée du Pont in 1805. Wool was an important commodity for mill owners, and Don Pedro sired enough lambs to become well-known. Thomas Jefferson sent a letter of condolence when Don Pedro died in 1811. His image is also on the weathervane on the roof of the museum.

As the country expanded, the need for powder grew, and the du Pont Company became the largest in America. Immigrants who had been starving in Ireland came to work in the mill. They worked sixteen hours a day, seven days a week, with two holidays a year: Christmas and the Fourth of July. When there was an explosion at the mill, anyone in the area lost his life. Sometimes the bodies were blown across the river; the expression "across the creek" came to mean that someone had died. Du Pont and his family took a risk in building their home so close to the mill. There were explosions that damaged the house, and his son Alexis was killed in one of the explosions. But du Pont's motto was "safety first," and he felt that there were fewer explosions because he lived on the site.

You can take a bus along the river or walk with a map in hand. Although the area looks like a park today, it was once a busy, dirty industrial site. The workers lived up the hill; archaeological digs have recovered artifacts that will reveal the everyday lives of these families. You can visit the **Gibbons-Stewart House,** which has been restored to represent the home of a foreman and his family; stop for lemonade and Mrs. Gibbons's cookies. The **Brandywine Manufacturers' Sunday School, Stable,** and **Springhouse** are all open to the public. The **Hagley Yard** itself is a series of reconstructed shops and mills strung along the river, each one demonstrating part of the carefully controlled manufacturing process needed to make a substance as volatile as gunpowder. The yard consists of the Millwright Shop, New Century Power House, Steam Plant, Eagle Roll Mill, Graining Mill, Birkenhead Mills, and Engine House.

The family house, Eleutherian Mills, contains furnishings that belonged to the family. Du Pont's great-granddaughter, Louise du Pont Crowninshield, was the last person to live in the house. The first floor remains much as she left it when she died in 1958. The artist who created the murals on the dining room walls had not been to America; he knew that Indians wore feathers on their heads, so he gave them peacock feathers. Follow the elliptical staircase up to the second floor, where there is an original Rembrandt in the Blue Room.

On the grounds outside the main house, the **Old Stone Office** served as a company office. Inside look at the old typewriter, with gold-leaf decoration; it even has characters on a cylinder, like modern typewriter print wheels. The garden has espaliered apple trees in a diamond shape and pear trees shaped into cones like those on a pine tree. Eight parterres on the inside contain flowers and vegetables; companion planting was used to ward off bugs. A compost pile grew huge pumpkins, some weighing over one hundred pounds. Deer, woodchuck, and rabbits still frequent the garden. A Conestoga wagon is on display.

Nearby **Nemours Mansion and Gardens** is a 102-room Louis XVI chateau on the estate of Alfred I. du Pont. The name was taken from the du Pont ancestral home of the same name in France. The mansion was designed by Carrère and Hastings of New York. It contains furnishings, tapestries, and paintings dating back to the fifteenth century. The gardens, developed from du Pont's travels in Europe, were based on French models. You must call ahead to make a reservation to see Nemours.

Route 141 or Route 9 will take you to New Castle.

Nemours Mansion and Gardens
Route 141
Wilmington 19899
302-651-6912

Old Court House
211 Delaware Street
New Castle 19720
302-323-4453

Old Dutch House
32 E. Third Street
New Castle 19720
302-322-9168

New Castle

Fort Casimir was the first name for this attractive town, then New Amstel, and finally New Castle. The **Green,** laid out by Peter Stuyvesant in 1655, when it was called Fort Casimir, is still there; weekly markets and "great fairs" were held on it. Restored buildings lining the sides of the Green include the **Old Court House, the Town Hall,** and the **Old Dutch House.** The Old New Castle Court House is one of the oldest courthouses in the United States. It dates from 1732 and was Delaware's colonial capitol and the meeting place of the State Assembly until 1777. Inside you'll see the original Speaker's chair, portraits of some of Delaware's prominent men, and a collection of excavated artifacts from the area. You will find signs all over town telling you what happened where. In **Packet Alley,** for example, you can read the following: "Packet boats from Philadelphia met stagecoaches here for Maryland, the chief line of communication from the north to Baltimore and the south. Andrew Jackson, Daniel Webster, Henry

George Read II
House
42 The Strand
New Castle 19720
302-322-8411

Historic Houses of
Odessa
Main Street
Odessa 19730
302-378-4069

Clay, David Crockett, Lord Ashburton, Louis Napoleon, Stonewall Jackson, Sam Houston, and Indians led by Osceola and Blackhawk en route to visit the Great Father in Washington all passed this way."

As you stroll around these streets, you will see window boxes filled with impatiens, heavy door knockers, painted shutters and doors, and a variety of iron fences. Another sign tells you that the site is the "Landing Place of William Penn. Near here Oct. 27, 1682 William Penn first stepped on American soil. He proceeded to the fort, performed livery of seisen [the act of taking legal possession of property], he took the key thereof. We did deliver unto him one turf with a twig upon it, a porringer with river water and soil in part of all."

The **George Read II House** is a Georgian house overlooking the Delaware River. The house was built between 1797 and 1804 by the son of a signer of the Declaration of Independence. Read wrote to his brother in 1802: "I have very nearly finished my new building which considering the magnitude of the undertaking is a very gratifying circumstance." The house has elaborately carved woodwork, gilded fanlights, and silver door hardware. Three rooms are preserved in the Colonial Revival style of the 1930s. The garden surrounding the house was developed in 1847 from the design of Andrew Jackson Downing.

New Castle has restaurants that fit right into its historical ambience: **The Arsenal on the Green** (Market Street; 302-328-1290) and **Jessop's Tavern** (114 Delaware Street; 302-322-4272).

Route 9 and Route 13 will take you to Odessa.

Odessa

Odessa has a historic district of restored and preserved eighteenth- and nineteenth-century homes. During the early nineteenth century, grain was shipped from this port. The name of the town came from the Ukrainian seaport Odessa, which also exported wheat. Up until 1855 the town had been called Cantwell's Bridge.

Winterthur Museum owns and operates two historical houses and the Brick Hotel Gallery. The **Corbit-Sharp House** was built by William Corbit, a Quaker tanner, in 1774. Some of the furnishings still in the house belonged to the Corbit family; others were made by local Delaware craftsmen. The **Wilson-Warner House** was owned by David Wilson, who was a local merchant and the brother-in-law of William Corbit. The house is furnished as it was when Wilson's son sold it in the early nineteenth century. The **Brick Hotel Gallery** contains the Belter collection of American-Victorian furniture.

The **Collins-Sharp** house is one of the oldest houses in Delaware, dating to the early eighteenth century. Educational programming takes place in this log and frame building. Cooking demonstrations using original recipes from the eighteenth and early nineteenth centuries are available. Hands-on hearth cooking is a favorite with children.

From Odessa take Route 299 and Route 9 to Bombay Hook.

> Brick Hotel Gallery
> Main Street
> Odessa 19730
> 302-378-4069
>
> Bombay Hook
>   National Wildlife
>   Refuge Information
> Center
> Route 9
> Smyrna 19977
> 302-653-6872
>
> Delaware Visitors'
> Center
> Federal and Court
> Streets
> Dover 19901
> 302-739-4266

Bombay Hook National Wildlife Refuge

Bombay Hook began its recorded history in 1679 with the sale of marshland to Peter Bayard by Mechacksett, chief of the Kahansink Indians. The refuge totals 15,122 acres of predominantly brackish tidal marsh. The rest of the area comprises freshwater pools, agricultural land, and swamp. Migrating and wintering ducks, geese, and the bald eagle live there; the tidal marsh provides them with a natural habitat and plenty of available food. Ornithological groups take field trips into the refuge, where more than 300 species have been sighted. You may also see whitetail deer, red and gray fox, river otter, muskrat, Virginia opossum, eastern gray squirrel, woodchuck, and beaver. The refuge has observation towers, nature trails, and an information center.

Dover

Dover was originally proclaimed the seat of Kent County in 1683 by William Penn. It became the state capital after the British captured New Castle in 1777. Take Route 13 and Route 113, turn west at the Court Street traffic light, and bear right at Legislative Hall onto Duke of York Street. At the end of Duke of York Street, drive straight into the parking lot at the **Delaware Visitors' Center.** You will see the **Green,** laid out by William Penn, where a portrait of King George III was burned after the ratification of the Declaration of Independence. (Delaware has the honor of having been the first state to ratify the U.S. Constitution in Dover, on December 7, 1787.) Look at the eighteenth- and nineteenth-century homes around the

Hall of Records
Legislative Avenue
Dover 19901
302-739-5318

Shadows of the Past
Tours
214 S. State Street
Dover
302-736-1419

Biggs Museum of
American Art
406 Federal Street
Dover 19903
302-674-2111

Green and north and south on State Street.

Delaware's **State House** is located on the Green. The building was restored in 1976 for Delaware's Bicentennial celebration; it contains a courtroom, a ceremonial Governor's Office, legislative chambers, and county offices. Look in the Senate Chamber for the large portrait of George Washington, commissioned in 1802. The State House remains the symbolic capitol of Delaware, although the General Assembly now meets in Legislative Hall. The **Hall of Records** (adjacent to Legislative Hall) houses important documents, including the original Royal Grant from King Charles II.

"Shadows of the Past" is offered by a former state police detective, John Alstadt, who combines his expertise at sleuthing crimes with the 0 of real historical figures. He gives free historical walking tours in Dover dressed in a Union soldier's greatcoat.

Listeners are entranced as he describes the goings-on in such places as the **Paton House**: A box of chocolates arrived from San Francisco in the summer of 1898. Two daughters of a Dover politician ate the candy, which was laced with arsenic, and died. The sender was a "Mrs. C," who turned out to be the California mistress of one of the daughter's husbands. He had announced that he was leaving her after their torrid love affair and she decided to get revenge. Instead she spent the rest of her life in prison.

The **King George Tavern** was famous for its changing signs—King George was pictured first, then after July 4, George Washington's image was painted on the sign.

There's also a headless woman in town who appeared to a cleaning lady in the **Sykes House.** And the ghost of Judge Samuel Chew continues to haunt the property he owned. People used to make fun of him by "chewing" sounds and children took delight in sneezing to annoy him.

If you visit before Halloween you may be in for Alstadt's "Haunted" tour, through which you will hear about eleven ghosts. Tours start at **John Bullen House.**

The Visitor Center is right around the corner from the State House. Upstairs, the **Biggs Museum of American Art** has a collection of paintings ranging from Gilbert Stuart, Thomas Cole, and Childe Hassam to Asher Durand. The collection includes furniture and silver as well as sculpture, needlework drawings, and ceramics.

The **Johnson Victrola Museum** details the story of recorded sound.

Eldridge R. Johnson invented a machine, then had to fight for the patent. He was successful and formed the Victor Talking Machine Company. The next improvement came about because people noticed that the horns collected dust—they were put inside the box and the victrola was born. You could also increase the volume by opening and closing little doors on the front of the box. Then a radio was added.

If you've wondered about the dog, Nipper was Johnson's brother's dog. He would jump up on a table and cock his head as if listening to the music. A friend painted the dog listening and the trademark was created, with "His Master's Voice" printed below.

The **Delaware Agricultural Museum and Village** takes visitors "Where Yesterday Meets Tomorrow." There's a 1700s log house built by Swedes from white oak logs. Motorized machines include an Allis Chalmers Model G Tractor, a John Deere Model L, a Groundhog Threshing Machine dated 1850, and more. Enter the Touch of History section and you can play and interact with all sorts of exhibits. One sign says, CLIMB INSIDE THE WAGON AND DRIVE THE HORSE TO MARKET, another DON'T RIDE THE HORSE AND WAGON TOO HARD, and TAKE A RIDE IN THE SLEIGH. We were entranced with the entire collection of Jehu Camper's "whittlin."

Outside, **Loockerman Landing Village** offers restored, historic buildings. An interpreter was sweeping the front porch of the 1893 farmhouse and escorted us through the house to see typical farm possessions. In another building, the blacksmith was pounding away. Other buildings include the Silver Lake Mill, a school, chapel, train station, Reeds General Store, and a barber shop.

The **Air Mobility Command Museum** is on Dover Air Force Base. Here's a chance to see all sorts of planes and even climb up into the cockpit of one.

The C-5 Galaxy is capable of transporting any of the Army's combat equipment, including the seventy-four-ton mobile scissors bridge. During the Persian Gulf crisis they delivered several helicopters and other minesweeping equipment to Navy vessels. A P51D "Mustang" is considered to be the best American Fighter during World War II. This one features Miss Kentucky State. A B-17 "Flying Fortress" was repainted by a talented artist to feature "sleepy time gal" once again. It is the sole remaining aircraft

Johnson Victrola Museum
Court and Federal Streets
Dover 19901
302-739-5316

Delaware Agricultural Museum and Village
866 N. DuPont Highway
Dover 19901
302-734-1618

Air Mobility Command Museum
1301 Heritage Road
Dover 19901
302-677-5938

John Dickinson
Plantation
Kitts-Hummock Road
Dover 19901
302–739–3277

Governor Ross
Mansion and
Plantation
Seaford Historical
Society
Seaford 19973
302–628–9500

from the 1948 Flying Bomb project. A C-17 "Globemaster" is one of the most recent acquisitions. It can land and take off from small, austere airfields with runways as short as 3,000 feet. The C-47 "Skytrain" is also called "Gooney Bird." It was the first aircraft to take part in the Berlin Airlift, supplying food to West Berlin.

We were amazed at the very small space for a gunner in his turret. After he had completed twenty-five missions he could go home for a year.

The highlight of this tour is the chance to enter a C-141 "Starlifter," which is the workhorse of the ABC. You'll see where supplies were strapped into the rear of the plane. Stretchers lined up down the center and a row of red bucket seats were on each side for passengers. Then climb up a small ladder into the cockpit and sit in the pilot's seat. Wow!

Restaurants in or near Dover include: **The Little Creek Inn** (2623 N. Little Creek Road, Dover; 302–730–1300) and **Sambo's Tavern** (Front Street, Leipsic; 302–674–9724).

Drive south on Route 1 to Kitts-Hummock Road and turn east to reach the **John Dickinson Plantation.** John Dickinson, sometimes called the "Penman of the Revolution," was a prolific writer for the colonists. It has been reported that he drafted the Articles of Confederation in 1778. This restored colonial home from Dickinson's boyhood contains furnishings of the period and a formal English garden.

In Seaford you can make an appointment to visit the Governor Ross Mansion dating from 1859. This eleven-room Italianate villa dates from the Civil War period. William Henry Harrison Ross was born in 1814 and was a Democratic governor of Delaware from 1851-1855. Because he was a southern sympathizer he left for England and stayed three years.

Lewes

Lewes dates back to Henry Hudson's discovery of Delaware Bay in 1609 and the subsequent settlement of a whaling colony on Lewes Creek in 1631. The unlucky colonists were murdered by the Indians, but more settlers arrived in 1659. Lewes led a maritime existence through its involvement with shipwrecks, pirates, and privateers during the Revolution and the War of 1812. Lewes was raided several times by pirates. In 1698 fifty men led by a French pirate plundered every house in Lewes and escaped with their booty. In 1708 pirates burned and sank three vessels off Cape

Henlopen within four days, causing William Penn's secretary to write, "The coast begins to be intolerably infested." In 1709 another French pirate made off with loot from the town. Later the government built the Delaware Breakwater and the Harbor of Refuge for ships to anchor in. Lewes prospered as a port with fish coming in and farm produce going out until the advent of the dual highway rolling down the center of Delaware. Today Lewes is the site of the **College of Marine Studies of the University of Delaware.**

> Lewes Historical
> Complex
> 110 Ship Carpenter
> Street
> Lewes 19958
> 302-645-7670
>
> Zwaanendael
> Museum
> Kings Highway &
> Savannah Road
> Lewes 19958
> 302-645-1148

The **Lewes Historical Complex** contains a group of restored buildings that have been moved into the area. The **Cannonball House Marine Museum** dates back to 1797. It was struck by a cannonball when the British bombarded Lewes in April of 1813. The **Early Plank House,** furnished as a settler's cabin, is probably the oldest building in the complex. The **Burton-Ingram House,** dating from 1789, is furnished with Chippendale and Empire antiques. Don't miss the **Thompson Country Store,** which was managed by the Thompson family from 1888 to 1962.

The **Zwaanendael Museum** looks as if it had been transplanted from Holland. In fact, the building is a replica of the town hall in Hoorn, Holland. It was constructed in 1931 to commemorate the 300th anniversary of the first settlement in Delaware. The H.M.S. *DeBraak* exhibit is exciting for those fascinated by nautical archaeology. The ship existed prior to 1781, when she sailed in Dutch naval operations from the North Sea to the Mediterranean. The British captured her in 1795, and the Admiralty converted her rig from a single-masted cutter to a two-masted brig-sloop. These ships were able to move into shallow waters and also assisted larger ships at sea. Her hull was covered with overlapping copper plates to keep marine organisms from demolishing the wooden bottom. A *kentledge,* consisting of iron ballast bars, provided weight below to provide stability. She carried two long guns, which fired six-pound projectiles, and fourteen guns called "smashers," which fired twenty-four–pound projectiles. Her smashers were very destructive at short range.

When sailing off Cape Henlopen in 1798, the vessel sank, perhaps because she was "overmasted" and therefore top-heavy. After her discovery in 1984, the state of Delaware provided specialists to study her hull and artifacts. Among the pieces recovered from the sea were barrel staves, barrel end pieces and hooping, earthenware and stoneware jars and pots. An exhibit entitled "Great Guns at Night" refers to April 6, 1813, when the

British began a long-range bombardment of Lewes because the people refused to supply the fleet with food and water. Hannah Wolfe Burton wrote that she began to hear many great guns at night until bedtime and on Wednesday "30 before breakfast, 15 while we were eating."

Other displays deal with more peaceful aspects of the town's history. The lighthouse built in the 1760s was made of granite and stood almost 70 feet tall; on April 23, 1926, it toppled into the sea. Also included in the museum's collection are small exhibits of silver, ceramics, and glassware that were owned by early Delawareans.

The **Lewes Chamber of Commerce** (120 Kings Highway, Lewes, DE 19958; 302–645–8075) has written a walking-tour guide complete with a map. This is a pleasant town to stroll through. Stop for lunch or dinner at **Fisherman's Wharf Lighthouse Restaurant** (by the drawbridge; 302–645–6271) or **Aurora Grill** (329 Savannah Road; 302–645–2327).

The **Lightship *Overfalls*** is on display at a wharf on Pilottown Road. The U.S. Coast Guard gave her to the Lewes Historical Society in 1973; she was one of the last lightships functioning on the East Coast. Drive for another mile on Pilottown Road to see the **deVries Monument and Fort Site,** which was the 1631 settlement of the whaling colony of Zwaanendael. The monument is placed on the site of the north bastion of the fort.

Cape Henlopen

One mile east of Lewes is Cape Henlopen. It has always been a crucial landmark for sailors and other seamen. Once you've made it around this low sand spit into Delaware Bay, you're home free. Although the stretch of beach from Cape Henlopen to the Maryland border is only 25 miles long, it was littered with more than 200 shipwrecks during the early years of our country. Pirate activity was also rampant here, and stamped silver bars from their hauls are still found by those who seek the best "coin beaches" in the country.

Legends abound about the *deBraak*, which foundered in 1798. In 1797 this ship was sent as an escort from Plymouth, England, to America and thence from the Delaware River to the Chesapeake. During a period of stormy weather, she and her crew became separated from the rest of the convoy, spotted a sloop that they could easily seize, and brought its cargo of cocoa and copper ingots on board. The vessel finally arrived off Cape Henlopen; a sudden squall capsized her, and she sank about 1 mile off Cape Henlopen light. The British Admiralty authorities in Philadelphia tried to salvage her, unsuccessfully. Yet her masts still showed above water, and everyone knew of the treasure she carried. She was salvaged in 1986.

In 1785 the *Faithful Steward* left Londonderry, Ireland, for Philadelphia. She carried 249 passengers, goods in her hold, and a large consignment of copper coins. When she went aground, her mainmast was cut away to lighten her. She got free but was unable to beat against a rising wind and gain sea room. She went aground again 10 miles south of Cape Henlopen, totally helpless in the huge seas of what may have been a hurricane. Residents of Lewes were not able to reach her and watched lifeboats coming ashore empty because there was no way to get passengers into them. Eventually the ship broke up, and four out of every five persons on board drowned. Coins from her cargo began washing up one hundred years later, no doubt adding to coins from other shipwrecks in the past.

Coin Beach
Delaware Seashore
  State Park
Cape Henlopen

Cape Henlopen
  State Park
42 Cape Henlopen
Drive
Cape Henlopen
19958
302–645–8983

Delaware Seashore
  State Park
Inlet 850
Rehoboth Beach
19971
302–227–2800

The **Coin Beach** is located just north of the Indian River Inlet. More coins have been found there over the years than anywhere else in the country. The U.S. Coast Guard searched the beach in this area after every storm in the 1930s and retrieved buckets of coins. Even a treasure chest reportedly 3 feet square and weighing 400 pounds surfaced, but it never reappeared.

Cape Henlopen State Park is a sandy peninsula with a 4-mile beach and crashing Atlantic waves. An 80-foot sand dune, the highest between Cape Hatteras and Cape Cod, rises above the beach. The park offers nature trails, crabbing, fishing, swimming, picnicking, tennis, basketball, softball, camping, a nature center, an aquarium, and World War II observation towers.

Rehoboth Beach

Have you ever had the chance to look over your toes at the beach while floating peacefully a few yards offshore? Try **Rehoboth Beach** early in the morning when the boardwalk shops and arcades are closed.

If you are a beach person, Rehoboth is a fine place to come—the white sand is free of stones and stretches for miles. There is one shop after another to explore, and arcades offer more diversion. The ambience of the boardwalk is low-keyed and pleasant for a family-oriented beach holiday.

But if you can't stand any sight of beach "civilization," head south for the more isolated beach of **Delaware Seashore State Park.** This narrow strip between ocean and bay provides miles of pristine beach, and you can

Fenwick Island State
Park
c/o Holts Landing
State Park
P.O. Box 76
Millville 19970
302–539–9060

Indian River
Lifesaving Station
Bethany Beach 19930
302–227–0478

camp there as well. The park offers a marina with docks and hookups. Another park awaits you close to the southern border of Delaware—**Fenwick Island State Park**—just before the high-rises of Ocean City, Maryland, bring the city back to the sea with a vengeance.

The **Indian River Lifesaving Station** dates from 1876. It was one of six built along Delaware shores to help shipwreck victims. Life as a surfman was hard, especially after they heard the dreaded cry, "Ship ashore!"

Step into the station and you will be in the Mess Room where seven men and the keeper had their meals. One was on duty at all times, walking along the 2½ mile stretch of beach to meet a man from the other direction. They had to look for any distress signal, such as debris in the breakers. A projectile was shot out to a vessel, the sailors on board pulled on the line, and people were hauled in by a breeches buoy.

Have you seen people wearing braided bracelets? A boat hook could be used to grab the bracelet and haul someone in. The surfmen were required to try to resuscitate those apparently drowned to bring them back. It was a very hard life for $1.33 a day.

After visiting the Indian River Lifesaving Station stop for lunch at **Mango's** (97 Garfield Parkway, Bethany; 302–537–6621).

For more information on the area, call the **Rehoboth Beach–Dewey Beach Chamber of Commerce** at 800–441–1329.

From this point you can proceed to Ocean City, Maryland, to link up with Itinerary I, or you can continue on to New Jersey. If you are going on to New Jersey, return to Lewes to take the Cape May/Lewes Ferry (follow the signs to the ferry) for a seventy-minute crossing of Delaware Bay. (For ferry information, call 302–645–6313 from Delaware; 609–886–2718 for New Jersey.)

ITINERARY I:

New Jersey

CAPE MAY

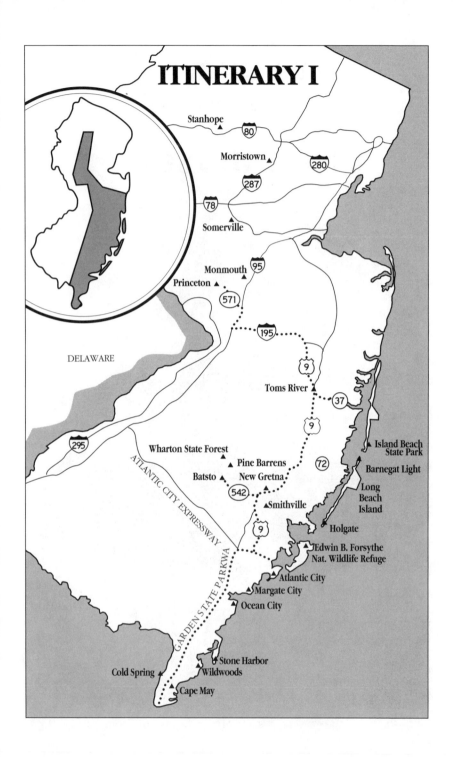

ITINERARY I

Stanhope ▲
80
Morristown ▲
280
287
78
Somerville ▲
Monmouth ▲ 95
Princeton ▲
571
DELAWARE
195
9
Toms River ▲
37
9
295
Island Beach State Park ▲
Wharton State Forest ▲
▲ Pine Barrens
Barnegat Light
Batsto ▲ New Gretna
542
72
Long Beach Island
Smithville ▲
ATLANTIC CITY EXPRESSWAY
9
Holgate ▲
▲ Edwin B. Forsythe Nat. Wildlife Refuge
Atlantic City ▲
GARDEN STATE PARKWA
Margate City ▲
Ocean City ▲
Stone Harbor ▲
Cold Spring ▲
Wildwoods
Cape May ▲

New Jersey

This itinerary through New Jersey links with itinerary H (Delaware) and itineraries J (Maryland) and K (Washington, D.C., and Virginia) along the Atlantic Coast.

≈ New Jersey ≈

Although some people think of New Jersey in terms of the megalopolis viewed from the New Jersey Turnpike, there is another, quiet side consisting of beaches, lakes, streams, pinelands, and marshes. The Appalachian Trail goes through the state. New Jersey is surrounded by water, except on the border it shares with New York. Vacationers enjoy the Delaware River, the Hudson River, and the barrier beaches along the Atlantic Coast.

Historically, New Jersey is packed with reminders of her past, dating from Henry Hudson's appearance in 1609. The Continental army crossed the state four times during the Revolutionary War.

For the purposes of this itinerary, we will begin in Cape May, head up the eastern coast, then turn west to Princeton and the Delaware River.

Cape May

Victoriana is in full swing in Cape May. Houses with lacy gingerbread woodwork racing up and down each peak look as if they'd just been painted. The entire town has been included on the National Historic Landmark list. You wouldn't think that a disastrous fire, the Great Fire of 1878, would have had such a silver lining. But when the ashes of the past had barely cooled, people started building their Victorian dream homes. Queen Victoria was responsible for the popularity of this architectural style both in England and the United States. Visitors from this country and abroad felt right at home as they vacationed in Cape May.

This ocean resort is the oldest in the United States. Cornelius Jacobsen Mey named the peninsula while on a trip of exploration from Holland in 1620; for the next hundred years, the village led a quiet agrarian life. Then came the explosion as vacationers discovered Cape May; in 1761 it became the first seashore resort in America. Famous visitors included Abraham Lincoln, Robert E. Lee, William Sherman, James Buchanan, Franklin Pierce, Ulysses S. Grant, William Harrison, P. T. Barnum, and John Philip Sousa.

Today a walking tour is the best way to see Cape May. Look for captain's walks, fretwork, cupolas, stained-glass windows, crowned dormers, rocking-chair porches, fancy fences, gazebos, and Victorian flower gardens. With several hundred houses to choose from, you and your camera can have a field day. Start your tour at **Cape May's Welcome Center,** where you can pick up a map and other information. This building was once a church; the "onion" dome on the tower is reminiscent of both the Orient and Bavaria. Visit the cluster of houses on Congress Street, including **Congress Hall** (Beach and Congress); **Annie Knight's and Joseph Evans's houses** (203 and 207 Congress Place), with captain's walks on their roofs; **Dr. Henry Hunt House** (209 Congress Place); and a "wedding cake" house, **Pink House** (33 Perry). Stroll down the mall, where shops line both sides of the street, and head onto Washington Street. **Alexander's Inn and Restaurant** (653 Washington) is said to be the oldest house in town. On the corner of Washington and Franklin is the **Fireman's Hall History Museum,** which houses a 1928 American La France fire engine. Across the street is the **Church of the Advent,** which has wonderful stained-glass windows. Dip down Washington to the **George Allen House** (720 Washington), designed by Samuel Sloan as an Italianate villa, and walk around the block to see it from all angles. Take Corgi to Franklin and jog to Hughes to a row of Victorian homes, beginning with Number 664 on the corner. This house is painted rose, gray, and white and is a photographer's dream, with no phone wires across its facade. Turn left on Stockton to the **Mainstay Inn** (635 Columbia), originally a gambling house and club known as Jackson's Clubhouse. From the corner of Columbia and Howard, you can see the **Chalfont Inn** (301 Howard), the only hotel that did not burn during the Great Fire (and therefore the oldest hotel in town). (See Inns appendix.) Cut across two blocks to Gurney Street and **The Abbey** (Columbia and Gurney); then stroll past a row of identical houses to the **Inn of Cape May** (Beach and Ocean), where Wallis Warfield, the Duchess of Windsor, had her coming-out party.

The **Emlen Physick House and Estate** was designed by the famous Philadelphia architect Frank Furness. The city of Cape May has leased this estate to the **Mid-Atlantic Center for the Arts;** if you're there in the summer, you can attend its theater (609–884–ARTS). Visitors during mid-October throng to the Victorian Week festival, presented by the Mid-Atlantic Center. There are house tours, boat trips, an antiques show, vaudeville, a marionette opera, a Victorian fashion show and lawn party, a grand ball, and more. The center also offers trolley tours, in either an enclosed

Cape May's Welcome Center
405 Lafayette Street
Cape May 08204
609–884–9562
The Depot
609 Lafayette Street
Cape May 08204
609–884–5508
Mid-Atlantic Center for the Arts
Emlen Physick House and Estate
1048 Washington Street
Cape May 08204
609–884–5404

bus or an open-air trolley, and an evening tour called "Mansions by Gaslight."

Twinings Tea Room (609–884–5404, ext. 138), also operated by MAC, is now a great place to have lunch, amid ornate iron grillwork on the horse stalls and natural wood paneling. Physick's grandfather, Philip Syng, was the silversmith who designed and made the inkwell used by the signers of the Declaration of Independence that is now on display in Independence Hall.

The carriage house was built in 1876, and the main house was begun in 1878. The stick-style construction, added to many gables, ridges, dormers, and chimneys, gives a cubical, top-heavy look to the house. Inside look for the different kinds of lincrusta wall-covering, an oil-based papier-mâché type of product (which, when made with molasses, attracted vermin and needed to be replaced!). The house has two different types of light fixtures: Electricity was used only until 10:00 P.M., when gas or candles were used. Look for the elegant soup tureen with three-dimensional carving; it was a housewarming present. The brass chandelier in the formal parlor has porcelain inserts. The house contains a collection of Victorian furnishings, clothing, toys, tools, and memorabilia. During the restoration process, a clock was stolen and later found by a dog underneath a local porch; it seems fitting that a man who kept fourteen dogs during his lifetime should have had his clock found by a dog.

Union Park Dining Room (at the Hotel Macomber, Beach Avenue and Howard Street; 609–884–8811) has gourmet cuisine in three dining rooms. The **Pelican Club** (at the Marquis de Lafayette Hotel, 581 Beach Drive; 609–884–3500) offers an extensive menu of sumptuous dishes. The view of the beach from its large windows on the sixth floor is one to remember. The **Mad Batter** (at the Carroll Villa Hotel, 19 Jackson Street; 609–884–5970) offers breakfast/lunch and dinner. Highly acclaimed for its changing, innovative menu, this is a place where guests will never go away hungry. Everything is fresh, attractively served, and delicious. The **Lobster House** (Fisherman's Wharf; 609–884–3064) offers dining rooms, take-out foods, a fish market, and a light menu in the Raw Bar. It's located right on a working fishing dock, and the fish couldn't be fresher.

Cape May Point

Cape May Point is the place to pick up "Cape May Diamonds," which are actually pieces of quartz that have been smoothed by the action of the waves; some people make them into jewelry. You might also be on hand when silver begins to surface from the *Juno,* a thirty-four-gun Spanish frigate that foundered off Cape May in 1802. In 1801 Spain was facing bankruptcy, so silver was shipped from Mexico to Spain on armed naval frigates instead of on the slower galleons. The *Juno* had over ten tons of Mexican silver on board as she headed for Spain; she encountered rough weather and put into San

> Cape May Point State Park
> Cape May Point
> 08212
> 609–884–2159

Juan, Puerto Rico, for repairs. She departed in October 1801 with 1,000 passengers, seamen, and soldiers on board. Gale winds swept away the mainsail, damaged a mast, and opened up seams in the hull. In an effort to lighten the sinking vessel, her anchors and many guns were tossed overboard. Emergency caulking and pumping below decks, and attempts to lash sails to the hull on the outside to slow the leaks, took the spirit right out of the entire crew. An American schooner, the *Favorite,* came upon the rapidly sinking ship, stood by to help as they saw her riding low, but then lost track of her during a storm. Although no one saw her position as she sank, some believe that she lies in 90 feet of water about 25 miles east of the mouth of Delaware off the tip of Cape May. The value of her silver has been estimated to be $4 million. The vessel's 7,100-pound anchor was snagged by a fisherman in June of 1968, 12½ miles off Cape May. It stands on the sea side of the Congress Hotel.

Cape May Point Lighthouse is one of the oldest functioning lighthouses in the country. As aficionados of historic lighthouses, we were happy to see it restored. You can climb the 199 steps to the top for a 360-degree view of Cape May. A number of lamps have been used in the tower, beginning with a classic lens installed in 1857 (now in the County Museum), a hydraulic float lamp from 1878, an incandescent oil-vapor lamp from 1910, and electrified lamps from 1938. Beginning that year lighthouse keepers were no longer required to live at the tower. The present light is visible 19 miles out at sea and flashes every ten seconds.

Cape May Point State Park offers a bird observatory, nature trails, a natural history museum, picnicking, and fishing. A museum on the grounds contains a tank with live lobsters, crabs, fish, and snails. Look for a smaller tank with a jaunty live seahorse strutting around. You'll also see fossil shells, a mastodon molar dredged off Cape May, a walrus tusk, ear bones of a right whale, honeycomb coral from the Devonian Age, and part of the rigging from an old sailing vessel. There is an exhibit of bird's nests, ranging from the smallest—a chipping sparrow who made a nest from wool left drying on a line by a weaver—to a large long-billed marsh wren nest. If you haven't seen Cape May diamonds before, you can see them here. You'll see clear, milky-clouded, orange-yellow, and smoky stones.

Take a walk on the boardwalk through the wildlife sanctuary, where you can enjoy sunshine without wind because of towering swamp grasses

Historic Cold Spring
Village
720 Route 9
Cold Spring 08201
609–898–2300

The Hedge Gardens
159 Fishing Creek
Road
Cold Spring 08201
609–886–5148

on both sides. You'll come out alongside several ponds, and there are benches for a rest while bird-watching.

After you emerge from your walk, join others on the Hawk Watch Platform. A posted list keeps you informed as to the number of species sighted to date. Cape May Point is said to be an ideal vantage point for bird-watching during migration, because of the location of this natural funnel. Active flights take place following a cold front—several thousand birds can be spotted in a single day. Roger Tory Peterson names Cape May as one of the dozen birding hotspots in North America.

Nearby, on the other side of the Cape May Canal, **Historic Cold Spring Village** is a re-created historical village. Fifteen restored buildings house crafts shops and a country store. Craftspeople are at work in their shops, and some of them give lessons at scheduled times. A working farm and petting zoo are also on the grounds. Nearby **The Hedge Gardens** exhibit more than 175 green sculptures made from hedges.

From Cape May heading north toward Atlantic City, you have two choices. You may take Route 9, the shore road along the barrier beach, which is often slow and exasperating, with many stoplights in built-up areas, but does provide some glimpses of the ocean. Your other alternative is the Garden State Parkway on the mainland proper, which provides faster, uninterrupted travel. The season, the weather, and your inclination should dictate the best choice on a given day.

The Wildwoods

Five miles of beaches and 3 miles of boardwalk at the Wildwoods add up to crowds during the season. The first beach area north of Cape May, it is one of the safest in New Jersey because the surf line stands 1,000 feet from shore. **Hereford Lighthouse** dates back to the 1800s and is listed on the National Register of Historic Places. The **English Cottage Gardens** that surround the lighthouse are beautiful, with more than 170 plant species. Here you may wander paths or rest on benches for quiet contemplation in this lovely "butterfly garden."

Follow Route 9 to Stone Harbor.

Stone Harbor

The **Stone Harbor Bird Sanctuary** provides a home for many species, including American egret, Louisiana heron, green heron, black crowned and yellow crowned night herons, cattle egret, and glossy ibis. Although visitors are not permitted inside the sanctuary, there is a visitors' center on Ocean Drive where you may spot birds flying and put coins into mounted binoculars to view birds.

The **Wetlands Institute and Museum** offers an observation tower, salt marsh trail, and Wetlandia Museum. This is the place to go to observe birds in a protected salt marsh and tidal creeks.

The **Cape May County Park and Zoo** offers 200 acres of natural habitat. The zoo is free and you can visit 180 species of animals. You might see Charlie Camel, Jerome Giraffe, Brutus & Tinkerbelle Cougar, Max & Ellie Lion, or Matilda & Dundee Wallaby, among others.

Leaming's Run Colonial Gardens is the place to wander through twenty-five blooming gardens on paths shaded by tall trees. Thomas Leaming, a New England whaler, purchased land in 1695 and built his home there. A stream runs through the property, and there's a gazebo and benches for a rest. Every year 10,000 flowers are planted in carefully planned gardens by color or species. You can savor a red and blue garden, an orange garden, an English garden, and many others. On the path you will pass the 1706 Leaming house; there are resident poultry living on the property. Hummingbirds are a special treat in August.

Stone Harbor Bird
  Sanctuary
111th to 117th
  Streets between
  2nd & 3rd Avenues
Stone Harbor 08247
609–368–5102 or
609–368–1211

Wetlands Institute
  and Museum
Stone Harbor
  Boulevard
Stone Harbor 08247
609–368–1211

Cape May County
  Park
Route 9 North
Cape May Court
  House 08210
609–465–5271

Leaming's Run
  Colonial Gardens
1845 Route 9 North
Swainton 08210
609–465–5871

Lucy the Margate
  Elephant
Atlantic Avenue
Margate City 08402
609–823–6473

Ocean City

Continue on Route 9 to Ocean City, which has been offering family vacations for more than one hundred years. Founded in 1879 by three Methodist ministers named Lake, the town was, and is, dry, which may account for its attraction to families. The beach is 8 miles long, and the port is popular with yachtsmen for fishing, sailing, and sightseeing.

Margate City

Lucy the Margate Elephant is worth a trip to Margate. One of the four "Victorian follies" built by James V. Lafferty in the 1880s, Lucy stands six stories high. You can walk inside, climb up the stairs in her legs, and

| Absecon Lighthouse |
| Rhode Island & |
| Pacific Avenues |
| Atlantic City 08404 |

visit a museum. She was originally designed to lure buyers to the real-estate development run by Lafferty. In the 1960s it looked as if she might be cast aside as Atlantic City went into decline, but with the help of many children Lucy was preserved.

Atlantic City

The Atlantic City Expressway leads from the Garden State Parkway or Route 9 to Atlantic City.

"On the Boardwalk of Atlantic City"—the rollicking tune lured summer visitors to the pleasures of Atlantic City in past eras. A decline beginning in the 1930s ravaged the town, but since the casino law of 1977, she seems to be recovering her old pizzazz.

In 1854, when the first railroad arrived, Atlantic City began to attract vacationers, and the first boardwalk was laid in 1870. The rolling chair, introduced in 1884 by a Philadelphia wheelchair manufacturer, is still a popular tourist vehicle for gliding along the boardwalk (you can also rent a bicycle). And yes, you can buy saltwater taffy in the shops along the boardwalk. Amusement piers house a variety of entertainments and frivolities. The beach itself is appealing: There is less undertow than usual because the configuration of the coastline shelters the beach somewhat; the Gulf Stream also makes both weather and water more temperate. Surfing is permitted, and lifeguards are on duty all summer. Fishermen haul in striped bass, flounder, kingfish, and snapper blues from the piers or the beach. You can also head out to sea in a charter boat to catch marlin, tuna, and bonito. Those interested in the less artificial aspects of the environment will want to visit **Absecon Lighthouse,** built in 1857. Stop by the new **Ocean Life Education Center** to experience sea life in two large aquarium tanks and to learn about ecotourism on the many computers.

The revival of Atlantic City has less to do with its benign climate and setting than with money. Visitors who are interested in gambling will find one place after another—all eager to take their money. Perhaps even more fun than gambling is watching the intent faces of those bound and determined to break the bank in a casino. You will see row after row of clanging machines in a glittering warehouse of illusions, each one with a strained but hopeful face before it. Or you can watch hands: At the gaming tables people extend their hands full of bills, which pass through the croupier's hands directly into a slot from which they can never be retrieved. Chips are thrown both by hands with sparkling diamonds and those with work-worn fingers. Roulette wheels turn; chips are scooped up, stacked, sold, distributed; and card games continue hand after hand. The rooms themselves are a mirage of glass, gold, mirrors, and bright lights. When you tire of gambling, you can watch a show, often with big-name performers; if you want to be sure to get into a particular performance, get your tickets in advance.

> Edwin B. Forsythe
> National Wildlife
> Refuge
> Route 9
> Oceanville 08231
> 609–652–1665
>
> Town of Historic
> Smithville
> Route 9
> Smithville 08201
> 609–652–7775

Edwin B. Forsythe National Wildlife Refuge

Just across the Absecon Inlet from Atlantic City lies the Brigantine barrier beach and, behind it, within sight of high-rise casinos, one of the most extensive protected salt marshes in the state. The **Edwin B. Forsythe National Wildlife Refuge** contains more than 22,000 acres of wetlands that attract flocks of migrating birds. You can walk on nature trails or drive through the refuge, which is reached by taking Route 9 north from Atlantic City through Absecon to Oceanville.

Smithville

Twelve miles north of Atlantic City, also on Route 9, you will find the **Town of Historic Smithville,** a restored village of sixty homes and shops collected from various locations in southern New Jersey. Each one dates from the 1800s and has been renovated for use in the village. The village is attractive, with winding streets, a lake, and many shops for you to explore. The **Towne Book Shoppe** (609–652–1999) has a well-chosen assortment of books.

Pine Barrens

From Smithville take Route 9 and the Garden State Parkway to New Gretna, then Route 542 west to **Batsto,** a jumping-off point for the Pine Barrens. Once the bottom of an ocean, the Pine Barrens are composed of hundreds of square miles of scrub oak and pine, blueberries and cranberries, and, believe it or not, wild orchids. It is also hard to believe that this wilderness of a million acres is located right in the middle of a megalopolis, just a few miles east of the Boston-Washington corridor. The Lenape Indians were probably the first to live there, but any traces of their existence have been swallowed up by the forest. Loggers probably moved in next, but again, not much remains of their existence. The discovery of bog iron inspired the construction of furnaces like the Batsto Furnace, built by

Batsto Historic Site
Wharton State Forest
Route 542
Hammonton 08037
609–561–3262

Atsion Recreation
 Area Ranger Station
Route 206
Atsion
609–268–0444

Charles Read in 1766. The Batsto Furnace was necessary as a supplier of munitions during the Revolutionary War. Glassworks also appeared on the scene for a short time but failed to be successful.

Joseph Wharton, from Philadelphia, bought many tracts of land in the barrens, totaling 99,672 acres around the Batsto River. The Batsto area of the **Wharton State Forest** is part of his estate. The village of Batsto (from the Swedish word *baatstoo,* meaning "steam bath") was founded by Swedish explorer Erik Mullica. The village has been renovated, and you can visit workers' cottages, post office, general store, gristmill, sawmill, ironmaster's mansion, and farm exhibits. When you get to the horse barn, look at the vertical slots in the walls, which were designed to prevent hay inside from molding. You may wonder about the workers' black homes, which are typical of the area. They were built of Jersey cedar clapboards that blacken with age and the weather.

Legends abound about the "Pine Robbers," who fled into the forest to safety. Some are based on historical fact; others are embellished fiction— believe what you will. Some say that Joe Mulliner, who was hanged in 1781, was the "Robin Hood" of the Pine Barrens. Apparently he was finally captured because he could not resist coming out of hiding to dance in a local tavern. Many stories have been told about a local "wizard" named Jerry Munyhon, who could make an ax chop wood without a hand to guide it, "catch" a bullet fired at him without being wounded, and inspire a rooster to pull a loaded wagon up a hill. "Pineys," the people who live deep in the forest, have tales to tell about the "Witch of the Pine," Peggy Clevenger. They say that she could turn herself into a rabbit and that she had a treasure of gold. Residents also tell about various monsters who inhabit the forest, including the Jersey Devil, who carried off farm and domestic animals, leaving cloven tracks behind.

If you've read John McPhee's *The Pine Barrens,* you will have some understanding about this part of New Jersey, which is so near a megalopolis and yet so isolated and rural.

Although you can drive through the Pine Barrens, you will probably get a better feel for this enchanted land if you choose to paddle along the network of rivers in the forest. The **Oswego, Wading, Batsto,** and **Mullica Rivers** are all popular canoe routes. Canoes can be rented from **Atsion Recreation Area.** We rented a canoe from **Adams Canoe Rental** (694 Atsion Road, Vincentown; 609–268–0189) and were taken by truck to the beginning of our trip on the Batsto. Although we did not see another person during the five hours we were on the river, we did see lots of turkey buzzards, herons, Canada geese, mallards, woodpeckers, and water bugs. The winding river housed beaver dams, but we didn't spot a beaver. Cedars along the shore interspersed with sandbars and sandy banks were just right for a lunch stop.

Long Beach Island

Retrace your way through the Pine Barrens back to the Garden State Parkway or Route 9. Head north to exit 63 or the town of Manahawkin, and take Route 72 across a long causeway to **Ship Bottom.** Long Beach Island is an 18-mile barrier isle ranging in width from several blocks to a mile. During the eighteenth century fishermen, sea captains, and pilots lived on the island. Shipwrecks are concentrated along this sandspit, which was lethal to those caught in a storm, misled by lights on shore, or hugging the coast to make a fast passage into New York. The beach at **Holgate,** at the southern end, has been inundated with coins. Those who have made a study of the effects of wind and weather patterns on the beach know that after a northeast storm, which scoops up sand and brings new sand to the top, the west winds of the following high-pressure system blow the top layers of sand away. Then the coins that are surfacing hold down a bit of sand as the surrounding loose sand blows away. This is the time to search for little mounds of sand—and a coin on top!

Years ago there was an island named Tucker's Island at the south end of Long Beach Island; Tucker's has now been entirely reclaimed by the sea. In the 1800s, according to legend, a chest of Spanish coins was taken from Tucker's Island. Two men rowed in from a waiting sloop, inquired about the location of two cedar trees in relation to a lighthouse, dug up a chest, tossed the coins into sacks, and sailed away in their sloop. The empty chest was found by the crew at the Life Saving Station . . . as well as a rusty cutlass.

It is likely that pirates (Captain Kidd included) were in and out of the sheltered waters behind the island, Little Egg Harbor, and Barnegat Bay, plundering when they could and stashing their treasure against a precarious future. In addition to pirates, the island attracted a particularly noxious breed of scavengers known as "wreckers" or "mooncussers." They walked their horses carrying lights at night, to simulate a vessel sailing close to shore. Wishing to cut their time going into New York, many captains veered closer to shore. The wreckers then reaped the benefits of their deception. One legend relates the story of the ghost who still walks the length of the island, sobbing. The girl who moans was forced to accompany her father, the leader of a wrecking group, as he removed rings and

Barnegat Lighthouse
Barnegat Lighthouse
State Park
Long Beach Island
08008
609–494–2016
Island Beach State
Park
Route 37
908–793–0506
Princeton University
Princeton 08540

valuables from the corpses washed up on shore. When she came upon the still body of her lover, who had joined the crew of that ill-fated ship, she went mad, and she still walks the beach in ethereal form on dark nights.

Marking the inlet at the northern tip of the island, **Barnegat Lighthouse,** affectionately known as "Old Barney," was built in 1857 when an earlier lighthouse dating from 1834 had collapsed into the sea. You can climb up 217 steps for a sweeping seascape of bay, barrier beach, and ocean.

Island Beach State Park

Retrace your way to the Garden State Parkway and head north to exit 82 at **Toms River.** If you have not yet had your fill of barrier beaches and would like to enjoy one that is undeveloped, take Route 37 to **Island Beach State Park.** This 10-mile strip of land offers nature trails, picnicking, fishing, and swimming without the commercialism of beach towns or the clutter of real-estate developments.

From this point you can head north through the older exurban beach and river towns on the way to New York City—Mantoloking, Point Pleasant Beach, Spring Lake, Ocean Grove, Asbury Park, Long Branch, Shrewsbury, Red Bank. Or take the Garden State Parkway to I–195 to Route 571 for a scenic trip through the countryside to Princeton.

Princeton

Princeton has a rural charm that fits the image of a small, Ivy League university town and has survived the astounding growth of high-tech research institutions and corporate headquarters in the surrounding countryside. As you drive into town from the north, west, or south, you will see one mansion after another, all beautifully landscaped with lush groundcover, gigantic old trees, and seasonal flowers. **Princeton University,** like its counterpart in England (Cambridge), has a campus with a sense of space and tranquillity that seems forever immune from the bustle of the town or the highway just 1 mile east. Many of its buildings also imitate those of Cambridge colleges like King's or Trinity—in the collegiate Gothic style with gray stone—or the red brick of the newer parts of St. John's, interspersed with a few Victorian brownstones and Greek Revival buildings. Nostalgia for the nineteenth-century sense of "college days" sometimes overwhelms a visitor who wanders through the campus on a warm spring afternoon or evening, while a visit during reunions in June immerses you in the world of F. Scott Fitzgerald. The highlight of that celebration, the P-rade, is a visual celebration of the generations marching by, the young following the old, class by class, behind banners and in costume; we recall one in which Jimmy Stewart stood out because he was a head taller than anyone else in the Class of 1932.

> Orange Key Guide
> Service
> Maclean House
> Princeton University
> Princeton 08540
> 609–258–3603

The town was founded in 1696 by Quakers, who named it "Prince's Town." The university began as a college in 1746 in Elizabeth; then it moved to Newark and finally to Princeton in 1756. Nassau Hall served as barracks and a hospital for American and British troops one after the other during the Revolutionary War. Washington was victorious in the Battle of Princeton on January 3, 1777; a monument at Mercer, Nassau, and Stockton Streets commemorates this battle. After the Revolution the Continental Congress met in Nassau Hall for six months in 1783.

You can take a free guided tour of the Princeton University campus by calling the **Orange Key Guide Service** three days in advance. The oldest building on the campus, **Nassau Hall,** was named for the House of Orange, which reigned in England when the college was founded; silencing its bell by climbing to the belfry and stealing the clapper was, for many years, an obligation of the new freshman class. The **Gothic Chapel** was built in 1928 and contains lovely stained-glass windows, which mountaineering students sometimes scale to worry their elders. The **Harvey S. Firestone Library,** built in the late forties, with an extensive later addition, contains individual study carrels for students working on senior theses; rare books; and a superb collection of books and manuscripts made accessible by an open-stack system. Among other notable buildings on campus worth a visit are the **Woodrow Wilson School of Public and International Affairs,** designed by Minoru Yamasaki and set off with a plaza, reflecting pool, and fountain. The newly expanded **McCormick Art Museum** now has enough galleries to display a larger portion of its wealth in collections of paintings, sculpture, and other art forms. The **James Forrestal Research Campus** was opened in 1951 to provide research facilities in the disciplines of applied mathematics, physics, and chemistry. It is located just beyond **Lake Carnegie,** east of the campus, and contains a cyclotron and other instruments for advanced research in atomic physics.

One entrepreneurial family, the Stocktons, were the seed of much of Princeton's later prosperity. Richard Stockton purchased large tracts of land, some of it from William Penn, in 1697. His grandson, Richard, a signer of the Declaration of Independence, built **Morven,** a Georgian mansion,

Drumthwacket
Stockton Street
Princeton 08540
609–683–0057

Bainbridge House
158 Nassau Street
Princeton 08540
609–921–6748

between 1751 and 1759. His grandson, Robert Field Stockton, became a commodore in the Navy, fought in the War of 1812 and the Mexican American War, helped build the Delaware and Raritan Canal and the railroad along it in the 1830s, became a U.S. senator, and spent much of the family fortune building three elegant mansions in Princeton.

Former Stockton land offers many opportunities for visitors interested in architecture. Declining family fortunes forced the subdivison of Morven land in 1890, just at the right moment to create one of the most beautiful residential districts in America. It was very appealing to residents of New York and Philadelphia, who could rusticate in a country town and still reach the cities conveniently by the main line of the Pennsylvania railroad. To appreciate the results, walk through the secluded section just northwest of Morven, especially on Library Place, Boudinot Street, Morven Place, Hodge Road, Lilac Lane, and Cleveland Lane.

Drumthwacket, a Greek Revival mansion built in 1834, is now the official residence of the governor of New Jersey. *Drumthwacket* means "Wooded Hill" in Gaelic. The house is open to the public on Wednesdays from noon to 2:00 P.M.

The Historical Society of Princeton has restored the **Bainbridge House,** which was built in 1766. It was the birthplace of William Bainbridge, who commanded the USS *Constitution* during the War of 1812. Two period rooms have been restored, and a special museum room has been developed for children. Visitors can also receive information on self-guided tours on eighteenth-century houses in town, the university campus, and a Revolutionary War route in the Princeton-Trenton area.

Those focused on Princeton's important role in the Revolution will enjoy **Battlefield State Park,** located 1½ miles southwest of the borough on Mercer Street. Here Washington was victorious in the Battle of Princeton on January 3, 1777, just after his victory at Trenton. The battlefield contains the **Thomas Clark House,** built by a Quaker farmer in 1770 and until recently, the tree marked **Mercer Oak,** where General Mercer fell mortally wounded before he was carried into the Clark farmhouse.

"Bagging the fox" didn't work for British General Cornwallis, who considered himself the hunter and George Washington the fox. Luckily the weather turned cold and froze the muddy tracks after Cornwallis and his troops had slogged through from Trenton. Washington and his men were able to make more speed, even though they were exhausted. A monument at the juncture of Mercer, Nassau, and Stockton Streets commemorates this victory.

Rockingham, also known as the Berrien Mansion, is where Martha and George Washington lived in 1783 while the Continental Congress was convening in Nassau Hall. Washington's "Farewell Address to the Armies" was written in Rockingham, which has been restored with period furnishings. The building is closed for restoration and will reopen at a new site; call for information.

Rockingham
Princeton 08540
609–921–8835

If you're ready for lunch, head for **Annex Grill** (128 Nassau Street; 609–921–7555), **Chesapeake Bagel Bakery** (179 Nassau Street; 609–921–8646), **Homestate Cafe or Gratella** (a Tuscan-style grill) in The Forrestal (100 College Road East; 609–452–7800), or **J. B. Winberie** (One Palmer Square; 609–921–0700).

Monmouth

East of Princeton lies Monmouth on Route 522. Mary Ludwig Hays, also known as "Molly Pitcher," is a heroine who took over firing her husband's cannon after he was wounded and overcome by heat during the Battle of Monmouth. She also carried water into the battlefield for the soldiers, earning her the nickname of Molly Pitcher. As a reward, she was presented to General Washington.

The long and crucial Battle of Monmouth took place in 100-degree heat on June 28, 1778. The 1777 American victory at Saratoga and the entry of the French into the battle on the American side set the stage. The French navy confronted the British early in 1778; the British fled Philadelphia, planning to regroup in New York. Almost 20,000 British troops and a 12-mile-long train started across New Jersey. However, Washington's army of 12,700 troops, trained at Velley Forge, were in hot pursuit.

The Americans had two choices: to attack or to harass the British. On June 27, while in the Village Inn in Englishtown, Washington decided to send 5,000 troops to attack, under the leadership of General Charles Lee, the rear guard. Washington's soldiers intercepted British General Sir Henry Clinton and his men as they were retreating from Philadelphia to Sandy Hook.

The fighting lasted until dusk. It was reported that 200 Americans and 300 British were killed or missing. About half of the casualties resulted from heat prostration. The Americans took a well-earned sleep; the British rested awhile and then continued retreating to Sandy Hook and New York City. An important battle in the War for Independence had ended.

Historians note that the goal of the British army was to find the

Monmouth
Battlefield State
Park
347 Freehold Road
Manalapan 07726
908–462–9616

American army in an open field and defeat it. However, each time the British came close, Washington made a brillant tactical decision. This battle was a military and political victory for the Americans. Von Steuben's training at Valley Forge had shaped the Continental volunteers into strong soldiers, the equals of the British regulars.

The **Visitor's Center** is the place to begin—a large electronic relief map provides an orientation so you can follow the route of the troops during the battle. An archaeological dig produced many artifacts, such as musket balls, ramrod tips, pipe fragments, buttons, buckles, coins, a shoulder box, and a Charlevoix musket.

Craig House, dating from 1710, is on the grounds; it was built by Archibald Craig for his family of eleven children and used as a field hospital by the British during the battle. There are two sections to the building: a Dutch-framed house built for John Craig's father between 1746 and 1747, which is now the kitchen, and an English-framed, two-story addition dating from 1770.

When Mrs. Craig heard that the British were approaching her farm, she took her children and two slaves and fled by wagon. Although she flung the family silver into the well to protect it, apparently the British found it.

Tennant Church, dating from 1751, stands on a hill that overlooks the battlefield, and you can get your bearings there. The churchyard contians bodies of Americans who died in the Battle of Monmouth. New headstones have replaced the old, crumbling ones, including that of Captain Henry Fauntleroy of Virginia, felled by a cannonball on his twenty-second birthday.

Sir Henry Clinton stayed at **Covenhoven,** at 150 West Main Street in freehold. The house has been restored and is open to visitors.

Monmouth Battlefield State Park is the scene of an annual firelock shoot and living history celebration in April and the annual reenactment of the Battle of Monmouth in June. Call for other special events.

From Princeton you can head to **Washington Crossing** on Route 206 and scenic Route 546 for exploration of the Delaware Canal area and Bucks County (see Itinerary G).

Somerville

You can also head north on route 206 to Somerville and **Duke Gardens.** In 1958 Doris Duke began creating her gardens. She traveled widely all over the world and brought back ideas from Italy, England, France, China, Japan, and more. Eleven gardens, all under glass, are offered to visitors. Statues and thematic pieces enhance the blooms. The effect is magnificent and each garden is meticulously maintained.

The Italian Garden is especially handsome with a number of sculptures, hibiscus, orchids, begonia, and tulips in the spring. The English Topiary Garden has mirrors with English ivy, pansies, a rock garden with primroses, and English herbs. The Desert Garden includes jade, barrow plant, century plant, Burbank prickly pear, and cactus. The Chinese Garden is very photogenic with camphor tree, a moon bridge, goldfish in the pond, wisteria, and a Chinese summer home. The Rain Forest is reminiscent of India and Africa with all sorts of tropical plants.

Duke Gardens
Route 206
Somerville 08876
908–722–3700

Village of Waterloo
Waterloo Road
Stanhope 07874
201–347–0900

Morristown National
Historical Park
Morristown 07960
973–539–2085

Stanhope

Continue on Route 206 to Stanhope and the **Village of Waterloo.** You can wander through this restored eighteenth- and nineteenth-century village. Homesteaders were on the site by the mid-1740s. By 1760, after iron had been found, the village had a four-fire, two-hammer forge, a grist- and a sawmill, and homes for workers, the ironmaster, and the forgeman. In 1812 Brigadier General John Smith bought the forge farm and named it Waterloo Foundry after Wellington, defeater of Napolean at Waterloo in 1815.

The Morris Canal used inclined planes to lift and lower boats. Waterloo was a lock and plane stop along the route. The village was a thriving inland port of fifteen houses by 1844. In 1847 a railroad was built to carry iron ore between mines and the ore docks at Waterloo.

Today many of the structures are open for visitors. You'll see the Methodist Church, a stone tenant house, several grand mansions, a tavern, a blacksmith shop, a sawmill, a gristmill, a canal museum, a weaving barn, antique carriages, an herb garden, and a Lenape Indian Village.

You can also enjoy cycling, hiking, boating, canoeing, rafting, fishing, golf, and hiking in the area. Several parks and forests offer the chance to get out and enjoy nature.

Morristown

The large **Morristown National Historical Park,** the first to be established in the United States, has three units. The **Ford Mansion** on Washington Place dates from 1772. General and Mrs. Washington lived there during the winter of 1779–1780, along with the owner, recently widowed Mrs. Theodosia Ford, and her four children. This large house is furnished with Chippendale furniture.

The **Washington Headquarters Museum and Library** documents the history of the period with an orientation film, exhibits, and an extensive collection of books and manuscripts relating to Revolutionary and colonial times.

Fort Nonsense, on Washington Street, was built by Washington's soldiers during the first encampment in 1777 as a defense for supplies in town. Cannons were placed to defend the north and south roads as well as the town. According to legend, Washington had his men build it just to keep them busy and less prone to desert—hence the name.

Jockey Hollow, the third site, located on Western Avenue 5 miles southwest of town, is the principal location of the later encampment. There the Continental Army spent the miserable winter of 1779–1780, enduring a succession of blizzards. Five reconstructed soldiers' huts represent the 1,200 that once filled the hollow. Today it is a wildlife sanctuary with hiking trails amidst flowers and woods. There you can also see the **Wick House,** a restored farmhouse once occupied by Major General Arthur St. Clair, commander of the Pennsylvania Line.

ITINERARY J:

Maryland

SMITH ISLAND

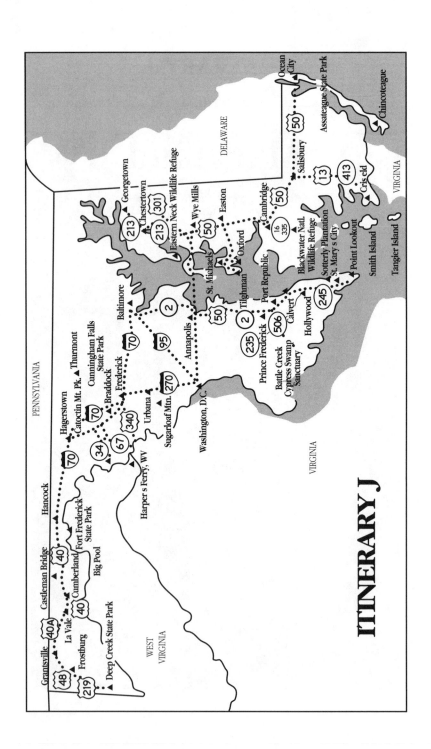

ITINERARY J

Maryland

This itinerary begins in historic Annapolis, a fine geographic center for explorations out in every direction. Chesapeake Bay divides southern Maryland (or the Western Shore) from the Eastern Shore, also called the Delmarva peninsula because Delaware, Maryland, and Virginia share the land between Chesapeake Bay and the Atlantic shore. Ocean City and Assateague Island National Seashore, at the most easterly point of Maryland, represent the extremes of beach hotels and wild seashore. Villages and towns along the Eastern Shore of Chesapeake Bay, from Crisfield in the south through Salisbury, Cambridge, Oxford, Easton, St. Michaels, and Chestertown, provide a full range of bayside communities, from those filled with working watermen to yachting centers. Touring south from Annapolis takes you to Prince Frederick, the harbors and shellfish of Solomons, the settlement at St. Mary's City, and Point Lookout. Heading north from Annapolis brings you to a rejuvenated Baltimore; then turning west toward the mountains takes you to the historic district in Frederick, Hagerstown, Cumberland, and Grantsville. Thus, in the span of 200 miles, you can move from Atlantic beaches through quiet bay villages and large cities to the Cumberland Mountains. In small compass, Maryland has it all.

≈ *Annapolis* ≈

Annapolis is a waterfront city with salt water washing right up into the City Dock. This narrow slip of water juts in to meet the bottom of Main and Cornhill Streets. Almost everyone gravitates at one time or another to the dock area—a busy place with fishing and pleasure boats going in and out. Annapolis has all the lure of an active port, as well as a rich historical heritage stretching back to its founding in the seventeenth century. A Kunta Kinte plaque on City Dock commemorates the 1767 arrival of slaves from Africa. Alex Haley wrote about this in *Roots*.

Annapolis was first established under the name of Providence, chosen by its Puritan settlers. Then a ship's captain was honored by the choice of his name, Proctor, for the town. Later it was called City by the Severn, the river on which it is located. Some records refer to it as Anne Arundel Town, Arrundell Towne, or Arundelton. In 1694 it became the capital of Maryland, when Governor Francis Nicholson moved the center of government from St. Mary's City to this centrally located site. He directed his commissioners "to survey and lay out in the most commodious and convenient parte and place of the said Towne six Acres of Land intire for the erecting a Court House and other buildings as shall be thought necessary and convenient." In 1694 Annapolis was chosen as the city's name to honor Queen Anne.

The city became an important and strategically located seaport, in addition to serving as the administrative center of Maryland during the Revolution. Ships sailed in and out of the harbor right past the blockade of English vessels. The Continental Congress met in the Maryland State House in 1783 and again in 1784 to ratify the Treaty of Paris, ending the Revolution. During the Civil War Annapolis was important as a shipping center, partial to the Union side in spite of the mixed sentiments that plagued all of Maryland during that internecine conflict. Later in the century the infant U.S. Naval Academy—which had been founded in 1845, at least partly in response to the uproar over the mutiny on the brig *Somers,* in which a midshipman had been hanged—began to grow toward its present stature as a rival of West Point.

Annapolis was laid out in terms of the best urban planning of its day; you can easily walk anywhere you need to go along a series of streets that are spokes radiating from two sister circles, State and Church, at the center. (Car-less, we did this for a year and know it works.) No one could have imagined the impact of the automobile on this plan when it was established in 1694. You may be lucky enough to find a parking place on one of the streets not restricted to those with a resident's permit, but beware of the time limit, which is two hours on Maryland Avenue and State Circle. Prince George Street, King George Street, and College Avenue are also zoned for two-hour free parking, and that may not give you enough time to complete your tour. Traffic police are active, and they do tow. There is a parking ramp between Main Street and Duke of Gloucester Street, near the foot of the hill. If you are touring in season, you may find it easier to park in the Navy–Marine Corps Stadium, just off Route 50/301, and take a shuttle bus into town; it runs every fifteen minutes and charges a nominal fee. The bus looks like a trolley car from the past. There is also parking at the Visitors' Center off Calvert Street.

You can begin to know Annapolis by visiting the Annapolis Visitor Center (26 West Street; 800–394–5717 or 410–280–0445). **Three Centuries Tours of Annapolis** (48 Maryland Avenue; 410–263–5401) offers a guided tour and **Historic Annapolis** (Paca House, 186 Prince George Street; 410–267–7619) offers an audio tour. This is the best way to see the city. Your family may enjoy being directed by a guide in colonial costume, who will pull relevant objects out of her basket as she reaches each new location. Our guide had a great deal of precise information, interspersed with anecdotes and stories, to make the history of Annapolis come alive. "Historic Annapolis Walk with Walter Cronkite," an audiocassette, is available from the **Historic Annapolis Foundation Museum** store and welcome center (77 Main Street, 410–268–5576). The **Treasury,** built in 1735, has the distinction of being the oldest public building in Maryland. There's also a mini-bus tour called "Discover Annapolis" (410–626–6000). It leaves from the Visitors' Center.

Annapolis will captivate architecture buffs, and it could serve as a useful school for students of the evolution of architecture in America. As you walk around Annapolis, you'll notice buildings marked with historic-district plaques that are color-coded according to date and style. Colors signify time periods as follows: provincial green (seventeenth century), terra cotta (eighteenth century), blue (Federal), verdigris (Greek Revival), aubergine (Victorian), and ochre (twentieth century). The earliest structures are plain seventeenth-century houses like the one at **130 Prince George Street.** This house was patterned after wooden-frame houses with little decoration, which were common in English villages. The gambrel roof is topped by the very large central chimney typical of colonial homes.

The Georgian period, from 1700 to 1780, presents carved classical motifs on a two-and-one-half-story building, with tall chimneys at the ends, a center doorway, and all windows and dormers symmetrical. Some of them, like the William Paca House (see later in this section) at **186 Prince George Street,** have a center block and an attached building on either end.

The Federal period, from 1780 to 1840, is typified by either brick or frame structures that are simple in design, two and one-half or three stories high, with steeply pitched roofs and tall chimneys usually placed at the ends. An example of this period may be seen at **223–225 Duke of Gloucester Street.**

The Greek Revival period, from 1825 to 1850, was derived from the Greek temple, with columns or pilasters on the facade below a triangular roof line, illustrated by the **Franklin Law Office** at 17 State Circle. The Gothic Revival style, from 1830 to 1880, used a pointed arch, buttresses, and rose windows; see **St. Mary's Church** on Duke of Gloucester Street. The Romanesque Revival style features heavy round arches and plain walls copied from northern Italian buildings, exemplified by **St. Anne's** on Church Circle. The Italianate or Bracketed style, from 1850 to 1900, is a popular Victorian Revival design, which was used in Annapolis at **132 Charles Street.** Flat facades and roofs with a carved wooden bracket under the cornice resemble the features of Italian palaces. Some Italianate houses have a peaked roof and a tower on one side and perhaps a bay window, as does the example at **243 Prince George Street.**

The French Second Empire period, from 1865 to 1890, is known for the mansard roof, sometimes covered with multicolored slates. The house at **195 Duke of Gloucester Street** is typical of this period. The Queen Anne period, from 1875 to 1890, may include gables, turrets, half-timbering, carved wood trim, and the use of several colors. Go to **138 Conduit Street** and **86–88 State Circle** for good examples of this style. Colonial Revival and Neo-Georgian styles date from 1895 to 1930, taking design features from the seventeenth century, Georgian, and Federal periods, as does the home at **59 Franklin Street.**

> Maryland State
> House
> State Circle
> Annapolis 21401
> 410–974–3400
>
> Governor Calvert
> House
> 58 State Circle
> Annapolis 21401

The **Maryland State House** was built in 1772 and has the honor of being the oldest state house in continuous legislative use in the United States. It also served as the U.S. Capitol from November 1783 to August 1784. George Washington resigned his commission as commander in chief of the Continental armies in the Old Senate Chamber. Patriotic fervor for this admired leader was expressed during a celebration the day before the resignation, given by Governor William Paca. Supplies for the evening were furnished by Mann's Hotel as follows: "ninety-eight bottles of wine, two and one-half gallons of spirits, nine pounds of sugar, a lot of limes, music and waiters, and a dozen packs of cards." A hogshead of rum (116 gallons) was provided by James Makubbin. Food included "15 pounds of loaf sugar, 176 pounds of bacon, 284 pounds of salt beef, 52 pounds of shoat, 126 pounds of mutton, 272 pounds of veal, 183 pounds of beef, 7 lambs and 12 fowls."

The official end of the Revolutionary War came with the signing of the Treaty of Paris in the State House in 1784. Charles Willson Peale painted a number of portraits for the State House, including one of George Washington with Tench Tilghman, his aide-de-camp, that hangs over the fireplace in the **Old Senate Chamber.** There's a bronze plaque on the floor marking the spot where George Washington stood when he resigned. An audiovisual program, guided tour, and exhibits are available. Don't miss the pitted iron cannon displayed on the lawn. Governor Calvert had a number of these cannons—which had been brought from England in 1634 by the first settlers—mounted on the fort at St. Mary's. Used to defend the settlers against Indians, Spaniards, Frenchmen, or pirates, the cannons eventually fell into the water, where they lay for 200 years, becoming pitted in the process. A sister to this cannon can be seen at St. Mary's.

If you are fascinated by "digs" of archaeological interest, walk into **Governor Calvert House.** From the entrance go straight back to a little room on the right, where you can walk on a glassed-in exhibition area that

St. Anne's Episcopal
Church
Church Circle
Annapolis 21401
410–267–9333

St. John's College
60 College Avenue
Annapolis 21401
410–263–2371

Chase-Lloyd House
22 Maryland Avenue
Annapolis 21401
410–263–2723

exposes the brick foundation of the heating system from the 1720s. This "hypocaust" probably heated a greenhouse and is one of the earliest heating systems in America. When the system was discarded, the brick outline was filled in with trash, such as bones, pins, buttons, hair, paper, lace, cloth, seeds, and fish scales. An earlier excavation of a lower level revealed bits of plates, cups, and bottles dating from the 1690s. (See Inns appendix.)

Walk up School Street to **St. Anne's Church.** An earlier Anglican church on the site dated from the 1690s; King William III contributed the communion silver with his coat of arms on it in 1695. In 1858 a fire destroyed the whole church except for the bell tower, the doorway, and the front wall. The church was rebuilt, and in 1866 a new bell was installed in the tower. In 1893 the **Sands Memorial Window** won first prize for ecclesiastical art at the Chicago World's Fair. The oldest grave in the cemetery is that of Amos Garrett, the first mayor of Annapolis, who died in 1727. You will see several gravestones there that were moved from other parishes for preservation.

The **Maryland Inn** fits into a small segment of the circle, extending pie-shaped out from the apex. It was built in the 1770s by Thomas Hyde. (See Inns appendix.)

From Church Circle walk along College Avenue to **St. John's College,** which was called King William's School when it was founded in 1696. There is a legend that the treaty of peace with the Susquehannock Indians was signed under the large, 400-year-old tulip poplar tree called the **Liberty Tree.** Later this tree was a popular place for the Sons of Liberty to meet when they wanted to consider separation from England. Because it was in the open, they could easily spot an outsider approaching in time to conclude their conversation. After the Revolution, when the Marquis de Lafayette returned to America in 1824, he reviewed the Maryland Militia under the tree. Francis Scott Key attended the school, and so did two nephews of George Washington, who graduated in 1796. It became a military school in 1884, and a liberal arts college in 1923, and developed its noted "Great Books" syllabus in 1937. Unfortunately, the Liberty Tree had to be cut down due to hurricane damage.

Turn right onto King George Street to reach the **Chase-Lloyd House,** which was partially built by Samuel Chase, a signer of the Declaration of Independence. In 1771 Chase sold his unfinished house to Edward Lloyd IV, who finished the building. Francis Scott Key married Mary Taylor Lloyd there in 1802. The house is now a home for elderly ladies, "where they may find a retreat from the vicissitudes of life." You can visit the museum on the first floor. You can't miss seeing the cantilevered stairway and the magnificent Palladian window. The Chase coat of arms decorates some of the family china on

Hammond-Harwood
House
19 Maryland Avenue
Annapolis 21401
410–263–4683

display. Look at the Italian marble mantel, which depicts Shakespeare receiving keys from the Goddess of Wisdom in the parlor.

Across the street is the **Hammond-Harwood House,** which was designed by William Buckland for Mathias Hammond in 1774. Although Buckland died during construction, the house was completed by his junior partner, John Randall. Hammond reportedly was having the house built for an unknown bride-to-be, who then eloped with someone else, so he resolved not to live in the house and left Annapolis abruptly in 1776. He died at the young age of thirty-eight; the mystery of his forlorn love has never been solved.

While the house was in the process of construction, a change was made to reduce the height so that Hammond's neighbor, Edward Lloyd, would have a view of the harbor and the city dock. This Georgian house displays semioctagonal pavilions at each end of the facade, an arched doorway, and recessed windows. Hammond had instructed the architect to design a house large enough for entertaining and yet cozy enough for family life during the cold winters. Hester Ann Harwood was the last person to live in the house, and when she died, the house and its contents were sold at auction. The house was purchased for restoration, and, fortunately, some of the original pieces of furniture were recovered and other period furnishings were found, including some pieces made by John Shaw, a respected cabinetmaker who lived nearby. Ask about the false doors, which were installed to provide symmetry. And you might like to find out more about the tunnel under the house that may have led to the water. Two ancient keys were also found under the floor, one labeled "To the Secret Chamber" and the other "To the Secret Burying Place." Doesn't that stir your imagination?

The house contains a number of portraits by Charles Willson Peale. In the dining room look for the "gib door," located below the window on the right; the window becomes a door leading into the garden. Look for the griffin heads and leaf arabesques over the doors, windows, and fireplace in this room. Upstairs in one of the bedrooms are portraits of Ann and Mary Proctor that were painted in 1789. Ann is holding her doll, and, in fact, the same doll sits in a high chair in front of the painting today.

The **William Paca House** is built in the Palladian style popular in

William Paca House
186 Prince George
Street
Annapolis 21401
410–263–5553

Charles Carroll
House
107 Duke of
Gloucester Street
Annapolis 21402
410–269–1737

English country houses. Palladian houses have wings spreading out from a central house. This house was designed to serve as a home and as an office for Paca, an active legislator. During the nineteenth century the house was occupied as a boardinghouse, and in the next century it was used as an elegant hotel, Carvel Hall. In 1966 the Carvel Hall addition was demolished, leaving the original Paca House intact. After a great deal of study, the house was restored to its appearance in the period Paca lived there, between 1765 and 1780. Because of the muddy streets during that time, this house did not have carpets, but the bright blue walls draw the eye upward. The house is furnished with period pieces, some of them owned by Paca. Pieces of the family silver were recovered, including George II silver salts and an ornate sugar bowl. Original oriental porcelain of the Nanking pattern is on display.

Carvel Hall once stood on the present site of the garden. During restoration some of Paca's original garden was discovered, and now the two-acre eighteenth-century garden has been completely restored. Look for the unusual Chinese trellis bridge, which matches the staircase in the house.

The **Charles Carroll House** was opened for visitors in May 1993. Charles Carroll the Settler owned the property of St. Mary's Parish, where the house and the church now stand. He built his home in the 1720s, perhaps using an older structure within the building. This two-and-a-half story house was then among the largest in Annapolis.

His son, Charles Carroll of Carrollton, was born in the house in 1737; it is the only surviving birthplace of a signer of the Declaration of Independence in Maryland. He studied with Jesuits in Maryland, Belgium, France, and England, then returned in 1765 to work in his father's business. He was very active among the patriots and served as a delegate to the Continental Congress for Maryland from 1776 to 1778, yet as a Catholic he was not allowed to vote. However, he was not only influential but was the wealthiest man in the colonies at that time.

The story of the Carroll House is not over yet. During archaeological exploration, the foundation of the "frame house," possibly a seventeenth-century building, was uncovered. Objects from the 1660s were unearthed in the adjacent "builder's trench," and broken dishes from the same era were also found on the property, near the Eastport bridge.

Inside the house, the east wing archaeological dig uncovered pieces from the late 1700s that may indicate that slaves lived and worked in that room. The collection of quartz crystals, polished stones, bone disks, and pierced coins provide a link with African-Americans, since both the pierced coins and bone disks relate to Kongo classical religion. Some tribes put transparent pieces such as glass near doorways to signify ancestral presence and protection.

> U.S. Naval Academy
> King George Street
> Annapolis 21402
> 410–263–6933

The house also provides an unusual experience for history buffs because the walls, floors, and woodwork have not been restored; you can see the original forms of construction right in front of your eyes. The oldest wooden staircase in Maryland is there, and the original floors are put together with iron pegs, then a sign of wealth.

Outside, an eighteenth-century cistern on the west side of the house was the first in a series of archaeological finds. Excavations continue in the gardens and along a 400-foot, eighteenth-century stone seawall. Core samples were taken to ascertain the makeup of the terraced gardens, which may eventually be restored to their original appearance. Workshops, concerts, and candlelight tours are scheduled at various times during the year.

The **U.S. Naval Academy** should be entered at Gate 1 at the corner of Randall Street. The **Armel Leftwich Visitors Center** is located just outside Gate 1 on King George Street. You may take a guided tour or stroll through on your own with the help of a map (ask for one at the gate). Since there is more for you to see than is reasonably possible in a short time, we will suggest a few highlights. Perhaps the most remarkable building is the **Chapel,** which dates from 1904 and is filled with stained-glass windows dedicated as memorials to naval heroes. Look for the Votive Ship, a fifteenth-century Flemish carrack, which hangs from the ceiling in the rear of the nave; the tradition of hanging a ship in church symbolizes the devotion of sailors to God. Walk downstairs to the crypt to see the sarcophagus of John Paul Jones, his commission, and his sword. Another building to visit is the **U.S.N.A. Museum,** located in Preble Hall. It houses collections of ship models, paintings, uniforms, swords, and relics from the career of John Paul Jones. On your way from the Chapel to the museum, don't miss the **Statue of Tecumseh,** known by midshipmen as the "God of the C," the grade every cadet needs to pass courses. Pennies are tossed at him; he also receives good-luck left-handed salutes. Before any athletic contest with arch rival Army, Tecumseh undergoes a makeup session and puts on war paint. Tecumseh is a copy of the figurehead on the wooden battleship *Delaware,* built in 1819.

Before you leave the grounds, stroll around the seawalls for views of harbor activity. Much of this land was reclaimed from the water for use as playing fields. The **Santee Basin** on the Severn River moors various fleets of sailboats used in training all midshipmen. The sailing team has 225 midshipmen and is the largest varsity team at the Naval Academy, one that has been very successful in intercollegiate competition. Boats moored in the basin include Naval Academy knockabouts, Shields sloops, International 420s, Lasers, and Windsurfers. Beyond the Sailing Center on the Annapolis Harbor side are a dozen 44-foot Luders yawls and a variety of larger ocean-racing boats that are actively campaigned in Chesapeake Bay and in the biennial Bermuda Race and other major worldwide ocean races. The Naval Academy feels that competitive sailing is one sport that presents most of the challenges the men will face as naval officers. From it they learn boat handling in relation to wind, waves, and current, other skills of seamanship, navigation, and the necessity of working together as a team.

The Annapolis harbor area is one of our favorite places to gaze at boats. Sailboats and powerboats are moored everywhere—along every inch of the City Dock as well as up the back creeks. It is a haven for some of the finest sailing yachts in the country as well as for historic sailing craft. During the 1950s we became familiar with the lines of the working skipjacks, the last type of working sailing vessel used on Chesapeake Bay. The skipjack, a hard-chined sloop with a mast raked sharply back that was developed during the 1860s, once numbered more than 1,000 on the bay; now only a handful go out for oysters. Two days a week oystermen may use motorboats, but they must use sails the rest of the week. The state of Maryland decreed this law in 1865 to protect the oyster industry from depletion. Skipjacks are now designated as the "state boat of Maryland"; if you're lucky you are likely to see some of them, although most are now moored in southern Maryland or on the Eastern Shore, or their larger two-masted cousins, the bugeyes, moored in the town dock. If you are eager to go out on the water, you will also find a number of charter companies and excursion boats along the dock. On the weekend in early October when the **Annapolis Boat Show** fills the City Dock is the time to see more sailboats than you can imagine; power boats take over the following weekend.

Stop for lunch in **Middleton Tavern** (City Dock; 410–263–3323), **Treaty of Paris** (Maryland Inn; 410–263–6340), **O'Leary's** (310 Third Street; 410–263–0884), or **Chart House** (300 Second Street; 410–268–7166). The **Market House** also offers seafood to eat in or take out; if soft-shell crabs are available, don't miss this delicacy of the bay.

❧ *Southern Maryland* ❧

You can take a tour of St. Mary's and Calvert counties by following this interesting itinerary.

Prince Frederick

To begin a tour of Southern Maryland from Annapolis, take Route 50 west to the junction with Route 2 at the edge of the city; then head south. Route 2 will join with Route 4 and lead into Prince Frederick, which was named for a son of King George II. Stop for a good dinner at the **Old Field Inn** (Main Street; 410–535–1054).

Battle Creek Cypress Swamp Sanctuary (follow Route 2 and Route 506 4 miles southwest of town) contains bald cypress trees that are 50 to 125 feet tall. This stand of trees is the northernmost location of this species in North America. An elevated boardwalk trail leads through the swamp. Look for the 1- to 4-foot "knees" on the cypress trees that stick out; they are part of the root system. Stop in the nature center for films, exhibits, and demonstrations.

Jefferson Patterson Park and Museum (located on Route 265 near Port Republic) contains archaeological sites dating back to 7500 B.C., nature trails, a museum, and a visitors' center. The Battle of St. Leonard's Creek was fought there during the War of 1812.

Calvert

Head south again on Route 2/4 to the **Calvert Cliffs Nuclear Power Plant,** where a converted tobacco farm has displays of fossils found in the area as well information on nuclear power. There you can trace the geologic history of Chesapeake Bay, from its formation to the present. Video games based on energy are available.

Calvert Cliffs State Park provides public access to Calvert Cliffs, well-known for Miocene fossils going back twenty million years. As animals died, they descended to the bottom of the sea and were preserved in layers of sediment. Fossils found on the beach include shark teeth, coral, whalebones, crocodile plates, and seashells. In 1968 a twenty-million-year-old whale skull was found that was about 5 feet long. You may keep any

---

Battle Creek Cypress
Swamp Sanctuary
2880 Gray's Road
Battle Creek 20678
410–535–5327

Jefferson Patterson
Park and Museum
Route 265
St. Leonard 20685
410–586–8500

Calvert Cliffs Nuclear
Power Plant
Visitors' Center
Route 2/4
Lusby 20657
410–495–4673

Calvert Cliffs State Park Lusby 20657 301–872–5389 Middleham Chapel Route 765 Lusby 20657 410–326–4948 Calvert Marine Museum Route 2 Solomons Island 20688 410–326–2042

fossils found lying loose on the beach or in the mud, but you may not dig into the cliff, because that would accelerate erosion. The cliffs rise 100 feet above Chesapeake Bay, almost straight up, and trees at the top with exposed roots lean over. During storms the wave action tends to wash away part of the cliff, and rockslides are particularly threatening to would-be beach collectors. Look up the cliffs to see the many layers of deposited and solidified sediments, each containing different kinds of fossils.

This is also a good place to learn more about the geologic history of Chesapeake Bay. During the Pleistocene epoch, glaciers were developing and causing the sea level to lower and expose sandy sediment. Later, as they melted, the various streams merged into a river, the Susquehanna, which carved a path through the sedimentary layers to the sea. Ocean levels rose again and flooded the mouth of the river. Thus what we know now as Chesapeake Bay is the drowned valley of the Susquehanna River. Calvert Cliffs reveal that history in a particularly dramatic way.

A mile north of the park, **Middleham Chapel** was founded in 1684 and is one of the oldest cruciform churches in Maryland. Many gravestones in the cemetery date from the 1700s.

Solomons Island

Nine miles down Route 2/4 lies Solomons Island, where the Patuxent River empties into Chesapeake Bay. The harbor, one of the deepest natural ports in the bay, is a mecca for boat-building, sailing, and fishing. Many bugeyes were built there during the nineteenth century, and it is loaded with boatyards and marinas today.

Calvert Marine Museum offers a three-part emphasis on paleontology, estuarine biology, and maritime history. The Calvert Cliffs are right next door, so to speak, providing a wealth of opportunity for exploration and collection of fossils. Exhibits on fossils of Calvert Cliffs in the Paleontology Room include a reconstructed ocean floor with fossil remains scattered about. Don't crack your head on the low-flying bird—it is just an extinct, pelicanlike, false-toothed marine bird. You're lucky that this one is only half-size, because the wingspan was up to 22 feet in real life. You can also see the jaws of a prehistoric crocodile there. In the Hall of Estuarine Biology, tidewater birds, fish, crabs, oysters, and other marine life are displayed as models. You can touch some of the species displayed on the "touch table" and look through a microscope to see minute creatures. Maritime Hall accents local maritime history and has a real log canoe on display. The M. M. Davis & Sons Shipyard collection was taken intact from a working shipyard; with everything in process it looks as though the men had just left their work for lunch. They have opened "Treasure of the Cliffs," a fossil exhibit.

An 1883 lighthouse that was moved from nearby Drum Point in 1975 is now poised on the dock at the entrance to the museum's basin. The **Drum Point Lighthouse** is called a "screwpile" cottage light and is one of only three that served Chesapeake Bay at the turn of the century left intact. The lighthouse was fully restored from the original architectural plans with the help of Anna Weems Ewalt, who was born in that very lighthouse. The doctor assisting her mother came by dory to the lighthouse, then located ⅛ mile offshore, the day before Anna's birth. Anna lived there until she was one year old and then returned every weekend to visit her grandparents in the lighthouse. She described watching her grandfather clean the lenses on the lighthouse lamp daily at dawn; it was quite a job because the kerosene flame smoked up the lenses. During a fog the bell had to be rung, which must have been earsplitting for the family to hear time after time after time. The mechanism for ringing it had to be wound by hand every two hours. Her grandfather used to tell the story of the time John Paul Jones's body was being transported back to Annapolis from France. He attributed the wild storm, which had all of the lighthouse windows leaking, to the fact that JPJ should not have been moved at all. During the cold winters the family lived in the kitchen, where the wood-burning range kept them warm. Anna's grandmother decorated the lighthouse for Christmas with holly, pyracantha, boxwood, and lots of handmade ornaments. Anna enjoyed decorating the lighthouse for the museum each year at Christmas. If you are at the museum when the lighthouse is open, you can climb up through the trapdoor into the rooms of the house itself, then up a narrow spiral staircase to the lenses.

The museum offers a cruise on the *William B. Tennison,* a historic Chesapeake Bay bugeye, during the season. She was built in 1899 at Crabb Island, Maryland, and her hull is "chunk built" of nine logs. Originally she sailed, but in 1907 she was converted to power. She worked as an "oyster buy-boat," going from one oyster bar to the next, loading on shellfish from the dredgers, and delivering them to the oyster house. The cruise takes you around the Solomons Inner Harbor, by the Chesapeake Biological Laboratory and the U.S. Naval Recreation Center at Point Patience, and under the Thomas Johnson Memorial Bridge.

There are a number of places to enjoy seafood in Solomons, includ-

Sotterley Plantation
Off Route 245
Hollywood 20636
301-373-2280

ing **The Lighthouse Inn** (410-326-2444), **Solomons Pier Restaurant** (410-326-2424), and **The Dry Dock** (410-326-4817).

From Solomons take the **Thomas Johnson Memorial Bridge** across the Patuxent River into St. Mary's County. This bridge was built in 1977 for $34 million and was named for the first governor of Maryland, who was born in Calvert County. Before the bridge was built, beginning in 1941, passengers were ferried to and from the Patuxent River Naval Air Station twice a day by Captain Leon Langley in *Miss Solomons*. After you have crossed the bridge, turn right on Route 235 to Hollywood and Route 245, where you turn right again to visit a remarkable plantation.

Hollywood

If you'd like to visit a tidewater plantation on the Patuxent River, head for **Sotterley.** Lord Baltimore issued a manorial grant in 1650 to Thomas Cornwallis, who arrived on either the *Ark* or the *Dove,* and James Bowles built the first house there in 1717. After Bowles's death, his widow married George Plater II, who named Sotterley after his ancestral home in Suffolk, England. George Plater III was a delegate to the Continental Congress and one of the first governors of Maryland. Because Sotterley was a port of entry for the colony, the resident of the house was also the customs officer. George Plater V was only five years old when he inherited the house, but he later lost it in a roll of the dice. He wanted to die in the house but didn't make it—his body was found in a nearby ditch. Some say that they can still hear hoofbeats, see footprints, and even hear the fatal roll of the dice— George is apparently a friendly spirit when he comes to visit his plantation.

Sotterley Plantation has a long low profile, tall chimneys, steep roofs, and a cupola. Set high on the ridge, the house commands a superb view of the Patuxent River. Inside it is famous for a Chinese Chippendale staircase and pine paneling with shell alcoves in the drawing room. Look for the set of four cut-crystal wall fixtures complete with prisms. In the dining room the Chinese lattice-back mahogany chairs match the Chinese trellis stair. The great hall has shell-topped alcoves on both sides of the fireplace. In the small, bright-red parlor, check for the secret staircase that leads to an upstairs bedroom. Sotterley is a working plantation, and you can visit the outbuildings, including tenant houses, smokehouse, and tobacco shed. Look for the "rolling road," where slaves rolled hogsheads of tobacco down to the dock. If you would like to return to appreciate the full ambience of the house, inquire about the dinners that are planned for special occasions during the year.

St. Mary's City

Historic St. Mary's
City Visitors' Center
Route 5
St. Mary's City 20686
800–762–1634 or
301–862–0962

Take Route 235 south to Route 489 and Route 5 to St. Mary's City, which was settled in 1634 under the royal charter of Lord Baltimore. Stop at **Historic St. Mary's City Visitor's Center** on Route 5. Did you know that St. Mary's was Maryland's first capital?

On November 22, 1633, 140 settlers boarded two ships, the *Ark* and the *Dove,* bound for Maryland. Seventeen were gentlemen who wanted to invest in the New World, and the rest worked after they arrived to pay for their passage. The ships had sailed from London in mid-October but were halted at the mouth of the Thames because they had not taken an oath of allegiance to the king. After all who were visible on board had taken the oath, the ships were allowed to sail. They landed in Cowes on the Isle of Wight to await departure on their four-month voyage across the Atlantic. Although the gentlemen investors may have had cabins, the rest of the contingent lived in a space about 100 feet by 30 feet, night and day, for those four months. They encountered a gale during their first days out, so they anchored in a harbor. Another vessel came down upon the *Dove,* however, which forced her to cut her anchor and sail out to sea. The *Ark* followed, and for a time they had fair winds. Another storm struck, and the ships were separated, each thinking the other had been lost, until they reached Barbados and were miraculously reunited. On March 25, 1634, the two ships landed on St. Clement's Island in the Potomac River. (A 40-foot cross stands there today as a memorial for those brave souls.) Within a few days the settlers had chosen the site that became Maryland's first capital, St. Mary's City. Governor Leonard Calvert sent a letter to England stating, "We have seated ourselves within one-half mile of the river within a pallizado of one-hundred twenty yards square." This group was firm in its resolve to guarantee religious and civil liberty for the settlers.

Unquestionably, the lives of those settlers were full of risks. To begin with, they had to survive four months in a tossing ship, with poor food and rampant disease. When they landed, they were exposed to new disease, such as malaria. Then most of them had to work for a number of years to pay for their passage before they could finally begin creating their own lives in the new land. These must have been hardy souls.

Today local people still bear the names of the early settlers, and some of them raise "sotweed," or tobacco, and "tong" for oysters, as their forebears did long ago.

Archaeologists have been finding remnants of the past (in the form of bits and pieces of porcelain, earthenware, bones, and other items thrown

Point Lookout State
Park
P.O. Box 48
Scotland 20687
301–872–5688

out as trash more than three centuries ago) that help them to piece together the lives of these settlers. Visitors are fascinated by a discovery—three lead coffins. In 1992 Project Lead Coffin undertook the process of determining whether the coffins still contained original air from the 1600s, taking a preliminary look inside by means of a fiberscope, lifting the coffins from the ground of Chapel Field, opening them, and analyzing the remains. NASA scientists were involved, and the procedure was carried out within a medical tent.

The small coffin contained the remains of a small female child, along with traces of finely woven linen. The second coffin contained an older woman, who is considered perhaps the best-preserved skeleton of a seventeenth-century colonist in North America. She was lying in a shroud with silk ribbons at her wrists, knees, and ankles. The third coffin revealed the skeleton of a man who wore a leather piece of clothing. The identity of the individuals has recently been established by Smithsonian Institution scientists: Governor Philip Calvert, his wife, Anne Wolsley, and an infant daughter, probably from the governor's second marriage. **Historic St. Mary's City** has reconstructed a village from the records of the settlement. You can look over workers' shoulders as they continue their archaeological quest. As you walk around the State House, Farthing's Ordinary, and the Godiah Spray Tobacco Plantation, you can witness reenactments of characters of the time. A replica of the *Dove* is moored on the river. She was reconstructed in time for the Bicentennial and commissioned in October 1978. Check with the visitors' center for information on the weekly schedule of events.

Point Lookout

Route 5 will take you to the southernmost tip of Maryland, Point Lookout. A visitors' center focuses on the Civil War, when a fort of earth was built there by Confederate prisoners of war. **Point Lookout State Park** offers fishing, hiking, beachcombing, swimming, and camping.

This is the conclusion of your tour of Southern Maryland. Return to Annapolis to continue on to Maryland's Eastern Shore or take Route 235 to Route 5 to I–95 to Washington, D.C.

∾ *Eastern Shore* ∾

Before the Chesapeake Bay Bridge east of Annapolis and the Chesapeake Bay Bridge and Tunnel from Norfolk to Cape Charles were built, the Eastern Shore was almost inaccessible to the major population centers nearby. Now that has changed, but the region still retains its aura of remoteness and timeless stability—almost as if the events and technologies across the bay in Washington and Baltimore were irrelevant to the relationships between men, boats, creeks, wildfowl, and fertile land. To get there from Annapolis, take Route 50 across the Chesapeake Bay Bridge.

Wye Oak State Park
Wye Mills 21679
410–820–1668

Wye Mill
Wye Mills 21679
301–827–6909 or
685–2886

Third Haven Friends
  Meeting House
405 South
  Washington Street
Easton 21601
410–822–0293

Historical Society
  Complex
25 South Washington
  Street
Easton 21601
410–822–0773

Wye Mills

From Route 50 take Route 213 to Route 662 to **Wye Oak State Park.** The Wye Oak tree is more than 450 years old; it reaches 95 feet high, has a trunk 21 feet in circumference, and stretches to a horizontal spread of 165 feet. This white oak is Maryland's state tree.

Wye Mill was built in 1671 and reconstructed in 1720, and then again in 1840. It is the earliest industrial-commercial building in continuous use in Maryland. Robert Morris, a major financier of the American Revolution, bought flour for the American troops in Valley Forge from the mill and paid 10,000 pounds sterling (about $50,000 in today's terms). Today visitors can see old equipment and new in Wye Mill.

Easton

Route 50 south will take you to Easton, which was settled in the late seventeenth century. The **Third Haven Friends Meeting House,** dating from 1682, is the oldest frame church still standing in America. It was built at the headwaters of the Tred Avon River, and people arrived by boat for the monthly meetings, which lasted all day long. William Penn preached there, and Lord Baltimore attended services there.

The **Historical Society Complex** contains an 1810, Federal-period town house; a Quaker cabinetmaker's cottage from the 1700s; period gar-

St. Mary's Square Museum
St. Mary's Square
St. Michaels 21663
410–745–9561
Chesapeake Bay Maritime Museum
Mill Street
St. Michaels 21663
410–745–2916

dens; and a museum. You can get information on the other colonial homes to see in town there.

November is the month of the annual **Waterfowl Festival,** held throughout downtown Easton. Paintings, carvings, rare books, duck stamps, old decoys, guns, and hunting gear are on display, and you can learn about goose calling or attend a carving seminar, various workshops, and auctions.

St. Michaels

Route 33 will take you to St. Michaels, which was known as Shipping Creek during the War of 1812. There is a legend that the people who lived in town foiled a British attack by snuffing out all lights at ground level and hanging lanterns in the tops of trees. This caused the British ships to aim their guns high and shoot over the town. The **Miles River** is very popular with sailors and fishermen, and St. Michaels offers extensive facilities for mooring, repairing, and storing boats. It is a favorite spot for those who want to refit or rebuild their boats, combining the availability of supplies and gear with the pleasures of a quiet, beautiful town.

St. Mary's Square is an attractive green that also serves as the center of many town activities. **St. Mary's Square Museum** has local historical displays; behind the museum is another building, called the "Teetotum" building, that looks like a top and contains more exhibits.

The **Chesapeake Bay Maritime Museum** is an eighteenth-century complex focusing on the maritime history of the area and the bay. As you enter the museum, you'll see an overview of the "drowned river," beginning with the Indians who made their canoes by burning and then scraping a log with oyster shells—a sample is on display, partly finished. Colonists arrived and planted tobacco, with sassafras as a secondary crop during poor tobacco-crop years. You can learn about the log canoes; unlike the Indians' canoes, these were racing machines, such as *Flying Cloud* or the 1892 *Island Blossom,* which look beautiful with their sails trimmed. More exhibits on the Chesapeake Bay skipjacks offer a look at a dying world, as they are dwindling in number. Watermen have worked long and hard for years, some families going back to the 1600s, and they live only in the Chesapeake Bay area. Among their superstitions are the belief that bad luck will come to a boat containing anything blue; a hatch cover upside-down; a red brick used as ballast; a leaf, nut, or twig from a walnut tree on board; a woman on board; changing the name of a boat; or watching three crows flying across the bow. These men must also work only under sail except two days a week, when a yawl boat may push with its motor.

The Waterfowl building displays decoys, guns, and a collection of stuffed birds. You'll learn how watermen went out in a white boat, wearing white clothing so the birds couldn't differentiate them from the light. Sandbags were placed behind some of the heavy guns so the kickback wouldn't damage the boat. Don't miss the 1910 guns that were really anywhere from three to eight barrels. Men went out in sinkboxes—boats with a hole in the middle to keep them more on a level with the top of the water. Some of the decoys are very old and valuable.

A large portion of the museum floats, including the sloop *J. T. Leonard,* a log-bottom bugeye, a skipjack, and a racing log canoe. The boat shed contains a variety of craft, including a Hampton-class loop, a Smith Island crabbing skiff, and a Pocomoke log canoe named *Lillian R.* There is no better or more pleasant place to study fine examples of major types of watercraft distinctive to the bay. The *Rebecca T. Ruark,* the only surviving oyster sloop keel still racing, dates from 1886. The 1879 **Hooper Straight Lighthouse** is also on display.

Don't miss the **Cannonball House** (not open for public tours), which achieved notoriety during the War of 1812. It seems that Mrs. Merchant was carrying her baby daughter down the stairs when a cannonball crashed through the roof, rolled across the attic floor, and careened down the stairs after her. The late James Michener lived in the village while writing *Chesapeake.* We enjoyed reading his account of the perfect crab cake in a local newspaper article.

We can recommend **Michael Rork's Town Dock** (125 Mulberry Street; 410–745–5577) or **The Crab Claw** (Navy Point; 410–745–2900) for a seafood meal. If you are willing to work at it, order steamed crabs; you will learn how to pry off the apron, top shell, and legs and eventually expose succulent crab meat. (A small mallet is handy for the claws.)

Take a cruise on *The Patriot* (410–745–3100). You'll learn about wildlife in the Chesapeake Bay area.

Tilghman

From St. Michaels Route 33 leads to Tilghman Island, home port of many vessels in the skipjack fleet. The watermen there harvest oysters in the fall and winter, catch eels for crab bait in the spring, and spend the summer crabbing, fishing, and clamming. The island was originally known as Great Choptank Island, but its name was changed when Matthew Tilghman became the owner. A local carpenter purposely built hexagonal houses there so that no one side would be fully exposed to the force of the wind. In the fall the southern tip of the island is loaded with birds migrating south.

Oxford

Oxford, situated at the mouth of the Tred Avon River where it joins the Choptank, has long been favored by yachtsmen because it's a sheltered place to anchor and good expertise is available on boat repairs. If you are returning from Tilghmans or St. Michaels, you can take the **Oxford-Bellevue Ferry,** which crosses to Oxford every twenty minutes (410-745-9023), or you can retrace your way along Route 33 to Route 50 and take Route 333 to Oxford.

Oxford was once a stamping ground for pirates, including Stede Bonner and Blackbeard Teach, when they needed repairs on their ships at Skillington's Shipyard. The town was second in size only to Annapolis during the early days of Chesapeake Bay civilization. Because of its location and sheltered anchorage, it was popular as a port of entry for the colony. London and Liverpool stores started branch stores in town where they exchanged goods for tobacco. Although Baltimore surpassed Oxford as a commercial port during the Revolution, Oxford bounced back after the Civil War, with steady business in shipbuilding, oystering, and fish-packing.

One of the town fathers, Robert Morris, for whom the main street is named, was killed unexpectedly by the wadding from a ceremonial cannonball; his son was a signer of the Declaration of Independence. The **Robert Morris Inn** (410-226-5111), located right on the river, has a fine reputation for dining and overnight stays. Apart from the food, you will enjoy looking at its architectural features. It was built in 1710 by ships' carpenters and has wooden-pegged paneling and hand-hewn beams. (See Inns appendix.)

Tench Tilghman, another Oxford resident, rode from Yorktown to Philadelphia on October 17, 1781, to tell the Continental Congress that Cornwallis had surrendered. As Washington's aide-de-camp he was well known for his bravery. He is buried in the Oxford Cemetery; a monument stands by his grave as a memorial. Look across the cove to see **Plimhimmon,** which was the home of his widow, Anna Maria Tilghman.

Cambridge

From Oxford return to Route 50, first on Route 333 and then on an unnumbered road heading due east where Route 333 swings north; then continue south to Cambridge. (Oxford and Cambridge are far closer here, and perhaps more compatible, than they are in England.) The town was founded in 1684, mostly for the purpose of collecting customs fees. High Street is brick paved and lined with houses from the eighteenth and nineteenth centuries. Stop in the **Dorchester County Historical Society** for a map of the walking tour. You may also want to drive along the Choptank waterfront on a marked tourist route. The Visitor Center in Sailwinds Park has exhibits of Eastern Shore life. Special events take place at Governors Hall.

Twelve miles south of Cambridge off Route 335, you will find the **Blackwater National Wildlife Refuge,** which was developed for migrating waterfowl in 1932. Blackwater is used by ducks and Canada geese, snow geese, eagles, ospreys, towhees, woodpeckers, brown-headed nuthatches, bobwhite, woodcock, warblers, vireos, orioles, and flycatchers. Some of the endangered species have also been spotted there, including the bald eagle, Delmarva fox squirrel, peregrine falcon, and red-cockaded woodpecker. The visitors' center has exhibits and films. You can drive along a 5-mile road, hike on one of the walking trails, cycle, and watch birds from an observation tower.

Dorchester County
Historical Society
909 LaGrange
Avenue
Cambridge 21613
410–228–7953

Sailwinds Park
200 Byrn Street
Cambridge 21613
410–228–7245

Blackwater National
Wildlife Refuge
Off Route 335
Cambridge 21613
410–228–2677

Ward Museum of
Wildfowl Art
909 S. Schumaker
Drive
Salisbury 21801
410–742–4988

Poplar Hill Mansion
117 E. Elizabeth
Street
Salisbury 21801
410–749–1776

Salisbury

Route 50 continues inland to Salisbury, which, unfortunately, suffered fires in 1860 and 1886; the historic district is now Victorian rather than colonial. The **Ward Museum of Wildfowl Art** highlights carvings of songbirds. The development of decoy carving is illustrated by the prolific work of Lem and Steve Ward; each decoy is a little different from the others. Their workshop has also been re-created. Visitors come into the museum through what looks like a rush-covered duck blind and are immediately enveloped in the sights and tape-recorded sounds of a marsh just before dawn. The sounds of wild Canada geese and the sunrise lead to flights of wildfowl. The museum displays some Indian rush decoys from the year 1000.

Newtown was the first residential area built after the fire of 1886. The oldest house in the city, **Poplar Hill Mansion,** which survived the fire, is located there. This Georgian house dates from 1805 and is furnished

J. Millard Tawes
Historical Museum
3 Ninth Street
Crisfield 21817
410–965–2501

with period pieces. Bull's-eye windows, a Palladian window on the second floor, dentil molding, and a fan-shaped window at the doorway are features of this home. A walking tour of the Newtown Historic District includes twenty-six houses. (Ask for walking-tour information at the chamber of commerce.)

From Salisbury you can go south for a side trip to Crisfield or east to Ocean City.

Crisfield

Routes 13 and 413 lead to Crisfield, a town built on oyster shells. On the piers you can sample oysters barely out of the water. Crisfield is also the center of the crabbing industry of Chesapeake Bay; there is even a crab on the water tower. Crisfield walking tours take place from **J. Millard Tawes Historical Museum.**

Passenger ferries are available from Crisfield to **Smith Island** and **Tangier Island;** cars are not allowed on either ferry. When you visit one of these remnants of the old life of Chesapeake Bay, you will be captivated by the absence of noise (apart from the motor scooters that have enabled children to re-create the noise of the modern world). Captain John Smith sailed to Smith Island in 1608 and named it. The people who live there now are descendants of the original settlers who left Cornwall in 1657; all of them still make a living from the sea, as they might have in southwestern England. Crab shanties on the docks and fishing boats portray an essential way of life there.

Captain John Smith reportedly named Tangier Island for the pirates of Tangiers. Then Joshua Thomas arrived on Tangier from Potato Neck on the mainland and converted everyone to Methodism. When 12,000 British troops camped on the island prior to the assault on Baltimore during the War of 1812, Thomas told them that they would not succeed—in fact, that God had told him they would fail. They returned in poor spirits following their defeat and admitted he was right. Today about 850 people live on the island, and all of them are involved in the fisheries.

If you visit either island by private boat, you will be treated to an extremely pleasant time warp as you enter harbors lined with fish shacks and houses on piles—but beware of the strong currents on the canals if you are docking across the stream; we spent half a day scraping off creosote from pilings at Tangier that left a memento on our topsides.

EASTERN SHORE

Ocean City

Route 50 east from Salisbury will take you to
Ocean City, where you can tickle your toes in the
Atlantic. This resort town offers a boardwalk, swimming, fishing, shopping, and entertainment. At the
south end of the boardwalk is the **Ocean City Life
Saving Museum,** which records the history of lifesaving efforts in town since 1891. Look for the artifacts
brought up from shipwrecks off the Delmarva coast,
including some dishes from the "China Wreck"; you
can investigate shipwrecks further with the staff. The
museum has a display of dollhouse models of the
buildings once situated in Ocean City, and it has an
aquarium.

The **Wheels of Yesterday Antique and Classic
Car Museum** houses all sorts of interesting cars.
Don't miss Jack Benny's 1928 Lincoln Touring Car.

Ocean City Life
Saving Museum
Ocean City 21842
410–289–4991

Wheels of Yesterday
Antique and Classic
Car Museum
Route 50/12708
Ocean Gateway
Ocean City 21842
410–213–7329

Assateague State
Park and National
Seashore
410–641–2120
(state phone) or
410–641–1441
(national park
phone)

Assateague

You can reach Assateague by following Route 50, Route 611, and the
Assateague Island Bridge. The Indian name *Assateague* means "place
across"; the island was once inhabited by a peaceful Indian tribe. It is part
of the barrier beach that runs along the coast from Florida to
Massachusetts. The island is 37 miles long and varies from ⅕ mile to 1½
miles in width. Some of the sand dunes are 30 feet high. The mystery of
shifting sands applies here, because there are many hulks from shipwrecks
buried underneath. The beach has only a slight undertow, making it rela-
tively safe for children in normal surf conditions.

There is much speculation about the origin of the wild ponies that
live on the island. In 1947 Marguerite Henry wrote *Misty of Chincoteague,*
a book that brought a great deal of attention to this interesting species.
One legend holds that the first ponies came ashore from a shipwrecked
Spanish galleon. It is thought that they adapted themselves to the hardships of exposure during the winter, with limited food and water, and
gradually evolved into hardy, small animals. There is a spot known as
Spanish Bar, located in Pope Bay, where some say the vessel met her end.
Other historians have a less romantic explanation: Horses belonging to
Eastern Shore planters in the seventeenth century were allowed to graze
on the island, and those that were not recovered developed into the breed
that exists today.

309

Chincoteague
National Wildlife
Refuge
8231 Beach Road
Chincoteague Island
23336
757–336–6122

There are actually two herds; the one in Virginia is kept within fenced marshes by the Chincoteague Volunteer Fire Company. If you're there in late July, you may see the Virginia herd rounded up for a swim. Most of the foals and yearlings are auctioned off. In this way population growth is controlled so that there are no more than 150 animals in each herd. In Maryland the ponies roam everywhere, including on the roads. Do not feed or touch them; they are notorious for kicking and biting.

The Assateague Island National Seashore was created by an Act of Congress and presidential signature on September 21, 1965. **Assateague State Park and National Seashore** (410–641–2120, state phone; 410–641–1441, national park phone) contains 680 acres, and federal and state agencies share responsibility for wildlife. The **Chincoteague National Wildlife Refuge** is at the southern end of this barrier beach. The National Park Service maintains a visitors' center at the north end of the island. Naturalists conduct canoe trips, guided nature walks, and clamming and fishing demonstrations daily during the season. The park offers picnicking, swimming, fishing, surfing, and camping. You can also reach the Chincoteague refuge at the southern end of the island by road from Chincoteague, Virginia.

From Assateague you can drive north along the coast into Delaware to join Itinerary H or continue on this itinerary by retracing your route on Route 50 west to Cambridge and north until it meets Route 213 to Chestertown.

Chestertown

If you want to see more Canada geese than you've ever seen in your life, go to Chestertown in the fall. We saw one "safe" pond, which was a city of geese that had spread its suburbs into the surrounding fields. Migrating geese must be grateful for this safe haven, where they can eat corn left in the fields and honk to each other. (Incongruously, another safe haven farther north is found in the corporate ponds and lawns of industrial New Jersey.) The noise they make is more like a symphony than cacophony to the initiated, with movements separated by pauses when the sounds completely stop for a fraction of a minute and then resume. Much of the Eastern Shore is charmed by these lovely birds, and you will see the motif on needlepoint pillows, decoys, lamps, writing paper, paintings, postcards, books, windsocks, wallets, purses, and jewelry.

Chestertown was founded in 1706 on the banks of the Chester River, although it had been designated as a town as early as 1668. Many waterfront homes were built during the 1700s, and a number of them are identified on a walking tour. (Other homes elsewhere in town are also on the tour.) Stop in the **Kent County Chamber of Commerce** for a brochure. The **Kent Office of Tourism** is located at 400 South Cross Street, Chestertown, MD 21620; 410–778–4606. The **Hynson-Ringgold House** dates from 1743 and is now the home of the Washington College president. At the end of that block and across the street is the **Customs House,** which has Flemish bond brick construction. Chestertown had its own version of the Boston Tea Party: On May 23, 1774, angry citizens boarded the brig *William Geddes,* moored in front of the Customs House, and threw the cargo of tea into the Chester River. The house across the street is called **Wide Hall;** this Georgian house

> Hynson-Ringgold House
> Cannon & Water Streets
> Chestertown 21620
>
> Washington College
> 300 Washington Avenue
> Chestertown 21620
>
> Eastern Neck Island Wildlife Refuge
> 1730 Eastern Neck Road
> Rock Hall 21661
> 410–639–7056

was the scene of much action during the Revolution because the owner, Thomas Smythe, was the head of Maryland's provincial government from 1774 until the state's first constitution emerged in 1776. An unusual free-standing staircase was built in the house. The house at **107 Water Street** was built by Richard Smythe between 1784 and 1787. Woodwork from one of the second-floor rooms now resides in the Winterthur Museum near Wilmington, Delaware, in what is known as the "Chestertown Room."

Washington College was founded in Chestertown in 1782 and is now the tenth-oldest institution of higher learning in America. George Washington was instrumental in the founding of the college and in 1789 received a doctor of law degree there.

If you're hungry, take a side trip west on Route 20 to the town of **Rock Hall,** which has been called the "Seafood Capital of Kent County." Over 1,000 skipjacks and bugeyes sailed out of Rock Hall during the early 1900s. **Waterman's Crab House** (410–639–2261), overlooking the harbor on Sharp Street Wharf, offers fresh seafood for lunch or dinner. Earlier, Tench Tilghman landed in Rock Hall on his way from Virginia to Philadelphia with the news that the Revolutionary War had ended. He was given a horse in Rock Hall and rode to Philadelphia calling, "Cornwallis is taken! A fresh horse for the Congress!"

Continue south on Route 445 to **Eastern Neck Island Wildlife Refuge,** a refuge for migrating birds during the spring and fall. The refuge was established in 1962 on 2,285 acres of marsh, ponds, and coves. This island was also one of the first places to be settled in the New World when, in 1650, Major Joseph Wickes built his home, "Wickliffe," there. Packet vessels sailed back and forth from the mainland to Bogle's Wharf on the east side of the island. Today the refuge offers environmental-education programs, and the observation tower, wildlife trail, and boardwalk are open to the public.

Georgetown

From Chestertown head north on Route 213 to Georgetown, the site of an episode involving a courageous young woman during the War of 1812. British troops were in the process of burning all of the homes in town on May 6, 1813, when they ran up against the determination of Miss Kitty Knight, a beautiful and accomplished woman. Many of the townspeople salvaged what they could from their homes and fled, but she replied to the command to leave, "I shall not leave; if you burn this house, you burn me with it." Although the torch ignited her house twice, she managed to extinguish the flames. The officer in charge at last deferred to her courage and spared her home as well as the one next door.

Because of its accessibility to Wilmington and Philadelphia, Georgetown and the whole Sassafras River have developed into a major boating center.

At this point you can head north for Wilmington or Philadelphia to join Itineraries H or G or continue on this itinerary by returning to Annapolis and then going on to Baltimore. The easiest route to the inner-harbor area from Annapolis is via I–97N to I–695 to I–95.

∼ *Baltimore* ∼

Baltimore evolved from early settlements at Jones Falls, now downtown, and Fells Point, an eighteenth-century shipbuilding center. Baltimore was an important port that produced many ships for the Continental navy during the Revolution. Privateers (privately owned armed warships) also used Baltimore for a base as they sailed out to demolish the British. During the War of 1812, the privateers again harassed the British and, in fact, seized 500 British merchant ships. The British were furious at these losses and became determined to destroy Baltimore.

During the summer of 1814, the British began to campaign in the Chesapeake. A fleet under Admiral Alexander Cochrane sailed up the bay, into the Patuxent River, then proceeded with infantry to Bladensburg, where they defeated American troops. They marched to Washington and burned the Capitol, the President's House, and other buildings. Back again on their ships, they sailed north in Chesapeake Bay, looking forward to getting rid of the "nest of pirates" in Baltimore. The citizens were aware of impending danger, however, and so dug trenches on Hampstead Hill, reinforced Fort McHenry, and made other preparations for defense. Church bells in town alerted the citizens,

> Fort McHenry
> Fort Avenue
> Baltimore 21230
> 410–962–4290

who took their positions as the British landed at North Point and started to march up Patapsco Neck. Colonel John Stricker and his men met the British on September 12 and fought the Battle of North Point. Although the Americans had to retreat, the British realized that a victory would not be so easy against such determined resistance. Also, their commander, General Robert Ross, was killed during that battle.

On the water the British began bombarding Fort McHenry for a period of twenty-five hours. Their 1,500 exploding shells did no essential damage to the fort, and eventually the British withdrew back to North Point. They sailed away in defeat, and Baltimore was saved. Francis Scott Key was on board a small ship just out of range of action but in full view of the fireworks. He wrote "The Star-Spangled Banner" on the back of a letter he had in his pocket, and it was published the next day. It became our national anthem in 1931.

Fort McHenry

You can visit Fort McHenry, which is designed in the French star shape, with five bastions to produce crossfire against attackers. **Fort McHenry National Monument and Historic Shrine** contains exhibits and brochures on the history of the fort and has an interesting video presentation about the events leading up to the Battle of Baltimore.

In addition, the Fort McHenry Guard, composed of volunteers and Park Service employees, presents programs on weekends during the summer. A drumroll calls the men to assembly, and as they take their places, visitors have the distinct feeling that they are watching men preparing to defend the fort again.

A fifteen-star–fifteen-stripe flag is raised, and the men report to their posts. The fun begins when a member of the garrison attempts to slip past a guard or someone from the outside tries to enter the fort. Guards need to be on their toes to spot an unauthorized attempt.

Those representing the Third Artillery Regiment wear dark-blue wool coats with gold trim and round felt hats topped with red plumes, and carry smooth-bore muskets. The Maryland Militia wear blue coats with red facings and half-moon–shaped hats. The Sea Fencibles group wear seaman's attire of 1814.

Baltimore Museum
of Industry
1415 Key Highway
Baltimore 21230
410–727–4808

Federal Hill
Key Highway &
  Battery
Baltimore 21202

Maryland Science
  Center and Davis
  Planetarium
601 Light Street
Baltimore 21230
410–685–5225

Harborplace and the
  Gallery
200 E. Pratt Street
Baltimore 21202
410–332–4191

Visitors can choose to interact with any of the divisions. Some of them will be in the barracks cleaning their weapons, playing games, or reading an 1814 newspaper. You'll think you're living in a different age as you question the members of the guard.

The **Baltimore Museum of Industry** is housed in an old oyster cannery, where you'll get a glimpse of the industrial history of the city. Hands-on exhibits intrigue young and old alike. Look for the 1906 steam tugboat, the *Baltimore.* There's a nineteenth-century print shop, cannery, machine shop, and garment loft.

Inner Harbor

Baltimore's recent renaissance has transformed the Inner Harbor into a real showplace. By the 1950s Baltimore realized that urban decay and decline were destroying the once-thriving inner city. One hundred businessmen formed the Greater Baltimore Committee and created a redevelopment plan to raise the city from the ashes of its past. More than seventy-five new or reconstructed buildings now line the attractive waterfront. You can start at one end of the Inner Harbor and spend all day learning about science or history and enjoying the sights, with plenty left over to see on another visit.

We suggest beginning your tour on **Federal Hill** in South Baltimore, where you can look across at the skyline of the Inner Harbor and the city beyond. This site was an observation point during the Civil War. For many years of Baltimore's maritime history, the lookout on the hill performed a useful service by keeping track of approaching ships that he could see but those in town could not. Then he would run up the appropriate flag on his pole to let shipowners know which vessel to expect.

Move around the harbor to the **Maryland Science Center and Davis Planetarium,** which houses a hands-on science experience on three floors. "Chesapeake Bay" is one of the permanent exhibits that appeals to all ages, with its 2,000-gallon tank teeming with estuarian life.

Harborplace and the Gallery are next, and we've found that if you wander through them before the rest of the tour, you may spend more time than you had planned. (But be sure to see them sometime.) Two glass-enclosed pavilions that look like steamship-pier headquarters house many shops and restaurants.

Next you'll come to the sloop *Constellation,* which was launched in 1854 as the last commissioned ship of the Civil War. She is the only surviving Civil War-era Naval vessel. She developed the reputation of a "Yankee Racehorse" after her first encounter with an enemy man-of-war, the frigate *L'Insurgente,* which she captured easily. She served as a training ship for midshipmen and finally saw active duty as a flagship of the Atlantic Fleet during World War II. Special tours and programs are held on cer-

> *Constellation*
> Pier One
> Pratt Street
> Baltimore 21202
> 410–539–1797
> (call ahead)

tain days including a "powder monkey" tour for kids, the "ship as a machine," "ward room chats" about topics such as the history of navigation, and history tours.

You can explore the various decks of our first warship to see the actual living space for the men, storage areas for munitions and gear, and various exhibits. The spar deck is the top deck, where the running rigging that controls yards and sails is belayed ready for use. From this deck men would clamber up the ratlines to lookout stations on the tops (platforms where sections of masts join), which were also used by marines firing rifles during combat. Or they would climb onto the yards to set, furl, reef, or change sails while balancing with their feet on a single footrope below the yard, using both hands for the sail as they leaned against the yard. Starting from the bow, the masts on this vessel are fore, main, and mizzen; moving upward from the deck on each mast, the sails are the course, topsail, topgallant, and royal.

Climb down from the spar deck to the gun deck, where the guns stand ready to poke out of gun-ports. Again starting from the forward end of the deck, you will see the galley, bilge pump, and captain's quarters in the aft section. The captain of the *Constellation* was lucky enough to have his own private, if primitive, toilet protruding over one side of the hull and his bathtub over the other. Go down one more level to the berthing deck, where the crew slept forward and the officers aft. The orlop deck is next, with the hospital in the forward section. Below that is the hold, with barrels of fish and dried, smoked, and salted meats, the powder magazine, and the sail loft. As you can imagine, space was at a premium, and rubbing elbows with your neighbor was more than a metaphor.

Life on board was sure to be crowded and might be boring after repeating the same routine day after day. Each sailor had duties to perform that were listed on a "station bill," so that he would know where to go when orders were given to get under way; bring the ship to anchor; tack, set, and furl sails; reef; and perform many other tasks of seamanship. Each man also had a station with a gun crew, where they trained every day so their teamwork would be perfect. Hours were divided into five four-hour watches and two two-hour dogwatches between 4:00 and 8:00 P.M. This schedule, still in use, allowed the watches to rotate so that a man would

315

World Trade Center
401 E. Pratt Street
Baltimore 21202
410–837–4515

National Aquarium in
  Baltimore
Piers 3 and 4
501 E. Pratt Street
Baltimore 21202
410–576–3800

not stand the same watch on any two days.

Every morning the boatswain piped "up all hammocks," which was answered by "rise and shine." At the order "lash and stow," each man lashed up his hammock and went above decks to stow it in the spar-deck nettings for the day. Next the men scoured the deck with "holystones and sand" until the deck was pronounced clean. When the ship was at anchor, some men cleaned the sides of the hull from platforms alongside the hull. At seven bells (7:30 A.M.) they cleaned up and fell into line for inspection. Next, sails were changed or trimmed, as needed, and the short pennant flown at night was changed for the 40-foot-long commission pennant flown during the day. At eight bells, after two or three hours of work, they were ready for breakfast. After breakfast the deck was swept, and they all went to their battle stations for drill and then to their work stations as carpenter, sailmaker, rigger, cooper, or tailor. On Thursday mornings they scrubbed their hammocks, and on Fridays they washed their clothes. On Wednesdays and Saturdays the barber was available for shaves and haircuts. Below decks the cooks scrubbed their pots for inspection. At 11:30 A.M. the sweepers were called again; then at noon grog and dinner were served. During the next few hours, some of the men had free time and others worked. After supper the entire crew gathered on deck to watch the sunset, spin yarns, and talk. At "stand by your hammocks," each man was ready to receive his hammock as numbers were called. Hammocks were slung on hooks below, the older crew retired, and the younger ones got out their accordions and banjos and gathered to sing and tell stories. The colors were hauled down at 8:00 P.M., and at 9:00 P.M. everyone not on watch turned in. On Sundays church services were held, and only necessary work was done on board.

You are sure to come away from your tour with a respect for the disciplined life these men shared. Life at sea never matched the romantic imaginings that brought farm boys down from the hills to enlist.

As you continue your circuit of the Inner Harbor, the top of the **World Trade Center** is a great place to go for a view of the entire area. Ride up the elevator to the **Top of the World,** where you can look out of large picture windows onto the city and harbor.

Next on your walking circuit is the **National Aquarium in Baltimore,** which provides visitors with a series of trips up escalators and moving ramps through five levels to view many varieties of marine life. A highlight is the dolphin show at the Marine Mammal Pavilion.

As you move up through the aquarium, you will see "Maryland: Mountains to the Sea" on Level 2, illustrated by living exhibits from the mountains, tidal marsh, Eastern Shore, and Atlantic Beach. Level 3 contains a gallery of animals who survive through changing their body shape, color, methods of feed-

> **Baltimore Maritime Museum**
> **Pier 3**
> **Baltimore 21202**
> **410-396-3453**

ing, or movement. Level 4 presents the different coastal environments, from the Atlantic to the Pacific. Look for the special "children's cove," where children can touch a variety of sea creatures. The South American Rain Forest on Level 5 is a moist, warm home to many crawling and flying creatures living in a green profusion of tropical plants. As you descend from it, you will have the chance to stare eyeball to eyeball at sharks and all sorts of fish in extensive tanks that surround your walkway down. This is an aquarium you'll want to visit and revisit; its exhibits are dramatically presented, and it is designed both to make you see the species and to understand its role in the ecological systems that surround it and us. Both in architecture and exhibit design, it is the most interesting aquarium we have ever visited.

At the end of the Inner Harbor circuit, the **Baltimore Maritime Museum** exhibits the lightship *Chesapeake,* built in Charleston, South Carolina, in 1930. With her bright red hull, she once marked major shipping channels in Delaware, Chesapeake Bay, and Massachusetts. Now large buoys have taken over the job from most lightships. The USS *Torsk* is a submarine built in Portsmouth, New Hampshire, in 1944, which saw action in Pearl Harbor, Guam, and the Sea of Japan in 1945. She was later used for training in New London, Connecticut, all along our Atlantic Coast, and in the Mediterranean and Norfolk, Virginia. She also participated in NATO exercises. She is 311 feet long, and her name came from the gadoid fish, which is like a codfish and found in the North Atlantic. The *Roger B. Taney,* a Coast Guard cutter that saw action during World War II, is a part of the museum. She was the only warship—out of 101—still afloat after the attack on Pearl Harbor on December 7, 1941. Also visit the Seven-Foot Knoll Lighthouse on Pier 5.

Take it easy by touring the harbor by water taxi or shuttle (call 800-685-8947 or 410-563-3901).

Fells Point

This early Baltimore community east of the Inner Harbor, which was founded in 1732, is now bustling with renovated and reconstructed buildings housing shops, pubs, and restaurants along the waterfront and surrounding

Babe Ruth
Birthplace
and Baseball Center
216 Emory Street
Baltimore 21230
410–727–1539

Camden Yards
333 W. Camden
Street
Baltimore 21201
410–685–9800

B & O Railroad
Museum
901 W. Pratt Street
Baltimore 21223-2699
410–752–2490

blocks. As a seaport Fells Point once had twenty ship-yards, including some that built the famous Baltimore clippers in the last quarter of the eighteenth century and the first quarter of the nineteenth. These fast schooners had the distinctive clipper bow and were the forerunners of the later, larger, square-rigged clipper ships developed for the California trade in the middle of the nineteenth century. Their fame rests on their success as blockade runners and privateers during the War of 1812—the success that led to the unsuccessful British attack on Baltimore in 1814. A replica of one of these beautiful ships, the *Pride of Baltimore II,* was commissioned on October 23, 1988, a few years after an earlier vessel with the same name was lost at sea. When the ship is not on extended cruises to Europe, she is moored in the Inner Harbor, where she receives visitors.

During the mid-1800s, Baltimore developed a series of ethnic neighborhoods, each quite distinct from the others. Waves of immigrants populated an Italian section, then Greek and Polish sections. The Italian, Greek, and Polish sections still exist in areas to the east and north of Fells Point. There is an abundance of good ethnic restaurants in each of them.

West Baltimore

If you admire Babe Ruth, be sure to visit the **Babe Ruth Birthplace;** it's one of the city's most popular spots for visitors. The "Sultan of Swat" was born there, and three adjoining houses are filled with memorabilia, photographs, and paintings. In the museum you can watch film clips of the Babe and Orioles' greats. Oriole Park at nearby **Camden Yards** is open year-round for visitors.

The oldest railroad station in the United States is located at Mt. Clare Station. This collection of railroad memorabilia here at the **B & O Railroad Museum** includes a cathedral-like roundhouse housing cars and locomotives; the oldest dates from 1829. Look for the model train, sure to delight everyone. You'll also see dioramas, prints, and telegraph equipment.

Mount Vernon Place

Mount Vernon Place is an elegant residential neighborhood with nineteenth-century mansions lining the square around the **Washington Monument.** It's the first architectural monument to George Washington.

You can't miss seeing this monument, which soars 178 feet into the air. Designed by Robert Mills, this monument was one of many dedicated to George Washington. The scene at the top depicts Washington resigning his commission as commander in chief of the Revolutionary army. What was then a rural setting at the edge of the city was chosen as the site for the

> Washington
> Monument
> 609 Washington
> Place
> Baltimore 21201
> 410–396–0929

monument, because the city fathers were worried about such a tall monument falling over. You can climb the 228 steps to the top for a fine view of the city.

From the monument cross to the west side of the square to the marble balustrade, where you will see two of a set of four bronzes by Antoine Louis Barye. The seated lion is also by Barye. To the left of the park is 1 West Mount Vernon Place, the **Thomas-Jencks-Gladding House.** This Classical Revival mansion has Italian Renaissance details. Along the same side of the square, Number 3 has heavy, carved wooden doors decorated with lions. Number 5 once housed the Walters collection of art, which has now been transferred to the larger Walters Art Gallery. Number 7 is actually four houses in one, owned originally by Mrs. Henry Barton Jacobs and now by the **Engineering Society of Baltimore.** Number 13 was where the Reverend Billy Sunday lived when he was trying to save Baltimore from perdition in 1916; it was then owned by Henri Pratt James.

As you turn right and cross the street, look for the **Boy and Turtle** fountain by Henri Grenier. Across Cathedral Street and to the north you will find **704 Cathedral Street,** the home of H. L. Mencken and his wife. The **Marburg House,** the home of Theodore Marburg, who was involved in drafting the covenants of the League of Nations, is at 14 West Mount Vernon Place. Number 8 was once owned by William Tiffany and is now the **Mount Vernon Club.**

Turn left at the corner to 700 North Charles Street, the **Washington Apartments,** which were originally designed to be eight stories high. A neighbor petitioned and won an ordinance prohibiting any building from rising higher than the Washington Monument. **Mount Vernon Place United Methodist Church** stands on the site of the house where Francis Scott Key died. The green serpentine stone has oxidized over the years. You can see that the spires are not as high as the monument. Number 14 East Mount Vernon Place was the home of William Patterson, whose daughter married Jerome Bonaparte, younger brother of Emperor Napoleon. Napoleon had the marriage annulled by the pope. Jerome went back to Europe in 1804, and Betsy stayed behind in Baltimore to have her baby; they never saw each other again. Numbers 33, 31, and 21 were

Walters Art Gallery
600 North Charles
  Street
Baltimore 21201
410–547–9000

Baltimore Museum
  of Art
Art Museum Drive,
  Charles Street at
  31st Street
Baltimore 21218
410–396–6330

Baltimore Zoo
Druid Hill Park
Baltimore 21217
410–396–7102 or
396–6165

owned by three Baltimore sisters, the granddaughters of Charles Carroll, a signer of the Declaration of Independence. The **Peabody Institute** owns the southeast corner of Mount Vernon Place.

The **Walters Art Gallery** is housed in a reproduction of the sixteenth-century Palazzo Bianco in Genoa. The collection includes more than 25,000 works of art dating back as much as 6,000 years. You can see Etruscan, Byzantine, Medieval, and Renaissance sculpture and painting, and the Chinese porcelain collection is extensive. The neighboring Hackerman House focuses on Chinese, Japanese, and Southeast Asian art.

Also on Charles Street you will find a number of shops and restaurants; it has been called "Culinary Corridor" or "Restaurant Row."

Head up Charles Street to the **Baltimore Museum of Art,** which has a special wing for modern art. The permanent collection contains more than 120,000 pieces of art. You'll see works from Europe, the Americas, Africa, Asia, and Oceania. The Cone Collection of prints and drawings is well known; Matisse, Picasso, and Cézanne are represented there. Don't miss the Alan and Janet Wurtzburger Sculpture Garden, with its concentration on the human figure.

In 1995 the **Baltimore Zoo** opened two new exhibits: a Leopard's Lair and a Chimpanzee Forest. The world's largest collection of African black-footed penguins lives there. You can ride on a zoo tram, and children will love the interactive children's zoo, named the best in the country. There's an African water hole filled with white rhinoceroses and zebras.

There is much more to see and do in Baltimore if you have some time to spend in this interesting city. For further information contact the **Baltimore Convention and Visitors' Bureau,** Pratt Street, Baltimore 21202; 410–837–4636.

❧ *Western Maryland* ❧

Route 70 will take you from Baltimore to Frederick, the town remembered for its "clustered spires" in John Greenleaf Whittier's poem, "The Ballad of Barbara Fritchie." From Frederick there are a number of pleasant trips you can take in any direction in the surrounding countryside.

Frederick

Originally called Fredericktown by the first English and German settlers in 1745, the town became a stop for wagon trains making their way through the Cumberland Gap and across the mountains to the west. Perhaps fortunately, because the settlers did not have the water transportation that was so easily available in eastern Maryland, they farmed their land instead of growing tobacco. Other communities found that tobacco soon depleted the soil, but the area around Frederick still has fertile soil.

> **Barbara Fritchie House and Museum**
> 154 West Patrick Street
> Frederick 21701
> 301–698–0630
>
> **Rose Hill Manor Museum**
> 1611 North Market Street
> Frederick 21701
> 301–694–1648

The early settlers were just as tenacious when they repudiated the Stamp Act in 1765. And during the Civil War, the citizens paid a ransom of $200,000 to Confederate General Jubal Early so that he would not destroy their city. Although they had hoped the federal government would reimburse them, nothing has been done yet. The Frederick Reimbursement Bill is presented year after year after year.

Stop in the tourism council office for information on a walking tour of the restored historic district and on other sights in town. You can see the **City Hall,** where the ransom was paid to Early in 1864; the **Historical Society of Frederick County** (301–663–1188), dating from 1830; the law offices of Roger B. Taney and Francis Scott Key; the **William Tyler Page Home** (the author of the American Creed); several interesting churches; and the **Court Square** area, dating from 1756.

Don't miss the **Barbara Fritchie House and Museum.** Whittier's version of the brief encounter between Confederate General Stonewall Jackson and Barbara Fritchie is the one we remember because it symbolizes a remnant of civility in a brutal and bloody war.

Inside Barbara's small house you can see a quilt made from flax she had spun on her spinning wheel, as well as her petticoat and jacket. Look for the large roller that looks like a rolling pin; it was used to roll the lumps out of a straw mattress. The famous window, with flag flying, is still there. The flag contains thirty-five stars, the last added for West Virginia. A silk dress belonging to Barbara is on display, as well as a doll dress she made for a young relative. The china teapot that she used to serve tea to George Washington in 1791 is there. Don't miss the knotted cane with which she shooed Confederate soldiers away from her porch after they had insulted her beloved Union flag.

One-way streets in Frederick can be frustrating, but work your way north past Governor Thomas Johnson High School to the **Rose Hill**

Manor Museum, which dates from the 1790s. This Georgian mansion was the home of Governor Thomas Johnson—who nominated George Washington as commander in chief of the Continental army—from 1794 until 1819. Now the house has been developed into a museum for children, where they can touch and play with nineteenth-century toys, try their hands at weaving, help make a quilt, and do a little colonial cooking. The guides are in costume and will help each child enjoy his or her experience there. The focus is on living history.

Stroll around the grounds to the blacksmith shop, carriage museum, log cabin, and farm museum. When you walk through the gardens, you are welcome to touch, smell, or taste mint, lavender, basil, oregano, and other medicinal and culinary herbs. The vegetable section provides produce to be used in the kitchen. Come to visit and experience a quilting bee, soap making, candle dipping, and cooking various dishes. Special events are held during the year, including an Easter egg hunt, fall festival, Halloween tour, needlework show, and Christmas open house.

If you're ready for lunch, head for **The Province** (129 North Market Street; 301–663–1441). **The Craftworks** (55 East Patrick Street; 301–662–3111) houses antiques on two full floors—whatever you're looking for has got to be there! (This concentration of antiques rivals **New Market,** noted as "The Antiques Capital of Maryland," located 8 miles east, which is also worth a visit.)

You may contact the **Tourism Council of Frederick County** (19 East Church Street, Frederick 21701; 301–663–8687) for more information about this area.

From Frederick you can take several excursions in different directions to see more of Western Maryland. A short excursion to the south leads to Sugarloaf Mountain (or you can go see it on your way to Washington, D.C.). To the north is Cunningham Falls State Park; to the west is Antietam National Battlefield; and to the northwest are Hagerstown and Cumberland.

Excursion South of Frederick

Heading south on Route 355 toward Urbana and Sugarloaf Mountain will take you to The **Blue Fox Inn** (Route 355; 301–831–4878) for lunch or dinner. Continue on another mile to the **Turning Point Inn** (3406 Urbana Pike; 301–831–8232) for dinner (or lunch by prior reservation). You can even spend the night here. (See Inns appendix.)

To reach the base of Sugarloaf Mountain, take Route 80 west from Urbana and turn south on Thurston Road shortly after crossing I–270. Then go west on Sugarloaf Road toward the village of Mt. Ephraim. Sugarloaf

Mountain, 1,282 feet high, is a great place to hike because you can see much of Frederick and Montgomery counties as well as parts of Virginia and West Virginia from the top. French trader and explorer Martin Chartier guided a Swiss nobleman, Baron Graffenried, over Sugarloaf Mountain in search of silver mines. "There is no more beautiful sight in the world," concluded Chartier. George Washington surveyed the area prior to 1769, and General Braddock passed through on his way to Fort Duquesne during the French and Indian War in 1769.

> Cunningham Falls
> State Park
> 14039 Catoctin
> Hollow Road
> Thurmont 21788
> 301–271–7574
>
> Catoctin Mountain
> Park
> Thurmont 21788
> 301–663–9330

Excursion North of Frederick

Route 15 north leads to Cunningham Falls State Park and the Grotto of Lourdes. On the way you can take a brief side trip to see one or two covered bridges. The one near Lewistown at Utica is the largest in Frederick County and has the original bowstring and Howe trusses still intact. To get to it leave Route 15 on the Old Frederick Road south of Lewistown and turn left when you reach Utica Road. The other covered bridge, called Loys Station Bridge, is north of Creagerstown; take Old Frederick Road through Creagerstown and continue another 2 miles. A map of the bridge route is available at the **County Tourism Office** (19 East Church Street; 301–663–8687).

Catoctin Furnace, located in **Cunningham Falls State Park,** was built by the James Johnson Company in 1774. It played an important role during the Revolution by producing weaponry for the Continental army. The iron plates for the *Monitor* were cast there during the Civil War period. The workers at the furnace lived in a stone-cottaged village, which is open as a National Register historic district. **Cunningham Falls,** a 78-foot cascading waterfall in a deep gorge, is located on the other side of the park. Cunningham Falls State Park offers picnicking, swimming, boating, fishing, and camping.

Catoctin Mountain Park, adjacent to Cunningham, is a national park. Check in at the visitors' center for information on hiking trails and other recreational activities. You can also drive 14 miles on the back roads of the Catoctin ridge; be sure to stop at the scenic overlook on the east side of Hunting Creek Lake. The National Park Service displays the **Blue Blazes Still,** a real still used during Prohibition, as part of an interpretive program. The presidential retreat **Camp David** is located within the park but is not open to the public.

Grotto of Lourdes
Emmitsburg 21727
301–447–5318

National Shrine of St.
Elizabeth Ann Seton
333 S. Seton Avenue
Emmitsburg 21727
301–447–6606

Washington
Monument State
Park
Monument Road
Boonsboro 21713

Greenbrier State
Park
Route 40
Boonsboro 21713
301–791–4767

Continue on Route 15, 8 miles north of Thurmont and follow signs to the **Grotto of Lourdes.** It is the first National Catholic Shrine in the United States and the oldest replica of Lourdes, France, in the Western Hemisphere. It is located on the side of the mountain above the campus of Mount St. Mary's College. A few miles farther on Route 15 will bring you to the **National Shrine of St. Elizabeth Ann Seton** on the grounds of the **St. Joseph Provincial House.** She was the first native-born American to be canonized by the Catholic Church.

Excursion West of Frederick

Head west from Frederick on Route 40, stay in the left lane, and bear left onto alternate Route 40. Continue up the mountain for 2 miles to the **Braddock Monument,** honoring General Edward Braddock, who did not survive his mission to liberate Fort Duquesne. The **Braddock Mountain** scenic overlook provides a panoramic view of the valley below. Continue on through **Middletown,** the home of Revolutionary War hero Sergeant Lawrence Everhart. During the Battle of Brandywine, Everhart was one of two soldiers who carried the wounded General Lafayette more than 2 miles for help.

A little farther along Route 40A you will come to **Old South Mountain Inn** (301–432–6155), which has served as a hotel, tavern, restaurant, stagecoach station, and private home. Across the street from the inn are four historical markers detailing the emplacement of troops there during the Civil War.

From Route 40A take Monument Road for 1 mile to **Washington Monument State Park** to see the monument that was the first memorial completed to George Washington. The citizens of Boonsboro built the monument in this park in one day on July 4, 1827.

The monument is quite close to **Greenbrier State Park,** which was developed by the state in the early 1960s. (Access to the park, however, is from Route 40, not Route 40A.) You can hike through a section of the Appalachian Trail or go picnicking, swimming, boating, fishing, or camping in the park.

Head back to Boonsboro and take Route 34 to Sharpsburg and follow signs to **Antietam National Battlefield,** where the bloodiest day of the Civil War took place during the Battle of Antietam (or Sharpsburg) on September 17, 1862. Clara Barton, after helping the wounded during that battle, exclaimed, "War is a dreadful thing. . . . Oh, my God, can't this civil strife be brought to an end?" In the battle 41,000 soldiers under Confederate General Robert E. Lee clashed with 87,000 soldiers of the Federal Army of the Potomac led by General George B. McClellan, who reputedly said, "If I cannot whip Bobbie Lee, I will be willing to go home." Bloody Lane was the area of greatest fatalities. At the end of that day, Federal losses were 12,410 and Confederate losses 10,700. Stop in the **Antietam National Battlefield Visitors' Center** to see a film on the action of that day.

> Antietam National
> Battlefield Visitors'
> Center
> Sharpsburg 21782
> 301–432–5124
>
> Harper's Ferry
> National Historical
> Park
> Harper's Ferry 25851
> 304–535–6223

Harper's Ferry, West Virginia

Route 67 will take you south to **Harper's Ferry, West Virginia.** In 1733 Peter Stephens set up a ferry service crossing the Potomac and Shenandoah rivers. Fourteen years later Robert Harper took over Stephens's ferry service and added a mill. During the 1790s President George Washington promoted the establishment of an armory in Harper's Ferry. The town's growth followed the construction of the Chesapeake and Ohio Canal and the Baltimore and Ohio Railroad in the 1830s.

In October 1859 John Brown's raid took place during the dead of night as twenty-two men took control of the armory, ending only when Robert E. Lee and Jeb Stuart took possession of the building. Brown was hanged at Charles Town on December 2, 1859. In 1861 the armory was burned so that it would not be available to the Confederates. As it happened, both the Union and Confederate sides occupied the town one after the other. In 1862 Stonewall Jackson captured the town; by then many of the townspeople had moved away because of the continued anguish of war in their area.

Harper's Ferry National Historic Park has been involved in a great deal of restoration, including more work after the floods in 1985. Stop in the visitors' center for information on historical sites to visit. The site of both the park and the town, on the steep hillsides of a peninsula overlooking the roaring rapids of two powerful rivers, is worth a visit in itself. Thomas Jefferson wrote that "the scene is worth a voyage across the Atlantic," and Carl Sandburg wrote, "Harper's Ferry is a meeting place of winds and water, rocks and ranges."

If you are interested in white-water trips, consider contacting one of these outfitters: **River & Trail Outfitters** (Route 2, Valley Road, Knoxville, MD 21758; 301–695–5177), **Blue Ridge Outfitters** (Box 750, Harper's

Hager House and Museum 110 Key Street Hagerstown 21740 301–739–8393
Fort Frederick State Park Route 56 Big Pool 21711 301–842–2155
C&O Canal Museum and Visitors' Center 326 E. Main Street Hancock 21750 301–678–5463

Ferry, WV; 304–725–3444), or **Harper's Ferry Riders** (Box 267, Knoxville, MD 21758; 301–834–8051). You can also canoe-camp along the Potomac and Shenandoah Rivers and the adjacent C&O Canal from Spring Gap Campground to Harper's Ferry, a distance of 115 miles. Most of this trip is flat-water. Or you can cycle and hike along the canal.

Hagerstown

The excursion northwest from Frederick begins with Hagerstown, reached by I–70 west. The town was founded in 1762 as Elizabeth Town to honor the wife of settler Jonathan Hager. Visit the **Hager House and Museum.** Sometimes called "Hager's Fancy," the house was built over a spring to ensure a source of water during an Indian attack. This stone house has eighteenth-century furnishings.

Fort Frederick State Park

Continue on I–70 to Big Pool and Route 56 to **Fort Frederick State Park,** which is the only remaining British stone fort in the country. It was begun in 1756 during the French and Indian War. Barracks have been reconstructed, and historical events are reenacted by military units in eighteenth-century costume. An orientation film and museum describe the historical development of the fort. The park offers cycling, camping, nature and hiking trails, boating, and fishing.

Hancock

Continue on I–70 to Hancock. The town has the distinction of being on the narrowest bit of Maryland in the western part of the state across the Mason-Dixon line from Pennsylvania. In fact, during the 1760s a seventy-three–year boundary dispute between the Penns of Pennsylvania and the Calverts of Maryland finally came to a head. It was resolved by the surveying of the Mason-Dixon line, which left only a 2-mile strip of land for Maryland between Pennsylvania and West Virginia. In 1839 the C&O Canal was completed to Hancock, bringing prosperity to the area. The next section, to Cumberland, was finished in 1850. You can visit the **C&O Canal Museum and Visitors' Center** to see models of canal boats and locks. A slide show and exhibits present the story of canal development.

The **Tonoloway Aqueduct** carried canal water over Tonoloway Creek; it is one of eleven aqueducts along the canal. You can hike along the towpath that runs from Georgetown to Cumberland. This 12-foot-wide path is overgrown in some places and may wash out after a heavy rain. Tent campsites are spaced every 5 miles along the 165-mile section from Carderock to Cumberland, and one is located midway between Seneca and Georgetown. Drive-in campgrounds are located at McCoys Ferry, Fifteen Mile Creek, and Spring Gap. Canoeing is available, with portages around the locks. For more information pick up a brochure at the **C&O Canal National Historical Park.**

If you visit Hancock in the fall, the air will be perfumed with the fragrance from apple and peach orchards around the town. In September there is a Canal Apple Festival to attend.

> C&O Canal National Historic Park
> Sharpsburg 21782
> 301–739–4200
>
> Rocky Gap State Park
> Route 40
> Cumberland 21502
> 301–777–2139
>
> History House
> 218 Washington Street
> Cumberland 21502
> 301–777–8678
>
> George Washington's Headquarters
> Riverside Park
> Cumberland 21502
> 301–777–8214

Cumberland

Six miles east of Cumberland on Route 40 is **Rocky Gap State Park,** located in a saddle between Evitts Mountain and Martin Mountain. The park offers fishing, boating, nature trails, hiking, picnicking, and camping.

Route 40 will bring you to Cumberland, which has a National Historic District composed of Federal and Georgian Revival homes. **History House** displays a primitive kitchen, a music room, and a library with a collection of genealogical materials. You can get information on a walking tour from **Allegany County Tourism** at Western Maryland Station Center, Cumberland, MD 21502; 301–777–5132.

George Washington's Headquarters was his first military headquarters. He began as an aide-de-camp to General Braddock and during the French and Indian War used the cabin as his headquarters. A taped narration is available while you view the exhibit from the outside.

Cumberland was the eastern end of the historic Cumberland Trail—our country's first road built with federal funds. It brought prosperity to Cumberland, which was a supply terminus for overland transportation. The B&O Railroad arrived in Cumberland in 1842, and the C&O Canal was completed in 1850. Take a stroll along the Fort Cumberland Trail around the site of Fort Cumberland.

The **Cumberland Narrows,** just west of town on Route 40A, is a sheer break in the Allegheny Mountains, with a rocky cliff rising 800 feet

LaVale Toll Gate
House
14302 National
Highway
LaVale 21502
301-729-3047

Casselman River
Bridge
Route 40
Grantsville 21550
301-895-5453

Penn Alps & Spruce
Forest
Route 40
Grantsville 21536
301-895-3332

above Wills Creek. There is a legend that Lover's Leap is the site of the tragic suicide of an Indian princess and English settler when they could not marry. Drive to the top of the eastern wall for a panoramic view of Cumberland and the Narrows.

A few miles west of the Narrows on Route 40A, the **LaVale Toll Gate House,** dating from 1835, was the first tollgate on the National Road in Maryland. Read the plaque to see how much was charged for wagons, animals, and pedestrians to pass through. The **Clarysville Bridge** is the only remaining original bridge from the National Road in Allegany County.

Grantsville

Farther along Route 40 **Stanton's Mill,** just east of Grantsville, is the oldest gristmill in Garrett County that is still operating. Its original grinding stones are on display. **Casselman River Bridge,** ½ mile east of Grantsville, was the longest single-span stone arch bridge in the country when it was built in 1813. Local people were sure that the bridge would collapse when the supporting logs were removed. The contractor loosened them the night before the opening ceremony and then stood under the bridge to prove his faith in its strength.

Continue west on Route 40. **Penn Alps & Spruce Forest** is a Mennonite crafts center and restaurant in an 1820 log house. Watch pottery being made, spinning, and clock-making.

This far-western part of Maryland is a fine place to come for outdoor living, with its mountains, waterfalls, and the largest freshwater lake in the state. You can come in the summer, spring, and fall for water sports and hiking, and again in the winter for skiing.

This is the western end of Itinerary J, which now turns back east to Washington (Itinerary K) via Route 40, I–70, and I–270. It is also easy to connect with Itinerary F (South Central Pennsylvania) by taking I–81 north from Hagerstown to Gettysburg.

ITINERARY K:

Washington, D.C., and Virginia

COLONIAL WILLIAMSBURG, VIRGINIA

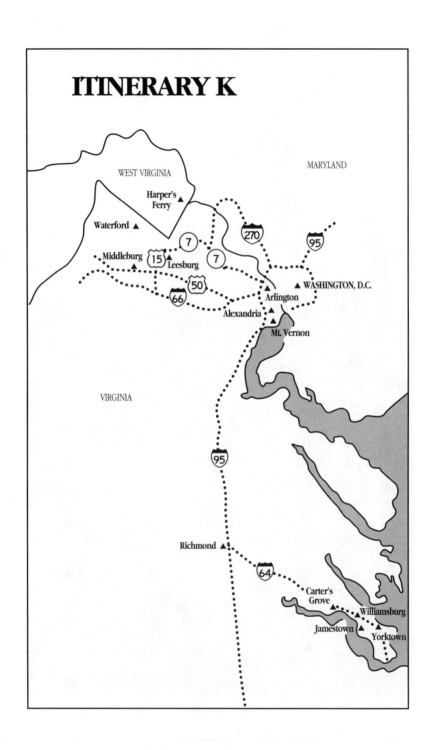

ITINERARY K

WEST VIRGINIA

MARYLAND

Harper's
Ferry ▲

Waterford ▲

Middleburg ▲

(7)

(270)

(95)

(7)

(15) Leesburg

(50)

(66)

WASHINGTON, D.C. ▲

Arlington ▲

Alexandria ▲

Mt. Vernon ▲

VIRGINIA

(95)

Richmond ▲

(64)

Carter's
Grove ▲

Williamsburg ▲

Jamestown ▲

Yorktown

Washington, D.C., and Virginia

Washington, D.C., Area

This last itinerary covers the Washington, D.C., area. The city itself is a museum of the history of our country. Most Americans, having been steeped in history as schoolchildren, want to visit Washington at some point. Years of watching historic events on television will make you feel you've been there before.

≈ *Washington, D.C., Area* ≈

The Washington, D.C., area may not be romantic to the government employees working there, but it certainly is to those who visit. Whether visiting for the first time or the fifteenth, visitors cannot help but be impressed by the beauty of the city's buildings, laid out according to a carefully articulated plan and meticulously landscaped with expanses of green lawn punctuated by flowering trees. The pervading sense of lives from the past that influenced our present well-being is ethereal yet real. Our founding fathers worked hard to provide a solid basis for the new, experimental nation and left us with a legacy to carry on, but they also lived hard, active lives and suffered defeats as well as successes. A visit to Washington should lead you backward into history, beyond the seeming permanence of the monuments to the struggles behind the achievements they memorialize.

In 1790 Congress was tied up with the thorny problem of where to situate our capital city. With diverse ideas ringing in his ears, George Washington settled the problem by choosing this site just 18 miles from his home at Mount Vernon. A 100-square-mile area was designated, and Major Pierre Charles L'Enfant, who had served on Washington's Continental army staff, was asked to design the city. Thinking of Paris, L'Enfant created scenic squares and circles with 160-foot-wide avenues spreading out like the spokes of a wheel.

George Washington died before he had a chance to live in the president's mansion, but President John Adams moved into the unfinished house in 1800. In 1814 the British burned the president's mansion, the Capitol, and the original Library of Congress. A thunderstorm fortunately put out the flames before the entire city went up in smoke. In 1815 rebuilding began. As the blackened planks of the mansion were repaired, they were also painted white, thus generating the name "the White House." Work progressed slowly, and in 1842 Charles Dickens could still write that the city had "spacious avenues that begin in nothing and lead nowhere, streets a mile long that only want houses, roads and inhabitants, public buildings that need but a public to be complete. . . ."

Because the site along the Potomac consisted of swampy, low ground with a canal running through it, floods were frequent. The Capitol was finished in 1863 as a symbol of unity (or perhaps tenacity) during difficult times. Abraham Lincoln commented, "If the people see the Capitol going on, it's a sign we intend the Union shall go on." After the Civil War the canal was filled and became Constitution Avenue. By 1874 Alexander Shepherd had improved sewers, sidewalks, and streets. Frederick Law Olmsted landscaped the Capitol grounds with thousands of trees. The Smithsonian Institution started to house exhibits from the 1876 Philadelphia Centennial in a Norman-Gothic castle in addition to the Arts and Industries Building.

The Washington Monument was in the process of construction for thirty-six years and was finally completed in 1884. A steam-driven elevator was available to take men to the top, but women and children had to walk up the 897 steps because of anxiety about the safety of the elevator. By the end of the nineteenth century, more buildings had been completed, including the Library of Congress, Union Station, the Corcoran and Renwick Gallery of Art, the Bureau of Printing and Engraving, the Post Office, the Treasury Buildings, and the National Portrait Gallery. The design of the parks began in 1901, and Japan sent 3,000 cherry trees as a gift in 1912.

The Botanic Gardens appeared in 1902, the Museum of Natural History in 1911, the Lincoln Memorial in 1922, and the Freer Gallery of Art in 1923. President Franklin Delano Roosevelt provided jobs in his WPA program during the Great Depression to build structures within the "Federal Triangle." In 1941 the National Gallery of Art was completed as a gift from Andrew Mellon. The Jefferson Memorial and the Pentagon were built in 1943, and the John F. Kennedy Center for the Performing Arts opened in 1971. The Smithsonian continued to make additions, including the Air and Space Museum, the Hirshhorn Museum, and the Sculpture Garden. The East Wing of the National Gallery of Art was designed by I. M. Pei and completed in 1979.

As in other cities, renovation of rundown areas has produced new parks, shops, and hotels. The Old Post Office has begun a new life as "The Pavilion," where a glass elevator whisks people up to an observation deck in the "clock tower."

Washington, D.C.

Before you leave home, contact the **Washington, D.C., Convention and Visitors Association** (1212 New York Avenue, N.W., Washington,

Washington
Monument
Washington, D.C.
202–426–6841

National Museum of
American History
Constitution Avenue
& 14th Street, N.W.
Washington, D.C.
20560
202–357–2700

D.C. 20005; 202–789–7000 or 800–422–8644) for information. Handy phone numbers include **National Park Service** (202–619–7222), **Dial-a-Museum** (202–357–2020), and **National Archives Exhibits** (202–501–5402).

We have been lucky enough to find a place to park in the touring areas of Washington—sometimes—but if you are there in high season, you may be wise to leave your car in a parking garage or in one of the suburbs and take the "Metro" into town. You can easily walk from one site to another, from the Capitol through the green Mall, parks, and gardens all the way to the Potomac. **Tourmobile Sightseeing** (1000 Ohio Street, S.W.; 202–554–5100) or the **Old Town Trolley** (2640 Reed Street, N.E.; 202–832–9800) are also available for rides from one site to another, and the Metro or a cab will take you to outlying places of interest.

How about an eagle's-eye view of the area from the top of the **Washington Monument** to begin your tour? It has been in the process of renovation and is now open again. Get there early (it opens at 9:00 A.M.) to avoid waiting in line. An elevator will take you up to the 500-foot level, where you can look out in all directions. Look for the Capitol to the east, the White House to the north, the Jefferson Memorial to the south, and the Lincoln Memorial to the west. (As you might imagine, the view sparkles with lights at night, so try to return then.) Then look slowly outward in each direction to identify major buildings and landmarks lying in concentric circles around the monument and the Mall; when your eyes have had their fill, you have the choice of walking down 897 steps or returning to ground by the elevator.

From the monument, begin your explorations of the riches of the Mall. (But you don't need to be "rich" to explore. Most of the buildings on the Mall are museums of the Smithsonian Institution and have no admission fee.) On the north side the **National Museum of American History** is particularly appealing to children, with its collection of vehicles, such as a 1913 Model T Ford, a Conestoga wagon, and a 280-ton steam locomotive. Don't miss Archie and Edith Bunker's chairs and end table from their TV series, which are displayed in a glass case on the second floor. On the third floor there's a model of the Capitol made entirely of glass rods by a fabrication process known as *lamp work*. The original Star-spangled Banner that flew over Fort McHenry in 1814 is in the museum, and don't miss George Washington's false teeth. Ball gowns worn by the First Ladies are on display. One of the most popular items, the Foucault Pendulum, is suspended from the ceiling of the fourth floor, illustrating the idea that the earth does rotate. Children can participate in the activities of several Discovery Corners.

By now you may be ready for lunch, so head out the Constitution Avenue side of the museum and turn onto 12th Street to the **Pavilion** in the **Old Post Office.** With specialty-food shops, restaurants, and food kiosks to choose from, you're sure to find a place for lunch, and you can watch entertainers or listen to music while you eat. While you're there, take a look at the 315-foot clock tower, which is the third-tallest building in the city.

Back on the north side of the Mall is the **National Museum of Natural History.** If you are fascinated by sixty-five-million-year-old dinosaurs, you have come to the right place. Don't miss "Uncle Beazley," a gigantic model of a Triceratops dinosaur that is stationed outside and loves to be climbed. Animals, fish, insects, birds, rocks, and minerals are displayed in this museum. The Hall of Gems contains, among other things, the 45.5-carat Hope Diamond and a diamond tiara containing 950 gems worn by the Empress Marie Louise. Children will enjoy the Discovery Room, where they can feel a variety of specimens. Look for the 5.03-carat red diamond, which was put on display in 1988, and the fossil of Tanytrachelus, a 200-million-year-old reptile.

The **National Gallery of Art** contains countless famous masterpieces that will entice both infrequent and experienced gallery-goers. If your time is limited, you can rent an Acoustiguide, which takes you to a selected number of paintings that most visitors want to see. Children can pick up a treasure-hunt form at the information desk in the West Building. Twentieth-century art is displayed in the East Wing, reached by an underground concourse. If you've waited for lunch, you might like to have it in pleasant surroundings beside the underground waterfall here.

Head up to the **Capitol,** past the **Reflecting Pool** and **Ulysses S. Grant Memorial,** which portrays the action of cavalry and artillery during the Civil War. The Capitol can be entered through the East Portico, where presidential inaugurations take place. Visitors can take a scheduled tour that begins every fifteen minutes or wander through on their own. Look at

Pavilion in the Old Post Office
Pennsylvania Avenue & 12th Street, N.W.
Washington, D.C. 20560
202-289-4224

National Museum of Natural History
Constitution Avenue & 10th Street, N.W.
Washington, D.C. 20560
202-357-2700

National Gallery of Art
Constitution Avenue & 4th Street, N.W.
Washington, D.C. 20560
202-737-4215

Capitol
Constitution & Independence Avenues
Washington, D.C.

Botanic Gardens
Maryland Avenue &
1st Street, S.W.
Washington, D.C.
20560
202–225–8333

National Air and
Space Museum
Independence
Avenue
& 6th Street, N.W.
Washington, D.C.
20560
202–357–2700

the frescoes high in the dome, with 15-foot-high statues that look life-size from the floor. John Trumbull, an aide to George Washington, painted four of the historical paintings on the Rotunda walls. Did you know that this is a whispering dome? There are a number of places where you can stand and hear people talking from across the Rotunda, which must be inconvenient at times for congressmen. Check to be sure that Congress is in session by observing the American flag flying over the south chamber for the House, or the north chamber for the Senate. If you would like to sit in the **Visitors' Gallery** in the Senate or the House, pick up a pass in the office of your senator or congressman. (To get to the offices, you can use the subway that connects the Capitol with the federal office buildings.) If you are from abroad, you can show your passport to receive a pass. Nearby, a popular spot for lunch is **The Monocle** (107 D Street, N.E.; 202–546–4488).

Just below the Capitol, across Maryland Avenue from the Reflecting Pool, the **Botanic Gardens** are housed in a Victorian-style greenhouse. Where else can you see a waterfall in the midst of a busy city? Four seasonal shows include azaleas in February, spring flowers in March and April, chrysanthemums in November, and poinsettias in December.

More buildings of the Smithsonian Institution fill most of the south side of the Mall. First you will come to the **National Air and Space Museum,** which may be counted among the most popular sites anywhere. There you can see the Wright brothers' 1903 *Kitty Hawk;* Lindbergh's *Spirit of St. Louis;* Amelia Earhart's *Vega;* the Apollo 11 *Columbia,* which took Neil Armstrong, Edwin Aldrin, and Michael Collins to the moon; and much more. The *Voyager,* which flew around the world without refueling, is in the south lobby. Look for the U.S. flag and flight patch that were found in the cabin debris of the *Challenger.* The Albert Einstein Planetarium presents a voyage into the expanse beyond the solar system. There is a display on balloons and airships that traces the development from early flights. The Langley Theater presents a number of films that are related to air and space travel.

Several of the Smithsonian museums have cafeterias or restaurants, but the newest is very dramatic. On the east end of the Air and Space Museum, you can't miss a large glass addition, which is actually two restaurants in one—a cafeteria on the lower level and the **Wright Place** (202–371–8777) above. You can dine with a view of the Capitol.

The **Hirshhorn Museum** looks like a doughnut because the design was planned to minimize sun damage to the works of art. The **Sculpture Garden** next to the museum features Auguste Rodin's sculpture *Burghers of Calais,* which dramatically portrays the town fathers wearing nooses around their necks as they hand over the keys of their city to British invaders.

The **Art and Industries Building** contains the pieces displayed during the Philadelphia Exposition of 1876. Victorian items of all kinds, furniture, pistols, silverware, and horse-drawn carriages are collected in this second-oldest building of the Smithsonian Institution.

Next to the Art and Industries Building is **The Castle,** which once was the only building of the Smithsonian. Designed by James Renwick, Jr., it was completed in 1855 and still has charm with its peaks and turrets. Children will love riding on the carousel located in front of The Castle. A Wurlitzer organ provides music. A visitors' center is there too.

The **Enid A. Haupt Garden,** behind The Castle, is the place to sit down and relax amid seasonal flowers. Then stroll into twin museums on the grounds, both built in 1987.

The **National Museum of African Art** devotes exhibits to the art of sub-Saharan Africa. The collection includes the Royal Benin Art exhibit of traditional court art. Look for the mask from Angola of a woman made from wood, fiber, and metal; a carved headdress from Somalia; a headdress from Nigeria made of wood, fiber, and red abrus seeds; a wooden figure of a Zairian Yombe woman holding her child; a Lower Niger bronze industry vessel; and a figure of an officer from the Cameroon grassfields.

Next door the **Arthur M. Sackler Gallery** includes work from China, South and Southeast Asia, and the ancient Near East. The collection includes Persian manuscripts as well as Chinese bronzes, jades, and lacquerware. Look for a gilt-and-silver bowl from the seventh century, a sculpture of an Indian goddess from the tenth century, and a bronze wine holder from the tenth century B.C.

The final building in the Smithsonian complex on the south side of the Mall is the **Freer Gallery of Art,** based on the collection of Charles Lang Freer of Detroit. As you emerge from the wonders of the

Hirshhorn Museum and Sculpture Garden
Independence Avenue and 7th Street, S.W.
Washington, D.C. 20560
202–357–2700

Art and Industries Building
900 Jefferson Drive, S.W.
Washington, D.C. 20560
202–357–2700

The Castle
1000 Jefferson Drive, S.W.
Washington, D.C. 20560
202–357–2700

National Museum of African Art
950 Independence Avenue, S.W.
Washington, D.C. 20560
202–357–4600

Arthur M. Sackler Gallery
1050 Independence Avenue, S.W.
Washington, D.C. 20560
202–357–3200

Freer Art Gallery
Jefferson Drive at
12th Street, S.W.
Washington, D.C.
20560
202–357–4880

United States
Holocaust Memorial
Museum
100 Raoul
Wallenberg
Place, S.W.
Washington, D.C.
20024
202–488–0400

White House
1600 Pennsylvania
Avenue, N.W.
Washington, D.C.
20500
202–456–7041

Smithsonian, pass the Washington Monument again and cross the Ellipse to the White House.

The **U.S. Holocaust Memorial Museum** is an angular building of three stories; an atrium, steel staircases, and catwalks provide a sense of foreboding and grim dislocation. Some of the angles may seem skewed, and the lines are reminiscent of real images from the death camps.

Every visitor receives an ID card bearing details of a victim, one who was the same gender and about the same age as the visitor. The card is updated at computer stations along the tour. You will find out something about this person and what happened to him and his family. At the end you will learn the fate of the victim.

Devices are used to disorient a visitor—for instance, a horizontal steel bar like those used at European borders forces movement along a detour. Watch your footing as you cross a bridge, a glass floor, cobblestones, and wooden flooring.

As you pass from the fourth floor down through to the main area, murals, exhibits, photographs, posters, and objects from the camps are on display. The Hollerith machine was used to classify citizens so that the Nazis could locate those they chose to exterminate. A freight car from Poland may have taken people to the camps. It stands silent. Personal possessions taken away are heaped in piles.

The Hall of Remembrance, with its skylight, is a place for quiet contemplation; candles may be left there. The Hall has six sides—one for each of the six million who died.

The **White House,** which celebrated its 200th anniversary in 1992, can be visited on a VIP tour if you contact your senator or congressman in advance for a ticket to go through earlier in the day than the more crowded regular tours. Friends also suggest getting in line at about 11:55 A.M. when the wait is usually shorter than it is earlier. As you are waiting in line to get in, be on the lookout for the president or one of his advisers driving in or out. (When we were last there, we were given the full treatment, with a helicopter landing the president on the lawn.)

The first room visitors see is the Library, which contains wall-to-wall books on American life. Portraits of American Indians meeting President Monroe in 1821 are displayed there. In the Vermeil Room you'll see gilded silver from Europe and America and a portrait of Eleanor Roosevelt.

Upstairs the tour takes you to the East Room, which you have seen on TV during performances and conferences. It is also the place where the body of John F. Kennedy lay in state. Cut-glass chandeliers from 1902 dazzle the eye in this white-and-gold room. Gilbert Stuart's painting of George Washington hangs on the east wall; Dolley Madison saved it during the great fire of 1814. Abigail Adams hung her laundry in this room, Theodore Roosevelt's children rollerskated on the parquet floors, and his guests watched wrestling and Japanese jujitsu performances.

The Green Room was the site of knitting and embroidery sessions by cabinet and diplomatic corps wives in ages past. Dolley Madison's silver candlesticks, a 1785 French clock on the mantel, the oldest portrait of Benjamin Franklin on public display (1767), and *The Last of the Mohicans* painting by Asher B. Durand enhance this 1810 Federal-style parlor.

Elliptically shaped, the Blue Room is often used by the president to receive heads of state and other guests. Gilded chairs covered with blue silk upholstery with an eagle on the back are eye-catching. The White House Christmas tree stands in this room every December.

The Red Room walls are covered by a red-satin fabric with an ornate gold border. Look for the musical clock given by the president of France in 1952. If you like intrigue, remember Rutherford B. Hayes's slim margin of one electoral vote in March 1877. Fearing that something might go wrong, President Grant encouraged Hayes to take the oath of office one day early; it was done in this room.

The State Dining Room is handsome, with floor-to-ceiling oak paneling dating from Theodore Roosevelt's tenure in 1902. Abraham Lincoln's portrait hangs above the mantel.

If you are there during the Christmas season, you may take the candlelit tour of the White House. On Easter Monday you can watch the famous Easter Egg Roll on the lawn. Children apparently gathered there as early as 1877 to roll eggs, and now they come every year. In 1981 each child received a wooden egg with the White House insignia on it as a prize. If you're ready for lunch after your tour, try **Garden Cafe** at the National Gallery (4th and Constitution, N.W.; 202–547–9401), the **Hay-Adams** (One Lafayette Square; 800–424–5054), **McCormick & Schmick's Seafood** (1652 K Street, N.W.; 202–861–2233), the **Morrison-Clark** (Massachusetts Avenue and 11th Street, N.W.; 800–332–7898), **Occidental Grill** (1475 Pennsylvania Avenue, N.W.; 202–783–1475), the **Old Ebbitt Grill** (675 15th Street, N.W.; 202–347–4801), or **Tony Cheng's Seafood** (619 H Street, N.W.; 202–371–8669).

The **Ellipse,** located between the Washington Monument and the White House, is the place to stroll in the midst of flowers and statues.

> Lincoln Memorial
> West Potomac Park
> at 23rd Street, N.W.
> Washington, D.C.

When we were last there, a group of Boy Scouts in uniform were darting around a monument of a man and a woman, with one Boy Scout in the center. They took time to dangle fingers, a foot, a stick, and a small boat in the pool. Further on we admired a statue of the Marquis de Lafayette, who visited in 1824.

Across the street stands **St. John's Church,** where presidents attend services. There is even a pew marked with a gold plaque reading "The President's Pew." The church dates from 1815. The Palladian window depicts the Lord's Supper in brilliant colors. The bronze bell was made from British cannons, and on VJ Day four parishioners rang it until the rope broke.

From the White House retrace your way across the Ellipse and turn right to stroll through the Constitution Gardens toward the **Vietnam Veterans Memorial,** the wall designed by Maya Ying Lin. Names of the 58,007 Americans who lost their lives in Vietnam are listed on the wall, in chronological order of death. The **Vietnam Women's Memorial** is located across from the Vietnam Veterans Memorial. Gienna Goodacre, a Santa Fe sculptor, created the bronze statue of three servicewomen and a wounded soldier. The Reflecting Pool leads to the **Lincoln Memorial,** which looks like a Greek temple with its thirty-six Doric columns. Daniel Chester French designed the statue of Lincoln and then supervised the carving done by the Piccarilli Brothers during a four-year period. Look carefully at Lincoln's hands, which stand for "A" and "L" in sign language. Did you know that there is a cave under the statue? This cavern is filled with stalactites and stalagmites created by the construction of the monument. You can explore it on a one-hour guided tour with the National Park Service if you bring your own flashlight and wear hiking boots. (Call 202–426–6841 for information.)

The **Korean War Veterans Memorial** is located adjacent to the Lincoln Memorial Reflecting Pool. It is composed of nineteen stainless steel statues; the figures wear ponchos and helmets and hold guns in their hands. They look as if they are stalking through unknown territory, hesitant and solemn. A granite slab is inscribed: "Our nation honors her sons and daughters who answered the call to defend a country they never knew and a people they never met."

Faces of about 2,500 men and women are etched on the accompanying wall, along with the inscription: "Freedom Is Not Free." During the day visitors find they can see the faces more clearly by casting their own shadows on the wall. This war, from 1950 to 1953, is sometimes called "the forgotten war." The Pool of Rembrance honors those who were killed, captured, wounded, or missing.

Look across the Tidal Basin to see the rounded **Thomas Jefferson Memorial,** just a pleasant walk away from the Lincoln Memorial, as befits the intentions of Washington's original planners. Fifty-four Ionic columns march around the circular structure, and the portico facing the Mall is supported by additional columns. Inside the memorial you will see a statue of Jefferson that reaches the height of 19 feet; Rudolph Evans was the sculptor.

A number of attractions are located within 1 or 2 blocks of the Mall area; those that are a little farther away are easily accessible by taxi or Metro.

> Jefferson Memorial
> Tidal Basin
> South end of 15th
> Street, S.W.
> Washington, D.C.
>
> Library of Congress
> 101 Independence
> Avenue, S.E.
> Washington, D.C.
> 20540
> 202–707–5000

One of the newest memorials in Washington was opened in May 1997. It is located on West Basin Drive on seven and a half acres. The focus is a sculpture of **Franklin D. Roosevelt** who sits with his dog, Fala. In his State of the Union Address in 1941, Roosevelt listed the "four freedoms" for the country: freedom of speech, freedom of worship, freedom from want, and freedom from fear. Those of us who were alive during his years remember listening to his fireside chats on the radio, underscored by his encouragement during difficult times.

This memorial is composed of sculpture, shade trees, a walkway, and rushing waterfalls. It is totally wheelchair accessible. Visitors can wander through a series of four outdoor "rooms." The first "room" after passing the bookstore is beside the Presidential Seal, which bears the inscription: "This Generation of Americans has a rendezvous with destiny."

The second "room" has a striking sculpture of five men standing in an urban breadline, with discouragement written all over their faces.

In the third "room," the War Room Fountain rushes beside the inscription, "I have seen war. I have seen war on land and sea. I have seen blood running from the wounded. . . . I have seen the dead in the mud. I have seen cities destroyed. . . . I have seen children starving. I have seen the agony of mothers and wives. I hate war." The statue of FDR with his dog is also here; it was created by Neil Estern. And the fourth "room" contains a statue of Eleanor Roosevelt. FDR's funeral cortege and an accompanying pool are also displayed in here. The Four Freedoms fountain completes the memorial.

The **Library of Congress,** across the street from the facade of the Capitol, contains priceless treasures of U.S. history. You can see an eighteen-minute slide show to become oriented before you take a tour of the stacks. Rare books include one of three remaining Gutenberg Bibles dating from 1455 and a fifteenth-century illuminated Bible manuscript from Mainz,

341

U.S. Supreme Court
E. Capitol Street and
Maryland Avenue,
N.E.
Washington, D.C.
20543
202–479–3030

National Archives
Pennsylvania Avenue
& 7th Street, N.W.
Washington, D.C.
20408
202–501–5205

Federal Bureau of
Investigation
10th Street &
Pennsylvania
Avenue, N.W.
Washington, D.C.
20535
202–324–3447

National Geographic
Society
17th & M Streets,
N.W.
Washington, D.C.
20036
202–857–7588 or
857–7000 (tape)

Germany. The Main Reading Room is striking, with three colors of marble leading up to the dome. The Juilliard String Quartet sometimes performs there, playing one or more of the five Stradivarius violins in the collection.

On the other side of East Capitol Avenue, facing the Library of Congress, is the **U.S. Supreme Court.** As the highest tribunal in the country, the Supreme Court is made up of nine members who hear 170 cases selected as being significant from more than 5,000 petitions each year. The justices are robed in black, a contrast against the red draperies, and they are in session two weeks each month from October to June.

The **National Archives,** just a block off the north side of the Mall, between the National Museum of Natural History and the National Gallery of Art, houses the Declaration of Independence, the Bill of Rights, the U.S. Constitution, and twenty-one floors of other documents. The most significant documents are sealed in helium for protection and are placed in the Rotunda near the Constitution Avenue entrance. You can take a tour on weekdays, or, if you make arrangements in advance, a "Behind the Scenes" tour is available.

The **Federal Bureau of Investigation** reportedly has 164,756,933 sets of fingerprints, and none of them match. The "Ten Most Wanted Lists" that you have seen on bulletin boards in your local post office are made up there. If you take a tour, you will see exhibits on crime detection and fingerprinting, as well as memorabilia taken from notorious criminals. You can see John Dillinger's death mask, a display of hollowed-out items used to transport microfilm, and samples of drugs, pipes, and needles. The lab has a serology section to study blood and a document area to identify handwriting, printing, fraudulent checks, and stolen art. We saw boxes labeled "Evidence: Do Not Disturb" waiting to be gone through. The firearms collection includes 5,000 revolvers, a rifle similar to the one that killed John F. Kennedy, and a cane that is really a 28-gauge shotgun. An oversized bullet model illustrates how bullets differ in striations after they are fired from different guns. More labs conduct analysis on hairs, fibers, paint, rubber, and other materials. The indoor target range presents demonstrations on target shooting.

The **National Geographic Society** is a bit off the beaten path but is still within walking distance of the FBI and the Mall. The Society has a variety of treats to offer visitors. The Explorer's Hall offers displays of exploration of the earth, sea, and sky. Look for a gigantic globe to set the stage for your tour. Hands-on displays encourage the visitor to relate to tornadoes, sea exploration, and more. There are artifacts from both the Peary and the Byrd polar expeditions. The 100th anniversary of the National Geographic Society was celebrated in 1992.

The **John F. Kennedy Center,** located on the riverfront, includes the Eisenhower Theatre, the Opera House, the Concert Hall, the American Film Institute Theatre, and restaurants. A sculpture of President John F. Kennedy is done in bronze. Go up to the rooftop terrace for a panoramic view. The Hall of States displays the flag of each U.S. state, and the Hall of Nations contains the flag of every nation recognized by the United States.

Don't miss the renovated **Union Station.** It had fallen into disrepair with leaking roofs and mushrooms growing on the floor, and its glory had faded. Restoration began in August 1986, and the building was opened with a gala celebration in September 1988. When Union Station opened its doors in 1907, it was the largest train station in the world. Daniel Burnham designed this structure, which cost $4 million to build. Thirty-six Roman legionnaires stood guard over the main hall; although they were designed naked, officials demanded the addition of shields. Seven pounds of gold leaf now glimmer from the 320 octagons in the ceiling of the main hall. Marble from Greece and Italy now covers the floors. The building houses many shops and restaurants, as well as outdoor cafes for people-watching.

One of the galleries in the **National Postal Museum** traces postal history from colonial days to the beginning of the twentieth century. In 1673 Francis Lovelace, the British governor of New York, established postal service between Boston and New York; the route was called the King's Best Highway and later the Boston Post Road. You'll see a representation of Benjamin Franklin, who was the colonial postmaster for the British. In 1775 the Royal Post was disbanded, and Franklin was named postmaster of the Continental Congress. The Pony Express began service in 1860 but lasted for only eighteen months.

John F. Kennedy Center
New Hampshire Avenue & F Street, N. W.
Washington, D.C. 20566
202–467–4600 or 800–444–1324

Union Station
Columbus Plaza
50 Massachusetts Avenue
Washington, D.C. 20002
202–289–1908

National Postal Museum
2 Massachusetts Avenue, N.E.
Washington, D.C. 20560
202–357–2700

Washington
Cathedral
Mount St. Alban at
Massachusetts &
Wisconsin Avenues,
N. W.
Washington, D.C.
20016
202–537–6200

National Zoological
Park
3000 Connecticut
Avenue
Washington, D.C.
20008
202–673–4800
natzoo.si.edu

The atrium houses a railway mail car, a stage coach, a Ford Model-A postal truck, and three small airmail planes, which hang from the ceiling. One is a 1911 Wiseman-Cooke flyer with fore and aft stabilizers; the 1939 Stinson Reliant has a grappling hook designed to grab mail sacks from the ground.

Can you believe that a little girl, four-year-old May Pierstoff, was "mailed" to her grandmother in Idaho? Fifty-three cents was the postage, and it was cheaper than sending her by train. It is no longer legal to mail human beings!

Don't miss the gallery of stamps and philately. More than 55,000 stamps are on exhibit—a fraction of the 16 million stamps in the collection. There's also a "time tunnel," where you walk along a dirt road with leaves rustling, and crows cawing, into a gallery.

Washington Cathedral (the Cathedral Church of St. Peter and St. Paul) is now completed. As you approach it, you will pass the Bishop's Garden, colorful with seasonal flowers. The cathedral spires are magnificent as they reach skyward. Inside, the stained-glass windows are brilliant with sunlight illuminating their hues. The west rose window can be called the jewel of the cathedral, with its vivid colors radiating out from a diamondlike center. The creator, Rowlan LeCompte, wrote, "The west rose seeks to sing its own hymn to the universe." He also designed the Maryland window, which depicts religious tolerance. Symbols of Maryland were carved into the Maryland Bay—a crab, starfish, oyster, terrapin, and a mother opossum with babies on her back. A statue of George Washington, by Lee Lawrie, stands 7 feet 6 inches tall in the Washington Bay. In the Baptistery stands the pink Tennessee-marble font. Two windows above the font depict the ceremony of baptism. Wood carvings on the choir stalls include Noah's Ark, St. George and the dragon, and Moses in the bullrushes. The Children's Chapel is like a miniature church for little ones. Needlepoint kneelers with a variety of animals, both wild and pets, appeal to children. You may be lucky enough to be at the cathedral for a carillon or pipe-organ concert.

The **National Zoological Park,** also called the **Washington Zoo,** is housed on 176 acres located at the southern end of Rock Creek Park. Follow six large poles, marked with animal signs, to each of the animal areas (orange for Lion Trail, brown for Elephant, black for Zebra, green for Crowned Crane, blue for Polar Bear, and yellow for Raccoon Trail). Among the most famous of the zoo's inhabitants in years past were Ling-Ling and Hsing-Hsing, the pandas sent from the People's Republic of China in 1972.

The Great Flight Cage houses all sorts of birds, and you can join them in their cage. When you get to the beaver area, you will find portholes in the glass so you can see their homes underwater. Don't miss the Zoolab learning center, where children can touch and handle all sorts of exhibits. Amazonia is a re-created microcosm of the world's largest rain forest.

Arlington National Cemetery Arlington 22211 703–607–8052
Arlington House Arlington 22210 703–379–2123

There are other areas in Washington to visit, such as **Georgetown** and **Foggy Bottom.** Once a tobacco port, Georgetown is now a very fashionable place to live. Boutiques, restaurants, pubs, and jazz clubs keep the place active far into the night. Georgetown University is also in Georgetown. Foggy Bottom was once a fume-clogged industrial area in the mid-nineteenth century, but no longer. The Kennedy Center for the Performing Arts, Watergate, and the World Bank have replaced Christian Heurich's brewery, among other things.

Diners come from miles around to try **Clyde's** (3236 M Street, N.W.; 202–333–9180), and **1789 Restaurant** (1226 36th Street, N.W.; 202–965–1789).

Arlington, Virginia

Arlington House and Arlington National Cemetery are located just across the bridge from the Lincoln Memorial. **Arlington National Cemetery** is best seen by Tourmobile because there is a vast amount of ground to cover, some of which is hilly. The **Tomb of the Unknowns** is a single block of white marble decorated with wreaths. Four U.S. servicemen from World Wars I and II and the Korean and Vietnam conflicts are interred there. The Changing of the Guard Ceremony is carried out every half hour in summer and every hour in winter. John F. Kennedy's grave is marked by the eternal flame and a slate headstone, and Robert F. Kennedy is also buried there.

Arlington House, also known as the **Custis-Lee House,** was the home of Robert E. Lee and his bride, Mary Custis, from 1831 to 1861. Martha Washington's son, John Custis, bought the land in 1778, and in 1802 his son, George Washington Parker Curtis, built the house. His daughter, Mary Anna Randolph Custis, inherited it and married Robert E. Lee. Lee wrote about Arlington House, "My affections and attachments are more strongly placed than at any other place in the world." The Lees went back and forth from army stations to Arlington. During the Civil War the Union army used the house as a headquarters. Property owners of homes occupied by Federal troops were still required to appear in person to pay their taxes; because the Lees could not appear, the house was confiscated in 1864. In February 1865

Newseum
1101 Wilson
Boulevard
Arlington 22209
888-NEWSEUM or
703-284-3544

Robert E. Lee was named general in chief of the Armies of the Confederate States, and he surrendered to Ulysses S. Grant on April 9 of the same year.

In 1925 Congress approved restoration of the house. Some of the furnishings belonging to the Lee family were returned. Look to the right into the family parlor to see Lee's traveling desk, which he carried from post to post. The green chairs in the parlor also belonged to the Lees. The ceiling lantern in the center hall is a copy of one that hangs at Mount Vernon. Robert E. Lee was accustomed to stroll through his rose garden each morning and pick a rose to lay beside the plate of each lady at breakfast in the family dining room. The dining room table, china, silver, and goblets all belonged to the Lees. Upstairs you will see the Lees' bedchamber, where he spent an agonizing night deciding whether he should support the Union his family had helped to build or follow the wishes of six generations of Lees in Virginia. A portrait painted by August Hervieu in 1831 of Mary Custis just before her marriage to Lee hangs in the parlor. Lafayette described the view from the front portico as the "finest view in the world."

As you walk up the incline toward the **Newseum,** you will pass through "Freedom Park," which tells the story of preserving freedom. Icons of freedom march up the path on patches of grass, including segments of the Berlin Wall weighing 2.5 tons. The statue of Vladimir Ilyich Lenin is permanently toppled, just as in Russia where people destroyed and beheaded his statues. Some cobblestones from the Warsaw Ghetto remind us of the hardship of those forced to live there.

A Cuban refugee kayak was used by two people who traveled in the boat for three days over stormy seas in their quest for freedom. There's a bronze casting of Martin Luther King Jr's Birmingham jail-cell door.

Women's Suffrage banners are next. During the suffrage movement, from 1848 to 1920, women marched, carried banners, and protested until they got the same voting rights as men.

A Native American circle of stones stands for unity and symbolizes tradition and ritual.

The Freedom Forum Journalists Memorial honors journalists who were killed while trying to report news—reporters, editors, photographers, and broadcasters who took their lives into their hands during conflict.

Inside the museum you can watch a film that describes great moments in our history. On Level 2 the "news globe" is the place to find your own newspaper; there are 1,841 newspaper nameplates from the U.S. and around the world. You can touch the Birthday Banner monitors to get news from the month and year of your birth.

The "interactive newsroom," also on Level 2, has computer stations and hands-on activities.

Head up to Level 3 to see exciting news stories in the news history gallery. Begin with the first newspapers from 1500 to 1720, then move on to the Revolutionary Press from 1720 to 1820.

Ramsay House
221 King Street
Alexandria 22314
703–838–4200 or
800–388–9119

Carlyle House
121 North Fairfax
Street
Alexandria 22314
703–549–2997

Alexandria, Virginia

Scottish merchants founded Alexandria in 1749 and named it after John Alexander, who had bought the land in 1669 for "six thousand pounds of Tobacco and Cask." George Washington surveyed the land when he was seventeen years old (along with John West, Jr.). Later he kept a residence in town, but his original home at 508 Cameron Street, built in 1765, no longer stands. The building on the site now is a replica and is privately owned. Washington was heavily involved in the communal affairs of Alexandria. He had a pew in Christ Church, organized the Friendship Fire Company, and served as Master of the Masonic Lodge.

The city had become one of the main seaports and trading centers of Virginia by the time of the Revolution. Slaves were sold in the market, yet there were also several free black communities in Alexandria. Blacks were known and valued as skilled artisans.

Today, visitors can soak in the ambience of colonial days as they walk the streets of Old Town Alexandria. Begin your tour at **Ramsay House,** the location of the Alexandria Convention & Visitors Association. William Ramsay and his wife Anne had eight children there; the original house was moved from another location. The gambrel roof is similar to those used on other colonial homes between 1675 and 1725. Ramsay was a good friend of George Washington, who walked in Ramsay's funeral procession. The visitor's center offers a video on Alexandria, brochures, help on planning sightseeing, and guided tours.

John Carlyle journeyed from Scotland in 1741 and became a successful tobacco merchant in Alexandria. During the French and Indian War, General Edward Braddock had his headquarters in the **Carlyle House.** He invited five colonial governors to meet with him, ostensibly to coerce them into raising money for their own defense in the war. They refused, and he sent a letter to London demanding that the colonists be taxed. Market Square in front of City Hall was a parade ground for colonial troops under Braddock's command. Braddock was later defeated at Fort Duquesne and died in that battle.

Turn left on Cameron Street, then onto Royal Street, and you'll come to the 1770 **Gadsby's Tavern,** where you can have a meal and tour the

Gadsby's Tavern
134 North Royal
 Street
Alexandria 22314
703–838–4242

Christ Church
118 N. Washington
 Street
Alexandria 22314
703–549–1450

Lee-Fendall House
 614 Oronoco Street
Alexandria 22314
703–548–1789

Boyhood home of
 Robert E. Lee
607 Oronoco Street
Alexandria 22314
703–548–8454

Lyceum
201 Washington
 Street
Alexandria 22314
703–838–4994

museum. George Washington was a frequent visitor here, and the annual Birthnight Ball took place there every year while he lived; it is re-enacted to this day.

The museum features a taproom where the main meal was served; it had board games such as backgammon, and men met there to talk politics and smoke clay pipes. Upstairs a sleeping room contains linen sacks filled with straw and a bedstead with a rope frame. Only men slept up there; no lady of quality would think of sleeping elsewhere than with friends or the local clergyman. Any man arriving after the beds were filled had to sleep on the floor. Perhaps fewer bedbugs were encountered on the floor than in bed!

Continue along Cameron Street to **Christ Church.** Begun in 1767 and finished in 1773, the church had galleries added in 1787 and a tower in 1820. George Washington's pew is marked with a silver tablet, as is that of Robert E. Lee. Washington's pew, number 60. Don't miss the cut-glass chandelier.

Turn right onto Washington Street to the **Lee-Fendall House.** Philip Fendall built his mansion in 1785. There Lighthorse Harry Lee worked on his farewell address from Alexandrians to George Washington as the latter left to become our first president. About thirty-five members of the Lee family lived in the house from 1785 to 1903, and many Lee possessions remain in the home.

Robert E. Lee's boyhood home stands in Oronoco Street. In 1804 Mary Lee Fitzhugh married George Washington Parke Custis, grandson of Martha Washington, in the drawing room. After twenty-seven years their daughter, Mary Ann Randolph Custis, wed Robert E. Lee. Lee had lived in the house during his student years, from 1812 to 1816, and again from 1821 to 1825. This 1795 Federal-style house is the site of celebrations, such as the January birthday of Robert E. Lee, the July fête in honor of the Fitzhugh-Custis wedding, and an October reception to commemorate the visit of the Marquis de Lafayette. As in all Lee houses, there are portraits of Lee and his wife.

Retrace your way back along Washington to the **Lyceum,** Alexandria's history museum. This Greek revival building was the first cultural center in Alexandria. Once occupied by Confederate and Union troops, the building is now a museum for Alexandria. Call ahead for a schedule of programs, exhibitions, and events.

348

Take Prince Street to Fairfax to see the **Stabler-Leadbeater Apothecary Shop.** George Washington and Robert E. Lee were among the patrons of the store, which was founded in 1792. One record states: "Mrs. Washington desires Mr. Stabler will send by the bearer a quart bottle of his best Castor Oil and the bill for it."

> Stabler-Leadbeater
> Apothecary Shop
> 105–107 S. Farifax
> Street
> Alexandria 22314
> 703–836–3713

Robert E. Lee was there talking with Mr. Leadbeater when J.E.B. Stuart gave him the order from the War Department to head immediately for Harper's Ferry and quell the John Brown insurrection. He said, "I am afraid this is only the beginning of more serious trouble."

When you're ready for a meal, try **Bilbo Baggins** (208 Queen Street; 703–683–0300), which is a cafe/restaurant with a wine bar and Sunday brunch; baked breads and desserts are a specialty. At **Gadsby's Tavern** (138 North Royal Street; 703–548–1288), costumed waiters and waitresses serve meals in the colonial dining room.

Mount Vernon, Virginia

Outside of the Washington, D.C., area but definitely a part of a visit to our capital is historic **Mount Vernon** (703–780–2000), located south of Alexandria, Virginia, and accessible from Route 1 south and Route 235. John Washington, George's great-grandfather, patented the Mount Vernon homesite in 1674. Augustine Washington, George's father, inherited the property in 1726, and in 1732 George was born. When Augustine Washington died in 1743, George's elder half-brother, Lawrence, inherited Mount Vernon. George Washington eventually inherited the plantation from Lawrence and then wrote, "No estate in United America is more pleasantly situated than this. It lies in a high, dry and healthy Country 300 miles by water from the Sea . . . on one of the finest Rivers in the world. . . ." In spite of this admiration for his own estate, he was not able to live there for years at a time while he was involved in fighting the French and Indian War and the Revolutionary War, as well as establishing the nation as its first president. When he was in residence, he studied the newest crop technology and was successful as a planter.

After George's marriage to Martha Dandridge Custis, widow of Daniel Parke Custis, he wrote, "I am now, I believe, fixed at this Seat with an agreeable Consort for Life and hope to find more happiness in retirement than I ever experienced amidst a wide and bustling World." Martha Washington spent eight winters with him during his northern encampments. He resigned his commission in 1783 and hoped to spend his remaining life at Mount Vernon. In 1789 he became president for the next eight years, which kept him away from Mount Vernon much of the time. When he finally did retire, he had only two and one-half years left at his beloved Mount Vernon before he died.

The mansion is a familiar sight to most Americans because photographs of this large white colonial building with its long, columned piazza have appeared frequently. George Washington added onto the smaller house he had inherited before his marriage to Martha and made other additions in later years. The large dining room is striking, with a Palladian window, green decor, and an ornate fireplace. Music played an important role in the social life at Mount Vernon; you will see a harpsichord in the little parlor. George Washington gave "one very good Spinit" to his stepdaughter, Patsy Custis, and her brother received a violin and "a fine German flute"; Nelly Custis was given a harpsichord in 1793, straight from London. The West Parlor has an ornate fireplace and mantel with the Washington coat of arms on the top, and five James Sharples paintings, including those of George and Martha Washington. The dining room has a gallery of portraits and a decorated ceiling. Upstairs George Washington's bedroom contains his unusually wide bed, in which he died in 1799.

Outside, visitors can explore the "dependencies." The kitchen, where a staff of two cooks and two waiters produced sumptuous meals, now houses a collection of utensils and cooking gear. According to one writer, "The dinner was very good, a small roasted pigg, boiled leg of lamb, roasted fowls, beef, peas, lettuce, cucumbers, artichokes, puddings, tarts. We were desired to call for what drinks we chose." Other buildings include the smokehouse, greenhouse, icehouse, storehouse, coach house, slave quarters, and a sixteen-sided re-created barn. A museum has been added to house the large collection of Washington artifacts.

George and Martha Washington are buried in the family vault on the estate. George directed that "the family Vault at Mount Vernon requiring repairs, and being improperly situated besides, I desire that a new one of Brick and upon a larger Scale, may be built at the foot of what is commonly called the Vineyard Inclosure—on the ground which is marked out—in which my remains, with those of my deceased relatives (now in the old Vault) and such others of my family as may chose to be entombed there, may be deposited."

Because of the popularity of Mount Vernon with tourists, we suggest you arrive early in the morning, tour the mansion, and then stroll around the grounds in uncrowded leisure.

Williamsburg, Virginia

| Colonial |
| Williamsburg |
| Box 1776 |
| Williamsburg |
| 23187-1776 |
| 800-HISTORY or |
| 757-220-7645 |

Another excursion from Washington takes travelers to **Colonial Williamsburg** via Interstate 95, 295, and 64. You can also plan a circle tour from Washington, going south to Williamsburg, across the Chesapeake Bay Bridge-Tunnel, north through the Delmarva peninsula, and then back across the Chesapeake Bay Bridge to Annapolis, Baltimore, or Washington.

Step back in time three centuries as you walk on the streets of colonial days in the footsteps of those who helped develop our nation. We suggest that you head for the Visitor Center, which is well marked as you come into town. A film, *Williamsburg—the Story of a Patriot*, provides orientation for your visit. Leave your car in the parking lot, and take a shuttle bus to the Historic Area. Duke of Gloucester Street is the "Main Street" of Williamsburg, and it runs for a mile between the Capitol and the College of William and Mary. Visitors can immerse themselves in the eighteenth century by wandering into buildings along this and adjoining streets.

Stop to chat with interpreters in costume, who are eager to tell you about their crafts. Max, in the Milliner's Shop, told us about the fans that George Washington ordered there. The milliner had the latest styles in clothing and was considered a fashion consultant, as she stitched new gowns for balls, changed the trim with the times, and suggested wearing "heartbreakers" (corkscrew curls).

Across the street, in the King's Arms Tavern, visitors are encouraged to exchange eighteenth-century news and views with the proprietress, the widow Jane Vobe. She assured us that she doesn't gossip but just tells what she hears—after all, one has to watch one's tongue or be put in the pillory. Cocking her ear, she wondered who might be listening but added that as long as you can hear slaves, you know they're working and not listening. She told Robert that he should really shave off his beard when he has time, as men with hair on their faces either have something to hide or are pirates. Men who want to stay in her fourteen-room inn pay 7½ pence for two-to-a-bed comfort. Meal costs can't exceed 1 shilling—dinner is served at two of the clock, and supper at nine of the clock, with the same food brought back redecorated. It pays to appear the first time food is served.

Having got into an eighteenth-century mood with two colorful characters, we headed for the **Capitol building.** As we stood by the green seats in the House of Burgess, we could hear "George Washington" explaining a bill that had to do with hogs. It seems that the hogs had been taking a bath in the drinking water, and he thought they should be fenced

351

in so people could drink clean water. Legislation had to be sent to the king in England, and so an answer could be expected in a few years. More seriously, he explained the Virginia Resolves against the Townshend Acts in 1769. "Patrick Henry" delivered his "Caesar-Brutus" speech, which offered a solution to the Stamp Act.

The Council Chamber is colorful, with a turkey-work carpet on the table. The portrait of Queen Anne reminds us that she had seventeen children, who all died in infancy except the Prince of Gloucester, who died at age eleven. The General Court was the place where pirates were sentenced to be "turned off," or hanged. People could be pardoned the first time, but a T (theft) or M (murder) was burned into the palm of the hand near the thumb.

One of the favorite buildings is the **Governor's Palace,** which housed seven royal governors and also the first two governors of the Commonwealth of Virginia, Patrick Henry and Thomas Jefferson. In 1780 the residence of the governor was moved to Richmond. The building was used as a hospital after the battle of Yorktown. In 1781 it burned completely.

Today visitors enter through a hall decorated with guns, swords, pistols, and muskets arranged in patterns. From his office to the left of the door, the butler managed visits from those who wished to see the governor. By their clothing and posture, he was able to screen the less important visitors, who waited in the hall; the more important ones, who were escorted into the parlor on the right; and the most important ones, who walked upstairs. Upstairs visitors can walk through several bedrooms with period furnishings. Don't miss the set of fashion prints—one for each month of the year. The Ball Room is where the governor sits at the "preferred" end, along with portraits of King George III and Queen Charlotte; when visitors bow to him, they are also bowing to the King and Queen.

The **Public Hospital,** in operation from 1773 to 1885, displays facilities once used to house the mentally ill, including a 1773 cell with a pallet on the floor over a lump of straw, a blanket, and a chamber pot— similar to a prison. The window was barred, and patients were chained to the wall. By 1845 each one lived in a small apartment with bed, table, chair, and a plaster wall. During this age of "moral management," patients were encouraged to spend time doing something—playing the violin, spinning, or playing cards, for example. The "custodial care" era lasted from 1862 to 1885. Patients were subjected to physical restraints and entertained with picnics and tea parties.

The **DeWitt Wallace Decorative Arts Museum** is accessible by walking through the hospital and downstairs. Collections include musical instruments, silver, pewter, ceramics, clocks, globes, furniture, paintings, costumes, and textiles. Favorites include an Aesop's fable candlestick, "The Tiger and the Fox," from 1765; a Greybeard face jug from 1645; a pair of lead-glazed earthenware rabbits from 1820; a turquoise tea urn from 1770; brass pipe tampers from 1650; wool crewelwork from 1750; and more. The **Abby Aldrich Rockefeller Folk Art Museum** opened after renovation and expansion in May 1992. She began collecting folk art in the 1920s. Today the collection includes shop signs, weather vanes, a carousel figure, portraits, furniture, chests, quilts, sewing tools, mariner's tools, and toys. We enjoyed the clown tobacconist sign from 1868, a group of weather vanes, a lion carousel figure, a monkey inkwell, a calico cat from 1900 to 1920, a 1907 to 1915 mechanical pump on three levels, and a 1795 Pennsylvania Dutch Easter rabbit, to name a few.

There are many places to have lunch or dinner in Williamsburg. Try the **Williamsburg Inn** (757–229–1000); also at the same phone number are **King's Arms Tavern, Chowning's, Mrs. Campbell's Tavern, Shields Tavern,** and **Williamsburg Lodge.**

If you're interested in trying "Christmas Away," Williamsburg is a great place. We saw people of all ages—some come every year—bringing their presents and a tree.

Carter's Grove, Virginia

Drive 8 miles east of Williamsburg on U.S. 60 to **Carter's Grove,** which is a plantation on the James River. The land was purchased by "King" Carter for his daughter Elizabeth. The original house was completed in 1755, and two wings were added in 1930 to connect the house with a kitchen on one end and a laundry on the other. The McCrea family purchased the house in 1928, and Mrs. McCrea lived there until her death in 1960. It is now owned by the Colonial Williamsburg Foundation, which conducted an archaeological search to discover signs of an early seventeenth-century settlement called Martin's Hundred. The **Winthrop Rockefeller Archaeology Museum** is an underground museum displaying artifacts from the dig. Mockleyware cooking pots from A.D. 200 to 900 are there, as are lead from casement windows with the words "John . . . 1625," a 1613 farthing coin, a seventeenth-century helmet, and the story of a woman, "Granny," who was partly scalped, with photos of her bones. Wolstenholme Towne was once part of Martin's Hundred, and some houses, stores, and the fort are now marked. An eighteenth-century slave quarter has been reconstructed on the site. Interpreters tell the story of the

Jamestown
Settlement
Box 1607
Williamsburg 23187
888–593–4682 or
757–253–4838

Jamestown Colonial
National Historical
Park
Box 210
Yorktown 23690
757–229–1733

African-Americans who lived there.

As we entered the mansion, we left our calling cards on the silver tray as people did 200 years ago. Portraits of the McCrea family hang on the dining room wall, including one of seventeen-year-old Molly McCrea in a yellow dress with flowers on the bodice. She died in 1960 at age eighty-four. The kitchen is a mixture of black iron pots in the large fireplace and an early Hotpoint electric stove. The Drawing Room is also called the "refusal" room because both Washington and Jefferson proposed to a lady there and both were refused.

Jamestown, Virginia

Jamestown Settlement is a re-creation of the nearby original site. It is just off Route 31, 6 miles from Williamsburg; it can also be reached from the Colonial Parkway. Jamestown was the first permanent colony in the New World, established by England in 1607. Three ships, the *Susan Constant,* the *Godspeed,* and the *Discovery,* brought the colonists to Jamestown; it took them five months to reach the New World. Replicas of the ships are usually moored at the dock for visitors to see.

Thatched houses were built inside the James Fort, along with public buildings and the church. The settlers were not used to farming, and after Captain John Smith sailed back to England in 1609, a "starving time" took many lives. They had almost given up hope when more settlers arrived from England with supplies and the urge to become wealthy with tobacco cultivation. By 1619 government had been developed, and Jamestown was the center until the capital was moved to Williamsburg in 1699.

Inside the re-created fort, interpreters dressed in colonial costume are going about their daily tasks, cooking, working on their houses, repairing weapons, and participating in military drills.

A re-created Powhatan Village offers the chance to see how the Indians lived, prepared food, made tools and weapons, and prepared for war. Some of their Tidewater Indian pipes and arrowheads are on display in the museum.

Be sure to see the twenty-minute orientation film before strolling through the museum. An actor speaks as one of the survivors of the Jamestown settlement. The museum contains three sections: the English Gallery, the Powhatan Indian Gallery, and the Jamestown Gallery. A variety of displays include weapons such as a sixteenth-century Iberian gunlock, a helmet, Spanish coins, a "bleeding bowl," a mortar and pestle, coffin handles, wine bottles, and Captain John Smith's original map. The King and Queen of England sent a ceramic jug to Pocahontas, and it is on display.

Although much of the original settlement site has been washed away by the James River, some ruins remain, including a 1608 glasshouse and the 1639 brick church tower. Archaeological excavations of the original fort are currently under way.

Visitors can also drive around a 3- or 5-mile loop to get a feeling for the type of terrain and environment the first settlers found. Audiotapes for the driving tour and the walking tour are available for rent in the gift shop.

Yorktown Victory Center
Box 1607
Yorktown 23187
888–593–4682 or
757–253–4838

Yorktown Battlefield
Colonial National
Historical Park
Box 210
Yorktown 23690
757–898–2410

Yorktown, Virginia

Visit **Yorktown Victory Center** for the sequence of events leading up to the victory of the American Revolution: from the 1763 Treaty of Paris (which increased British holdings in our country), the Boston Tea Party, the First Continental Congress, and the conflicts with Britain to the battle at Yorktown, when the British surrendered. A film, "A Time of Revolution," gives a picture of the events. Learn about life on board a ship from the artifacts taken from the *Betsy,* a British merchant ship sunk in the Siege of Yorktown, in the "Yorktown's Sunken Fleet" display.

The "Witnesses to Revolution" gallery includes portrayals of six persons—an African-American patriot, a loyalist, a Quaker pacifist, two Continental army soldiers, and the wife of a Virginia plantation owner. Information was gathered from their personal diaries and correspondence.

Outside, the Continental Army Camp offers interpreters who explain the life of those in the camp. Soldiers' tents, two officers' tents, a weapons tent, and a cooking center have been re-created. You may be there for a military drill, demonstration of musket loading and firing, or food preparation.

A typical farm is represented by the outline of a house and a separate kitchen. Herbs and vegetables are grown in the garden and corn and tobacco in a nearby field.

Visitors can take two driving tours around the battlefield and the encampment area. The 7-mile Battlefield Tour includes the British Inner Defense Line and Hornwork, Grand French Battery, Second Allied Siege Line, Redoubts 9 and 10, the Moore House, where surrender terms were

The Loudoun
Museum
14–16 Loudoun
Street, S.W.
Leesburg 20175
703–777–7427

negotiated, and the Surrender Field. The 9-mile Allied Encampment Tour begins at the American Artillery Park, includes Washington's Headquarters, French Cemetery, French Artillery Park, and French Encampment Loop, and ends at the British Redoubt.

The city of Yorktown includes more historic sites. On Main Street the Dudley Digges House was home for a lawyer who served as council member for Virginia during the Revolution. The 1692 Thomas Sessions house is the oldest house in Yorktown. On Nelson Street stands the Captain John Ballard house and the Edmund Smith House. Back on Main Street is the "Scotch Tom" Nelson House, a Georgian mansion that was also home to his grandson, Thomas Nelson, Jr., who signed the Declaration of Independence. This house, with cannonballs still in its side, is occasionally opened by the Park Service. In the next block you'll pass the Pate House, Customhouse, Somerwell House, a reconstructed Medical Shop, and the Swan Tavern, which is now an antiques shop. Grace Church on Church Street is noted for the grave of Thomas Nelson, Jr., in the churchyard.

Leesburg, Virginia

Leesburg was an outfitting post during the French and Indian War, and George Washington had a headquarters there. During the War of 1812, the Declaration of Independence, the Constitution, and other important papers were stored in the cellar of a nearby mansion when Washington went up in flames under British attack.

Many historic buildings still stand in an attractive and hospitable town that has no artificial trappings designed to attract tourists. The surrounding countryside in Loudoun County is beautiful, with rolling hills, old mills, plantation mansions, restaurants, and bed-and-breakfasts from the colonial era. There has been so little change in the county that some of the secondary roads are still gravel—all within an hour of Washington's Beltway. The **Loudoun Tourism Council** may be contacted at 108-D South Street; S.E., Leesburg, VA 20175; 800–752–6118.

The **Loudoun Museum** has a video that provides an orientation for a visit to Leesburg and the area. Indians were in residence for many years, leaving behind arrowheads and pottery, now on display in the museum. The Powhatans were members of the Algonquin tribe, and they lived in the river valleys; Iroquois came from the north and raided the county.

King Charles I granted land to seven of his faithful followers in 1649, but when the monarchy ended and Cromwell took over, they were not able to claim their land. By 1660, when Charles II had claimed the throne, new grants were issued. But the land was slow to settle, perhaps because of fear of Indians. Then the Treaty of Albany in 1722 ordained that the Indians could not come east of the Blue Ridge or south of the Potomac without permission.

By 1757 Thomas Lord Fairfax had surveyed Leesburg, and seventy half-acre lots were plotted. George Washington had been hired at the age of seventeen, in 1749, to survey land in the area. Silversmiths, blacksmiths, and traders kept the town's tavern busy. Stephen Donaldson was the first silversmith in Leesburg; he built a log building in 1763 that is now the gift shop next to the Loudoun Museum. By 1760 the town that had been *Georgetown* was renamed *Leesburg* for Thomas Lee.

Local farmers provided food for George Washington's Continental Army. Citizens gave clothing and wagons and also sent men to the war. Two generations later, during the Civil War, General Robert E. Lee's men were fed and housed in Leesburg after the Battle of Manassas.

The best way to get a sense of Leesburg's heritage is on foot. "A Walk Around Leesburg" brochure is available in the museum shop or by calling Historic Leesburg (888–777–1758). Visitors can stroll around a six-block area to get a feeling for the rich historical background of the city. At 29 West Market Street is a Federal-style stone house that served as a girls' school. In 1825 Lafayette visited Leesburg, and the girls performed a dance for him on the courthouse lawn. At 20 West Market Street is the site of an "ordinary," now the Laurel Brigade Inn, both an inn and a restaurant. The long section at the rear of the building was probably built as a ballroom to entertain Marquis de Lafayette in 1825.

Dr. Jacob Coutsman, the first doctor in Leesburg, lived at 19 East Market Street. The deed was filed in 1758. His office was located at 23 East Market Street and has interesting Flemish-bond brickwork with arches over the openings.

The **Episcopal Graveyard** on Church Street contains the grave of General Armistead Thomson Mason, who lost his life in the Mason/McCarty duel. The two men were cousins with very different political views who chose to settle their dispute in Bladensburg, Maryland, because dueling was against the law in Virginia. The weapons chosen were muskets with one ball each. Mason was killed and McCarty was injured in the arm.

At 4 East Loudoun Street is a 1759 Georgian-style house with a Colonial Revival porch, one of the oldest in Leesburg. John and Fleming Patterson came from Scotland to build the house and settle there. Hessian soldiers imprisoned in the house drew caricatures of Washington, Patrick

Henry, and other Revolutionary War leaders on the walls. The **Patterson House** was Captain Henry McCabe's ordinary in the late 1770s. George Washington enjoyed a dinner there of jowls and greens, prepared by Mrs. McGill. Lafayette was toasted by the mayor of the town in 1825 on the front steps. The building is open by appointment with Town and Country Realty.

The **Courthouse,** dating from 1757, is located on the corner of King and Market streets. The bell in the cupola tolled the news of the Boston Tea Party with its very first peals. In 1774 Loudoun freeholders, protesting the Stamp Act, created the Loudoun Resolves, which were taken to Philadelphia to the Continental Congress in September 1774.

The **Gray-Benedict-Harrison home** dates from 1759. The Flemish-bond front combines Georgian and Federal styles. Major John Orr lived in the home at 7 East Cornwall Street from 1858 to 1869. It is said that there is a tunnel from the courthouse to his home that protected important papers and sometimes Confederate soldiers. Money during the war had his name on it and also a picture of a reclining dog at the top of each bill. It was called "dog money."

John Janney lived at 10 East Cornwall Street in a 1780 house. He was known for handing General Robert E. Lee his sword to take command of the Confederate troops during a ceremony at the State Capitol. Janney's office stands at 4 East Cornwall Street.

Reverend John Littlejohn lived at 11 West Cornwall Street. During the War of 1812 the Declaration of Independence and the Constitution were taken by wagon to this home just before the British burned Washington. Then they were transferred to a cellar vault in Rokeby House in the nearby countryside.

Sir Peter Halkett had his headquarters in a stone house at 24 West Loudoun Street before the 1755 Battle of Monongahela. It is probable that George Washington had his headquarters there during the French and Indian War. Henry Clay campaigned in the area in 1832, and there is a pencil inscription on the wall: "Hon. Henry Clay of the United States Senate and would be President of the United States." The stone house is now a great place to have an elegant afternoon tea. Call 703–779–2933 for information.

All of Leesburg turns out for its annual August Court Days. Visitors will see Thomas Jefferson, George Washington, and the Town Crier strolling the streets. Interpreters dressed in colonial costumes walk through the crowds, getting everyone involved in conversations of the day.

During the mid-1700s, circuit judges traveled from town to town, and by the late 1700s, they held "court days" on specific days. The local people looked upon these days as a time to "make merrie" and enjoy the gossip about various court cases. There are colonial dances, musketry practice, and re-enactments of that era. The Bluemont Concert Series presents wonderful music during the Court

Morven Park
Old Waterford Road
Leesburg 20178
703-777-2414

Days. Craftspeople come from all over the Mid-Atlantic region to display and sell their wares. For more information call the **Loudoun County Visitor Center** at 703–777–0519 or 800–752–6118.

The first **Morven Park** building was a fieldstone farmhouse dating from 1781. Thomas Swann, a governor of Maryland, had arrived by the late 1700s and connected the old house with two others. Westmoreland Davis and his wife, Marguerite, bought the house from the Swann family. Davis was also governor from 1918 to 1922. Inside, visitors can view a Renaissance great hall, a Jacobean dining room, and a French drawing room. The trophy-billiard room is decorated with an Asian snow tiger and other wildlife. The 1550 tapestries depicting the second Punic War were made in Brabant in Belgium for the Hapsburg family. The house is filled with lovely furnishings, such as a collection of Italian *cassones* or storage chests. The portraits are of family members; there are also many landscape paintings from the Hudson River School.

Don't miss the **Museum of Hounds and Hunting,** which is appropriate for this area of Virginia's hunt country. The **Carriage Museum** displays vehicles through the ages, all kept in pristine condition.

If you're there at Christmas, you'll see a 16-foot tree in the Great Hall and fragrant greens decorating the house. Christmas carols waft through the air and refreshments are served; call ahead for information.

Waterford, Virginia

To the west, the almost untouched Quaker village of **Waterford** was settled in 1733 by Amos Janney. The area is still accessible by a dirt road, which winds through lovely country; it can also be reached by a faster road for those in a hurry. Janney built a grist mill around 1733 and the area was soon a thriving farming community.

Mill End, across from the mill, is a Federal-style house built after 1814 that was the home of a number of millers. It is guarded by a stone lion in front.

The **Hague-Hough House,** located across from the mill and up the paved road past the lion, dates from 1745, when Francis Hague built his home like an Irish cottage. William Hough added a two-story brick house and a wing in 1790. The **Samuel Means House,** on Bond Street, was built

Oatlands Plantation
20850 Oatlands
Plantation Lane
Leesburg 20175
703-777-3174

by Manlon Janney around 1762. The **Thomas Moore House,** also on Bond Street, was begun in 1750 as a log house. Moore operated a tanyard in front of his house. The **Francis Pierpoint House,** on the north side of Main Street near the mill, was built by Richard Richardson of Frederick County, Maryland. The stone fireplace in the courtyard is all that stands of his original home. The Joseph Janney House, also on Main Street, dates from 1796. It was a log house covered with clapboard.

Oatlands Plantation was built in the early 1800s for George Carter, the great grandson of "King" Carter. It is said that Thomas Jefferson once said feet and stairways were not exciting, and so Carter took out the central stairway in the house. Unfortunately, he had to sell the house, and the Eustic family bought it. They restored the house and lived there for six months of the year. The detail work around the ceiling and the hand carving over the doors are worth noting. Sixty-five percent of the windows contain original glass. The den contains mementoes of this horse-loving family, including a trophy won at a steeplechase in Ireland. The dining room is beautiful, with collections of silver and china. The Louis XV roll-top desk in the octagon room is an original. The morning room is highlighted with a Louis XIV desk.

The garden at Oatlands is fragrant with boxwood and alive with colorful flowers. There's a gazebo, a reflecting pool and a bowling green.

Christmas at Oatlands features fragrant "kissing balls (like mistletoe)," a tree decorated with traditional popcorn and paper chains, and dolls dressed for the occasion. Call ahead for candlelight tours and living-history vignettes which take place Saturday evenings.

Middleburg, Virginia

Middleburg was the place where Joseph Chinn inherited a stone house on the site of the Red Fox Inn. The corner was dubbed "Chinn's Crossroads." The town was established in 1787 by Colonel Leven Powell. It was named so because it is halfway between Alexandria and Winchester. For more than two hundred years, the town has been a popular place for travelers to stop for a meal and a room for the night. The Red Fox Inn and Tavern is said to be the oldest original inn in America. George Washington stopped there around 1748 as he was surveying for Lord Fairfax.

General Jeb Stuart met Colonel John Mosby and the Rangers there. Mosby and Stuart spent the night before the battle of Gettysburg dancing to country music. Stuart received a fine sorrel horse from Mosby, taken from a Yankee officer. The inn was a headquarters during the Gettysburg battles and a hospital as well.

Cyclists and walkers will want to enjoy the **Washington & Old Dominion Railroad Regional Park,** which extends for 45 miles, from Alexandria to the foothills of the Blue Ridge Mountains. You'll see 450 different wildflower species along the way at dif-

Harper's Ferry National Historical Park
Box 65
Harper's Ferry 25425
304-535-6029

ferent times of the year, and 100 species of birds. Visitors can also exercise at the Parcourse fitness stations along the trail. For a Trail Guide call 703-729-0596.

Harper's Ferry, West Virginia

"John Brown's body lies a-moldering in his grave . . ." but not in Harper's Ferry. Although he was hanged near Harper's Ferry, his body lies in Lake Placid. This wild-eyed, bushy-headed and -bearded man was an abolitionist who had promoted his beliefs with violence, in Kansas and elsewhere. On October 16, 1859, Brown arrived in Harper's Ferry with twenty-one men to liberate slaves. Of course he counted on being able to capture the U.S. arms stashed in the armory at the ferry landing.

During their surprise attack, the twenty-one men took the armory and barricaded themselves inside the guard house, dubbed "John Brown's Fort." A train came through and Brown made a mistake when he allowed it to leave—the engineer raised the alarm and Col. Robert E. Lee arrived with marines to seize the fort. Brown was tried, found guilty of murder, treason, and insurrection, and hanged in nearby Charles Town on December 2, 1859. On the way to the gallows he prophesied the Civil War, which started sixteen months later at Fort Sumter in Charlestown, South Carolina.

Harper's Ferry is located at the junction of the Shenandoah and Potomac rivers, with the Blue Ridge Mountains sloping down to meet the rivers. Peter Stephens arrived in 1733 and began running a ferry service. Robert Harper, a millwright, was on his way to build a meeting house near Winchester, Virginia, when he met a man who said he would show him a shortcut through "The Hole." There he met Peter Stephens and bought his squatter's cabin. The land itself belonged to Lord Fairfax, so Harper presented himself in person at the Lord's residence and bought the land. Harper settled in 1747 and continued Stephens's ferry operation. He built a large stone house on High Street, which still stands.

Today, visitors arrive at the National Park Service Visitors' Center within a landscaped park. Rangers present talks and programs as well as tours. Shuttle buses run down into Harper's Ferry every ten minutes. The town is small and the historic buildings stand within a two-block area. The Stagecoach Inn, built in 1826, is the first place to stop for information from a ranger. You might also wish to select a book or two from the park book-store.

Stroll down Shenandoah Street to the Provost Office, where you'll see a sign that says SHOW YOUR PASS. (The Union Provost Guard once provided security for the town.) Next door, the Dry Goods Store displays all sorts of necessary items for residents. The Master Armorer's House is now an artillery museum displaying the story of gun-making. Don't miss the unfinished "mystery" letter, which seems to refer to a new revolving rifle capable of firing sixty rounds per minute before the handwriting fades away.

Continue down Shenandoah Street to the John Brown Museum on the corner, where you can see a slide show detailing John Brown's raid. Among the displays is a glass case with "Weapons of the Raid," including a Harper Ferry #1842 musket, a Maynard Revolver, and a Sharps Carbine (perhaps used by one of his men during fighting in the "Bleeding Kansas" episode).

The U.S. Arsenal was burned at the beginning of the Civil War in 1861, but Arsenal Square marks the site. John Brown's Fort, once the armory fire-engine house, still stands on the corner. The original site of the firehouse is now the site of Brown's Monument up on the hill. Walk to **The Point,** the edge of the rivers, for a lovely view of rushing water with mountains as a backdrop. When we were there a canoeist was swirling around at the junction. The Appalachian Trail crosses near The Point.

Retrace your footsteps and turn right onto High Street to the Black History Exhibit, the Civil War Museum, the John Brown Wax Museum, and several places for lunch. We had lunch at the **Garden of Food** (304–535–2202), outside under shady umbrella tables. Then we walked diagonally across to a path leading to the Harper House. Don't miss walking down the unusual stone steps that were cut into the natural rock, leaving its swirls and patterns intact.

This concludes Itinerary K. You will probably find that you've only scratched the surface and will want to head off in another direction for more exploration. Happy traveling!

APPENDIX

Inns, Hotels, and Bed & Breakfast Establishments in the Mid-Atlantic States

The following list of inns and bed & breakfast accommodations includes a selection ranging from those that are inexpensive to establishments worthy of a "big splurge" occasion. We have tried to include those with an interesting historical past or a beautiful setting.

On the whole, inns and B&Bs in the United States are more expensive than their counterparts in Europe, but they are more appealing than comparable motel accommodations. Some of them offer special rates during their off-peak times, such as weekends in cities and weekdays in the country, or at quiet times in their seasonal cycle through the year. Prices will vary, but all of them offer personal attention to make your stay pleasant; for once you will be something more than twenty to forty bytes on a computerized reservation list. Your host or hostess may offer you a glass of sherry, fresh fruit in your room, flowers, bath oil in the bathroom, or a foil-wrapped chocolate on your pillow. You may find that your hosts will offer you an hour of conversation during an evening, and you may become friends and return year after year. B&B hosts and guests share one quality that appeals more and more to most Americans: They like to talk and to meet new friends in each region they visit. So it is no wonder that those who have traveled widely prefer staying in someone's home rather than in an anonymous hotel owned by a corporate chain. Almost all of the inns and B&Bs serve complimentary breakfast, but only the inns serve lunch and dinner. Occasionally we have listed accommodations that do not fit the criteria for inns or B&Bs but are nevertheless the most appealing accommodations in the area.

In no case do we intend to be comprehensive. We recommend good places that we know something of without prejudice to equally good places that we are ignorant of, many of which we hope to discover in future travels. Our listings of accommodations are neither inclusive nor exclusive—but only an adjunct to the book's itineraries for the convenience of those who do not wish to spend much of their time finding a good place to sleep.

Delaware

Dover

Cowgills Corner Bed & Breakfast, 7299 Bayside Drive, Dover 19901. Phone: 302–734–5743; fax: 302–734–5245. This working farm includes a flock of sheep, beef

cattle, and working border collies. Two queen-size bedrooms share a bath.
Little Creek Inn Bed & Breakfast, 2623 N. Little Creek Road, Dover 19901.
Phone: 302–730–1300, fax: 302–730–4070; www.littlecreekinn.com. This three-story
Italianate home is decorated with antiques. Some rooms have Jacuzzis.

Laurel

Spring Garden, RD 5, Box 238A, Delaware Avenue Extended, Laurel 19956.
Phone: 302–875–7015. This B&B offers rooms decorated in colonial or Victorian style.
Antiques shop in the barn. Ask Gwen North about the inn-to-inn biking tour.

Lewes

Bay Moon Bed & Breakfast, 128 Kings Highway, Lewes 19958. Phone:
302–644–1802. This B&B is located one block from the canal.

Inn at Canal Square, 122 Market Street, Lewes 19958. Phone: 888–664–1911 or
302–644–3377; fax: 302–644–3377; www.beach-net.com/canalsquare.html. The Inn is
located on a canal, and there's even a stationary houseboat available. Most rooms
have balconies.

John Penrose Virden House Bed & Breakfast, 217 Second Street, Lewes 19958.
Phone: 302–644–0217. This home is right in the center of the historic district.

Wild Swan Inn, 525 Kings Highway, Lewes 19958. Phone: 302–645–8550. Wild
Swan is located 1 mile from the bay.

New Castle

Armitage Inn, 2 The Strand, New Castle 19720. Phone: 302–328–6618; fax:
302–324–1163. Armitage Inn is located in the historic district.

Terry House Bed & Breakfast, 130 Delaware Street, New Castle 19720. Phone:
302–322–2505. This Federal townhouse overlooks Battery Park and the Delaware
River.

Wilmington

Hotel du Pont, 11th & Market Streets, Wilmington 19801. Phone: 800–441–9019
or 302–594–3100; fax: 302–656–2145; www.preferredhotels.com. This 1913 hotel has
more than 800 works of art, hand-carved walnut doors, Italian roseal marble, and
sgraffito medallions in the ballroom.

Inn at Montchanin Village, Route 100 & Kirk Road, Montchanin 19801. Phone:
302–888–2133, fax: 302–888–0389; www.montchanin.com. The village is on the
National Register of Historic Places. Guest rooms are in original homes for Dupont
Company powder mill workers from the 1800s.

Maryland

Annapolis

Historic Inns of Annapolis, 16 Church Circle, Annapolis 21401. Phone:
410–263–2641, 800–638–8902 from Maryland, 800–847–8882 outside of Maryland; fax:
410–263–3813. www.annapolisinns.com. Five historic inns located in the center of
town, with restaurants.

Prince George Inn, 232 Prince George Street, Annapolis 21401. Phone:

410–263–6418; fax: 410–626–0009. This centrally located inn offers four Victorian town house rooms all decorated differently.

Antrim
Antrim 1844, 30 Trevanion Road, Taneytown 21787. Phone: 800–858–1844 or 410–756–6812; fax: 410–756–2744; wwww.antrim1844.com. This Greek Revival building was built as a wedding gift for the daughter of Andrew Ege.

Baltimore
Abacrombie Badger, 58 W. Biddle Street, Baltimore 21201-5502. Phone: 410–244–7227; fax: 410–244–8415; badger-inn.com. Located across the street from the Meyerhoff Symphony Hall, this B&B is also near Antique Row.

Admiral Fell Inn, 888 South Broadway (Fells Point), Baltimore 21231. Phone: 800–292–4667 or 410–522–7377; fax: 410–522–0707; www.admiralfell.com. Dating from the late 1800s, this inn is decorated with antiques and period pieces.

The Biltmore Suites Inn, 205 West Madison Street, Baltimore 21201. Phone: 800–868–5064 or 410–728–6550; fax: 410–728–5829; www.biltmoresuites.com. 1880s-renovated building contains seventeen units with cooking facilities and private baths. Antiques from England.

Mr. Mole B&B, 1601 Bolton Street, Baltimore 21217. Phone: 410–728–1179; fax: 410–728–3379; www.mrmolebb.com. This 1870s guest house is filled with antiques and offers suites and bedrooms.

Berlin
Atlantic Hotel, 2 North Main Street, Berlin 21811. Phone: 800–814–7672 or 410–641–3589; fax: 410–641–4928; www.atlantichotel.com. This 1895 Victorian hotel is on the National Register of Historic Places. Antiques, oriental rugs, and Tiffany lamps add to the Victorian flavor.

Chesapeake City
Inn at the Canal, 104 Bohemia, Chesapeake City 21915. Phone: 410–885–5995; fax: 410–885–3585; www.innatthecanal.com. Located in historic district; built for the Brady family, who operated tug boats on the canal.

Chestertown
The White Swan Tavern, 231 High Street, Chestertown 21620. Phone: 410–778–2300; fax: 410–778–4543. The 1733 tavern was active for many years.

Easton
The Tidewater Inn, Dover and Harrison Streets, Easton 21601. Phone: 800–237–8775 or 410–822–1300; fax: 410–820–8847; www.tidewaterinn.com. There are 119 rooms in this brick building, a spiral staircase, and an outdoor pool.

Frederick
The Turning Point Inn, 3406 Urbana Pike (Route 355 near Urbana), Frederick 21701. Phone: 301–874–2421; fax: 301–874–5773; www.theturningpointinn.com. This is a lovely Victorian mansion built by Dr. Perry in 1910, with a giant pear tree.

Havre de Grace
Vandiver Inn, 301 South Union Avenue, Havre de Grace 21078. Phone:

800–245–1655 or 410–939–5200; fax: 410–939–5202; www.vandiverinn.com. The Vandiver Inn dates from 1886. The innkeeper is also the chef and is a graduate of the Culinary Institue of America.

Oxford

Oxford Inn, Box 627, Oxford 21654. Phone: 410–226–5220; www.oxfordmd.com/oxfordinn.com. Located at the head of Town Creek with views of the harbor as well, this inn offers a variety of accommodations, including suites.

Robert Morris Inn, P.O. Box 70, The Strand, Oxford 21654. Phone: 410–226–5111; fax: 410–226–5744; www.robertmorrisinn.com. Dating from the early 1700s, the inn was once the home of Robert Morris, a friend of George Washington. Thirty-six rooms, some have fireplaces and antique furnishings.

St. Michaels

The Inn at Perry Cabin, P.O. Box 247, Route 33, St. Michaels 21663. Phone: 800–722–2949 or 410–745–2200, fax: 410–745–3348; www.preferredhotels.com. Inn used to be a riding academy whose resident thoroughbred, named "Spectacular Bid," once won the Kentucky Derby.

The Parsonage Inn, 210 North Talbot Street, St. Michaels 21663. Phone: 800–394–5519 or 410–745–5519; www.parsonage-inn.com. Once a parsonage, this 1883 building was built of bricks from the owner's brickyard. It is now a seven-room bed-and-breakfast inn with Victorian decor.

St. Michaels Harbour Inn and Marina, 101 North Harbor Road, St. Michaels 21663. Phone: 800–955–9001 or 301–745–9001; fax: 301–745–9150; www. harbourinn.com Located on the water with a spectacular view of the lighthouse and maritime museum across the harbor.

Wades Point Inn, Box 7, St. Michaels 21663. Phone: 410–745–2500; www. wadepoint.com. A nineteenth-century home, built by a shipwright, on the water.

Tilghman

Chesapeake-House, Tilghman 21671. Phone: 410–886–2123; fax: 410–886–2599; www.chesapeakehouse.com. This 1856 inn on the water attracts fishermen.

Tilghman Island Inn, Tilghman Island 21671. Phone: 800–866–2141 or 410–886–2141; fax: 410–886–2216; www.tilghmanislandinn.com. On the water over-looking Knapps Narrows, which joins the Choptank and the Chesapeake.

New Jersey

Cape May

The Abbey, Columbia Avenue and Gurney Street, Cape May 08204. Phone: 609–884–4506; fax: 609–884–2379; www.abbeybedandbreakfast.com. This Gothic villa has a 60-foot tower and seven guest rooms furnished with Victorian antiques.

The Chalfonte, 301 Howard Street, Cape May 08204. Phone: 609–884–8409; fax: 609–884–4588; www.chalfonte.com. This inn provides rocking chairs on the porch, 103 rooms, and traditional southern cooking served family-style.

The Mainstay, 635 Columbia Avenue, Cape May 08204. Phone: 609–884–8690;

fax: 609–884–1498; www.mainstay.com. A twelve-room Victorian inn that was once an elegant gentleman's club now has Victorian furnishings.

Hope

Inn at Millrace Pond, Route 519, Hope 07844. Phone: 800–746–6467 or 908–459–4884; fax: 908–459–5276. www.innatmillracepond.com. This 1769 building is on the National Register of Historic Buildings.

Lambertville

Chimney Hill Farm Estate, 207 Goat Hill Road, Lambertville 08530. Phone: 609–397–1516; fax: 609–397–9353; www.chimneyhillinn.com. This 1820 stone house is located high on a hill above Lambertville. Four suites are in the Ol' Barn, and there are eight rooms in the main house.

Newton

The Wooden Duck, 140 Goodale Road, Newton 07860. Phone: 973–300–0395; fax: 973–300–0395; www.woodenduckinn.com. This B&B is on seventeen acres of fields and woodlands. Look for the collections, such as ice cream scoops and decoys.

North Wildwood

Candlelight Inn, 2310 Central Avenue, North Wildwood 08260. Phone: 800–992–2632 or 609–522–6200; fax: 609–522–6125; www.candlelight-inn.com. This Queen Anne Victorian home is filled with antiques. Wraparound porch.

Princeton

The Forrestal at Princeton, 100 College Road East, Princeton 08540. Phone: 800–222–1131 or 609–452–7800; fax: 609–452–7883; www.forrestal.com. Located in a park, the building is architecturally exciting with brick and strategic glass windows. Walking, jogging trails, tennis courts.

Nassau Inn, Palmer Square, Princeton 08540. Phone: 800–862–7728 or 609–921–7500; fax: 609–921–9385; www.nassauinn.com. A tradition in Princeton, this inn is wonderful for a getaway weekend. Its location can't be beat.

The Peacock Inn, 20 Bayard Lane, Princeton 08540. Phone: 609–924–1707; fax: 609–924–0788; www.peacockinn.tripod.com. Dating from 1775, this three-story inn has housed F. Scott Fitzgerald, Albert Einstein, and Bertrand Russell.

Spring Lake

Hollycroft, 506 North Boulevard, Spring Lake 07762. Phone: 800–679–2254 or 732–681–2254; fax: 732–280–8145; www.hollycroft.com. Built as a private summer retreat nestled in holly on Lake Como.

Sea Crest by the Sea, 19 Tuttle Avenue, Spring Lake 07762. Phone: 800–803–9031 or 908–449–9031; fax: 732–974–0403; www.seacrestbythesea.com. Filled with family heirlooms and antiques. Borrow a bicycle and head for the boardwalk.

Stanhope

The Whistling Swan Inn, 110 Main Street, Stanhope 07874. Phone: 973–347–6369; fax: 973–347–3391; www.whistlingswaninn.com. This Victorian inn is full of swans—and other collectibles. Sleep in the art deco room, the oriental room, or the forties "swing" room, to name a few. Near Lake Musconetcong.

Woodbine

Henry Ludlam Inn, 1336 Route 47, Woodbine 08270. Phone: 609–861–5847; www.newjerseybbinj.com. This eighteenth-century B&B was built by shipwrights. It is just south of the Pine Barrens.

New York

Albany

Century House Inn, 997 New Loudon Road, RD 1, Box 287, Cohoes 12047. Phone: 518–785–0931; fax: 518–785–3274; www.thecenturyhouse.com. This inn has a colonial theme. It is located north of Albany on Route 9.

The Desmond Americana, 660 Albany Shaker Road, Albany 12211. Phone: 800–448–3500 or 518–869–8100; fax: 518–869–7659; www.desmondhotels.com. The hotel looks like an eighteenth-century village. Located near the airport.

Alexandria Bay

Bonnie Castle Resort, Holland Street, P.O. Box 219, Alexandria Bay 13607. Phone: 315–482–4511 or 800–955–4511; fax: 315–482–9600; www.bonniecastle.com. Built in 1877 as a mansion for Dr. Josiah Holland.

The Ledges, P.O. Box 245, Alexandria Bay 13607. Phone: 315–482–9334; www.thousandislands.com/ledges. Once an estate on nine acres, The Ledges provides a quiet atmosphere on the shore of the St. Lawrence River. Free dockage for guests with boats.

Amagansett

Gansett Green Manor, Box 799, Main Street, Amagansett 11930. Phone: 631–267–3133; fax: 631–267–2177; www.gansettgreen.com. Gardens and fountains add to the restful atmosphere here. Many rooms have kitchens and patios.

The Mill Garth Inn, Box 700, Windmill Lane, Amagansett 11930. Phone: 631–267–3757. This historic inn offers lawns and gardens for the pleasure of guests.

Auburn

Springside Inn, Route 38, Auburn. Phone: 315–252–7247; fax: 315–252–8096; www.springsideinn.com. A boarding school in the 1850s, then part of the Underground Railroad during the Civil War, the inn has been operating since 1919.

Bear Mountain Park

Bear Mountain Inn, Route 9W, Bear Mountain Park 10911. Phone: 845–786–2731; fax: 845–786–2543. This lodge looks like a European chalet. Recreational facilities are nearby.

Blue Mountain Lake

The Hedges, Blue Mountain Lake 12812. Phone: 518–352–7325; fax: 518–352–7672. This rustic retreat features stone and log cottages furnished with oak and typical Adirondack pieces.

Hemlock Hall, Blue Mountain Lake 12812. Phone: 518–352–7706; www. hemlockhall.com. Cottages on the lake nestled in the forest setting of birch, balsam, and pine attract guests during the summer season.

Bolton Landing

Boathouse Bed & Breakfast, 44 Sagomore Road, Bolton Landing 12814. Phone: 518–644–2554; e-mail: boathousebb@aol.com; www.boathousebb.com. This 1917 boathouse was built for George Reis. He won the gold cup on Lake George in 1934 and 1935 in his *El Lagarto*.

Melody Manor Motel, P.O. Box 366, Bolton Landing 12814. Phone: 518–644–9750; www.melodymanor.com. This is a pleasant resort on the west side of Lake George, offering pool and lake swimming, water-skiing, and tennis.

The Sagamore, Bolton Landing 12814. Phone: 800–358–3585 or 518–644–9400; fax: 518–644–2626; www.thesagamore.com. This is just the place for a splurge or a getaway weekend on beautiful Lake George.

Canandaigua

Oliver Phelps Country Inn, 252 North Main Street, Canandaigua 14424. Phone: 800–724–7397 or 716–396–1650; www.oliverphelps.com. This Federal home was built by Nathaniel Norton near the historic Granger Homestead.

Thendara Inn & Restaurant, 4356 East Lake Road, Canandaigua 14424. Phone: 716–394–4868; fax: 716–396–0804; www.gatewaygroup.com. Built as a retirement home for Senator John Raines, the inn dates from 1900. It is right on the river.

Cazenovia

Brae Loch Inn, Route 20, Cazenovia 13035. Phone: 315–655–3431; fax: 315–655–4844; www.cazenovia.com/braeloch. Entering the Brae Loch is like stepping into a bit of Scotland. Nine guest rooms.

Lincklaen House, Box 36, 79 Albany Street, Cazenovia 13035. Phone: 315–655–3461; fax: 315–655–5443; www.cazenovia.com/lincklaen. Dating from 1835, this house features Williamsburg chandeliers, painted wood panels, delft tiles, chandeliers, and three fireplaces on the ground floor.

Chestertown

The Friend's Lake Inn, Chestertown 12817. Phone: 518–494–4751; fax: 518–494–4616; www.friendslake.com. Built in the 1860s, the inn has brass beds, Americana antiques, and quilts. Some rooms have a lake view.

Landon Hill Bed & Breakfast, Landon Hill Road, Chestertown 12817. Phone: 888–244–2599 or 518–494–2599; fax: (call first) 518–494–7423; www.bedbreakfast.net. This Victorian home dates from the 1880s and overlooks Chestertown. Guests can walk into the village or hike up into the mountains.

Clarence Hollow

Asa Ransom House, 10529 Main Street, Clarence Hollow 14031-1684. Phone: 716–759–2315; fax: 716–759–2791; www.asaransom.com. Dating from 1853, the inn is on the grounds of an 1803 gristmill built by Asa Ransom.

Cold Spring Harbor

Hudson House, 2 Main Street, Cold Spring 10516. Phone: 914–265–9355; fax: 914–265–4532. This 1832 building contains fourteen guest rooms, antique furnishings, the Half Moon Bar reminiscent of Henry Hudson, and some balconies.

Cooperstown

The Cooper Inn, Main and Chestnut Streets, Cooperstown 13326. Phone: 800–348–6222; fax: 607–547–9675; www.cooperinn.com. Affiliated with The Otsega Resort Hotel.

Inn at Cooperstown, 16 Chestnut Street, Cooperstown 13326. Phone: 800–437–6303 or 607–547–5756; fax: 607–547–8779; www.cooperstown.net/theinn. Built as an annex to the Fenimore Hotel in 1874, the inn is in the center of the Historic District.

JP Sill House, 63 Chestnut Street, Cooperstown 13326. Phone: 607–547–2633; www.cooperstownchamber.org/jpsill. On the National Register. Contains marble fireplaces and authentic handprinted Victorian wallcoverings.

Lyoncher B&B, 8 Eagle Street, Cooperstown 13326. Phone: 607–547–2709 or 5194. Two guest rooms, a family-style apartment, and a cottage. Walk to town.

The Otsega, 60 Lake Street, Cooperstown 13326. Phone: 800–348–6222 or 607–547–9931; www.otsega.com. Offers golf, swimming, and tennis and a lake view.

Corning

Rosewood Inn, 134 East First Street, Corning 14830. Phone: 607–962–3253; www.rosewoodinn.com. Built in 1855 in Greek Revival style, this inn retains the charm of the past. The rooms are furnished in period pieces; two suites are available.

Diamond Point

Canoe Island Lodge, Lake Shore Drive, Diamond Point 12824. Phone: 518–668–5592; fax: 518–668–2012; www.canoeislandlodge.com. Offers lake swimming, water-skiing, barbecues on an island, sailing, and tennis. It has a lodge and cottages.

Dolgeville

Adrianna Bed & Breakfast, 44 Stewart Street, Dolgeville 13329. Phone: 800–335–4233 or 315–429–3249; www.bedbreakfastNYS.com. This home, decorated with a wildflower theme, is in the foothills of the Adirondack Mountains.

Dundee

The Red Brick Inn, RD2, Box 57A, Dunde 14837. Phone: 607–243–8844; www.bbonline.com/ny/redbrick. The innkeeper also makes wine and champagne; you can visit his cellar to see the bottles quietly aging. Rooms are attractive.

East Aurora

The Roycroft Inn, 40 South Grove Street, East Aurora 14052. Phone: 716–652–5552; fax: 716–655–5345; www.someplacedifferent.com. The Roycroft Arts and Crafts Community was founded by Elbert Hubbard in 1895 and the Roycroft Inn opened in 1905. It was renovated and re-opened in 1995. Some of the original furniture is there.

East Hampton

Bassett House, P.O. Box 1426, East Hampton 11937. Phone: 631–324–6127; fax: 631–324–5944; www.easthampton.com. Built in 1830, this house has a charm all its own. Decorated with a red-leather barber's chair, three stuffed bears, a stoplight, an oriental picture, and a wooden sea chest.

The Huntting Inn, 94 Main Street, East Hampton 11937. Phone: 631–324–0410, fax: 516–672–2107; www.whiteinn.com. Located in the center of town, the inn offers pleasant country gardens.

Fredonia

White Inn, 52 East Main Street, Fredonia 14063. Phone: 716–672–2103; fax: 716–324–8751. The twenty guest rooms have been decorated with designer wallpapers and furnished with antiques and prints. There is a full restaurant.

Garrison

The Bird and Bottle Inn, Nelson's Corners, Old Albany Post Road, Garrison 10524. Phone: 800–782–7837 or 845–424–3000, fax: 845–424–3283; www.birdbottle.com. Once a stagecoach stop before the Revolution, the inn maintains colonial charm with fireplaces, wide-plank floors, and antique furnishings.

Geneva

Belhurst Castle, Box 609, Geneva 14456. Phone: 315–781–0201; fax: 315–781–0201; www.belhurstcastle.com. The 1885 castle was built with materials from Europe. Decorated with stained-glass windows, porcelain figurines, and antiques.

Geneva on the Lake, 1001 Lochland Road, Route 14S, Geneva 14456. Phone: 315–789–7190 or 800–3GENEVA; fax: 315–789–0322; www.genevaonthelake.com. Italian Renaissance villa offers elegance on ten acres of gardens and woods.

Hadley

Saratoga Rose, 4174 Rockwell Street, Hadley 12835. Phone: 800–942–5025 or 518–696–2861; www.saratogarose.com. Decorated with antiques; some rooms have Jacuzzis. A carriage house in a separate building.

Hague

Ruah Bed & Breakfast, 34 Lake Shore Drive, Hague 12836. Phone: 800–224–7549 or 518–543–8816; www.ruahbb.com. This 1907 home was built by Henry Watrous, a prankster who created the Lake George monster hoax. The house has Victorian furnishings and large windows looking out on the lake and gardens.

Trout House Village Resort, Route 9N, Hague 12836. Phone: 800–368–6088 or 518–543–6088; www.trouthouse.com. Located with beautiful views of Lake George; a variety of log cabins and rooms in the lodge available.

Inlet

Holl's Inn, Inlet 13360. Phone: 315–357–2941; www.hollsinn.com. Holl's Inn is probably the last traditional Adirondack inn in the Fulton Lakes Chain. It has been run with warm hospitality by the Holl family since 1935.

Ithaca

Buttermilk Falls Bed & Breakfast, 110 East Buttermilk Falls Road, Ithaca 14850. Phone: 607–272–6767; fax: 607–272–6767. The Rumsey family has lived in this house for five generations. Hike beside the falls up to Pinnacle Rock.

Rose Inn, 813 Auburn Road, Route 34, P.O. Box 6576, Ithaca 14851. Phone: 800–756–ROSE or 607–533–7905; fax: 607–533–7908; www.roseinn.com. In 1809 "The House with the Circular Staircase" was built as a home for Abraham Osmun. Nine guest rooms with period furniture.

Keene

The Bark Eater, Alstead Mill Road, Keene 12942. Phone: 800–232–1607 or 518–576–2221; www.barkeater.com. At one time a stagecoach stop, the Bark Eater has been welcoming guests since the 1800s. The rooms are furnished with country antiques, and there is a cottage with a sleigh bed.

Lake George

Dunham's Bay Lodge, 2999 State Route 9L, Lake George 12845. Phone: 800–79 LODGE or 518–656–9242; fax: 518–656–9250; www.dunhamsbay.com. The indoor pool is large and pleasant in all weather. This lodge on the lake attracts swimmers, sailors, and those who want to relax.

Roaring Brook Ranch & Tennis Resort, Luzerne Road, Lake George 12845. Phone: 800–882–7665 or 518–668–5767; fax 518–668–4019; www.roaring bookranch.com. Resort offers tennis, badminton, sauna baths, swimming, riding, archery, basketball, volleyball, table tennis, hiking.

Tall Pines Motel, Route 9, Lake George 12845. Phone: 800–368–5122 or 518–668–5122; fax: 518–668–3563; www.tallpines.com. Located minutes from Lake George, Tall Pines features a pool. The bike trail is across the road.

Lake Luzerne

The Lamplight Inn, 2129 Lake Avenue, Lake Luzerne 12846. Phone: 800–262–4668 or 518–696–5294; www.lamplightinn.com. 1890 Victorian inn. Another home nearby is available for families or couples.

Lake Placid

Adirondack Loj, Box 867, Lake Placid 12946. Phone: 518–523–3441; fax: 518–523–3518; www.adk.org. The Adirondack Mountain Club operates several lodges in the area, including Adirondack Loj, 8 miles south of Lake Placid.

Interlaken Inn, 15 Interlaken Avenue, Lake Placid 12946. Phone: 800–428–4369 or 518–523–3180; www.innbookslakeplacid.com. Eight rooms decorated with Victorian furnishings welcome guests.

Lake Placid Lodge, Whiteface Inn Road, Lake Placid 12946. Phone: 518–523–2700; fax: 518–523–1124; www.lakeplacidlodge.com. Once an Adirondack camp dating to 1895, located on the shores of Lake Placid and has views of Whiteface Mountain. Adirondack style with birchwood furniture.

Mirror Lake Inn, 5 Mirror Lake Drive, Lake Placid 12946. Phone: 518–523–2544; fax: 518–523–2871; www.mirrorlakeinn.com. In January 1988 a fire destroyed the entire 105-year-old main building; an 1895 grandfather clock and the grand piano were saved from the fire to grace the new building.

Lew Beach

Beaverkill Valley Inn, Lew Beach 12753. Phone: 845–439–4844; fax: 845–439–3884; www.beaverkillvalley.com. 1893 country inn. Outdoor tennis courts, indoor swimming pool, and miles of woodland trails. Anglers come in the autumn.

Montauk

Gurney's Inn, Old Montauk Highway, Montauk 11954. Phone: 800–8–Gurneys or 516–668–2345; fax: 516–668–3576; www.gurneysinn.com. The inn dates from 1926, when Carl Fisher began as innkeeper.

Mumford

Genesee Country Inn, 948 George Street, Mumford 14511. Phone: 800–697–8297 or 716–538–2500; fax: 716–538–4565; www.geneseecountryinn.com. An 1880s plaster mill, which later manufactured hubs, handles for hammers, and wheel spokes. A creek wanders through the property.

New Paltz

The Mohonk Mountain House, Lake Mohonk, New Paltz 12561. Phone: 800–772–6646 or 845–255–1000 or 255–4500; fax: 845–256–2161; www.mohonk.com. Established in 1869 by the Smiley family, this place offers views of the mountains, cliffs, and crystal-clear lake.

New York

The Algonquin, 59 West 44th Street, New York 10036. Phone: 800–555–8000; fax: 212–944–1419; www.canberleyhotels.com. As you drink tea, have a cocktail, or eat dinner, know that the literary spirits of years ago were there before you.

The Essex House, 160 Central Park South, New York 10019. Phone: 888–645–5697 or 212–247–0300; fax: 212–315–1839; www.westin.com. The hotel is located across from Central Park.

Hotel Salisbury, 123 West 57th Street, New York 10019. Phone: 888–692–5757 or 212–246 1300; fax: 212 977–7752; www.NYCsalisbury.com. Located opposite Carnegie Hall, and Central Park is not far away.

The Mayflower Hotel, 15 Central Park West at 61st Street, New York 10023. Phone 800–223–4164 or 212–265–0060; fax: 212–265–0227; www.mayflower hotel.com. Located right on Central Park with its greenery and early morning walkers.

Le Parker Meridien, 118 West 57th Street, New York 10019. Phone: 800–543–4300 or 212–245–5000; fax: 212–307–1776; www.parkermeridien.com. Located just south of Central Park and close to Fifth Avenue.

Rihga Royal Hotel, 151 West 54th Street 10019. Phone: 800–937–5454 or 212–307–5000; fax: 212–765–6530; www.rihga.com. The building is architecturally interesting, with its horizontal bay windows set into brick and granite.

Sheraton Manhattan, 790 Seventh Avenue, New York 10019. Phone: 800–325–3535 or 212–581–3300; fax: 212–541–9219; www.sheraton.com. Located near the Museum of Modern Art and two blocks from Radio City.

Trump International Hotel & Tower, One Central Park West, New York 10023. Phone 888–448–7867 or 212–299–1000; fax: 212–299–1150; www.trumpintl.com.

Overlooks Central Park at Columbus Circle. Great views and European-style kitchens. The Warwick, 65 West 54th Street, New York 10019. Phone: 800–223–4099 or 212–247–2700; fax: 212–957–8915; www.warwickhotel.com. Built by William Randolph Hearst in 1927 for Marion Davies, who had a suite on the 27th floor.

North Creek

Copperfield Inn, 224 Main Street, North Creek 12853. Phone: 800–424–9910 or 518–251–2500; fax 518–251–4143; www.copperfieldinn.com. Located in the Adirondacks, the inn is convenient to winter and summer sports. A shuttle will take you to Gore for skiing.

North River

Garnet Hill Lodge, Thirteenth Lake Road, North River 12856. Phone: 518–251–2444; fax: 518–251–3089; www.garnethill.com. Named for the garnet mine nearby, the lodge was built in 1936 as a residence for miners. Now it attracts skiers in winter and vacationers who want to enjoy Thirteenth Lake in summer.

Pittsford

Oliver Loud's Inn, Bushnell's Basin, Pittsford 14534. Phone: 716–248–5200; fax: 716–248–9970; www.frontiernet.net/~rchi. The 1812 building was moved to its present location on the Erie Canal in 1986. Oliver Loud was the first innkeeper in 1813.

Poughkeepsie

Inn at the Falls, 50 Red Oaks Mill Road, Poughkeepsie 12603. Phone: 800–344–1466 or 845–462–5770; fax: 845–462–5943; www.innatthefalls.com. B&B has elegant rooms and suites in English contemporary, or country styles.

Rhinebeck

Beekman Arms, Route 9, Rhinebeck 12572. Phone: 800–361–6517 or 845–876–7077; fax: 845–876–7077; www.beekmanarms.com. This 1766 hotel claims to be the oldest in America. George Washington did sleep here, as did a number of other leaders from the past. Includes the Delamater House down the street.

Rochester

Strathallan, 550 East Avenue, Rochester 14607. Phone: 800–678–7284 or 716–461–5010; fax: 716–461–3387; www.strathallan.com. Once an apartment complex, the Strathallan contains suites, kitchens, and balconies.

Woodcliff the Lodge, Box 22850, Rochester 14692. Phone: 800–365–3065 or 716–381–4000; fax: 716–381–2673; www.woodclifflodge.com. Woodcliff is set on top of a hill with views of the Bristol Hills.

Rome

The Beeches-Paul Revere, 7900 Turin Road, Rome 13440. Phone: 800–765–7251 or 315–336–1776; fax: 315–336–7270; www.thebeeches.com. Dates from 1924. Like a European country home. The Paul Revere Lodge is down a green lawn in the midst of trees.

Round Top

Winter Clove Inn, Round Top 12473. Phone: 518–622–3267; fax: 518–622–3267; www.inns.com. Five generations of the same family have been welcoming guests since 1850 to this peaceful mountain setting.

Sag Harbor

The American Hotel, Main Street, Sag Harbor 11963. Phone: 631–725–3535; fax: 631–725–3573; www.theamericanhotel.com. Built in 1846, the hotel is located in the middle of Sag Harbor, so you can walk wherever you want to explore.

Saranac Lake

Hotel Saranac, Saranac Lake 12983. Phone: 800–937–0211 or 518–891–2200; fax: 518–891–5664; www.hotelsaranac.com. Wonderful service in this hotel run by Paul Smith's College.

Saratoga Springs

The Adelphi Hotel, 365 Broadway, Saratoga Springs 12866. Phone: 800–860–4086 or 518–587–4688; fax: 518–587–0851; www.adelphihotel.com. Built in 1877, the Adelphi was part of the social life of the summer season in Saratoga. Victorian furnishings.

Batcheller Mansion Inn, 20 Circular Street, Saratoga Springs 12866. Phone: 800–616–7012 or 518–584–7012; fax: 518–581–7746; www.batchellermansioninn.com. George Batcheller built this home in 1873. It is decorated in Victorian style.

Brunswick B&B, 143 Union Avenue, Saratoga Springs 12866. Phone: 800–585–6751 or 518–584–6751; www.mannixmarketing.com/brunswick. 1886 Victorian Gothic decorated with antiques and lace. Rocking chairs on the porch.

Gideon Putnam Hotel, Spa State Park, Saratoga Springs 12866. Phone: 800–732–1560 or 518–584–3000; fax: 518–584–1354; www.gideonputnam.com. This 1930 building is in Spa State Park.

Union Gables, 55 Union Avenue, Saratoga Springs 12866. Phone: 800–398–1558 or 518–584–1558; fax: 518–583–0649; www.uniongables.com. This restored Queen Anne home is right on Union Avenue.

The Washington Inn, South Broadway at Fenlon, Saratoga Springs 12866. Phone: 518 584 9807; fax: same as phone; http://hometown.aol.com/washingtoninn/index.html. On a hill under spruces, two late 1800s Victorian houses.

Wayside Inn, 104 Wilton Road, Greenfield 12833. Phone: 800–893–2884 or 518–893–7249; fax: 518–893–2884; www.waysideinn.com. This 1786 inn was once a stop on the Underground Railroad. Furnished with pieces from the Middle East, Europe, and Far East.

The Westchester House, 102 Lincoln Avenue, Saratoga Springs 12866. Phone: 518–587–7613; www.westchester-bb.saratoga.ny.us. This Victorian house in a residential neighborhood is furnished with antiques. Paths lead through colorful gardens.

Schroon Lake

Schroon Lake Bed & Breakfast, Route 9, Schroon Lake 12870. Phone: 800–523–6755 or 518–532–7042; fax: 518–532–9820, www.schroonbb.com. The porch offers wicker rockers with a mountain view.

Silver Spruce Inn, Route 9, Schroon Lake 12870. Phone: 518–532–7031; www.silverspruce.com. This 1790s building had additions when it became a corporate estate in the 1920s. Much of the acreage of the original property is in the

Adirondack Park. Guest rooms have cedar panelling and bathrooms a la The Waldorf Astoria.

Scotia

Glen Sanders Mansion, 1 Glen Avenue, Scotia 12302. Phone: 518–374–7262; fax: 518–374–7391 or 518–733–6997; www.glensandersmansion.com. Parts of the mansion date from the 1680s; the 1713 Great Room is now the main dining room..

Shelter Island Heights

Ram's Head Inn, Box 638, Shelter Island Heights 11965. Phone: 631–749–0811; fax: 631–749–0059; www.shelterislandinns.com. Located on Coecles Harbor, the inn provides sailboats, a paddle boat, and a kayak. Guests can arrive in their own boats.

Skaneateles

The Sherwood Inn, 26 West Genesee Street, Skaneateles 13152. Phone: 800–374–3796 or 315–685–3405; fax: 315–685–8983; www.thesherwoodinn.com. Built in 1807 as a tavern; fifteen guest rooms are fitted with period furnishings from the early nineteenth century through the Victorian age.

Stanfordville

The Lakehouse, Shelley Hill Road, Stanfordville 12581. Phone: 845–266–8093; fax: 845–266–4051; www.lakehouseinn.com. This getaway retreat for special occasions is located in the woods on a lake. Rooms have antiques, four-poster beds, and Jacuzzis.

Stephentown

Berkshire Mountain House, Wyomanock Road, Stephentown 12168. Phone: 800–497–0176 or 518–733–6923; fax: 518–733–6997; www.berkshirebb.com. This contemporary inn is located on fifty acres. Mountain views are superb.

Tarrytown

The Castle at Tarrytown, 400 Benedict Avenue, Tarrytown 10591. Phone: 914–631–1980; fax: 914–631–4612; www.castleattarrytown.com. This elegant stone castle is a spectacular hotel with all amenities. Each room is furnished with antiques and objects d'art.

Upper Saranac Lake

The Wawbeek, 553 Panther Mountain Road, Upper Saranac Lake 13986. Phone: 800–953–2656 or 518–359–2656; fax: 518–359–2475; www.wawbeek.com. Picturesque log cabins are located on forty private acres.

Warrensburg

Merrill Magee House, Warrensburg 12885. Phone: 888–MMHINNI or 518–623–2449; fax: 518–623–3990; www.webny.com/merrillmageehouse. This nineteenth-century Greek Revival house has a guest house composed of ten elegant rooms with fireplaces.

Westport

All Tucked In, 53 South Main Street, Westport 12993. Phone: 800–ALL–TUCK or 518–962–4400; fax: 518–962–4400; www.alltuckedin.com. Nine rooms and a comfortable common room.

The Inn on the Library Lawn, Westport 12993. Phone: 888–577–7748 or 518–962–8666; www.theinnonthelibrarylawn.com. This Victorian B&B has large bay windows overlooking the lake.

Victorian Lady, 57 South Main Street, Westport 12993. Phone: 518–962–2345; www.adirondackinns.com/victorianlady. This home has many personal collections that have been in the families of the owners.

Westport Hotel, Westport 12993. Phone: 518–962–4501. Decorated with antiques and stenciled walls. The restaurant is available to the public.

Pennsylvania

Bedford
Jean Bonnet Tavern, Route 30, Bedford 15522. Phone: 814–623–2250. Jean Bonnet ran this public house from 1780. It is near Bedford Village.

Bethlehem
Wyndor Hall Inn, Old Philadelphia Pike, Bethlehem 18018. Phone: 800–839–0020 or 610–867–6851; fax: 610–866–2062; www.bedandbreakfast.com. This 1812 late Georgian-style stone home is furnished with antiques.

Canadensis
The Pine Knob, Box 295, Route 447, Canadensis 18325. Phone: 800–426–1460 or 717–595–2532; fax: 717–595–6429; www.pineknobinn.com. This pre–Civil War inn features antique furnishings, lots of books, and a grand piano.

Chadds Ford
Brandywine River Hotel, Box 1058, Chadds Ford 19317. Phone: 610–388–1200; fax: 610–388–1200; www.virtualcities.com/pabrn.htm. Located in an historic colonial area, the hotel is convenient for touring.

Champion
Seven Springs Mountain Resort, Champion 15622. Phone: 800–452–2223 or 814–352–7777; fax: 814–352–7911; www.7springs.com. The Dupres built their first home in 1932, as well as many log cabins, and now the resort includes a hotel.

Cresco
Crescent Lodge Country Inn, Paradise Valley, Cresco 18326. Phone: 800–392–9400 or 717–595–7486; fax: 717–595–3452; www.crescentlodge.com. Family-run for forty years, the inn's newest building increased the estate.

Ephrata
Historic Smithton, a Bed & Breakfast Country Inn, 900 West Main Street, Ephrata 17522. Phone: 717–733–6094; www.historicsmithtoninn.com. Each bedroom in this inn has its own fireplace and a sitting area with comfortable chairs, reading lamps, and a writing desk.

Erwinna
The Golden Pheasant Inn, River Road, Erwinna 18920. Phone: 800–830–4474 or 610–294–9595; fax: 610–294–9882; www.goldenpheasant.com. Built in 1857 for

bargemen on the canal, the inn now offers fourteen guest rooms. There are two Victorian dining rooms and a greenhouse dining area.

Fogelsville

Glasbern, Pack House Road, Fogelsville 18051. Phone: 610–285–4723; fax: 610–285–2862; www.glasbern.com. This country inn includes a renovated nineteenth-century bank barn. Rooms include old beams and wide-board floors.

Greensburg

Mountain View Inn, 1001 Village Drive, Mountain View Village, Greensburg 15601. Phone: 800–537–8709 or 412–834–5300; fax: 412–834–5304; www.mountainviewinn.com. The Mountain View truly does have a wonderful view.

Gwynedd

William Penn Inn, Route 202 and Sumneytown Pike, Gwynedd 19436. Phone: 215–699–9272; fax: 215–699–4808; www.philanet.com/wmpenn. The 1714 building has been expanded to include several dining areas.

Hershey

Hotel Hershey, Hotel Road, Hershey 17033. Phone 800–533–3131 or 717–533–2171; fax: 717–534–8887; www.preferredhotels.com. This historic hotel sits on a hilltop close to a town built around chocolate.

Kennett Square

Longwood Inn, 815 East Baltimore Pike, Kennett Square 19348. Phone: 610–444–3515; fax: 610–444–4285. The family-owned and -operated inn is located near Longwood Gardens.

Kintnersville

Bucksville House B&B, 4501 Durham Road and Buck Drive, Kintnersville 18930. Phone: 888–617–6300 or 610–847–8948; fax: 610–847–8948; www.bucksvillehouse.com. Captain Nicholas Buck built this house in 1795.

Lewisburg

The Pineapple Inn, 439 Market Street, Lewisburg 17837. Phone: 570–524–6200; www.kdweb.pineappleinn. This Federal-style house was built in 1857 by the architect Louis Palmer.

Lititz

General Sutter Inn, 14 East Main Street, Lititz 17543. Phone: 717–626–2115; fax: 716–626–0992; www.generalsutterinn.com. The inn was founded in 1764 by the Moravian church. John Augustus Sutter arrived in Lititz to find a cure for his arthritis.

Lumberville

Black Bass Hotel, Route 32, Lumberville 18933. Phone: 215–297–5815; fax: 215–297–0262; www.blackbasshotel.com. The hotel was built in the 1740s for traders and traveling businessmen; in the 1830s it was popular with passengers on canal boats. Collection of royal commemorative pieces.

Malvern

General Warren Inne, Old Lancaster Highway West, Malvern 19355. Phone:

610–296–3637; fax: 610–296–8084; www.generalwarren.com. This eighteenth-century inn is south of Valley Forge.

Mercersburg

The Mercersburg Inn, 405 South Main Street, Mercersburg 17236. Phone: 717–328–5231; fax: 717–328–3403; www.mercersburginn.com. Built as a residence in 1910, this mansion contains a handsome marble stairway and mahogany paneling. Antiques include four-poster beds with canopies.

New Hope

Centre Bridge Inn, Box 74, New Hope 18938. Phone: 215–862–2048 or 862–9139; fax: 215–862–9139; www.centrebridgeinn.com. The nine guest rooms contain colonial furnishings, and some have four-poster beds. River views are abundant.

Hotel du Village, corner of North River Road and Phillips Mill Road, New Hope 18938. Phone: 215–862–9911 or 862–5164; fax: 215–862–9788. Located on land granted to the Ely family by William Penn in the seventeenth century.

The Inn at Phillips Mill, North River Road, New Hope 18938. Phone: 215–862–2984. Originally a stone barn built in 1750, the inn has been restored and now offers five bedrooms furnished with antiques and quilts on four-poster beds.

Logan Inn, 10 West Ferry Street, New Hope 18938. Phone: 215–862–2300; www.loganinn.com. The inn dates from 1727; George Washington visited it.

The Wedgwood Inn, 111 West Bridge Street, New Hope 18938. Phone: 215–862–2570; fax: 215–862–2570; www.new-hope-inn.com. Built in 1870 over the ruins of an earlier structure where General Alexander Lord Stirling encamped in December 1776.

Newtown

Brick Hotel, Washington Avenue and State Street, Newtown 18940. Phone: 215–860–8313; fax: 215–860–8084; www.brickhotel.com. This house was once owned by an aide to Napoleon Bonaparte. It dates from 1764.

Temperance House, 5–11 South State Street, Newtown 18940. Phone: 800–446–0474 or 215–860–0474; fax: 215–860–7773; www.temperancehouse.com. The eighteenth-century building was once the site of temperance meetings.

Orrtanna

Hickory Bridge Farm, Orrtanna 17353. Phone: 800–642–1766 or 717–642–5261; fax: 717–642–6419; www.hickorybridgefarm.com. In the foothills of the Appalachian Mountains, the farm has rooms in the farmhouse and cottages in the woods on the bank of a stream. A good location for touring Gettysburg.

Paradise

Revere Tavern and Inn, Route 30, Paradise 17562. Phone: 800–528–1234 or 717–687–7683; fax: 717–687–6141; www.bestwestern.com. The inn is located in the heart of Pennsylvania Dutch country.

Philadelphia

Four Seasons Hotel, One Logan Square, Philadelphia 19103. Phone: 215–963–1500; fax: 215–963–9506; www.fourseasons.com. Sumptuous rooms appeal to guests with their individual decorating and tasteful furnishings.

The Independence Park Inn, 236 Chestnut Street, Philadelphia 19106. Phone: 800–624–2988 or 215–922–4443; fax: 215–922–4487; www.independence parkinn.com. A mid-nineteenth century Victorian inn with beautiful lobby.

The Park Hyatt Philadelphia 1415 Chancellor Court, Philadelphia 19102. Phone: 800–233–1234 or 215–893–1776; fax: 215–732–8518; www.hyatt.com. The hotel dates from 1904 when it was built by George Boldt, who had built the Waldorf.

Philadelphia Marriott Hotel, 1201 Market Street, Philadelphia 19107. Phone: 800–228–8920 or 215–625–2900; fax: 215–625–6000; www.marriot.com. This hotel is located right across from the Convention Center. Independence Historic Park is only four blocks away.

The Ritz-Carlton, 17th and Chestnut, Philadelphia 19103. Phone: 800–241–3333 or 215–563–1600; fax: 215–567–2822; www.ritzcarlton.com. The hotel was named for its founder, Cesar Ritz, who was born in Switzerland.

The Rittenhouse, 210 West Rittenhouse Square, Philadelphia 19103. Phone: 800–635–1042 or 215–546–9000, fax: 215–732–3364; www.Rittenhousehotel.com. Each spacious guest room is decorated with beautiful furnishings and fresh flowers. Every room has a fax machine and a desk.

Thomas Bond House, 129 South Second Street, Philadelphia 19106. Phone: 800–845–2663 or 215–923–8523; fax: 215–923–8504; www.winston-saleminn.com/phila. Was once the residence of a Philadelphia physician.

Pittsburgh

The Priory, 614 Pressley Street, Pittsburgh 15212. Phone: 412–231–3338; fax: 412–231–4838; www.thepriory.com. Once home to Benedictine priests; built 1888.

Westin William Penn Hotel, William Penn Place, Pittsburgh 15230. Phone: 800–228–3000 or 412–281–7100; fax: 412–553–5252; www.westin.com. Elaborate ornamentations were copied from the Château of Fontainebleau.

Scranton

Lackawanna Station Hotel, 700 Lackawanna Avenue, Scranton 18503. Phone: 800–347–6888 or 570–342–8300; fax: 570–342–0380; www.radisson.com. Inside a 1908 railroad station; on the National Register of Historic Places.

South Sterling

The French Manor, Huckleberry Road, South Sterling 18460. Phone 800–523–8200 or 717–676–3244; fax: 717–676–9786; www.thesterlinginn.com. A sister hotel to The Sterling Inn. In a secluded location with great mountain views.

The Sterling Inn, Box 2, South Sterling 18460. Phone: 717–676–3311 or 800–523–8200; fax: 717–676–9786; www.thesterlinginn.com. The living room is filled with sofas, chairs, and books.

Strasburg

Historic Strasburg Inn, Route 896, Strasburg 17579. Phone: 800–872–0201 or 717–687–7691; fax: 717–687–6098; www.historicstrasburginn.com. A country inn located on fifty-eight acres.

Strasburg Village Inn, One West Main Street, Strasburg 17579. Phone: 800–541–1055 or 717–687–0900; www.strasburg.com. A National Historic Inn with Williamsburg rooms and suites.

Washington, D.C.

Adams Inn, 1744 Lanier Place, N.W., Washington, D.C. 20009. Phone: 800–578–6807 or 202–745–3600; fax: 202–319–7958; www.adamsinn.com. A turn-of-the-twentieth-century bed-and-breakfast, near the National Zoo.

Doubletree Guest Suites, 801 New Hampshire Avenue, N.W., Washington, D.C. 20037. Phone: 202–785–2000; fax: 202–785–9485; www.doubletree.com.

Grand Hyatt, 1000 H Street, N.W., Washington, D.C. 20001. Phone: 800–233–1234 or 202–582–1234; fax: 202–637–4797; www.hyatt.com. Atrium lobby has a waterfall and pool. Underground passage connects the hotel to Metro Center.

Hay-Adams Hotel, One Lafayette Square, N.W., Washington, D.C. 20006. Phone: 800–424–5054 or 202–638–6600; fax: 202–638–2716; www.hayadams.com. The hotel was built in 1927 in Italian Renaissance style. Beautiful antiques, gold leaf, and Medici tapestry.

Holiday Inn Capitol, 550 C Street, S.W., Washington, D.C. 20024. Phone: 800–HOLIDAY or 202–479–4000; fax: 202–479–4000; www.basshotels.com. The hotel is located just one block away from the Smithsonian.

Hotel Washington, Pennyslvania Avenue, N.W. at 15th Street, Washington, D.C. 20004. Phone: 800–424–9540 or 202–638–5900; fax: 202–638–4275; www.hotelwashington.com. The White House is only a block away.

Kalorama Guest House, 1854 Mintwood Place, N.W., Washington, D.C. 20009. Phone: 202–667–6369; fax: 202–319–1262. Victorian dating from 1880; decorated with period furnishings and artwork.

Loews L'Enfant Plaza, 480 L'Enfant Plaza, S.W., Washington, D.C. 20024. Phone: 800–23–LOEWS or 202–484–1000; fax: 202–646–4456; www.loewshotels.com. The hotel is located near the Smithsonian with all its wonders. The decor is nineteenth-century French style.

Morrison-Clark, Massachusetts Avenue and Eleventh Street, N.W., Washington, D.C. 20001. Phone: 800–332–7898 or 202–898–1200; fax: 202–289–8576; www.morrisclark.com. Within the hotel is an 1876 mansion.

Renaissance Mayflower Hotel, 1127 Connecticut Avenue N.W., Washington, D.C. 20036. Phone: 800–HOTELS1 or 202–347–3000; fax: 202–466–9082; www.renaissancehotels.com. This 1925 historic hotel is located four blocks from the White House.

Wyndham Hotel, 1400 M Street, N.W., Washington, D.C. 20005. Phone: 800–VISTA–DC or 202–420–1700; fax: 202–785–0786; www.wyndham.com. This hotel contains a spectacular, fourteen-story, glass-canopied atrium lobby.

Virginia

Alexandria

Morrison House, 116 S. Alfred Street, Alexandria 22314. Phone: 800–367–0800 or 703–838–8000; fax: 703–684–6283; www.morrisonhouse.com. Eighteenth-century manor house located in Old Town. English tea served in the afternoons.

Chincoteague

Island Belle Motor Lodge, Beach Road, Box 585, Chincoteague 23336. Phone: 800–615–6343 or 804–336–3600; www.chincoteague/belle. The lodge is not far from the Chincoteague Wildlife Refuge.

Refuge Motor Inn, Box 378, Chincoteague 23336. Phone: 800–544–8469 or 804–336–5511; fax: 804–336–6134; www.refugeinn.com. The motor inn is located just across the bridge from Chincoteague Wildlife Refuge.

Leesburg

The Laurel Brigade Inn, 20 West Market Street, Leesburg 22075. Phone: 703–777–1010; fax: 703–777–9001; www.laurelbrigade.com. A pub during colonial days; Marquis de Lafayette had dinner there.

Norris House Inn B&B & Stone House Tea Room, 108 Loudoun Street S.W., Leesburg 22075. Phone: 800–644–1806 or 703–777–1806; fax: 703–771–8051; www.norrishouse.com. In the historic district. Afternoon tea is served in the Stone House.

McLean

Ritz-Carlton, Tysons Corner, 1700 Tysons Boulevard, McLean 22102. Phone: 800–241–3333 or 703–506–4300; fax: 703–506–2694; www.ritzcarlton.com. The lobby has an antique Louis XV marble fireplace, paintings, and paneled walls.

Middleburg

Red Fox Inn & Mosby's Tavern, 2 East Washington Street, Middleburg 22117. Phone: 800–223–1728 outside VA or 703–687–6301; fax: 703–687–6187. Dating from 1728, the complex offers period furniture with modern facilities.

Williamsburg

Colonial Williamsburg Hotels, Williamsburg 23187–1776. Phone: 800–HISTORY (447–8679) or 757–229–1000; fax: 757–565–8797; www.history.org. Includes The Williamsburg Inn, Providence Hall, Colonial Houses & Taverns, Williamsburg Lodge, Williamsburg Woodlands, and Governor's Inn. All are within the Historic Area, or just outside it, and some are on Duke of Gloucester Street.

Kingsmill Resort, 1010 Kingsmill Road, Williamsburg 23185. Phone: 800–832–5665 or 757–253–1703; fax: 757–253–8246; www.kingsmill.com. Built on land owned by Richard Kingsmill in 1736. Deer can be seen in the woods.

Index

About the Authors

Patricia and Robert Foulke have traveled together for forty-seven years, including four fellowship and sabbatical years in Europe, a three-month voyage in the Mediterranean, and numerous trips in the United States to research articles and update their guidebooks. They have written books on New England, the Mid-Atlantic states, and Europe within the last fifteen years. Their travel articles have appeared in the *Rotarian,* the *Christian Science Monitor,* the *Hartford Courant, Oceans Magazine, Greek Accent,* the *Detroit Free Press Magazine,* the *San Francisco Examiner,* the *Boston Globe, St. Petersburg Times, Off Duty Magazine, British Heritage,* the *Boston Herald, SAIL, Walking Magazine, International Living,* the *Glens Falls Post Star, Hawaii Magazine, Camping & Walking, Vista USA, Sea History, Saab Soundings, Canoe & Kayak,* and *Senior Magazine.*

Robert completed his undergraduate work at Princeton University and received a Ph.D from the University of Minnesota. He is a professor emeritus of English at Skidmore College in Saratoga Springs, New York. Patricia earned her master's degree at Trinity College in Hartford, Connecticut, and taught elementary school, remedial reading, special education, and writing classes until her retirement. The Foulkes live in Lake George, New York.